Teaching
Elementary
Social Studies

Pearl M. Oliner
Humboldt State University

Teaching Elementary Social Studies

A Rational and Humanistic Approach

HARCOURT BRACE JOVANOVICH INC.
New York Chicago San Francisco Atlanta

ISBN: 0-15-588052-7

Library of Congress Catalog Card Number: 76-504

Printed in the United States of America

Picture Credits

Irene Bayer/Monkmeyer *146.* Marion Bernstein/Editorial Photocolor Archives *311.* Raimondo Borea *261.* Forsythe/U.S.D.A. *242 (left).* Owen Franken/Stock, Boston *119.* Ellen Galinsky *200.* Greenberg/Monkmeyer *187.* Nancy Hays/Monkmeyer *162, 341.* Kenneth Karp *2, 10, 38, 49, 55, 76, 89, 95, 107, 126, 127, 135, 153, 167, 205, 211, 263, 265, 273, 278, 287, 298, 339, 353.* Jan Lukas/Photo Researchers *171.* Nestor/Monkmeyer *29.* Donald Wright Patterson, Jr./Stock, Boston *140.* Marjorie Pickens *216, 326.* Bruce Roberts/Photo Researchers *315.* Hugh Rogers/Monkmeyer *221.* Nancy Rudolph *114, 230.* Blair Seitz/Editorial Photocolor Archives *182.* Shackman/Monkmeyer *233, 335.* Suzanne Szasz *244.* Mary M. Thacher/Photo Researchers *193.*

For Sam, Ron, David, and Ian

For John, then Devon and Tim

Preface

There are basically two schools of thought regarding what the social studies should be. One group of educators sees the goal of the social studies to be the learning of selected elements of the social sciences, the assumption being that such knowledge is useful in its own right. The essence of this view was once expressed in a definition offered by Edgar Wesley: "the social studies are the social sciences simplified for pedagogical purposes." The other group believes that the goal of the social studies should be citizenship education, with emphasis on the development of those rational habits of mind and humane attitudes that enable individuals to make informed decisions about social and personal matters.

Some of the advocates of both these schools feel that their positions cannot be reconciled. It is a basic premise of this book, however, that no genuine conflict exists between them. The social sciences are clearly the foundation of the social studies. But it seems more than reasonable that the criteria by which the specific elements of the social sciences are selected should largely—although not exclusively—reflect the usefulness of that material in helping young people become purposeful, knowledgeable human beings and responsible citizens.

The social studies have been charged with one of education's most important responsibilities: cultivating the individual's understanding of the social environment. This environment encompasses not only the local community but the nation and, increasingly, the world. The growing interdependence of people all over the earth makes understanding and cooperation more important than ever before. Such global issues as pollution, the consumption of energy, and the peaceful resolution of conflict are imperative concerns of the social studies. The curriculum *must* deal with the problems that threaten our very existence.

But we will need more than good intentions and moral indignation. Solving these problems requires complex skills and solidly based knowledge. To paraphrase psychologist Jerome Bruner, relevance depends on the ability to mobilize what is known toward ends that are of importance. The study of spatial location, for example, is not very inspiring, but without it we cannot really comprehend such universal problems as hunger and war, much less solve them.

A decade ago, generous federal funding enabled educators to launch valuable programs of research and to collaborate in the development of new and more effective methods of teaching. However, the products of this period of investigation have not yet been fully synthesized or widely disseminated among either pre-service or in-service teachers. One of the principal objectives of *Teaching Elementary Social Studies* is to bring together the essential elements of this new material in a systematic way.

Ultimately, this is a book about how and what to teach. It is divided into five parts that deal with those two questions from different perspectives. The first part, Cognitive Concerns, concentrates on the intellectual aspects of social studies education. Chapter 1 examines the concept of inquiry and the teaching strategies that promote it; Chapter 2 deals with the subject matter of the new social studies curricula, which are organized around specific concepts and generalizations rather than around collections of facts.

The second part of the book, Humanistic Concerns, considers the intellectual and affective needs of individual students and society. Children, no less than adults, have different interests and skills; these should not be stifled under a blanket of uniform requirements but encouraged through curricula that are divergent and responsive. Chapter 3 describes ways in which instruction can be adapted to the needs of the individual student. Chapter 4 covers the current range of ideas on the teaching of values, describing the various approaches in detail and evaluating the advantages and disadvantages of each. Chapter 5 addresses the question of relevance in the social studies and shows how social issues can be used as an effective basis for organizing a humanistic curriculum.

The third part, Skills and Techniques, translates the how and what of teaching into practical classroom terms. Chapter 6 provides an overview of the basic skills that are required in the social studies, detailing just what these are and giving examples of ways in which they may be taught. Chapters 7 and 8 cover the variety of instructional resources available to the teacher, beginning with the most simple and concrete and finishing with the most complex and abstract.

The fourth part of the book consists of a single chapter on evaluation, with emphasis on the techniques of criterion-referenced evaluation — which, because it assesses student progress in relation to clearly stated objectives, is far more effective than the traditional forms of evaluation. This chapter also offers techniques for assessing the other major elements of the educational process, including the teacher, the textbook, and even the community.

The final part, The Unit Plan, deals with the organization of day-to-day teaching through unit and lesson plans. The types, forms, and elements of these plans are treated in detail and examples are given. The final part also functions as a summary of the book, bringing together the principal points from each of the earlier chapters.

I would like to acknowledge the help of many people in the preparation of this book. I owe special thanks to two colleagues who played major roles in the writing of certain chapters: Barbara Maxon, who contributed substantially to chapters 7 and 8, which cover instructional resources, and Thomas Price of Humboldt State University, who developed the classroom activities involving social issues for Chapter 5. Among those who read portions of the manuscript and made valuable suggestions, I would like to thank John McGill of the University of Illinois at Urbana-Champaign, Gary McKenzie of the University of Texas at Austin, Arthur Peterson of Everett Junior High School in San Francisco, Frank Ryan of the University of California, Riverside, and Helen Sagl of Indiana University at Bloomington. I am especially indebted to Elizabeth Léonie Simpson of the University of Southern California and to Gary Burke of Harcourt Brace Jovanovich, who were responsible for my writing this book, and to those who helped put it all together: William Dyckes and Andrea Haight, the editors who carefully polished the manuscript; Nancy Kirsh, the designer of the book; Lois Paster, who was in charge of the illustration program; and photographer Kenneth Karp, who took many of the pictures especially for this book. And finally, I would like to thank my husband, Samuel Oliner, and my sons, Ron, David, and Ian, for their cooperation and support during the many months in which this book was written and edited.

Contents

Part II
Humanistic Concerns   **75**

8 Visual and Verbal Experiences 245

Part IV

Evaluation   **277**

9 Evaluation 279

Part V

The Unit Plan   **325**

10 Unit and Lesson Plans   327

I

Cognitive Concerns

Inquiry

Although social studies educators today are almost unanimous in advocating *inquiry,* there is no real consensus regarding the meaning of the term. Inquiry is a complex concept and a crucial one. It has been the core of most of the new developments that have occurred in the social studies over the last few years and underlies much of the material in this book.

Some Basic Attributes of Inquiry

Inquiry is, first of all, *a teaching strategy*—that is, a systematic approach to learning designed to achieve a definite objective. The objective may be a long-term one, such as the study of the effects of technology on our lives, or a short-term one, such as learning to read map symbols.

Second, inquiry is *intended to involve the students as much as possible.* Curiosity and active involvement encourage learning; passivity hinders it. Inquiry requires a high level of consistent student involvement. It is not a one-shot technique to be called on from time to time.

Third, inquiry *requires thinking*—particularly higher-level thinking. Involvement of itself is not necessarily an indication of inquiry. Students may talk a great deal, paint a mural, read, or jump around—but unless thought accompanies these processes, they are not inquiry. The essence of inquiry is the planned involvement of students in thinking.

These three points raise a great many questions, some of which will be answered in this chapter. First, however, we will have to deal with the two most basic ones: What's so important about thinking? Just what *is* thinking?

The Value of Thinking

If we believed that we live in the best of all possible worlds, educators might reasonably be quite content to merely reproduce existing patterns—to teach youngsters to do exactly as we have done in the past in order to perpetuate what is. Thinking would be entirely unnecessary. But since few people agree with this assumption, we have come to believe that thinking is a mechanism for inducing the changes needed for improvement.

If the best minds of our century agreed on the reasons for the world's imperfections and on their solutions, we might be able to dispense with thinking. The best we might do then would be to marshal our educational expertise to effectively teach these solutions as catechism or prescriptions. But since authorities do not agree—and there is even doubt regarding exactly who the authorities are—thinking is a way of introducing new ideas.

If truth were monolithic and universally recognized, thinking could be dispensed with. Truth, however, is pluralistic—as varied as the beliefs of different groups and individuals in different times. Even scientific "truth" is tentative and subject to changing information. Thinking is a means of evaluating "truth" statements—of testing whether they are internally consistent, logically sound, based on empirical reality, and can be independently validated.

Finally, thinking is an intensely human and pleasurable activity. Imposing intellectual order on disorder, gaining new insights, proposing new solutions are all satisfying activities—so deeply satisfying, apparently, that despite frequent concerted efforts throughout history to suppress it, thinking has proved as sturdy a drive as motherhood. But effective thinking, like effective mothering, needs a supportive environment to flourish.

What Is Thinking? Psychologists have devoted considerable energy to determining precisely what thinking is, and their work is by no means complete. New evidence and paths of investigation emerge each year. The contribution of J. P. Guilford, who identified some fifty different primary mental abilities that human beings use in thinking, is particularly pertinent to this discussion.[1] Guilford classified the primary mental abilities in three major categories: (1) the *contents,* or kind of information dealt with, (2) the *operations* performed on the information, and (3) the *products* of the operations. The mental abilities that concern us here are those of the second category, which are the most relevant to inquiry. Guilford identified five types of operations.[2]

Memory: those abilities involved in the retention or storage of information.

Cognition: those abilities that have to do with comprehending—the discovery or recognition of information.

Convergent production: those abilities used to generate *determined* information from other information. (This kind of thinking proceeds toward a determined or conventional answer.)

Divergent production: those abilities used to generate *varied* information from given or known information.

Evaluation: those abilities used in making decisions about the goodness, accuracy, or suitability of information.

Social studies teachers have traditionally called primarily on memory and cognition, somewhat on convergent production, and least of all on divergent production and evaluation abilities. And this is very significant.

Memory, cognition, and *convergent production* abilities are most useful in confirming knowledge that is given us. If we are expected to learn, for example, that culture affects the use of economic resources, we call on memory to store this information, on cognition to understand it, and on convergent production abilities to examine data with a view toward supporting it. Hence these abilities lend themselves to preserving what is known and to maintaining the status quo.

[1]J. P. Guilford, "The Structure of the Intellect," *Psychological Bulletin,* 53:4 (July 1956), pp. 267–93.
[2]Robert Wilson, "The Structure of the Intellect," in Mary Jane Aschner and Charles W. Bish, eds., *Productive Thinking in Education* (New York: NEA and Carnegie Corporation of New York, 1965), p. 21.

Divergent production and *evaluation* abilities, on the other hand, are most useful in generating new knowledge and suggesting needed change. We would use these abilities to challenge, rather than support, the statement that culture affects the use of economic resources, for they lend themselves to a critical examination of data and are intended to lead to alternative explanations.

Both preserving the old and generating the new are important. Social studies classrooms, however, have been primarily oriented toward preserving. If inquiry is to be encouraged, educators must call upon divergent production and evaluation abilities more frequently. A teacher concerned with helping pupils develop a full range of intellectual abilities must ensure that they engage in all kinds of mental operations.

Stimulating Thinking Through Questions

It is widely assumed that simply exposing people to experiences inevitably leads them to think, but this is neither necessarily nor inevitably the case. It is quite possible to have a variety of experiences with different people and places and not really think about them. Perhaps the most obvious example of this is school itself. Despite the fact that children and teachers are in almost daily contact, they frequently know very little about each other. The feelings, attitudes, significant life experiences — even physical appearance — of others may never be considered.

One way to stimulate thinking is to ask certain kinds of questions: "What are your feelings about this?" "How can you be sure this is right?" "Is this an adequate description?" Questions such as these can focus attention on experiences that might otherwise be overlooked. Some individuals may generate these questions by themselves; others need help. But either way, the question is one of the most basic tools for promoting thinking.

If we are to stimulate a fuller range of mental abilities, we must take care to ask questions that are appropriate for each ability. Chart 1 – 1 gives a number of examples of questions that can be used to stimulate the mental abilities identified in Guilford's list.

We cannot be certain, of course, that questions designed to stimulate particular mental abilities will always really do so. It may well be that a question like "How can we solve the problem of urban congestion?" which is intended to stimulate divergent production, may really be stimulating memory for a student who happened to read an article about this very thing and remembers what was said. However, if the teacher asks a large number of how-can-we-solve questions, it is highly probable that the pupils will eventually be forced into divergent production.

Educational Objectives

The work of Guilford and other educational psychologists has not only enlarged our understanding of the mental abilities, it clearly has implications for education. As a result of their work, major efforts have been made to develop ways to modify teaching practices to make use of the full range of mental abilities.

The first step that had to be taken before all of this could proceed, however,

---

Chart 1–1
Stimulating Mental Abilities with Questions

Questions to Stimulate Memory
What is the population of New York?
What did you learn about the American Indian last year?
According to our text, why is it important to conserve energy?

Questions to Stimulate Cognition
Write a summary of the paragraph *in your own words*.
What is the main idea in this essay?
What important things does this picture show?

Questions to Stimulate Convergent Production
Make a bar graph using these figures.
What is the only conclusion we can reach with the information we have?
Since we now know what makes a statement either a fact or an opinion, is the following statement a fact or is it an opinion?

Questions to Stimulate Divergent Production
What other types of solutions can we propose?
What other conclusion can we reach?
Can you think of another reason why this might have happened?

Questions to Stimulate Evaluation
Is this information consistent with other information we have?
What makes you think so?
Do we have enough information to make a conclusion? Why or why not?
Is the information correct? What makes you think so?

---

was to determine the relationship between the mental abilities that had been identified by Guilford and the objectives of the schools. This was a potentially difficult task, for the schools did not seem to be very sure just what it was they were trying to do. Over the years, many new programs of study had been launched by curriculum developers and teachers, who had specified thousands of educational objectives. But the language they used to describe these objectives was vague and often ambiguous, so very little progress had really been made. In a book published in the same year as Guilford's article, Benjamin Bloom wrote of this problem: ". . . some teachers believe their students should 'really understand,' others desire their students to 'internalize knowledge,' still others want their students to 'grasp the core or essence' or 'comprehend.' Do they all mean the same thing?"[3]

Bloom and his associates hoped to resolve this problem by establishing a very precise classification system. When their work was published, however, it became apparent that it could be combined with Guilford's and put to other uses that were equally if not more important.

[3]Benjamin Bloom, ed., *Taxonomy of Educational Objectives: Handbook I, Cognitive Domain* (New York: David McKay, 1956).

The Bloom group divided educational objectives into three domains. The first of these, cognitive — or intellectual — objectives, are the ones that pertain to Guilford's work. Under this heading, Bloom's *Taxonomy* lists six major categories, which might be summarized as follows:

Knowledge: objectives that require the recall of various kinds of information.

Comprehension: objectives that require the translation of a communication from one symbolic form to another (e.g., paraphrasing, converting from visual symbols to verbal symbols) or the interpretation and extrapolation of a communication.

Application: objectives that require the use of abstractions, such as principles or generalized methods, to solve a particular and concrete problem.

Analysis: objectives that require breaking a communication down into its constituent elements so that relationships among these elements are made clear.

Synthesis: objectives that require the combining of parts in an original way in order to form a whole.

Evaluation: objectives that require the making of judgments about the value of material and methods in accordance with some set of standards.

Bloom and his associates found that these categories form an ascending scale of complexity and that each is dependent on the one before it. That is to say, until students have knowledge of something we cannot expect them to comprehend it, until they comprehend it they cannot apply it, until they apply it they cannot analyze it, and so on up the scale. Figure 1–1 represents this hierarchy diagrammatically.

Figure 1–1
A Hierarchy of Educational Objectives

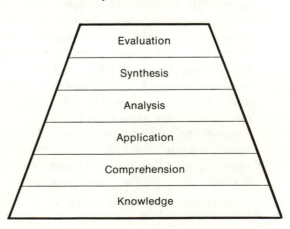

**Mental Abilities
and Educational
Objectives**

It is readily apparent that a relationship exists between the educational objectives identified by the Bloom group and the mental abilities identified by Guilford. Chart 1–2 represents this relationship by matching the educational objectives with each of the mental abilities that presumably need to be stimulated in order to achieve them.

**Chart 1–2
The Relationship of Educational Objectives to Mental Abilities**

Bloom's List of Educational Objectives		Guilford's List of Mental Abilities
Knowledge	*depends on*	Memory
Comprehension	*depends on*	Cognition
Application	*depends on*	Divergent or Convergent Production
Analysis	*depends on*	Divergent or Convergent Production
Synthesis	*depends on*	Divergent or Convergent Production
Evaluation	*depends on*	Evaluation

This relationship has two significant implications. First, it suggests that the more complex educational objectives correspond to the more complex mental abilities. As inquiry is primarily associated with the more complex mental abilities, we may therefore assume that the educational objectives in an inquiry strategy would also be primarily those of the upper levels: evaluation, synthesis, and analysis. The second implication is that the mental abilities form a hierarchy similar to that discovered by the Bloom group in educational objectives. This point is crucially important in the teaching of thinking: we cannot stimulate the higher levels of thinking until we have dealt with the lower ones.

Suppose, for example, that we wanted students to evaluate the accuracy of a Mercator projection. Exactly what would they have to be able to do in order to achieve this level of thinking? Obviously they must have *knowledge* of map reading—that is, they must be able to recall the conventions regarding the translation of written and pictorial map symbols into spoken ones. Second, they must be able to *comprehend* these symbols—to paraphrase and interpret them. Third, they should be able to *apply* appropriate principles of map construction in order to interpret the map correctly (e.g., principles relating to longitude and latitude, designation of geographic boundaries, scale construction). Fourth, they need to be able to *analyze* the map by identifying major components and their relationships to each other (e.g., hemispheres and continents, scale and its relationship to actual size). Fifth, they would have to be able to *syn-*

thesize what they know so that they have available mentally a concept of what a "map" is and what makes some maps better than others. Finally, they would have to be able to *evaluate* the accuracy of the map by comparing it with the globe and understanding wherein and why distortions arise.

Teaching Strategies for Educational Objectives

There is no certain evidence that students must go through all these steps before being able to make evaluations, but logic suggests that they will probably go through most of them. This leads us to the next issue: How can we design teaching strategies in the social studies so that students can successfully achieve all levels of educational objectives?

If we assume that students need to achieve lower-level objectives before they can achieve higher-level ones, it follows that questions need to be arranged in such a manner as to ensure that this will occur. Thus any strategy, no matter whether it intends to stimulate evaluation or merely comprehension, should probably begin with questions intended to stimulate knowledge.

While there is no definitive "best" sequence of questions in a teaching strategy, some are better than others. Chart 1–3 offers a series of possible sequences that can be used to stimulate the different levels of objectives.

Each of the questioning sequences shown in Chart 1–3 plays an important role in encouraging inquiry. An inquiry strategy, however, will incorporate more than one of them. Hence it is more appropriate to refer to them as substrategies—that is, component parts of an inquiry strategy.

Chart 1–3
Questioning Sequences for Each of the Educational Objectives

A Knowledge Strategy

Student Objective	*Guiding Questions*	*Example*
To identify what needs to be known.	What exactly do we need to know?	What is it that we need to know about Bangor, Maine? Population? Industries? History?
To recall specifics.	Who knows something about this?	Who knows the population? Major industries?
To recall sources of knowledge.	How did you learn this?	Where did you get the information?
To recall divergent knowledge claims.	Does everyone agree this is so?	Does everyone agree? Why not?
To verify knowledge where necessary.	Do we need to check this? What sources can we use?	Do we need to check this? Where can we find the information?

Other Types of Knowledge Questions

Of terminology:	Can you pronounce this word? Which words describe this best?
Of facts:	When did this happen? Who were the people involved in it?
Of conventions:	What symbols do map makers use to indicate population density? Where would we find books on the Civil War in the library? How can we find the word "city" in the dictionary? What type of information could we find in an atlas?
Of trends and sequences:	What has been happening to population growth in the United States since the beginning of the twentieth century? How do human bodies change over time?
Of classification and categories:	What do we call books about things that didn't really happen? What do we call a body of land surrounded on all sides by water?
Of criteria:	How can we tell if a statement is true? How can we tell if a problem is important?
Of principles and generalizations:	Why do people all over the world have different eating habits? Where are food stores generally located?
Of theories and structures:	According to _____, what are the causes of war? What are the major divisions of the local government?

A Comprehension Strategy

Student Objective	Guiding Questions	Examples
To select content that requires further clarification.	What needs to be clarified?	What words don't you understand? Is the main idea clear?
To demonstrate comprehension by translation from one symbolic system to another.	Can you put this in different words? How would you draw this?	How would you define "role" in your own words?
To interpret.	What are the most important ideas? Points? Conclusions?	What is the most important part of the definition of "role"?
To extrapolate.	If these ideas are right, what is likely to happen?	If each person has a role in the family, does this mean that fathers' roles will be the same in all families?

Other Types of Comprehension Questions

To translate:	Tell what the (picture, graph, play, article) says in your own words.
	Illustrate the ideas in the (story, play, article) by (drawing a picture, acting out the parts, preparing a chart).
To interpret:	What are the most important points in the (picture, model, map, graph, cartoon, film)?
	Which of the following (statements, pictures, graphs, enactments) most closely resembles what you have (observed, read, heard)?
To extrapolate:	What would be the most likely (conclusion, trend, consequence) given what you have (observed, read, heard)?
	Given this (generalization, concept, principle, idea), what would you say would happen in this situation?

An Application Strategy

Student Objective	Guiding Questions	Examples
To comprehend the example.	What is happening here?	What is happening in this picture?
To interpret the example.	What are the most important parts? Points? Facts?	What is the most important part of this picture?
To apply knowledge of principles.	What principle, concept, generalization does this illustrate?	What idea have we learned that is illustrated in this picture?

Other Types of Application Questions

Of rules:	What procedures are best to follow (in preparing your research project, in composing your mural, in solving a controversy)?
Of concepts:	Given what you know about (how a house is made, what an opinion is, what a nonrenewable resource is), what would you call this?
Of relationships and generalizations:	Given what we have learned about (the relationship of price to supply and demand, the roles of fathers and mothers in families), what is likely to happen if (the price of sugar continues to rise, more mothers go out and work)?

An Analysis Strategy

Student Objective	*Guiding Questions*	*Examples*
To identify the main elements of written materials, pictures, graphs, problems.	What parts are included in this description? Picture? Graph? Problem?	What are the important parts of this graph?
To comprehend each part.	What is the meaning of each?	What does the horizontal line stand for? The vertical line?
To classify parts.	What is included in each part?	What information is given for each country?
To identify the relationship among parts.	How are the parts alike? Different? Connected?	How does the amount of energy used by each person in the United States compare with the amount of energy used by each person in Mexico? Who uses more?
		How many times more energy is used per person in the United States as compared with Mexico?
To identify trends.	What does this show? What can we conclude?	What can we say about the amount of energy used in different countries?

Other Types of Analysis Questions

Of elements:

What are the (facts, assumptions, hypotheses, values, distortions, conclusions and supporting evidence) in this textbook's version of Washington's crossing of the Delaware?

What (important events, characters, results, behaviors) are included in this account of Columbus's voyage to America?

What are the (feelings, values, attitudes) of the (writer, painter, photographer, speaker)?

What are your (feelings, values, attitudes)?

Of relationships:

How are parts related (chronologically, spatially, conceptually, as cause and effect)?
How is land related to capital?
How are houses related to homes?
Does poverty cause little education or does little education cause poverty?

Of organization:

How does the (illustration, style, print, order) support the main idea?

What techniques does the (author, photographer, speaker, filmmaker) use to convince people that (energy sources are running low, air pollution is not a real problem, the character is not quite as honest as he might be)?

In what (sequence, conceptual order, logical order) are the main ideas presented?

A Synthesis Strategy

Student Objective	Guiding Question	Examples
Recall learnings.	What did you note? Observe?	What did you note about the Italian immigrant experiences? The Jewish immigrant experience?
Analyze common and divergent elements.	In what ways were these similar? Divergent?	What things did they have in common? In what ways were they different?
Conceptualize by labeling and defining common relationships.	What shall we call these similar things? What does this include?	What shall we call the common experiences?
Hypothesize about the relationships among concepts.	What can we say about the relationship between _____ and _____?	What can we say about the relationship of immigration to poverty? Immigration and life styles? Immigration and settlement patterns?
Propose a plan to test the hypotheses.	How can we find out if these are really so?	How can we find out if the same applies to all immigrant groups?
Generalize about relationships.	Do our hypotheses hold up? Do we need to change them? How?	Do these ideas apply to Irish immigrants? Puerto Rican immigrants? Do we need to change our ideas? How?
Propose plans.	Does this relationship present a problem? How can we handle it?	Can anything be done to prevent these problems from occurring again? How?
Produce a unique communication.	How can you present your ideas? A mural? Scrapbooks? Team reports? A display?	How would you present the things you have learned and felt to others?

Other Types of Synthesis Questions

To produce a unique communication:	Can you (make a speech; present a pantomime; write a story, poem, report; compose a song) about (the Navajos' first contacts with a pioneer family, economic roles among the Ashanti) that includes your own ideas and feelings?
To produce a plan or propose a set of operations:	How can you (test, evaluate, check, confirm) whether (a change in diet can alter height, noise affects people's behavior, there is likely to be a greater number of people living in cities in the future)? What can we (propose, construct, design) to (overcome the problems of older people, teach people how to stop polluting the environment, help government meet the needs of special groups)?
To derive a set of abstract relations:	How can we (group, classify, arrange, organize) the (life styles of women in different cultures and periods, economic products and services, governmental relationships in the United States)? What can we (hypothesize, generalize, predict) about (culture and the use of the environment, families and economic needs, rules and people's behavior)?

An Evaluation Strategy

Student Objective	*Guiding Questions*	*Examples*
Identify what needs to be evaluated.	What do we need to evaluate? Why?	You have read many different accounts of the "discovery" of America. Should we accept them all? Why?
Identify and define standards for evaluation.	What standards should we use to evaluate? What do they include?	What standards should we apply? Probability? Accuracy? Evidence? Remains? What is meant by each?
Propose plans for collecting appropriate data.	Where can we find evidence for each standard?	How can we find the evidence we need? Within the accounts? Outside sources?
Make judgments.	Which, can we conclude, best meets the standards? Why?	Which account is best? Why?

Sample Questions to Guide Internal Evaluation

Do the (facts, maps, diagrams, photographs, figures) appear (accurate, to exclude other evidence, documented, probable)?

Are the (conclusions, generalizations, impressions) supported by evidence?

Are the (conclusions, generalizations, impressions) warranted on the basis of the evidence offered?

Are (meanings, definitions, facts, conclusions) always used in the same way?

Is it (logical, clear, reasonable, plausible, precise, probable)?

Sample Questions to Guide External Evaluation

How does the (generalization, theory, fact, photograph, map, graph) compare with the best models in the same field?

To what extent does it meet values such as (justice, equality, beauty, utility, fairness)?

Which of the proposed means will meet goals (the best, the cheapest, the fastest, with least harmful side effects to others and the environment)?

What are the probable (consequences, effects, results) of each?

Thinking and Inquiry Processes   One final piece needs to be put into place before a specific description of inquiry strategies can begin. We need to be able to identify what types of activities take place when we think. The following list of processes has been suggested by John Michaelis, who calls them *inquiry processes*:[4]

recalling	analyzing	defining the problem
observing	comparing	exploring values
classifying	interpreting	hypothesizing
defining	integrating	gathering data
contrasting	synthesizing	proposing solutions
generalizing	evaluating	testing solutions
inferring	predicting	making decisions

[4]John Michaelis, "Process of Inquiry in Each Mode," in R. Jones, ed., *Social Studies for Young Americans* (Dubuque, Iowa: Kendall/Hunt, 1970), p. 93.

Chart 1–4
The Relationship of Inquiry Processes
to Educational Objectives and Mental Abilities

Educational Objective	Mental Ability	Inquiry Process
knowledge	memory	recalling
comprehension	cognition	observing interpreting inferring

application	convergent or divergent production	classifying
		    (based on given principle)
		predicting
		    (based on given principle)

analysis	convergent or divergent production	classifying
		    (where principle is
		    not given)
		defining
		contrasting
		comparing
		analyzing
		gathering data
		exploring values

synthesis	convergent or divergent production	conceptualizing
		generalizing
		integrating
		synthesizing
		hypothesizing
		predicting
		    (where principle is
		    not given)
		proposing solutions

evaluation	evaluation	evaluating testing solutions making decisions

---

Some of the terms that Michaelis uses are the same as those used by Bloom, a fact that suggests that inquiry processes can probably be broken down into the same categories. The educational objective *knowledge* would, for example, probably employ the inquiry process *recall*. Comprehension, which is more complex, would appear to call on the inquiry processes of observing, interpreting, and inferring. Chart 1–4 is an attempt to match the various inquiry processes to the lists of educational objectives and mental abilities.

Inquiry Strategies

An inquiry strategy is intended to promote conditions under which students will: (1) make use of all their mental abilities, (2) spend much of their time in pursuit of higher-level educational objectives, and (3) engage in multiple inquiry processes. Figure 1–3 translates the relationships of four different types of strategies into visual terms. The top of the figure represents a maximal inquiry situation and the strategy that promotes it is an inquiry strategy. As we go down the figure, we move further and further away from an inquiry situation. However, since many of the components of inquiry still occur within the middle ranges of the figure, those strategies that promote these components are called "modified inquiry" strategies. Near the bottom of the figure there is very little

Figure 1–3
Instructional Strategies and Their Associated Student Processes

Instructional Strategy	Process	Objective	Ability
Inquiry	evaluating testing solutions making decisions	evaluation	evaluation
Modified Inquiry	generalizing integrating synthesizing hypothesizing predicting (where principle is not given) proposing solutions	synthesis	convergent and divergent
	classifying (where principle is not given) defining contrasting comparing analyzing gathering data exploring values	analysis	convergent and divergent
	classifying (based on given principle) predicting (based on given principle)	application	convergent and divergent
Modified Expository	observing interpreting inferring	comprehension	cognition
Expository	recalling	knowledge	memory

student inquiry. The strategy that tends to prevail in these conditions is an "expository" strategy, that is, a strategy in which the teacher or text is doing most of the work and may be engaging in inquiry, but the students show little evidence of inquiry. Of course, the students may be silently engaged in inquiry under an expository strategy—but we see no evidence of it. This does not mean that teachers should never employ an expository strategy; it may be very useful to do so on occasion. But extended usage of the expository strategy tends to discourage inquiry.

Constructing the figure in this way suggests something else about an inquiry strategy—that while most of the time will be spent in higher-level inquiry, some of the time will nevertheless have to be spent in lower-level cognition. Lower-level cognitive skills are essential as a foundation for higher skills.

An Optimal Inquiry Strategy

It is generally believed that students will engage in most of the processes of inquiry and use most of their mental abilities if they have to:

identify an issue
develop tentative hypotheses
gather and evaluate evidence
test hypotheses
draw tentative conclusions

Suppose, for example, that the issue in which a student was interested was how and why clothing had changed over time. He might begin by looking at drawings of clothing styles in the United States. This might lead to the discovery of different patterns and the tentative hypothesis that men's clothing had become simpler or that women's hemlines had risen. But then the student might begin to read about clothing changes in other parts of the world and decide that the patterns that had been observed appeared to be truer of western Europe and the United States than of Africa or Samoa. The idea that clothing changes are related to such things as war, climate, and the economy will probably occur during these readings. The student might compare and evaluate the ideas of different writers and arrive at some satisfactory conclusion—or abandon the effort without any final resolution. This type of activity is circular and can go on indefinitely. The sequence is illustrated in Figure 1–4.

Several factors make this an optimal inquiry strategy. First, it suggests to students the tentativeness of knowledge. Conclusions are rarely definitive—one simply tries to make the best judgment possible at the time based on as much evidence as one can find and the best evaluation one can make. Second, it suggests that the inquiry process does not begin at any particular point. It may as well begin with the identification of an issue as with a tentative conclusion. Third, it suggests that the sequence of steps in an inquiry strategy is uncertain. The arrows in Figure 1–4 point in both directions. Even so, it is not complete. The figure should in fact include two-way arrows connecting *all* of the activities. For example, gathering evidence might lead to other issues or a tentative con-

Figure 1–4
Student Activities Under an Optimal Inquiry Strategy

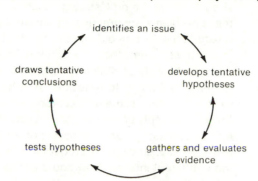

clusion might suggest an entirely new hypothesis. The fourth factor that contributes to making this an optimal strategy is the fact that a student engaged in such activities would probably also be engaged in higher thinking for most of the time—and therefore would probably also be engaged in most of the processes of inquiry.

To illustrate the inquiry strategy by way of contrast, let us examine student activities under an expository strategy. They would probably look like Figure 1–5.

The disadvantages of this type of strategy are clear. For one thing, the linear progression encourages students to believe that learning stops when the teacher finishes presenting material. Moreover, the primary activity the students appear to be engaged in is *receiving* the product of someone else's inquiry—which requires no more than simple memory and cognition.

Figure 1–5
Student Activities Under an Expository Strategy

receives an issue

↓

receives an hypothesis

↓

receives evidence and an evaluation of evidence

↓

receives tests of hypotheses

↓

receives conclusions

Some Issues   Despite the apparent attraction of an optimal inquiry strategy of the type just described, there are enough problems associated with it to suggest that it should not be the *only* strategy used in the social studies classroom. Some of these problems are practical in nature. An optimal inquiry strategy is premised on student selection of issues to be studied. If students study only those things that interest them, then the schools must have available many resources on graduated levels of difficulty—and this is extremely unlikely. Another problem is that it is difficult to assess what is happening in such a situation. How can we be sure, for example, that students are really engaging in higher thinking? They may simply be reading and observing sporadically—without really analyzing or evaluating—and perhaps not even acquiring essential comprehension skills. Finally, since every student in a classroom might theoretically be exploring a different interest, how could one teacher realistically respond to them all?

Equally important are the philosophical questions the strategy poses. Probably the most important issue is the justifiability of a social studies program based exclusively on student interests. True enough, student interests are vital to curriculum selection, but is this sufficient? Is it not also important to ensure that students grapple with social concerns, develop critical skills, and learn what scholars in various disciplines have already learned? Can we be sure students will do so when their studies are determined exclusively by their own interests? Moreover, many student interests are at least in part the result of a lack of awareness of alternatives. Does the school not have a legitimate responsibility to broaden this awareness? And finally, should we expect students to learn everything through inquiry? Or is there some knowledge that has already been explored extensively by others that the student might acquire in a quicker and more efficient way?

It appears then that there must be limits to the use of the optimal inquiry strategy and that it must be balanced with other forms of teaching. At least part of the time students should be engaged in learning material that has been selected for them—preferably through strategies that are designed to promote higher-level thinking.

Modified Inquiry Strategies   Implicitly or explicitly, all instructional materials place limitations on inquiry. They necessarily select the issues and data that the students are to explore and incorporate some sort of teaching strategy. In the past, most textbooks employed the basic expository strategy described above. But lately an increasing number have come to use *modified* inquiry strategies—that is, strategies that are not optimal but which are nevertheless inquiry oriented.

Two broad questions tend to guide modifications of inquiry strategies:

1. How much guidance should the strategy incorporate?
2. In what sequence should the steps of inquiry be arranged?

The first question has to do with the degree to which the conclusions of the lesson are predetermined. A lesson may be intended to reach a very definite conclusion, such as "the colonists won their independence by fighting a war," in which case the strategy is *closed.* Or it may be intended to stimulate the students to reach conclusions of their own, as is the case when asking "what other things could the colonists have done to show their unhappiness with England?" In this case the strategy is *open.*

The second question has to do with the way in which the conclusions are reached. A lesson may begin with some concrete detail and attempt to generalize from it (as when the teacher begins by reciting Patrick Henry's famous speech in order to make a point about nonviolent protest in general). In this case the strategy is *inductive.* Or the lesson may begin with a more abstract idea and proceed to a more concrete one (as when the teacher begins with a definition of nonviolent protest and its techniques and then goes on to cite specific acts of the colonists), in which case the strategy is *deductive.*

As every strategy must answer both of these questions, four different combinations tend to occur: (1) closed deductive, (2) open deductive, (3) closed inductive, or (4) open inductive. Each of these types of modified inquiry strategies will be dealt with in detail later in this chapter, but for the moment it would be best to examine the individual elements in greater detail.

A Closed Strategy   A closed strategy tends to impose predetermined issues, contents, and conclusions. Although it may include some opportunities for divergence, it emphasizes convergent thinking.

Issues are usually identified with precision in the form of a statement or generalization, rather than a question or problem. For example, the units developed under the consultantship of Hilda Taba for the Contra Costa County Schools in California begin with "main ideas" stated in the form of declarative statements, e.g., "Civilizations change when they meet a new culture. These changes may be one of degree."[5] "People of primitive cultures are extremely dependent upon their immediate environment and their own skills; people of a modern culture use the skills of others and are much less dependent on their environment."[6]

However, the form of the statement is not sufficient to impose a closed strategy. It must continue in ways that direct students toward convergence. The Taba units, for example, employ a strategy that is tightly structured to lead students to the main idea. Although the strategy incorporates many opportunities for higher-level thinking and multiple processes of inquiry, they emphasize convergence rather than divergence.

The following example is taken from the Harcourt Brace Jovanovich Concepts and Values series. The lesson is the introductory one in a unit called "We Look at Ourselves." It begins with some fairly open-ended questions: What are twins? How are brothers and sisters alike? However, the objective of the unit is to have the students arrive at a specific conclusion: "Individuals resemble each other."

[5]Contra Costa County Schools, *Latin America,* Grade 6 (Pleasant Hill, Calif.: Office of Superintendent of Schools, 1963), p. vi.

[6]Contra Costa County Schools, *A Study in Comparative Communities,* Grade 3 (Pleasant Hill, Calif.: Office of Superintendent of Schools, 1963), p. xi.

AN INTRODUCTORY DISCUSSION: pages 2 and 3

Before reading the text on these two pages, you may want to begin a discussion of human variability by asking:

T • Does anyone know some twins?
  • What are twins?
C • Two people who look alike.
  • Two people born at the same time.
T • How many of you have a brother or sister?
  • How are brothers and sisters alike? different?
C • They may look sort of alike.
  • They have the same parents.
  • They aren't the same age.
  • They may have different-colored hair.

Now ask the class to study pages 2 and 3. Ask:

T • Which picture shows twins? brother and sister?
  • How can you tell?
  • Can a boy and a girl be twins?

WORKING WITH THE PICTURES

Ask the class to look at page 2 and read the text. Then, ask:

T • How might the twin girls be different from each other?
C • They might not like the same things.
  • One might be fatter than the other.

Follow the same questioning sequence as the children turn their attention to page 3. Ask:

T • How are both pictures alike?
C • Both show two children.

• Both show a girl.
• All the children are wearing clothes.

WORKING WITH "THE BIG IDEA": pages 12 and 13

At this point, each child has probably begun to understand the concept of human variability. Most likely, each will be able to predict that children everywhere may look different, but that they are similar in many ways. "The Big Idea" provides an opportunity for the children to summarize their understandings developed through their work in this unit.

You may want the children to look at the words "The Big Idea" in their books and try to explain what this phrase means. One acceptable response would be:

C • The important thing.

You can explain that the pages in this book with the words "The Big Idea" at the top show what the important parts of the unit are.

Now ask the children to study the pictures on pages 12 and 13. You can ask:

T • What are some big ideas here?
C • All kinds of different people.
  • All kinds of different places.
  • All the kids are having fun.
  • Children look different in some ways; the same in other ways.

Next, work with the text questions.

From *Principles and Practices in the Teaching of the Social Sciences: Concepts and Values,* Blue (Level One), 2d ed., by Paul F. Brandwein et al. (New York: Harcourt Brace Jovanovich, 1975), pp. 47, 61. Reprinted by permission.

The goal of the unit is accomplished in the final lesson, in which the students are asked to identify "The Big Idea." In short, the objective of the lesson and the entire unit is to have students arrive at a closed, or convergent, answer.

Advantages and Disadvantages

There is nothing wrong with closed strategies that emphasize convergent learning. At times, they are essential. A legitimate purpose of education is to transmit validated information and ideas, and closed strategies are an efficient means for accomplishing this.

However, not all learning should proceed in this manner. For one thing, there are many important ideas that are either tentative or incomplete. (For example, only partial explanations can be offered to account for the origins of war.)

For another, if all learning is structured toward convergence, students soon become aware that they are required to produce desired answers and weary of the game of outguessing the teacher or text. They may ultimately simply avoid the risk of being "wrong" by retreating into silence. Most important, students who are always taught with closed strategies will become accustomed to continual deference to authority and learn to suppress divergent thinking.

An Open Strategy   An open strategy tries to avoid imposing predetermined issues, content, and conclusions. It emphasizes divergent thinking. However, all modified inquiry strategies must impose some convergence; issues, some content, and some conclusions are chosen in advance.

When the issue is an unresolved problem, the strategy tends to incline toward openness. For example, the problem "How can we influence people to behave more kindly toward each other?" has clearly not been resolved in society; hence it tends to promote open inquiry. However, even when the issue is a question or concept to which answers are to some degree predetermined, it is still possible to incorporate a more open strategy. The primary requisite of an open strategy is that it involve students in divergent thinking a good deal of the time.

Among the textbooks that employ open strategies is the Holt Databank series. The Process Objectives proposed in this particular example tend to promote divergent thinking. The accompanying lesson plan suggests a strategy for implementing one of the Process Objectives.

OBJECTIVES

1. Information Objectives
   1.1 There is a sufficient amount of historical evidence to support Christopher Columbus' claim that he discovered the New World on his famous voyage in 1492.
   1.2 There is a considerable amount of historical evidence to suggest that other groups of people may have or actually did discover the New World before Columbus.
   1.3 There are many different kinds of historical evidence available to scholars—journals, eye-witness accounts, maps, sagas and other elements of oral tradition, archeological findings, etc.

2. Process Objectives
   2.1 Patterns to begin investigations
      2.1.1 Students will investigate the discovery of the New World by six different groups of people—Columbus and his followers, the Indians, the Vikings, the Chinese, the Phoenicians, and the Egyptians.
      Evaluation: During the course of the unit, students will be asked the question "Who discovered America?" They will locate and examine evidence in their textbooks and in the *Databank* and independently draw their own conclusions.

DAY 4/ Did the Indians Discover America?

Materials in the Databank
Data Pack 1: Did the
Indians discover America?

TODAY'S LESSON

Today the class will work in groups with DATABANK materials which will help them decide whether it is possible or probable that the Indians arrived in the New World before Columbus. You may also want the class to decide if it is possible or probable that the Indians came from Asia, and if they arrived 12,000 or more years before Columbus.

WORKING WITH THE DATA PACK

Tell the students that today they will work in groups, using Data Pack 1 to decide if it is possible or probable that the Indians arrived in the New World before Columbus. Make sure that the class understands the meaning of "possible" and "probable." Give an example. On a dark, damp, cloudy day, sunlight is possible. On a dark, damp, cloudy day rain is probable. When something is probable there is strong evidence or clues like the darkness, dampness, and clouds in the example. But the clues don't guarantee that it will rain. When you say that something is possible, you mean that it *could* happen, but there are no good clues or strong evidence.

Explain that some scientists think the Indians arrived in America more than 12,000 years ago, coming from Siberia. Tell the class that they will examine the facts to see if this is possible or probable.

Briefly run through the types of evidence in the data pack: the fact sheet on Card 3, the artifacts on Card 4, the theory of migration on Card 5, and the maps on Card 6. Now explain that Card 1 states the problem.

Divide the class into groups and give each group a copy of Data Pack 1: *Did the Indians Discover America?* Before the groups begin

work, point out that the questions on Card 2 will help them answer the question "Did the Indians discover America?"

Tell the class that they will have fifteen minutes to arrive at their answers. Emphasize that group members should feel free to express differing opinions, and that each group should choose a representative to tell the class what it has decided. One of the representatives may report that the migration was possible, another that it was impossible, and still another that it was probable.

While the groups are working you may want to write some of the key words on the chalkboard to guide the discussion later. You will probably want to go from group to group to see how they are proceeding in their examination of the evidence and to offer help wherever needed.

DISCUSSING THE DATA PACK

Before representatives give their reports, ask the class some of the questions on Card 2 to make sure that they understand the information on the datacards. Since this is the first time they are dealing with archeological evidence, you might remind them of the evidence they examined in the preceding days— Columbus' journal—and ask them what kind of evidence they have just examined.

As the representatives report, have them support their views with reference to evidence examined in the data pack. Tell them that historians are required to do the same thing when they report their findings or theories. When all reports have been given, you may want to ask the class if anyone has changed his or her mind. If so, why?

By the end of the lesson, the students should understand the theory that the Indians discovered America more than 12,000 years ago, even if they do not agree with it.

CARBON-14 DATING

If there is time, tell the class about Carbon-14 dating, a scientific method of finding out how old certain archeological findings are.

Carbon-14 dating, a testing device, was invented by Dr. Willard F. Libby. It can date objects as old as 250,000 years, with an error margin of only 250 years. The test is possible because of the presence of an unstable isotope, or different form of carbon, called Carbon-14, in all living matter. The isotope is produced in the atmosphere when nuclei of nitrogen—a gas in living matter—atoms are struck by cosmic rays. The resultant Carbon-14 is then absorbed by plants, and by man, who lives directly or indirectly on plants. Dr. Libby discovered that the death of a plant or animal started the disintegration of its Carbon-14 content at a fixed rate. This could be measured in comparison with Carbon-14 in living plants or animals, and the death rate of the test matter determined. Dating charcoal from an old hearth, for example, would reveal the approximate time the wood was used, since it had lost its life, or "died" when it was thrust into the fire to roast a mammoth steak.

DATA PACK IDENTIFICATION

Data Pack 1: Did the Indians Discover America?

A brief identification of the cards in the data pack appears here for your convenience:

Card 1 states the problem, the group's task, and outlines the available information and evidence they will use.

Card 2 contains questions about each card; the questions will help focus the group's inquiry.

Card 3 has facts about the Sandia Cave and about other archeological findings in North America and Siberia.

Card 4 has pictures of flint spear points found in Sandia Cave and flint spear points found in Siberia.

Card 5 offers information about where the Indians might have come from and how they might have come to North America.

Card 6 has two maps, one showing the distance between Asia and America from 10,000 to 25,000 years ago, and another showing the distance between Asia and America today.

Card 7 is a map of other places in the New World where scientists have found Indians remains many thousands of years old.

FOR THE DATABOOK

Now that the class has been introduced to the idea that Columbus may not have been the first person to discover America, the students are ready to consider others who may have been first. Today, you will introduce your class to the possibility that the Indians discovered America.

Remind the class that Columbus found Indians here when he arrived. When did the Indians arrive? Some scientists think that Indians arrived in America at least 12,000 years before Columbus. They think that the Indians came from Asia on a land bridge that once existed where the Bering Strait is today.

Ask the students to discuss what sorts of evidence they would look for to prove or disprove the idea that the Indians of America came from Asia more than 12,000 years ago. After they have had sufficient time to share their ideas, explain that there is geological evidence for the existence of the land bridge, that there is a strong physical similarity between the Indians of America and the remains of the ancient inhabitants of Siberia as well as the Siberians of today, and that similar flint tools, many thousands of years old, have been found in Siberia and America. Does the class now believe that the Indians might have been the first to discover America?

Advantages and Disadvantages

A modified open inquiry strategy permits students to relate to issues in terms personally relevant for them. Since they need not be continually engaged in "outguessing" the teacher or text, the students can develop their own ideas. The acceptance of divergence creates a climate in which students do not feel threatened or anxious. Higher-level thinking is thus more likely to occur. Finally, it provides opportunities for student feedback to teachers, so that teachers get to know what their students really think.

However, because this is a modified open strategy, there are potential difficulties that need to be recognized. Texts generally attempt to provide direction for a maximum number of contingencies, both in terms of teacher questions and student answers. As a result, some teachers may be inclined to depend on the text too heavily and overlook the opportunities to generate their own questions based on actual student responses. Teachers may also prefer to use divergent questions as means for eliciting convergent answers. They may also restrict the entire social studies program to the issues specified in the text and not attempt to supplement them with other issues emanating more directly from student interests.

An Inductive Strategy

An inductive strategy arranges the sequence of learning so that it proceeds from the more particular to the more general, or from the more concrete to the more abstract. The inductive strategy tends to be favored in the elementary grades. In the example opposite, taken from a fifth-grade unit in the Laidlaw series, students are led to the major concepts after a series of questions of graduated abstractness. They begin with experiences taken from their own lives, then proceed to form hypotheses about other groups of people, and conclude with a reading in which the ideas are more fully developed.

Advantages and Disadvantages

An inductive strategy tends to be in accord with what is generally known about how young children learn. It enables them to conceptualize on the basis of concrete experiences and helps them to avoid the empty "verbalization" of abstractions that may have little meaning for them. Moreover, it tends to involve students in more synthesizing activities, and, therefore, higher educational objectives.

The major disadvantage of an inductive strategy is that it requires considerably more time to execute than the other strategies do. If all learning were to proceed inductively, a great many things of importance would have to be omitted from the curriculum simply because of lack of time. Moreover, it is not at all certain that all effective learning needs to be restricted to this one approach. While an inductive strategy is generally to be preferred over a deductive one in the elementary classroom, there are occasions when a deductive strategy is appropriate.

TEACHING HELPS — Unit Introduction, Pages 92–94

CONCEPTS

1. Americans today or their ancestors once had a native land other than where they now live.

2. People who came to America brought with them many of their beliefs and customs.

Recommended Procedure

Getting Started Ask if any members of the class know of someone, perhaps a famous person they have read or heard about, who lived in another country before coming to the United States. Be prepared to suggest someone you know or have read about. Using a map or globe, have pupils try to locate where these people came from.

Developing the Lesson Ask the class if they know of reasons why people from many different countries of the world have come to the United States to live. Have the pupils turn to page 92 and observe the picture. Ask pupils such questions as the following. (1) What might we learn about the culture of the people in this picture by looking at the clothes they wear? (2) Do you think the people in this picture or their ancestors have always lived in our country?

Lead the pupils to these ideas: Americans today or their ancestors once had a native land other than the one they are now living in. The first people to become Americans were from countries overseas.

Have the pupils study page 93 to find out (1) how people who came to our country are alike today and (2) the kinds of things people brought with them when they came to America. Complete the study of page 93 by having a pupil read aloud the last paragraph on the page, which tells what pupils will be studying about in this unit.

Concluding the Lesson After discussing page 93 suggest to the pupils that they may enjoy going on a make-believe trip with one of the early famous explorers they will be studying about. Take time to read and discuss page 94, helping the pupils realize that doing Part 1 of the class project may take several weeks. Mention that the project has other parts on pages 113, 125, and 141.

Going Further Encourage each pupil to find or make a picture that shows a group of Americans, preferably Americans of various ethnic groups. Have each pupil write at least one sentence under his picture which tells how the people are alike.

From *The Social Studies and Our Country: Concepts in Social Sciences,* Teacher's Edition, Grade 5 (River Forest, Ill.: Laidlaw, 1970), p. 45. Reprinted by permission of Laidlaw Brothers, A Division of Doubleday & Company, Inc.

A Deductive Strategy   The sequence of learning in a deductive strategy is arranged so that it proceeds from the more general to the more particular, or from the more abstract to the more concrete. In the example from the series *Our Working World*, on page 28, the student begins with the reading of the text, which identifies the concept "city" and describes its elements. After the children analyze what they have read, the strategy calls for a rereading of the text. Only in the final stages does the study of a generalized "city" become more concrete in the form of a case study of the city of Chicago.

The Concept Unit

To help the children get an idea of some of the important elements that go to make up a city, the teacher can have them read the concept unit "What Is a City?" on page 18 of the text. After they have read the unit, the teacher should raise the following questions for discussion. The purpose of this discussion is not to have the children simply repeat the statements in the concept unit, but rather to awaken a lively interest in the nature of cities.

1. Why is a city like a workshop?
2. What is done with the goods and services produced?
3. What do we mean when we say that the city is a trading place?
4. How do cities get their food?
5. What is a specialist? (One who has learned to perform a particular job well.)
6. Why do cities have so many different specialists? Do these many specialists make the city a good place to produce and trade goods and services? Why?
7. Do people come to the city from other areas? Why?
8. Are there many neighborhoods in a city? Do people do all their working, shopping, and playing in their own neighborhood? How do they get from one neighborhood to another? How are neighborhoods alike? (They all have land, buildings, and people). How are neighborhoods different?
9. Is the city a definite place marked off with a boundary?
10. How is the land used? How does the use of land affect the beauty and safety of the city?
11. Do the people of the city have a voice in their government?
12. In what ways do cities change? Are changes sometimes made by government?

The above discussion should act as an introduction to the lesson. After the children have completed the work of the lesson, including whatever activities they may choose to do, they should return to the concept unit, reread it, and again discuss its more important points. This time the discussion should be more extensive, and the children should draw on what they have learned in the course of their work, citing examples to back their opinions.

The Case Study

To help the children discover many of the characteristics of cities as they show themselves in a real-life situation, the teacher can have them read the case study "People Make the City: Chicago," on page 26 of the text. Afterward the class can use the case study as a basis for the following series of inquiries and discussions, which should give them greater insight into, and understanding of, the life of the city.

From *Our Working World—Cities at Work* by Lawrence Senesh, Teacher's Guide Grades 1–3, pp. 15–16. © 1966, 1967, Science Research Associates, Inc. Reprinted by permission of the publisher.

Advantages and Disadvantages

A deductive strategy begins with a verbal conclusion on a fairly high level of abstraction. By well-directed questioning, students can be made to grapple with high-level abstractions. Since a good deal of information is transmitted through high-level abstractions, experience in analyzing them is important. Moreover, a deductive strategy can be very efficient—that is, it can convey information quickly.

There are several major disadvantages. For one, students may be led to concentrate on analytical skills to the exclusion of synthesizing and evaluating skills. And since a deductive strategy begins at the more abstract level, it may lead to student "verbalization" rather than personally meaningful statements based on concrete experiences. Finally, since it is the material rather than student ideas that tends to remain the focus of attention, this strategy may lead to apathy on the part of the students.

Four Modified Inquiry Strategies: A Synthesis

As was explained earlier, the amount of guidance a strategy incorporates determines whether it is open or closed, and the sequence in which the steps of the strategy are arranged determines whether it is inductive or deductive. And as both of these questions must be answered in every case, four basic combinations tend to occur: (1) closed deductive, (2) open deductive, (3) closed inductive, and (4) open inductive. The sequence of steps generally associated with each strategy is identified on the top of the next page.

**Sequences Associated with the
Four Modified Inquiry Strategies**

Closed Deductive
A. Teacher or text presents conclusion.
B. Teacher or text presents supporting evidence.
C. Students analyze evidence.
D. Students apply conclusions.

Open Deductive
A. Teacher or text presents conclusion.
B. Teacher or text presents supporting evidence.
C. Students analyze evidence.
D. Students evaluate evidence.
E. Students develop alternative conclusions.

Closed Inductive
A. Teacher or text presents problem or issue.
B. Teacher or text presents evidence.
C. Students analyze evidence.
D. Students draw conclusions.
E. Students apply conclusions.

Open Inductive
A. Teacher or text presents problem or issue.
B. Teacher or text presents evidence.
C. Students analyze evidence.
D. Students evaluate evidence.
E. Students develop tentative hypotheses.
F. Students propose plans for testing hypotheses.
G. Students propose conclusions.

*Moving from One
Strategy to Another*

Textbooks are frequently—often justifiably—accused of presenting inert materials in dull and routine ways. This has led some people to dismiss them as essentially worthless and to insist that students would be better served without them. In my judgment, this is an error because it mistakes the function of the textbook. The textbook is merely one of several instructional tools, and what is really required is that teachers learn to modify them to fit the needs of their strategies.

The simplest modification is to replace the strategy used by the book with the one the teacher would prefer to use. This is easier than it sounds and usually quite effective. It involves identifying the strategy in the book and then adapting the material by applying the other strategy in a series of questions of a specific type. The example on the next three pages is taken from a textbook series that includes more than one type of teaching strategy. This particular lesson, however, is basically an expository one. The students are primarily expected to receive information. Nevertheless, it can easily be made more provocative through the use of the four basic strategies, as will be shown.

CONCEPT:

SPATIAL LOCATION ◄

Where on earth is your state?

**Where is your state
in relation to other places?**

Every place on the earth has a location. Geographers use many different symbols on globes and maps to show the space a state takes up on the earth's surface. This space is a state's spatial location.

Using maps and globes, geographers can find the exact location of your state. Your state is a particular piece of land on the earth's surface. No other state has that piece of land. Two states never have the same location.

Using maps and globes, geographers also can find the location of your state in relation to natural features such as oceans. Geographers can tell what direction your state is from another state.

Study of a State: Physical Geography/Concept: Spatial Location **15**

[*continued*]

► EACH STATE HAS
AN EXACT LOCATION

Can you describe the location of your state? Can you tell exactly where it is? When you know the facts below and on the next page, you will be able to describe the exact location of your state.

Geographers can use the North Pole, the South Pole, and the Equator as points of reference to help them locate any place on the earth. Find these points of reference on the global map below. You can see that North America is located between the North Pole and the Equator. Is it in the Northern Hemisphere or in the Southern Hemisphere?

Look at the global map on the opposite page. Between what two north-south lines is North America located? Between what two east-west lines is most of North America located? No other continent on earth has this location.

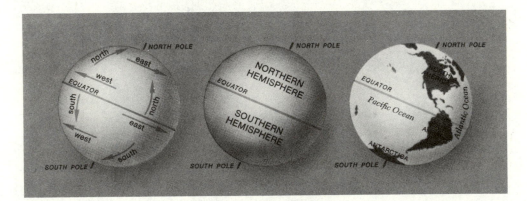

Understanding Points of Reference

What are the poles?
The North Pole is the place on the earth that is farthest north. The South Pole is the place that is farthest south. From any place on the earth, north is always the direction toward the North Pole. South is the direction toward the South Pole. When you face the North Pole, east is at your right and west is at your left.

What is the Equator?
The Equator divides the earth into two equal parts. Since the earth is a sphere, each part is a half sphere, or hemisphere.

The Northern Hemisphere is the half of the earth between the Equator and the North Pole. The Southern Hemisphere is the half between the Equator and the South Pole.

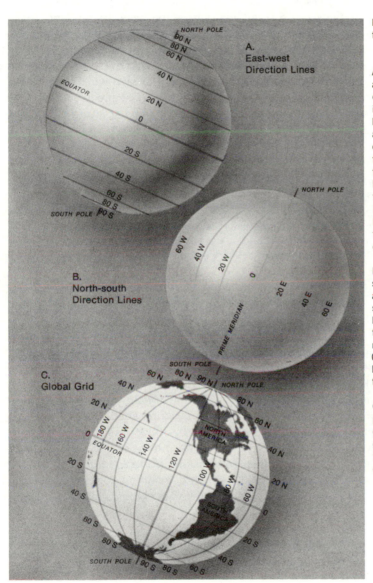

A.
East-west
Direction Lines

B.
North-south
Direction Lines

C.
Global Grid

Facts that help geographers find exact location

A. Lines that go east and west around the globe are east-west direction lines. The Equator is the 0 east-west line. The North Pole and the South Pole are each numbered 90. All east-west lines are numbered from 0 to 90 north and south from the Equator. East-west lines between the Equator and the North Pole are north of the Equator. Are the east-west lines between the Equator and the South Pole north or south of the Equator?

B. Lines that go north and south between the North Pole and the South Pole are north-south direction lines. Prime Meridian is a special name for the 0 north-south line. All north-south lines are numbered 0 to 180 east from the Prime Meridian and 0 to 180 west from the Prime Meridian.

C. When north-south lines are placed over east-west lines, a global grid is formed. The global grid can be used to find the exact location of any place on earth.

Study of a State: Physical Geography/Concept: Spatial Location   **17**

From *Investigating Man's World: Regional Studies* (Grade 5) by Paul R. Hanna, Clyde F. Kohn and Clarence L. Ver Steeg, pp. 15–17. Copyright © 1970 by Scott, Foresman and Company. Reprinted by permission of the publisher.

Modifying the | The simplest way to modify an expository strategy is to transform it into a
Expository Strategy | *closed deductive strategy.* The basic difference between them is that the latter requires the students to do some analyzing. First have the students read the text, then ask them some basic questions to assess knowledge (e.g., What points of reference do geographers use? When you face the North Pole, is east to your right or left?) and comprehension (e.g., Is the northern hemisphere larger than the southern hemisphere? Describe in your own words what a global grid is). Students are now ready to do some analysis (see the questions in Modification 1, below). The lesson concludes with students applying the principles they have learned.

Modification 1: *Moving toward a closed deductive inquiry strategy*

Teacher or text presents conclusions and supporting evidence.
Students read the text.

Students analyze evidence.
Teacher: What is the most important idea here? What information do you need to know in order to describe where you are on the earth? Who would be interested in this information? Would an airplane pilot need to know? Why? How could a pilot find out? What purpose does the equator serve? Could I find the equator if I went to look for it? What do you suppose the word "hemisphere" means?

Students apply conclusions.
Teacher: How would you describe the location of South America? Africa? China?

By providing an opportunity to challenge the conclusions of the text, the lesson can make use of an *open deductive strategy.* One begins in the same way as above but takes the lesson a step further. After students have done some analysis, ask them to evaluate the evidence and the conclusions. For example, the teacher might ask if this is a good way to describe spatial location. Students would then have to develop some criteria by which "goodness" can be assessed. They might suggest simplicity, the need to be able to locate any place on earth, clarity, and so on. Conclude by asking students to develop alternative ways of locating places on earth. They can do so in a large group discussion, individually, or in small groups. They should present their suggestion to the entire class when done.

Modification 2: *Moving toward an open deductive strategy*

Teacher or text presents conclusions and supporting evidence.
Students read the text.

Students analyze evidence.
Teacher: What is the most important idea here? What information do you need to know in order to describe where you are on the earth? Who would be interested in this information? Would an airplane pilot need to know? Why? How could a pilot find out? What purpose does the equator serve? Could I find the equator if I went to look for it? What do you suppose the word "hemisphere" means?

Students evaluate evidence.
Teacher: Do you think this is a good way of describing where you are on the

earth? Why or why not? Do you think it is an important thing to know? Why or why not? Do you believe the writer of the text is telling you the truth about the way geographers describe location on the earth? What makes you think so? How could you find out? Do you think the writer presents these ideas clearly? How would you improve the text?

Students develop alternative conclusions.
   Teacher: Can you think of other ways to describe your location on the earth? What advantages and disadvantages does your way have?

The *closed inductive strategy* requires some basic modification right at the start. Begin with concrete experiences rather then abstract conclusions, using objects such as balls and globes and visual materials. You might begin by posing a problem and using the pictorial materials in the text as a means of generating pertinent questions that lead to appropriate conclusions. When you are reasonably sure that the students have induced essential principles, ask them to read the text and apply these principles to solving the problem posed at the beginning.

Modification 3: *Moving toward a closed inductive strategy*

Teacher or text presents problem.
   Teacher: My name is Wrang Janher. I come from the planet Mars. I have been invited by the President of the United States to meet him in Washington, D. C. We are going to discuss how to avoid war between our two planets. It is very important that I get there on time. Can you tell me how to get there? I am ready to give a reward of 300 maridols (Martian money) to the person who gives me the best directions, plus a free vacation on my planet this summer.

Teacher or text presents evidence.
   Teacher: Look at the pictures in your textbook on pages 16 and 17. What information do they give us? What do the words next to the pictures say? What is a "hemisphere"? What is an "equator"? Where is it? What does 60W mean? 20N? What is the Prime Meridian? Where is it?

Students analyze evidence.
   Teacher: What are the most important ideas in these pictures? What purpose does the equator serve? Could I find it if I went to look for it? What purpose does the Prime Meridian serve? Could I find it if I went to look for it? What does "hemisphere" mean?

Students evaluate evidence.
   Teacher: Let us read how the textbook explains these ideas. Do you think this is a good way of describing where you are on the earth? Why or why not? Do you think it is an important thing to know? Why or why not? Do you believe the writer of the text is telling you the truth about the way geographers describe location on the earth? What makes you think so? How could you find out?

Students draw conclusions.
   Teacher: How do these ideas help us find our way from one place to another? What then is one way of directing our visitor from Mars?

Students apply conculsions.
   Teacher: How would you describe the location of South America? Africa? China?

The same lesson taught via an *open inductive inquiry strategy* begins and develops the same way as the closed inductive strategy. It differs from the closed strategy in that it provides an opportunity for students to challenge the conclusions.

Modification 4: *Moving toward an open inductive inquiry strategy*

Teacher or text presents problem.

Teacher: My name is Wrang Janher. I come from the planet Mars. I have been invited by the President of the United States to meet him in Washington, D. C. We are going to discuss how to avoid war between our two planets. It is very important that I get there on time. Can you tell me how to get there? I am ready to give a reward of 300 maridols (Martian money) to the person who gives me the best directions, plus a free vacation on my planet this summer.

Teacher or text presents evidence.

Teacher: Look at the pictures in your textbook on pages 16 and 17. What information do they give us? What do the words next to the pictures say? What is a "hemisphere"? What is an "equator"? Where is it? What does 60W mean? 20N? What is the Prime Meridian? Where is it?

Students analyze evidence.

Teacher: What are the most important ideas in these pictures? What purpose does the equator serve? Could I find it if I went to look for it? What purpose does the Prime Meridian serve? Could I find it if I went to look for it? What does "hemisphere" mean?

Students evaluate evidence.

Teacher: Let us read how the textbook explains these ideas. Do you think this is a good way of describing where you are on the earth? Why or why not? Do you think it is an important thing to know? Why or why not? Do you believe the writer of the text is telling you the truth about the way geographers describe location on the earth? What makes you think so? How could you find out?

Students develop tentative hypotheses.

Teacher: In what way do these ideas help us find our way from one place to another? What then is one way of directing our visitor from Mars? Are there some other ways?

Students propose plans for testing hypotheses.

Teacher: How can we find out which way is best? What happens when we do this? What advantages are there? What disadvantages? How about this way?

Students propose conclusions.

Teacher: Which way then is best? Why?

Summary

Although a great deal of complicated material had to be covered in this chapter in order to explain the bases of inquiry, it is a relatively simple matter to summarize it. There are essentially two areas covered, one that deals with what might be called the anatomy of thinking and one that deals with the basic forms of the inquiry strategy.

In order to teach effectively, one must be aware of the following points:

1. There are different types of thinking, each of which is associated with a different type of learning.
2. Different ways of phrasing questions encourage the different types of thinking.
3. Some types of learning are more basic than others and must be achieved before the others can be attempted.

Teaching strategies arrange questions and activities in particular sequences so as to encourage the different types of thinking. Inquiry is the best strategy to use in teaching because it makes students active participants in the teaching process and encourages higher-level thinking. The best, or optimal, inquiry strategy is one that enables the students to select their own issues, find their own evidence, and draw their own conclusions. However, this is not always practical or desirable, and in many cases one must modify the inquiry strategy.

The two essential decisions to be made in modifying an inquiry strategy are: To what degree should the students be encouraged to draw their own conclusions? Should the lesson proceed from specifics to generalities or the other way around? The modification that comes closest to the optimal one is that which imposes the fewest conclusions and allows the students to begin with concrete things from which they induce more general principles.

Concepts and Generalizations

Ask the average person what should be taught in the elementary social studies and chances are the answer will be something like "the facts of history and geography." This is probably what most of us did indeed learn, but it is far from adequate in today's world.

Why the emphasis on history and geography? It is true that they are among the oldest of the social sciences, but if age were an index of significance, why not include economics, which has a long and honorable history? And what about the numerous other disciplines that have emerged more recently and that have radically enlarged our conception of human beings and their society, including but not limited to sociology, anthropology, psychology, and social psychology? Why shouldn't these be included in the elementary social studies?

And what facts should be included? It is obviously impossible to teach them all, so which should be omitted? Those relating to the Soviet Union? Black Americans? Women? Moreover, many so-called facts turn out to be quite slippery upon close inspection. For example, virtually every elementary school child has been taught that Columbus discovered America. But as native Americans point out, how could he have "discovered" it when their ancestors were already here? And as some historians have suggested, the Vikings or even the Chinese may have arrived before Columbus.

If, then, the average response is not satisfactory, we must seek another one.

The Social Science Disciplines

Social studies educators generally agree that the social science disciplines constitute the principal content of the social studies. Differences of opinion exist as to whether social studies is supposed to include more than just the social science disciplines, but there is little disagreement regarding the general importance of the disciplines to the social studies. Although there are many criteria whereby a social science discipline can be identified, there is one highly pragmatic one: that which is included as a legitimate area of study in the social science departments of universities is generally acknowledged as a social science discipline.

At present, the disciplines of knowledge as reflected in universities are usually incorporated in four broadly defined areas: mathematics, the humanities, the natural and life sciences, and the social sciences. The social sciences focus on the scientific study of the *social* behavior of human beings. Social science disciplines generally included in universities can be briefly described as follows:

Anthropology, although potentially the broadest of all fields of study, is still usually limited to cultural concerns in the elementary social studies. It focuses on the values, history, customs, behavior — in a word, the way of life — of human groups around the world.

Economics is concerned with the choices people make regarding the use of scarce resources, production, and distribution of commodities.

Geography is the study of the areal differentiation and integration of physical, biotic, and cultural elements of the Earth's surface.

History is concerned with selecting and interpreting significant past events.

Political science is the study of political processes, including the acquisition and maintenance of power and political socialization (the process whereby people are taught their political attitudes and behaviors).

Psychology focuses on the study of individual behavior, including biological bases, motivation, personality, learning, and abilities.

Sociology deals with groups in society. It examines their organizational patterns (structure) and the causes and consequences of these patterns.

Social psychology focuses on the individual within groups: attitudes, behavior, self-conception, and interaction.

The disciplines social scientists consider acceptable today are not necessarily the same as those of even a few years ago, nor will they necessarily be those of tomorrow. It took several decades, for example, for sociology and psychology to be incorporated as legitimate disciplines of study in the universities. And what prophet could have foreseen even in the 1960s that "futurology," the study of the future, might someday be considered a respectable academic discipline? In short, the disciplines of knowledge are not permanently fixed—and curricula for school children can therefore not be permanently fixed either.

The Structure of Disciplines

Lest the reader assume from the above that the recognition of a discipline by a university is based on caprice or politics, I hasten to add that this is not the case—at least not entirely. Disciplined knowledge is distinguished from nondisciplined knowledge by its structure, and structure, as Irving Morrissett has said,

> is the arrangement and interrelationship of parts within a whole. A structure can refer to the relationship of concepts to each other: for example, the concepts "economic system" and "political system" may be related to each other in a structure called a "social system." Conversely, a concept may itself have a structure. The concept "economic system" can also be thought of as a structure, having component concepts such as "money" and "spending" which are structurally related to each other.[1]

Stated another way, the essential parts of a structure of a discipline are its concepts and generalizations. And it is concepts and generalizations, rather than facts, that have become the organizing core of most of the new social studies curricula.

Concepts

A concept is an abstraction based on an element or criterial attribute shared by two or more objects. Consider S. I. Hayakawa's "Abstraction Ladder" (reproduced in Figure 2–1). The subject of the ladder is "Bessie the Cow." The real Bessie is a dynamic organism consisting of particles of matter in motion. What

[1]Irving Morrissett, "The New Social Science Curricula," in Irving Morrissett, ed., *Concepts and Structure in the New Social Science Curricula* (Lafayette, Ind.: Social Science Education Consortium, 1966), p. 4.

Figure 2–1
Abstraction Ladder

Start reading from the bottom UP

8. "wealth"

8. The word "wealth" is at an extremely high level of abstraction, omitting *almost* all reference to the characteristics of Bessie.

7. "asset"

7. When Bessie is referred to as an "asset," still more of her characteristics are left out.

6. "farm assets"

6. When Bessie is included among "farm assets," reference is made only to what she has in common with all other salable items on the farm.

5. "livestock"

5. When Bessie is referred to as "livestock," only those characteristics she has in common with pigs, chickens, goats, etc., are referred to.

4. "cow"

4. The word "cow" stands for the characteristics we have abstracted as common to cow_1, cow_2, cow_3 . . . cow_n. Characteristics peculiar to specific cows are left out.

3. "Bessie"

3. The word "Bessie" (cow_1) is the *name* we give to the object of perception of level 2. The name *is not* the object; it merely *stands for* the object and omits reference to many of the characteristics of the object.

2.

2. The cow we perceive is not the word, but the object of experience, that which our nervous system abstracts (selects) from the totality that constitutes the process-cow. Many of the characteristics of the process-cow are left out.

1. The cow known to science ultimately consists of atoms, electrons, etc., according to present-day scientific inference. Characteristics (represented by circles) are infinite at this level and ever-changing. This is the *process level*.

SOURCE: *Language in Thought and Action*, 3rd Edition, by S. J. Hayakawa, copyright © 1972 by Harcourt Brace Jovanovich, Inc., and reproduced with their permission.

we perceive of Bessie when we look at her is just a part. When we compare what we perceive of Bessie with other objects, we note that she along with some others has four legs, chews cud, gives milk, etc. We decide that these attributes shall be the determinants of a concept we call "cow," and all objects possessing these attributes shall be "cows."

For other purposes, however, the concept "cow" is inadequate. We note, for example, that sheep, goats, and cows have the communal attribute of being domesticated animals. We conceptualize this relationship in the term "live-stock." And so on up the ladder. Each new concept is based on the sharing of some criterial attribute.

Each ascending concept on the ladder is more and more abstract—that is, each one blurs more of Bessie's unique characteristics. Hence, while Bessie herself remains unique, each ascending level of abstraction tells us less and less about her. What is the advantage of this process?

For one thing, it is of enormous advantage in organizing our experiences. Without such concepts as "cow," we would be unable to see how one animal (or object) relates to another. Without the concept "wealth," we would be unable to see how livestock, farm assets, and assets in general are related.

For another, the process provides us with a very efficient shorthand way of talking about our experiences. Instead of simply saying, for example, "John is wealthy," one would be forced to say "John has twenty-six cows, fifty tractors, and one million dollars in the bank." Now these specifics are the facts of John's wealth and without them we cannot really understand what John's wealth is. But for purposes of efficient communication, the concept is very useful.

Finally, the higher the level of abstraction, the more powerful it is in relating things. Another way of stating this is to say that more powerful concepts subsume many subconcepts. "Wealth" includes the concepts "assets," "farm assets," "livestock," "cows," as well as "Bessie."

Concepts in the Social Sciences. Given that concepts are powerful and efficient ways of organizing our experience, it appeared eminently reasonable to social studies educators to use them as the organizing core of the social studies curriculum. The problem remained, however, to identify the most powerful concepts in the social sciences.

Social science concepts are high-level abstractions that are particularly fruitful in guiding social science inquiries. The concept "cow" is obviously not suitable—it is neither a very powerful concept nor a particularly fruitful one in guiding social science inquiries. Social scientists can describe human social behavior quite adequately without necessarily understanding or using the concept "cow." But other concepts do appear to be essential, and major efforts have been made in the 1960s and 1970s to identify these concepts.

One particularly valuable effort began with a survey of some eighty articles written by noted scholars in the various social science disciplines. A total of 329 concepts were identified, but when the list was reduced to those concepts that were identified at least four times by four different scholars, only 89 remained. That list is reproduced in Chart 2–1.

Chart 2–1
Social Science Terms by Disciplines

Social Science Terms	f	Geo.	Pol. Sci.	Econ.	Anthro.	Soc.	Psych.
areal association	4	x	—	—	—	—	—
attitudes	11	x	x	—	x	x	x
behavior	22	—	x	x	x	x	x
capital	6	—	—	x	—	x	—
capitalism	9	—	x	x	x	x	x
change	22	x	x	x	x	x	x
citizenship	9	x	x	x	—	x	—
class	6	—	x	—	x	x	x
climate	10	x	—	—	x	x	—
communism	4	—	x	x	—	—	—
community	8	—	x	—	x	x	x
competition	6	—	—	x	x	—	x
consumer	8	x	—	x	—	—	—
culture	25	x	x	—	x	x	x
custom	7	—	x	—	x	x	—
decision-making	4	—	x	—	x	—	—
democracy	11	x	x	x	x	x	x
demography	7	x	x	—	x	x	x
distribution	6	x	—	x	x	—	x
drives	5	—	—	—	x	x	x
employment-unemployment	6	—	—	x	—	—	—
environment	18	x	x	—	x	x	x
ethnocentrism	5	—	—	—	x	x	x
evolution	6	—	—	—	x	—	—
exchange	5	—	—	x	—	x	—
family	9	—	—	—	x	x	x
freedom	6	—	x	—	—	—	—
goods & services	7	x	—	x	—	x	—
government	15	x	x	—	x	x	—
gross national product	4	x	—	x	—	—	—
groups	23	x	x	x	x	x	x
growth	8	x	x	x	—	—	—
habit	4	x	—	—	x	x	—
income	6	—	—	x	—	—	—
industrialization	11	x	x	x	x	—	—
inflation	7	—	x	x	—	—	—
institutions	20	x	x	x	x	x	x
interaction	16	x	—	—	x	x	x
interdependence	8	x	—	x	x	—	—
international relations	13	x	x	x	—	—	—
labor	10	x	—	x	—	x	—
land	6	x	—	x	—	x	—
landforms, distrib. of	6	x	—	—	—	—	—
law	12	—	x	—	x	x	x
leadership	4	—	x	—	—	—	x

Social Science Terms	f	Geo.	Pol. Sci.	Econ.	Anthro.	Soc.	Psych.
markets	4	—	—	x	—	—	—
mobility	8	—	x	—	x	x	x
money	7	—	—	x	—	—	—
monopoly	4	—	x	x	—	—	—
motivation	11	—	x	—	x	x	x
nationalism	6	—	x	—	x	—	—
needs	11	x	—	x	x	x	x
norms	12	—	x	—	x	x	x
personality	15	—	—	—	x	x	x
place	9	x	—	—	—	x	—
political parties	8	—	x	—	—	—	—
population	8	x	x	x	—	—	—
power	16	x	x	x	—	x	—
price	7	—	x	x	—	—	—
production	11	x	x	x	—	—	x
profit	5	—	—	x	—	—	—
public opinion	5	—	x	x	—	—	—
race	10	—	x	—	x	x	x
region	9	x	—	—	—	x	—
resources	18	x	—	x	x	x	—
rights	10	—	x	—	—	x	x
role	24	x	x	x	x	x	x
scarcity	4	—	—	x	—	—	—
social process	10	—	x	—	x	x	—
social structure	10	—	x	—	x	x	x
socialism	6	—	x	x	—	—	—
socialization	12	—	x	—	x	x	x
society	13	x	x	—	x	x	x
specialization	4	—	—	x	—	x	—
stability	5	—	—	x	—	—	—
state	4	x	x	—	—	—	—
status	8	—	—	—	x	x	x
supply and demand	6	—	x	x	—	—	—
surface features	5	x	—	—	—	—	—
symbols	6	—	x	—	x	—	x
systems	21	—	x	x	x	x	x
taxation	7	—	x	x	x	—	—
technology	6	x	x	x	—	—	—
trade	11	x	x	x	x	—	x
values	16	—	x	x	x	x	x
vegetation	4	x	—	—	—	—	—
wages	5	—	—	x	x	x	x
wants	4	x	—	x	—	—	—
welfare	7	—	x	x	—	—	—
Terms in discipline		40	51	50	47	48	38

[f = the number of articles in which the term appeared]

SOURCE: Research project done by Robert H. Ratcliffe, cited in *New Approaches to and Materials for a Sequential Curriculum of American Society for Grades Five to Twelve,* Vol. I (Washington, D.C.: U.S. Department of Health, Education, and Welfare, Office of Education, Bureau of Research, July 1970), pp. 133–35.

As the list indicates, many concepts appear to be basic to more than one discipline.[2] Indeed, only fourteen concepts failed to be identified as basic to more than one discipline, and these were predominantly in the area of economics. However, even these concepts appear important in more than one discipline. For example, the concept "capitalism" is named by several disciplines, but "employment," "money," and "profits" were named only by economists. It is doubtful whether "capitalism" can be understood without reference to these latter terms.

Another effort was undertaken by Roy Price, who, together with the staff of the Syracuse University Social Studies Curriculum, identified the following thirty-four concepts as the most useful for a social studies program:[3]

Substantive Concepts

sovereignty

conflict—its origin, expression, and resolution

the industrialization-urbanization syndrome

secularization

compromise and adjustment

comparative advantage

power

morality-choice

scarcity

input-output

saving

the modified market economy

habitat

culture

institution

social control

social change

interaction

Value Concepts

dignity of man

empathy

loyalty

government by consent of the governed

freedom and equality

Aspects of Method

historical method and point of view

the geographical approach

causation

observation, classification, and measurement

analysis and synthesis

question-answer

objectivity

skepticism

interpretation

evaluation

evidence

Hilda Taba developed a program for kindergarten through eighth grade based on the following eleven concepts.[4]

causality

conflict

cooperation

cultural change

differences

interdependence

modification

power

societal control

tradition

values

[2]The writers of the list rejected the word "concept" because they could not agree on its meaning. Instead they used the word "term," which they defined as "a word or phrase used in a recognized sense in a particular subject." For our purposes here, the words "term" and "concept" are interchangeable.

[3]As reported by Verna S. Fancett, "Social Science Concepts and the Classroom," in Berry K. Beyer and Anthony N. Penna, eds., *Concepts in the Social Studies,* National Council for the Social Studies Bulletin 45 (Washington D.C.: National Educators Association, 1971), pp. 14–16.

[4]Hilda Taba, Mary C. Durkin, Jack R. Fraenkel, and Anthony R. McNaughton, *A Teacher's Handbook to Elementary Social Studies* (Reading, Mass.: Addison-Wesley, 1971), pp. 24–27.

And the new California Social Sciences Education Framework recommends the following concepts as guidelines for the K–12 program:[5]

citizenship	multiple causation	morality
justice	needs	change
freedom	property	conflict
diversity	authority/power	interdependence
culture	scarcity	environment
resources	social control	truth

It is apparent from these lists that no consensus exists regarding the most powerful concepts to serve as the core of a social studies curriculum. But a comparison of the lists also reveals interesting points of agreement. Many of the concepts identified by the several groups are indeed similar. And current programs in the social studies tend to reflect many of them.

Subconcepts   The concepts identified above are very high-level abstractions — hence they include many subconcepts. If identifying the powerful social science concepts has been difficult, identification of the subconcepts has proved even more so. Nonetheless, efforts have been made in this direction and all written materials in the social studies are explicitly or implicitly guided by their own assumptions regarding the proper subconceptual scheme. To illustrate the nature of subconcepts, the following are excerpted from John Michaelis, who calls them "concept clusters."

Concepts

Power authority, unit, regime, state, sovereignty, system, demands, decision making, party, government, constitution, law, rules, political behavior, processes, services

Concept Clusters

Tasks of Government: external security, internal order, justice, public services, freedom (under democracy)

Processes: rule making (legislative), rule applying (executive), rule adjudicating (judicial)

Levels of Government: local, state, national, international

Public Services: police, fire, postal, education, health, welfare, sanitation, conservation, recreation, labor, business

Types of Government: democratic, authoritarian; parliamentary, presidential; unitary, federal

Themes: maintaining civil liberties, the rights of minorities, the general consent of the governed, due process of law, separation of powers[6]

The following concepts and subconcepts were used in a seventh grade in the Montgomery, Alabama school system, which was interested in developing a "cultural" approach to the study of human groups. Teachers were able to use these in studying any human group, no matter how complex.

[5] *Social Sciences Education Framework for California Public Schools,* Report of the Statewide Social Science Framework Committee (Sacramento, Calif.: California State Board of Education, 1974), pp. 20–28.
[6] John U. Michaelis, *Social Studies for Children in a Democracy,* 5th ed. (Englewood Cliffs, N.J.: Prentice-Hall, 1972), p. 165.

Concept: Culture

Subconcept: Social activities—family, tribe, marriage, home festivals, recreation, class

Subconcept: Economic activities—market, labor, contract, production, ownership, commerce

Subconcept: Political activities—state, government, legislature, executive, judicial

Subconcept: Religious activities—church, sacred writings, ritual, ethics, congregation

Subconcept: Aesthetic activities—arts, architecture, dance, drama, crafts, music, painting

Subconcept: Intellectual—school, science, technology, literature, communication[7]

Generalizations

Concepts are indeed high-powered abstractions, but concepts by themselves do not make the relationships among things explicit. Generalizations do. Generalizations are statements about the explicit relationships between or among concepts. Since they relate one abstraction to another, they are more abstract than either.

The word "generalization" implies that the statement of relationship applies generally or universally. The strength of a social science lies in its ability to make reliable generalizations—that is, statements of relationships or patterns which are supported by facts and apply universally. The ultimate aim of social science is to discover all those universal patterns whereby human beings relate to their human and nonhuman environments. Social scientists have not yet accomplished this aim—and some doubt they ever will. But they have been able to identify some generalizations, even though they are rarely able to state these relationships with precision.

Consider the following examples of generalizations in the social science disciplines taken from various sources:

Every geographic area is affected by physical, biotic, and societal forces. (Geography)

Natural resources and the supply of goods and services to satisfy needs and wants are limited. (Economics)

Social problems and institutions of today have roots in the past. (History)

Social classes have existed in every society. (Sociology)

Individuals differ from one another in personal values, attitudes, personalities, and roles; yet at the same time the members of a group must possess certain common values and characteristics. (Psychology)

Human beings have many different ways of meeting similar needs. (Anthropology)

All societies have developed ways of establishing and maintaining a social order. (Political science)

Note that each example states a relationship between or among concepts. In the first one we note that a geographic area (a concept) is affected (a relationship) by physical, biotic, and social forces (concepts). In the second we learn that natural resources and the supply of goods and services (concepts) are lim-

[7]Sharryl Hawke, "A Cultural Approach to the Teaching of Social Studies," *Profiles of Promise,* No. 22. (Boulder, Colorado: ERIC/Clearinghouse for Social Studies/Social Science Education and the Social Science Education Consortium, Inc., 1974).

ited (a relationship) in relation to the satisfaction of needs and wants (concepts). And so on. Each of these generalizations presumes to apply universally—and both common sense and, more importantly, available evidence suggest they do.

But note, too, that the examples do not identify the nature of the relationship very rigorously. True enough, geographic areas are "affected"—but exactly how are they affected? True enough, natural resources and the supply of goods and services are "limited"—but exactly which resources and which goods and services are limited in relation to whose needs and wants? Moreover, it is very difficult to identify generalizations that really do apply universally. The bulk of social science research has taken place in the United States and to a lesser degree in western Europe. The study of ethnic and racial relations, for example, has been primarily done in the United States. Hence, currently accepted generalizations in this subject area are based on a very small sampling of the earth's population. We really cannot be sure that they apply elsewhere.

Despite their limitations, however, generalizations are powerful statements about human experience. They do, after all, make certain relationships explicit and are applicable in many situations. Hence, along with concepts, they have been made part of the organizing content core of the new social studies curriculum. Some educators, however, prefer to call them "concept statements" or "main ideas" because of their shortcomings.

The reader may well wonder at this point if the social sciences contain enough generalizations to warrant their usage as an organizing content core.

The fact is that the social sciences contain thousands of them. A report issued by the California State Department of Education identified several hundred,[8] Paul R. Hanna and John R. Lee were able to identify more than three thousand,[9] and several hundred are to be found in a notable collection by two eminent social scientists, Bernard Berelson and Gary A. Steiner.[10] The problem, then, for educators, is not to find enough generalizations, but to choose those that appear most worthwhile in providing a content curriculum core.

Identifying Important Generalizations

One way to make this determination is to eliminate those generalizations that appear to be neither universal nor reliable. For example, "Stable political organization improves the quality of life shared by its citizens" is one of the organizing generalizations identified in one textbook series.[11] It may well be argued, however, that a stable political system may simply perpetuate quality for some and oppression for others. Some totalitarian regimes have proved to be quite stable—but it is highly doubtful that political opponents have felt this stability adding to the quality of their lives. Or consider this one in the Wisconsin program: "The varied backgrounds of many groups that came to this country have blended to form a national culture with regional differences."[12] Its converse is equally true. Many groups have not blended—some have been maintained as separate culture enclaves, while others have been virtually obliterated or ignored. Perhaps most difficult to detect are those generalizations that fit our own biases, as, for example, "Democracy satisfies the most wants for the most people," or "Human survival depends on an adequate analysis of our ecosystem." Those of us who like democratic forms of government prefer to believe the former, but we have no conclusive evidence to support it. The second statement seems reasonable enough, and this writer subscribes to it, but it is really a statement of belief with little evidence.

Hilda Taba suggested the following criteria in determining generalizations for the social studies:

1. *Validity:* Do they adequately represent the concepts of the discipline from which they are drawn?
2. *Significance:* Can they explain important segments of the world today, and are they descriptive of important aspects of human behavior?
3. *Durability:* Are they of lasting importance?

[8]California State Curriculum Committee, *Social Studies Framework for the Public Schools of California* (Sacramento, Calif.: California State Department of Education, 1962).
[9]Paul R. Hanna and John R. Lee, "Content in the Social Studies: Generalizations from the Social Sciences," in John U. Michaelis, ed., *Social Studies in Elementary Schools,* Thirty-Second Yearbook (Washington, D.C.: National Council for the Social Studies, 1962), pp. 62–89.
[10]Bernard Berelson and Gary A. Steiner, *Human Behavior: An Inventory of Scientific Findings* (New York: Harcourt Brace Jovanovich, 1964).
[11]In the series *Principles and Practices in the Teaching of the Social Studies,* Level 4 (New York: Harcourt Brace Jovanovich, 1970), T-17.
[12] *A Conceptual Framework for the Social Studies in Wisconsin Schools* (Madison, Wis.: Wisconsin Department of Public Instruction, 1964) and *A Scope and Sequence Plan for the Social Studies in Wisconsin Schools* (Madison, Wis.: Wisconsin Department of Public Instruction, 1964).

Chart 2-2
Subgeneralizations by Grade in the Wisconsin Program

Major Generalization: People living in groups develop a culture. This includes their particular patterns of behavior and the resulting material products. (Anthropology)

Grade	Subgeneralization
K	Families and schools provide the opportunities for young people to learn.
1	People in the same neighborhood usually have similar cultural traits—language, customs, values and beliefs, and ways of doing things.
2	Communities close together tend to be more alike culturally than those farther apart since they usually have greater opportunities to learn from each other.
3	Although people everywhere have similar needs and desires, their ways of meeting them differ according to their cultures. Ways of living different from our own are not necessarily worse or better than ours—they are merely different.
4	There are some similarities and differences in the cultural patterns of various Wisconsin communities.
5	The varied backgrounds of the many groups that came to this country have blended to form a national culture with regional differences.
6	Cultural differences among groups stem from their different backgrounds, experiences, and environments and may represent different stages of development.

SOURCE: *A Conceptual Framework for the Social Studies in Wisconsin Schools* (Madison, Wis.: Wisconsin Department of Public Instruction, 1964).

---

4. *Balance:* Do they permit development of student thinking in both scope and depth?
5. *Appropriateness:* Are they suited to needs, interests and maturational level of students?[13]

Obviously, answers to these questions depend on judgments. But if the teacher, along with others, can answer "yes" to all of the above for a given generalization, chances are it would be adequate in a core.

Subgeneralizations   In much the same way that concepts can be broken down into subconcepts, generalizations can be further analyzed into subgeneralizations. Characteristically, a program of study will identify several major generalizations that are to be mastered at the end of several years of study. At each grade level, however, a subgeneralization of the larger generalization may be taught, as in the representative example in Chart 2-2, taken from the Wisconsin program in the discipline of anthropology.

[13]Taba et al., *A Teacher's Handbook,* pp. 28-30.

Organizing Curricula Around Concepts and Generalizations

In recent years, more and more school systems have begun to structure social studies curricula around major concepts and the generalizations that accompany them. The entire sequence of social studies, from kindergarten up through and including senior high school, is organized so that specific concepts will be introduced and examined at each grade level. Typically, the structuring process begins with the identification of the major social studies concepts. Then, generalizations that elaborate on each concept are developed, and several of them are selected for use with each concept, as in the following excerpt on the subject of confict:

> Conflicts are evidences of disagreement and can arise out of differences as to what ought to be achieved in a given situation as well as to the most effective way of securing an agreed upon end.

> The desire for and the use of power by individuals and groups with differing moral commitments and competing principles often lead to conflict.

> Differing interests and purposes about the allocation of resources in a complex society inevitably stimulate conflict.

> Conflict can have a positive function in assuring that a large variety of views are expressed, arousing interest in an issue, and assisting in value clarification and decision-making.

> Unless conflict is expressed within generally accepted limits and managed by the social system under fair and equitable rules and procedures, it can be disfunctional and socially destructive.[14]

Just as choice of concepts may vary from curriculum to curriculum, so may the accompanying generalizations—even for the same concept. The following example taken from the Taba program also includes the concept of conflict, but the generalizations are somewhat different:

> Interaction among individuals or groups frequently results in hostile encounters or struggles.

> Conflict is characteristic of the growth and development of individuals and of civilization as a whole.

> There are culturally approved and disapproved means for resolving all varieties of conflicts.

> Irrational conflict is reduced by recognition of the inevitability of differences and of the difficulty of determining their relative value.

> In most situations, some form of compromise is necessary because of the serious consequences of sustained conflict.[15]

Whatever concepts are chosen, ultimately some allocation is made in terms of grade level. Sometimes a single concept with different generalizations or sub-generalizations will be taught at each grade level. Sometimes different concepts will be taught at different grade levels.

---

[14]California State Curriculum Committee, *Social Sciences Education Framework*, p. 27.
[15]Taba et al., *A Teacher's Handbook*, p. 24.

Single-Discipline Patterns

Some current programs are organized around the concepts and generalizations of single disciplines. For example, *Man: A Course of Study*[16] focuses mainly on anthropology, while the *Elementary Economics Project*[17] concentrates on economics. Other single-discipline programs are identified in Chart 2–3. Sometimes the study of a single discipline is planned for an entire year's work. More often such programs are planned as supplementary work for a number of years. The advantage of a single-discipline approach is that it affords students an opportunity to explore an area in depth. However, critics of this approach point out that the object of social studies instruction is not to enable students to gain mastery in one discipline, but to enable them to perceive how the integration of the perspectives of many disciplines helps in the understanding of human behavior.

Interdisciplinary Patterns

An interdisciplinary program is organized around concepts that are basic to more than one discipline. As suggested above, such concepts are not difficult to find—indeed, they are common. The emphasis in interdisciplinary programs which are currently the most popular approach at the elementary level—is to explore the concept from the vantage point of many disciplines. Thus, for example, power can be studied from more than a political viewpoint. In the interdisciplinary format, it will probably be studied from an economic, a sociological, and possibly an historical viewpoint as well. It is quite true that an interdisciplinary format may encourage fragmented and surface learning; a student will not get the fullest sense of any of the individual disciplines. One way to overcome this disadvantage is to allow for intervals in which single disciplines are pursued in depth, while other intervals may provide for a more integrated approach. Since many existing single-discipline programs are planned as supplementary activities, this compromise is now feasible without requiring too much preparation by individual teachers.

Traditional Patterns

The idea of organizing a social studies curriculum around the concepts and generalizations of the social sciences is a radical departure from the past. In order to understand it and evaluate it fully, some comparison with past practice is necessary.

The traditional social studies program of the decades immediately preceding the sixties was organized on an "expanding horizon" concept. It was assumed that students' orientations to their spatial and temporal world became increasingly broader as they matured, and the content selected for study reflected this assumption. The common pattern of organization was as follows:[18]

[16] *Man: A Course of Study* (Cambridge, Mass.: Educational Development Center, 1968).
[17] University of Chicago Industrial Relations Center, *Elementary Economics Project* (Galien, Mich.: Allied Education Council, 1967).
[18] Richard R. Gross, "Social Studies," in *Encyclopedia of Educational Research,* Chester W. Harris, ed. (New York: Macmillan, 1960), p. 130.

Chart 2–3
Examples of Social Studies Programs

With Single-Discipline Emphasis*

Program	Discipline	Grade Level	Format	Publisher
University of California, Los Angeles, *Committee of Civic Education*	Civics, Geography	4–12	Supplementary Multiyear	Ginn and Co., 191 Spring Street, Lexington, Mass. 02173
University of Chicago, Industrial Relations Center, *Elementary Economics Project*	Economics	4–8	Supplementary Multiyear	Allied Education Council, P.O. Box 78, Galien, Mich. 49113
University of Georgia, *Anthropology Curriculum Project*	Anthropology	K–12	Supplementary Multiyear	Anthropology Curriculum Project, University of Georgia, 107 Dudley Hall, Athens, Ga. 30601
University of Michigan, *Elementary Social Science Education Program*	Social Psychology	4–6	Supplementary Multiyear	Science Research Associates, Inc., 259 E. Erie St., Chicago, Ill. 60611
Tufts University, *Lincoln Filene Center for Citizenship and Public Affairs*	Political Science	K–12	Multiyear	Lincoln Filene Center for Citizenship and Public Affairs, Tufts University, Medford, Mass. 02155

With Interdisciplinary Emphasis

Program	Grade Level	Format	Publisher
Boston Children's Museum, *MATCH Program*	1–6	Supplementary units	American Science and Engineering, Inc., 20 Overland St., Boston, Mass. 02215
Investigating Man's World	K–6	Multiyear	Scott, Foresman & Co., 1900 E. Lake Ave., Glenview, Ill. 60025
University of Minnesota, *Project Social Studies*	K–12	Multiyear	Green Printing Co., 631 Eighth Ave. North, Minneapolis, Minn. 55411
Taba Program in Social Science	1–8	Multiyear	Addison-Wesley Publishing Co., Inc., Jacob Way, Reading, Mass. 01867
The Social Sciences: Concepts and Values	1–9	Multiyear	Harcourt Brace Jovanovich, Inc., 757 Third Ave., New York, N.Y. 10017

*For an evaluation of some of these programs, see *Social Education* 36:7, November 1972.

Grade	Topic
1	Home and School Life
2	Community Helpers
3	The Larger Community and Other Communities
4	State History and Geography
5	United States History and Geography
6	Other Regions and Countries of the World
7	History and Geography of the Eastern and Western Hemispheres
8	United States History

Typically, units of study would then be identified within each of the grade levels and appropriate content selected. Figure 2–2 illustrates some of the representative components that might have been included in a unit on Mexico.

The traditional social studies format was attacked on several grounds. For one thing, the notion of an "expanding horizon" was challenged on the basis that children today have greater access to the spatially and temporally removed than did their peers of a pretelevision era. Hence, while it appeared reasonable that horizons did expand with maturity, it also appeared reasonable that the in-

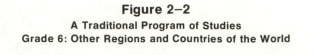

Figure 2–2
A Traditional Program of Studies
Grade 6: Other Regions and Countries of the World

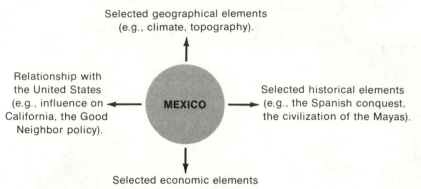

Selected geographical elements
(e.g., climate, topography).

Relationship with
the United States
(e.g., influence on
California, the Good
Neighbor policy).

MEXICO

Selected historical elements
(e.g., the Spanish conquest,
the civilization of the Mayas).

Selected economic elements
(e.g., industries, agriculture).

troduction of foreign places and the past (as well as the future) could be included much earlier in the program.

Second, the content components of many units left much unexplained. Why, for example, were the particular components identified in Figure 2–2 chosen for study? Answers to this query might take the form "students need to understand Mexico" or "appreciate the Mexican heritage." But "understanding" and "appreciation" can be achieved via many routes. How was this one justified above all others?

Third, the sequence of learning content—the content selected from grade to grade—appeared to be largely arbitrary, not developmental. How, for example, did the content studied in grade 5 help the student learn about Mexico in grade 6? What connecting threads were there in this organizational format that would allow for increased depth and complexity of learning as the child matured?

Current Patterns   Focusing on concepts and generalizations as organizing threads of the social studies curriculum eliminates some of these weaknesses. Because concepts and generalizations have wide applicability, specific content areas that can be used as illustrative vehicles are quite flexible. Even primary-grade children (kindergarten–grade 3) can learn about conflict, for example, in many varied settings: their own families, an urban or rural family in the United States, a Parisian family, an African family, a Puritan family. This allows for the early introduction of places far and near, as well as of historical events. (Compare the example in Figure 2–3 with that in Figure 2–2.)

The fact that concepts and generalizations are selected for their power in explaining human behavior suggests another important reason for learning them.

Figure 2–3
A Program Organized around Generalizations
Grade 6: Focus on Generalizations in Anthropology

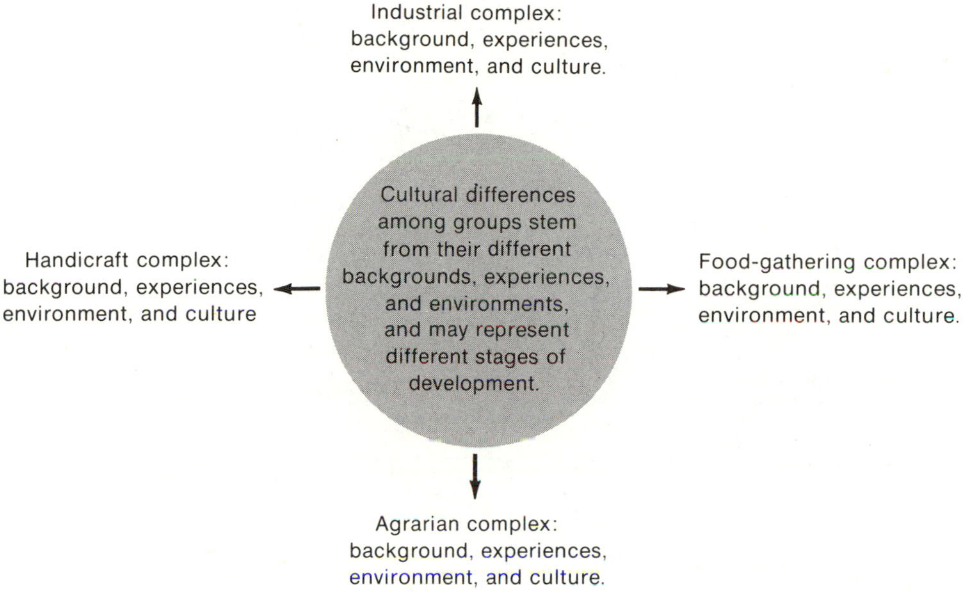

Industrial complex:
background, experiences,
environment, and culture.

Handicraft complex:
background, experiences,
environment, and culture

Cultural differences
among groups stem
from their different
backgrounds, experiences,
and environments,
and may represent
different stages of
development.

Food-gathering complex:
background, experiences,
environment, and culture.

Agrarian complex:
background, experiences,
environment, and culture.

SOURCE: Adapted, with modifications, from *A Conceptual Framework for the Social Studies in Wisconsin Schools* (Madison, Wis.: Wisconsin Department of Public Instruction, 1964) and *A Scope and Sequence Plan for the Social Studies in Wisconsin Schools* (Madison, Wis.: Wisconsin Department of Public Instruction, 1964).

Content would have to be justified on the basis of this power, which enables us to eliminate the random treatment of human behavior that has appeared to be a characteristic of traditional programs.

Finally, powerful concepts and generalizations lend themselves to structuring a sequence of learning experiences in an orderly fashion from grade to grade. Since each is made up of many subcomponents, each, developed sequentially, lends itself in a cumulative fashion to the eventual mastery of the whole. Therefore a few well-chosen concepts and generalizations can serve as the organizing threads of the entire curriculum from kindergarten through twelfth grade. Many of the new programs are indeed fashioned in this manner, and the average number of concepts upon which they are based is probably no more than thirty — and frequently less. (See Figure 2–4 for an illustration of how three concepts can be developed with increasing complexity in varied settings from grades one through eight.)

Figure 2–4
The Spiral Development of Three Key Concepts

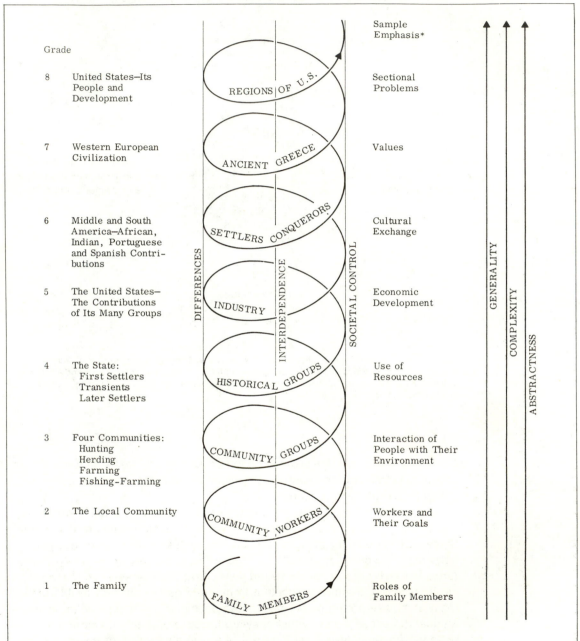

*The sample shown on this chart does not represent the emphasis for the year's program.

SOURCE: Hilda Taba et al., *A Teacher's Handbook to Elementary Social Studies* (Reading, Mass.: Addison-Wesley, 1971), p. 21. Reprinted by permission.

Conceptualizing and Generalizing Inquiry Strategies

Verbalizing a concept or generalization is not the same as conceptualizing or generalizing. Verbalizing is merely a demonstration of knowledge, while conceptualizing and generalizing are *synthesizing* activities. It is possible to teach children a lot of very impressive verbalizations. It is another matter to help them conceptualize or generalize.

To recapitulate the categories of educational objectives listed in Chapter 1, synthesizing requires not only knowledge but also comprehension, application, and analysis. Hence any strategy that presumes to have students conceptualize or generalize must perforce include at least some of these other objectives.

Like other high-level objectives, conceptualizing and generalizing can be taught by both expository and inquiry methods. However, since expository strategies give no overt evidence of student thinking, inquiry strategies are preferable—particularly when dealing with powerful concepts and generalizations.

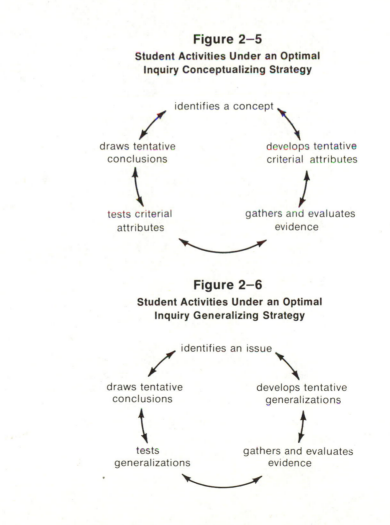

Figure 2–5
Student Activities Under an Optimal
Inquiry Conceptualizing Strategy

identifies a concept

develops tentative criterial attributes

gathers and evaluates evidence

tests criterial attributes

draws tentative conclusions

Figure 2–6
Student Activities Under an Optimal
Inquiry Generalizing Strategy

identifies an issue

develops tentative generalizations

gathers and evaluates evidence

tests generalizations

draws tentative conclusions

An optimal conceptualization strategy is illustrated in Figure 2–5 and an optimal generalization strategy in Figure 2–6. They are, of course, virtually the same as the optimal inquiry strategy (Figure 1–4), and they offer the same advantages and disadvantages. They must often be modified—for much the same reasons as discussed in Chapter 1—and the four types of modification used to adapt inquiry strategies are equally applicable for conceptualization strategies (shown below) and generalization strategies (shown on page 70).

Sequences Associated with the
Four Modified Conceptualization Strategies

Closed Deductive

A. Teacher or text presents a concept.
B. Teacher or text identifies the criterial attributes of the concept.
C. Teacher or text presents examples and nonexamples of the concept.
D. Students analyze examples and nonexamples.
E. Students generate additional examples and nonexamples.

Open Deductive

A. Teacher or text presents a concept.
B. Teacher or text identifies some of the criterial attributes of the concept.
C. Teacher or text presents examples and nonexamples of the concept.
D. Students analyze examples and nonexamples.
E. Students evaluate criterial attributes.
F. Students modify and/or develop other criterial attributes.
G. Students evaluate modifications and new criterial attributes.

Closed Inductive

A. Teacher or text presents examples and nonexamples in which criterial attributes of a concept are embedded, but does not identify them.
B. Students analyze examples and induce communal elements (criterial attributes).
C. Students group examples according to induced criterial attributes.
D. Students label groups.
E. Students generate additional examples and nonexamples.

Open Inductive

A. Teacher or text presents examples and nonexamples in which criterial attributes of a concept are embedded, but does not identify them.
B. Students analyze examples and induce communal elements (criterial attributes).
C. Students group examples according to induced criterial attributes.
D. Students label groups.
E. Students evaluate criterial attributes and labels.
F. Students modify and/or develop other criterial attributes and labels.
G. Students evaluate modifications and new criterial attributes.

Some Examples of Strategies

The following are examples taken from assorted materials. Each represents essentially one of the above strategies. Look at each one carefully and decide how you would classify them. Compare your answers with those given after Example E.

Example A

[Our Working World: Neighbors at Work. Grade 1.]

[Students listen to recorded lesson in which some criterial attributes of a "neighborhood" are identified. Teacher asks the following questions after recorded lesson is completed.]

1. What can we find in every neighborhood? (Land, buildings, people.)
2. Why are neighborhoods different? (Because the land is different; the land is used differently; the people are different.)
3. Why did Stephen like his neighborhood better than the big-city neighborhood?
4. Why do people like to come back to their own neighborhood?
5. What can we learn from the song? (The teacher may play the song again before the children answer.)

[Several activities follow of which the following constitute but a part:]

1. To help the children discover that one way of looking at a neighborhood is to think of it as the area within walking distance of one's home, the teacher can ask each child to draw pictures of nearby places to which he walks. (This concept of the neighborhood applies more to cities and towns than to rural areas.) Such places may include friends' homes, stores, parks, the school, and churches. The teacher can discuss with the children that people who live within walking distance of their homes are their neighbors, and the area within walking distance is their neighborhood.
2. To make the children aware of the principal elements that make up a neighborhood, the teacher can use the pictures drawn in Activity 1 as the basis for a class discussion. The discussion should bring out that every neighborhood has people and land, and that people use the land for buildings, streets, parks, playgrounds, and so forth.

   The children can prepare a display of the pictures from Activity 1 and title it "People, Land, Buildings, and Streets Make Up Our Neighborhood." The display itself can be discussed and the children should see that since the neighborhood is the area in which they most frequently walk, it is the one they know most about. They should see that the more one gets to know a place and the people there, the better one feels.

• • •

18. The following activities can be completed in the Activity Book.
   a) 1A: "Different Ways Land Can Be Used." The children should be able to match each picture with its title, indicating some of the varieties of land use. After completing the activity, the class can discuss examples of various land uses in their own community.

From *Our Working World: Neighborhoods* by Lawrence Senesh. © 1973, Science Research Associates, Inc. Reprinted by permission of the publisher.

Example B

[**The Concept of Culture. Grade 4.** Pupil text.]

Culture Defined

All of the things that make up ways of living are called *culture*. The way people eat; the houses they live in; the way they make a living; the language they speak; the way they buy and sell things; and the way they worship God are all part of their way of living or their *culture*.

There are many different ways of living. The life of the American Indian, the Eskimo, and the person who lives in an American city are very different. These three people eat different kinds of food, get their food in different ways, speak different languages, and even wear different kinds of clothes.

Although there are many different ways of living, or *cultures*, all people have to do some things in order to live. All people must have food and water. All people must protect themselves from dangers such as cold weather, floods, and storms. All people must sleep. All people must learn to live with other people in their families and groups. Most people want other people to like them because they want friends.

[**The Concept of Culture.** Pupil Study Guide.]

II. CONCEPT OF CULTURE
  A. Anthropological terms I must use:
     culture   social organization
     economy   technology
     religion   values
  B. Key ideas I am to look for and learn about are:
     1. What is culture?
     2. What is the relation of biological drives to culture?
     3. Why is culture man's method of adapting to his environment?
     4. How is culture learned?
     5. What are some traits that all people possess?
  C. Things I can do:
     1. Collect pictures of types of tools used in various cultures to share with the class.
     2. Collect pictures which visually demonstrate the way man:
        (a) adjusts to his environment
        (b) modifies his environment.
     3. Read stories about children in other cultures. Find out how they do things differently from the manner in which we do them in our culture.

From *The Concept of Culture*, Pupil Text, Publication No. 16, and Pupil Study Guide, Publication No. 17, Anthropology Curriculum Project (Athens, Ga.: University of Georgia, 1965).

Example C

[J. Baboon Sounds and Human Speech]

3. MESSAGE-SENDING ACTIVITY

This activity will help children distinguish between messages that can be sent without language and messages that require it. They then consider various kinds of messages that language enables us to communicate.

Before class copy the following messages onto index cards and prepare dittoed "Language Messages."

MESSAGES TO PUT ON THE CARDS:

1. I'm hungry.
2. I hurt my leg.
3. I'm screaming mad!
4. I like you.
5. I'm embarrassed.
6. I'm so frightened!
7. I took a bath yesterday.
8. Last year, John used to cheat.
9. It will rain tomorrow.
10. Your refrigerator is running.
11. I'll be DeVore and you be the baboon.
12. You're wrong to say that baboons live for hundreds of years.
13. Can you come to my house after school?
14. The spider asked the princess to marry him.
15. My grandfather is not here.
16. It will be difficult to live on the moon.
17. Our eggs cannot be beaten.
18. Let's pretend we're spacemen.
19. It's not true that Mars has people on it.
20. Who's the best swimmer?
21. The giant had three eyes right on top of one another like a traffic light—only one was blue, one was orange, and the middle one was the color of dried blood.
22. I sent the book to Washington.
23. We made a club house when we were little.
24. I shall get the money.
25. He made a stone walk.
26. He likes to make believe he's a famous drummer.
27. No, Mexico and New Mexico are not the same place.
28. Do you have hand brakes on your bike?
29. In the middle of the night the fairy flew into the room and scattered her magic glow dust into every one of Nancy's shoes.
30. Our TV is in the repair shop.

The "Language Messages" are the sentences from the preceding list that can be communicated only with language. One "power" of language is identified for each group of sentences in parentheses. Do not copy these on the sheets for children. Notice that each of the messages may have several language powers but that all the messages in each group have at least one power in common. It is not important for the children to use the same words as those in parentheses to explain the language powers.

[*continued on the next page*]

LANGUAGE MESSAGES

What power of language does each group of sentences show?

I took a bath yesterday.
Last year John used to cheat.
We made a club house when we were little.

These sentences show that language lets us talk about

_____.

(THINGS THAT HAVE ALREADY HAPPENED: THE PAST.)

It will rain tomorrow.
It will be difficult to live on the moon.
I shall get the money.

These sentences show that language lets us talk about

_____.

(THINGS THAT HAVEN'T HAPPENED YET; THE FUTURE; PREDICTIONS.)

I'll be DeVore and you be the baboon.
Let's pretend we're spacemen.
He likes to make believe he's a famous drummer.

These sentences show that language lets us talk about

_____.

(SITUATIONS THAT DON'T REALLY EXIST.)

You're wrong to say that baboons live for hundreds of years.
It's not true that Mars has people on it.
No, Mexico and New Mexico are not the same place.

These sentences show that language lets us say things that

_____.

(ARGUE OR DISAGREE WITH SOMETHING; CONTRADICT.)

Can you come to my house after school?
Who's the best swimmer?
Do you have hand brakes on your bike?

These sentences show that language lets us say things that

_____.

(ASK QUESTIONS.)

The giant had three eyes right on top of one another like a traffic light—only one was blue, one was orange, and the middle one was the color of the dried blood.

In the middle of the night the fairy flew into the room and scattered her magic glow dust into every one of Nancy's shoes.
The spider asked the princess to marry him.

These sentences show that language lets us talk about

_____.

(THINGS THAT DON'T EXIST, OR ARE NOT "REAL.")

[continued on the next page]

My grandfather is not here.
Our TV is in the repair shop.
I sent the book to Washington.

These sentences show that language lets the speaker say something about things that

(ARE OUT OF HIS SIGHT.)

CHALLENGE:

Your refrigerator is running.
Our eggs cannot be beaten.
He made a stone walk.

These sentences show that language lets us say things that

(HAVE DOUBLE MEANING.)

a. Messages that can be sent without language.
Explain to the class that they are going to play a game about human communication and the messages humans can send.

Distribute the cards, explaining that everybody has a message and that no one should show his card to anyone else. Most of the messages need language to be communicated. But a few of the messages can be sent without language. Ask the children who think they have messages that can be communicated without language to raise their hands. Then ask those children, one at a time, to communicate their messages without language to the class. (They can use sounds and gestures but not signs used in charades because these signs represent words.) Keep a list on the board of the messages communicated.

After all the children who can communicate their messages without language have done so, examine the list on the board and ask children to consider what all of these messages have in common. The children should realize that these messages are all expressions of immediate feelings or physical needs. They are all responses to a present situation.

b. Kinds of messages that language enables humans to communicate.
Divide the class into groups of three or four, giving each group a dittoed "Language Messages" sheet. Explain that these messages are the ones that couldn't be acted out and they need language to be communicated. They are to consider "What special powers does language have?" while looking over each group of sentences. The sentences in each group have one special "power" in common—for example, allowing us to communicate about the future.

As the children finish their sheets, discuss the conclusions each group has reached. You might want to compile a class list of the powers of language on the board. Children can add additional sentences as examples of the various powers.

From "Baboons," in *Man: A Course of Study*, Teacher's Manual (Cambridge, Mass.; Educational Development Center, 1968), pp. 60–65.

Example D

Lesson 1
What Do We Know About Friendliness?

Purpose of Lesson 1
- To motivate students to explore this behavior with objectivity.
- To demonstrate that friendliness is not always appropriate.
- To identify the three parts of the behavior—feelings, intentions, actions.

Item 1

The first objective is to clear up any confusion or hesitation that pupils might have about the idea of studying a topic like friendliness scientifically.

You could say something like this: "Contrary to what many think friendliness is not always the best or most appropriate behavior, any more than unfriendliness is always bad and inappropriate. Both are legitimate subjects for the social scientist to study, because he wants to learn about human behavior.

"Almost everyone has an intuitive notion about what constitutes friendliness. Yet few people realize the different aspects involved; these are the feelings and intentions *behind* a person's actions. Equally important is the way in which another person perceives that behavior. It might be different from what the first person intended. For example, one person may have friendly feelings and intentions that are the inside causes for his actions. But another person may interpret his behavior as the opposite of what was intended. This kind of interaction can become quite complicated. One person can feel unfriendly and have unfriendly intentions, but act in a friendly way. Another can have both friendly feelings and intentions, but behave in a way that's considered unfriendly."

Three short behavior specimens are contained in the first reading selection. They illustrate some of the dimensions discussed above. The questions that appear at the conclusion of each episode should foster a lively class discussion.

The children should be encouraged to make value judgments about these behaviors. You can initiate these by asking the pupils, "Did you like the way the story ended? Why? Was the behavior of the characters good or bad? Why?" The purpose of value inquiry is to provide the student with an opportunity to discuss his own values openly and share them with others. Allow each child to express his values. Avoid stating your position or taking sides. Review "Conducting Value Inquiry in Class" in *The Teacher's Role in Social Science Investigation*, pages 21–37.

In the first reading selection, "Don't Be Mean to My Dog," the situation is one in which many people would consider unfriendly behavior fully justified, even appropriate. The episode should help pupils see that unfriendliness as a behavior is not always out of order.

In the second, friendliness prevails and is so perceived. In a way, it contains the beginnings of a circular process based on friendliness.

In "The Bully," the appropriateness of George's friendliness toward Bud

[*continued on the next page*]

is questionable. Was it really right, under the circumstances, for George to invite Bud to have a root beer with him? Was his friendliness a good thing?

Read "Friendly and Unfriendly Behavior"
on pages 89–93 of the Resource Book.

From *Social Science Laboratory Units*, Teacher's Guide by Ronald Lippitt, Robert Fox, and Lucille Schaible. © 1969, Science Research Associates, Inc. Reprinted by permission of the publisher.

Example E

THE CLASS IN THE NEIGHBORHOOD

Description

The class goes on a walking tour to survey the school neighborhood.

Objectives

To make the children aware of their own neighborhood.

To give the class a real experience which it can draw upon and refer to in subsequent and more abstract lessons.

Materials and Arrangements

Some paper and pencils for the children to make notes on the trip.

It is very helpful to arrange for some room mothers or fellow teachers to go along on the trip. It will make a great difference to you and the children, in terms of enjoyment and what is learned. For a class of 30 children, try to recruit at least two or even three people to assist you. With 4 assistants you could break the class down into 5 teams.

Some ways of organizing:

1–3 adults	class as a body
4 adults	2 groups of about 15 children
5 adults	5 groups of children

Procedure

Almost any neighborhood will lend itself to this lesson—whether it is in the heart of the city, the suburbs, or even in the country. All neighborhoods have their own unique characteristics. The trip should be used to bring these out so that comparisons can be made with various kinds of city neighborhoods.

1. *Know the neighborhood yourself:* Some advanced scouting will enable you to plan and time the trip. Take note of special neighborhood features. Perhaps make arrangements for the children to stop in at an office, store, or factory to give them a better idea of what actually goes on in the neighborhood. Try as much as possible to make the children aware of life in their neighborhood.

2. *Before the walk:* Sometime before the day of the tour, find out what

[*continued on the next page*]

impressions and information the children already have about the neighborhood. Outline these on a chart which can be added to or modified after the trip, thereby giving the children a chance to "see" what they've found out about the neighborhood.

Assign specific fact-gathering tasks to teams of two or more children. Let the teams decide for themselves what they are going to find out. Here are some possibilities to offer:

- find out what sounds there are in the neighborhood and how often they are heard.
- list the different types of buildings and spaces.
- what are the different smells in the neighborhood?
- what's up high?
- what's on the ground?
- how many different kinds of living things are there, besides people?
- what's in back of things?
- how many signs are there and what do they say?
- what things are moving in the neighborhood? how do they move? where are they going?
- what is changing in the neighborhood?
- what's under things?
- meet some people and find out where they live and where they are going.
- what are the best things in the neighborhood?
- what are the scariest things?
- what are the biggest and smallest things?
- how many different things are there to feel in the neighborhood (textures, etc.)?
- what things in the neighborhood are there to wonder about?

Each team should be equipped with paper and pencil to list and record their findings.

Also, before you go, try to have a planning session with your assistants to fill them in on team assignments and routes.

3. *On the walk:* Help the children gather their data: introduce them to people, point things out to them, and above all have a good time. If the class is divided into groups, they can take different routes to cover more of the neighborhood.

4. *After the walk:* Pull things together in a class discussion: What did the teams find out? What puzzled or surprised the children? What would they like to learn more about? What did they like best?

How would the children characterize the neighborhood? Are they left with any overall impression? Are there similar neighborhoods shown in the serial photograph or in the picture pool?

From the MATCH Program, *The City,* Teacher's Guide (Boston: American Science and Engineering, 1969), pp. 20–21. Reprinted with permission of Children's Museum, Boston, Massachusetts, and American Science and Engineering, Inc., Boston, Massachusetts.

Answers to the Strategy Examples

If your answers correspond to the ones below, you have understood the criteria that differentiate instructional strategies.

Example A is a closed deductive strategy. The criterial attributes of the concept "neighborhood" are identified for the student. Students are led to more concrete activities (drawing pictures of nearby places and discussing their own neighborhood) after the more abstract criteria are presented.

Example B is not an inquiry strategy at all; it is an expository one. The text presents all the information and students are required, in the questions that follow, to do little more than show comprehension.

Example C is a good example of a closed inductive strategy. The students are first given many concrete examples and nonexamples before they are asked to induce the criterial attributes of human speech. It is a closed strategy because the objective is to have students arrive at predetermined or convergent answers.

Example D is essentially an open deductive strategy. The teacher introduces the concept "friendly and unfriendly behavior" and suggests one criterial attribute—in this case, related to intention. Questions that are asked at the end of each reading, however, invite much divergence. The lesson begins with the teacher presenting some abstract ideas that are given more concrete reference in the readings that follow.

Example E makes a good contrast with Example A since it deals with the same concept. This example, however, uses an open inductive strategy. The lesson is not based on predetermined criterial attributes; students are asked to induce their own. They begin with the concrete experience of walking and observing in the neighborhood and arrive at abstractions later on.

Modified Inquiry Generalizing Strategies

Identifying teaching strategies would be a pointless exercise if the reader were unable to actually use them in the classroom. The steps identified below are suggested sequences for *generalizing* strategies in the four modes of modified inquiry. They are essentially elaborations of the sequences identified at the end of Chapter 1. Each strategy includes additional steps, and each is adapted specifically to fit the teaching of a generalization.

Both deductive strategies begin with the teacher or text presenting the generalization and elaborating on it by explaining the concepts and giving examples. The closed deductive strategy, however, concludes with students applying the generalization, while the open deductive strategy ends with the students modifying the generalization and evaluating their modifications. In short, the former stresses convergence; the latter, divergence.

The inductive strategies begin with concrete examples in which the generalization is embedded but not identified. In both cases the students induce the generalization after analyzing the examples. The closed inductive strategy concludes with the application of the generalization. In the open inductive strategy, however, the students propose modifications and proceed to evaluate their own contributions.

Sequences Associated with the Four Modified Generalization Strategies

Closed Deductive

A. Teacher or text presents the generalization.
B. Teacher or text elaborates on the embedded concepts.
C. Teacher or text presents examples in which the generalization applies.
D. Students analyze examples.
E. Students apply the generalization by identifying additional examples and/or making predictions based on the generalization.

Open Deductive

A. Teacher or text presents the generalization.
B. Teacher or text elaborates on the embedded concepts.
C. Teacher or text presents examples in which the generalization applies.
D. Students analyze the examples.
E. Students evaluate the generalization.
F. Students propose modifications and/or new generalizations.
G. Students propose ways to test the modifications and new generalizations.
H. Students gather appropriate evidence.
I. Students evaluate the modifications.

Closed Inductive

A. Teacher or text presents examples in which the generalization is embedded, but does not identify the generalization.
B. Students analyze examples and explore relationships.
C. Students induce the generalization.
D. Students evaluate the generalization on the basis of given examples.
E. Students apply the generalization by identifying additional examples and/or making predictions based on the generalization.

Open Inductive

A. Teacher or text presents examples in which the generalization is embedded, but does not identify the generalization.
B. Students analyze examples and explore relationships.
C. Students induce the generalization.
D. Students evaluate the generalization on the basis of given examples.
E. Students propose new evidence.
F. Students suggest modifications and/or new generalizations.
G. Students propose ways to test the modifications and new generalizations.
H. Students gather appropriate evidence.
I. Students evaluate the modifications.

Moving from One Strategy to Another

When using prepared materials, teachers have the option of proceeding in the manner recommended or adapting the materials to their own needs. Read the materials carefully before beginning instruction. Identify the recommended strategy and consider alternative approaches that might be more interesting or useful for your particular group of students. Rearranging the sequence can frequently result in heightened student involvement and motivation. Chart 2–4 uses a low-level generalization (''workers produce goods or services'') to demonstrate how such modifications can be made.

Chart 2–4
Modified Generalization Strategies: An Example

A Closed Deductive Strategy

Teacher states and explains the generalization

Teacher: Today we are going to learn what workers produce. Workers produce either goods or services.

Teacher elaborates on embedded concepts

Teacher: Workers do all kinds of jobs. There are doctors, teachers, clerks, woodcutters, bricklayers, secretaries, welders, and so on. There are over three thousand different types of jobs that people do in the United States. All these workers produce either goods or services. By "goods" we mean something that can be touched or seen, an object. By "services" we mean helping other people. For example, the things we eat are goods. The farmer who grows the food is producing goods. But the truck driver who brings the food from the farm to the store is performing a service.

Teacher gives examples

Teacher: Here is a picture of a carpenter. He is building furniture. He is producing goods. Here is a picture of a dentist. She is fixing the child's teeth. She is producing a service.

Students analyze examples

Teacher: Why do we call what the carpenter is making "goods"? Why do we call what the dentist is doing a "service"? How is what the carpenter and the dentist are doing the same? How is it different? What does a carpet layer produce? What does an architect produce?

Students generate additional examples

Teacher: What other workers produce goods? What other workers produce services?

An Open Deductive Strategy

Teacher states and explains the generalizations

Teacher: Today we are going to learn what workers produce. Workers produce either goods or services.

Teacher elaborates on embedded concepts

Teacher: Workers do all kinds of jobs. There are doctors, teachers, clerks, woodcutters, bricklayers, secretaries, welders, and so on. There are over three thousand different types of jobs that people do in the United States. All these workers produce either goods or services. By "goods" we mean something that can be touched or seen, an object. By "services" we mean helping other people. For example, the things we eat are goods. The farmer who grows the food is producing goods. But the truck driver who brings the food from the farm to the store is performing a service.

Teacher gives examples

Teacher: Here is a picture of a carpenter. He is building furniture. He is producing goods. Here is a picture of a dentist. She is fixing the child's teeth. She is producing a service.

Students analyze examples

Teacher: Why do we call what the carpenter is making "goods"? Why do we call what the dentist is doing a "service"? How is what the carpenter and the dentist are doing the same? How is it different? What does a carpet layer produce? What does an architect produce?

Students evaluate the generalization

Teacher: Can you think of examples in which workers produce neither goods nor services? How about what you are doing right now? How about cooking supper? Are these services? Whom do they serve? How about someone who is reading a book?

Students suggest modifications or new generalizations

Teacher: Should we change the sentence "Workers produce goods or services"? How?

Students propose ways to test modifications

Teacher: How can we find out if the changes we have made are correct?

Students investigate

Teacher: Who will go ahead and do it?

Students evaluate modifications

Teacher: Is this better? Why or why not?

A Closed Inductive Strategy

Teacher presents examples

Teacher: Let's look at these pictures.

Students analyze examples

Teacher: What do you see in these pictures? How are some alike? How are some different? How are all of them alike? Can we say all the people are working? Why or why not? What is different about what they're making? What is the same about what they're making?

Students induce generalization

Teacher: Can you tell me in one sentence what workers do? Can you tell me in one sentence what they produce?

Students evaluate generalization

Teacher: Is what we've said true on the basis of the pictures we have?

Students apply generalization

Teacher: What other workers produce goods? Services? What does an architect produce? How about a carpet layer?

An Open Inductive Strategy

Teacher presents examples

Teacher: Let's look at these pictures.

Students analyze examples

Teacher: What do you see in these pictures? How are some alike? How are some different? How are all of them alike? Can we say all the people are working? Why or why not? What is different about what they're making? What is the same about what they're making?

Students induce generalization

Teacher: Can you tell me in one sentence what workers do? Can you tell me in one sentence what they produce?

Students evaluate generalization

Teacher: Can you think of any exceptions? How about what you are doing right now? How about cooking supper? Is this work? Are you producing goods or a service? Whom do they serve? How about someone who is reading a book?

Students suggest modifications or new generalizations
Teacher: Should we change the sentences we wrote before? How?

Students propose ways to test modifications
Teacher: How can we find out if the changes we've made are correct?

Students investigate
Teacher: Who will go ahead and do it?

Students evaluate modifications
Teacher: Is this better? Why or why not?

Summary

A question that is at least as important as *how* to teach is *what* to teach. In other words, just what is the content of social studies education? Traditionally, the content has been rather vague—sometimes little more than the accumulation of such knowledge as was deemed useful by those who designed the curricula. Frequently this boiled down to a set of specific facts whose importance seemed questionable at best.

The current view of the "what" of education places much less stress on specifics and more on powerful abstractions. For one thing, facts are no longer as dependable as they once seemed; even such classic social studies standbys as "Columbus discovered America" need to be presented with a great deal of caution. For another, many people have finally come to the conclusion that the principal content of education should be those ideas that best help explain human existence.

Such focus as existed in the traditional approach to teaching social studies was generally based on the idea of an "expanding horizon," a view of learning in which each grade represented not only a step up but a broadening of awareness, beginning with the home and community and working up to foreign countries. It was only reasonable that such an approach would be questioned in an age in which most schoolchildren had seen the surface of the moon broadcast live on television, but it was inevitable that it would be challenged for its loose structure.

If we are to make sense of what we learn, the material must be developed within a structure of some sort—and the bases of structure are concepts and generalizations. Concepts are those things that have attributes in common and generalizations are statements about how one concept is related to another concept. Generalizing may be popularly considered a bad habit, but it has definite advantages. If enough reliable generalizations can be made about the relationships of human beings to each other and to the rest of the world, some real progress may be made in dealing with our problems—just as the increasing number of reliable generalizations about the human body (a concept) and disease (another concept) has led to progress in dealing with health problems.

Inquiry can be an integral part of the concept/generalization type of organization. (Indeed, one would probably have little success trying to get concepts and generalizations across in an expository way.) The conditions that apply to leading students to formulate concepts and generalizations are therefore the same as those that apply to inquiry, and the appropriate strategy modifications—discussed at length in Chapter 1—are likewise the same.

Humanistic
Concerns

Individualizing
Instruction

One of the major concerns of recent years has been to discover the means to individualize instruction so as to meet diverse student needs and interests. Three overriding questions are implicit in this quest: (1) In what ways are children likely to be similar? (2) In what ways are children likely to be different? (3) How can instruction be designed to satisfy similarities and differences?

How Children Are Similar

Despite the unchallengeable assertion that the individual is unique, it is equally true that individuals have much in common. Through intensive studies of maturing children, psychologists have made us aware that much of cognitive, emotional, physical, and social change is a developmental process marked by identifiable sequences. These sequences tend to be similar for all people, although the age at which they occur and the precise form they take may vary greatly among individuals.

Piaget   One of the most noted investigators of cognitive development, Jean Piaget, has identified four primary stages of cognition, each associated with an approximate age level.[1]

From birth to the age of two, the child is in what Piaget calls the *sensorimotor stage.* The child learns about the world through the senses and by the direct physical manipulation of objects. The child is literally self-centered and cannot distinguish between his or her own self and external reality. Toward the end of this stage, the child begins to perceive an objective world outside the self.

The next stage, which Piaget terms the *preoperational stage,* lasts roughly from the second to the seventh years. It is marked by great advances in language growth that enable the child to learn about the world through mental manipulation. Although still primarily egocentric (interested only in his or her own point of view), the child is beginning to understand other points of view. Thinking is largely intuitive, and the child makes frequent assertions without trying to support them factually. Notions of causality are still primitive at this point.

The *concrete operational stage,* from seven to eleven, is the period during which the child becomes able to distinguish between his or her own point of view and those of others. Time, space, causality, and conservation (the idea that transforming the shape or appearance of a thing does not change its mass or substance) are understood now. Intuition is transformed into operations (internalized actions that modify knowledge). At the heart of these operations is the ability to reverse—to be aware that conditions can be reversed to return to their original state. But the child can only perform operations with concrete objects with which he or she has had direct experience.

[1]Jean Piaget and B. Inhelder, *The Growth of Logical Thinking from Childhood to Adolescence* (New York: Basic Books, 1958).

After eleven, the child is in the *formal operational stage.* He or she can deal with abstractions—theoretical problems, hypotheses, probabilities, and so on. Ideas can be manipulated even when they are not supported by perception or experience. Indeed, the adolescent often rejects reality and seeks to reform it. Rather than discourage youthful plans for the reform of society, adults should promote them. Such plans are very important in developing creativity among the young, who discover soon enough that adaptions must be made if they are to be used in the real world.

Although not all developmentalists agree with Piaget regarding precisely what happens at each of these stages, they do share the view that growth is to a large extent determined by maturation—that is, it is independent of training or teaching. Moreover, such changes are age-linked. Hence how and what we teach needs to be suitable for the age level under consideration.

Bruner   Jerome Bruner attributes more importance than Piaget to the influence of the external environment on development.[2] He believes teachers can do a great deal to accelerate the rate of growth. Bruner says that there are three successive systems of representation through which intellectual development occurs. The teacher's mode of communicating information has to fit the learner's age and experience as well as the intrinsic nature of the subject matter. Very young children understand things best through *enactive* representation—that is, through actual actions. Approximately by age three, children can understand things through *iconic* representation—that is, through visual imagery like pictures or diagrams. The most advanced form of representation is *symbolic*—experience is translated through words. While people continue to use all three forms of representation to comprehend experiences throughout their lives, it is important to emphasize the appropriate ones for particular age levels.

Maslow   Abraham Maslow has postulated a hierarchy of needs that people must satisfy in order to grow emotionally and cognitively.[3] This hierarchy is illustrated in Figure 3–1. Failure to satisfy needs leads to deficiency motivation—that is, to behavior that will seek to get rid of the deficiency. Thus a child who feels unsafe and unloved will spend a great deal of time seeking safety and love. Movement from one stage to another is a pleasurable, self-satisfying process resulting in general health and well-being. But growth will occur only as deficiency needs are satisfied. The child whose more basic needs are satisfied will show a healthy curiosity about the world and learning. Conversely, a child whose physiological, safety, love and belonging, esteem, and self-actualization needs are not satisfied will have little desire to learn.

[2]Jerome S. Bruner, *Toward a Theory of Instruction* (Cambridge, Mass.: Harvard University Press, 1966).

[3]Abraham H. Maslow, "A Theory of Human Motivation." *Psychological Review,* Vol. 50 (July 1943), pp. 370–96.

Figure 3–1
Maslow's Hierarchy

Aesthetic needs

Desire to know and understand

Need for self-actualization

Esteem needs

Love and belonging needs

Safety needs

Physiological needs

SOURCE: Abraham H. Maslow, "A Theory of Human Motivation," *Psychological Review* 50:370–96. Copyright 1943 by the American Psychological Association. Reprinted by permission.

Age-level Characteristics

Each developmental stage in the maturing individual is accompanied by new needs, abilities, and learnings. Each step includes physical, social, and emotional changes—as well as cognitive ones. It is obviously impossible to predict with any certainty the developmental pattern of any individual. Nevertheless, there are characteristics that are generally common to age groups. The following is a summary of age-level characteristics that occur in most children.[4]

Preschool and Kindergarten: 3–6 Years

At this age, children are extremely active physically and require periods of rest to compensate for their great exertion. Large muscles are more developed than small ones. Tying shoes, buttoning coats, and writing are almost impossible. They have difficulty focusing on small objects and eye-hand coordination is poor. Girls are usually ahead of boys in all areas of development, with the possible exception of size. Right- or left-handedness is usually established.

Socially, friendships are usually limited to one or two "best" friends, but these may change frequently. Play groups are not too well organized and tend to change often. Although quarrels are frequent, they tend to be of short duration. There is great pleasure in dramatic play and beginning awareness of sex roles.

Emotional development is at a volatile stage—emotions are expressed freely and outbursts of anger are common. A vivid imagination frequently leads to grossly exaggerated fears. Competition for adult affection breeds jealousy.

Mentally, students are developing rapidly in the acquisition of language. They enjoy talking to each other and in front of groups. Imagination and fantasy are at their peak.

[4]Summarized primarily from Robert F. Biehler, *Psychology Applied to Teaching,* 2nd ed. (Boston: Houghton Mifflin, 1974), ch. 4.

Primary Grades:
6–9 Years

Children continue to be very physically active during this stage. Suppressed energy may be released in fidgeting, nail-biting, and similar behavior during periods of sedentary activity. Fine coordination may still be poor. Difficulty still exists in writing and focusing on small objects. Common childhood diseases are most likely to occur during this period. The accident rate is also at a peak because children in this age group tend to underestimate dangers.

Although friendship patterns are still likely to be characterized by "best friends," greater selectivity is usually evident in the choice of friends. Games are more organized, but there is great emphasis on "rules." Quarrels are still frequent as are physical aggression, competition, and boasting. Although the difference in interests of boys and girls becomes more pronounced at this age, there is great variation in behavior from one classroom to another because of influences exerted by teachers.

Emotionally, children become very sensitive during this period. Criticism, ridicule, and failure can be devastating. Despite their own sensitivity, they are quick to hurt others. Generally, students are eager to please the teacher and want to do well in school, for which reasons they require frequent praise.

Eagerness to learn is common. Learning occurs primarily through concrete manipulation of materials. Eagerness to talk is still evident and there is much experimentation with language—including obscene language. Concepts of reciprocity, fairness, and right and wrong develop during this period.

Elementary Grades:
9–12 Years

This period is marked by a growth spurt, more evident among girls than boys. Many girls reach puberty, and with the appearance of secondary sex characteristics, concern and curiosity about sex increases. Fine coordination develops during this period; hence there is much pleasure in arts and crafts and in musical activities. Rough play is evident among boys, often resulting in injuries because incomplete bone growth cannot yet sustain heavy pressure.

Peer groups begin to replace adults as sources of behavior standards and the recognition of achievement. Interests become more sharply divergent between the sexes—frequently resulting in "battles" between them for recognition and achievement, as well as the exchange of insults. Team games become more popular, along with class spirit. Crushes and hero worship are common.

This is the period when the conflict between adults and the group code begins to emerge. "Moral relativism" replaces the absolute imperative of rules as youngsters begin to understand the need for exceptions. Frequently they set very high standards for themselves—sometimes unreal standards—hence feelings of frustration are common. While the desire for independence grows, the need for adult support is still strong—therefore irrational and unpredictable behavior often results.

Curiosity still remains strong; children frequently become "collectors" during this age. During the early part of this period children are still in the concrete operational stage, but toward the end formal thinking begins to emerge.

Teaching Suggestions for Helping Students Learn

1. Concrete learning experiences should predominate during the primary grades. Increased use of iconic and symbolic representations should occur during intermediate and upper elementary grades, but concrete experiences should continue to be used throughout.

2. Opportunities for engaging in abstract thinking should increase with age.

3. Experiences should be provided that help youngsters understand other points of view.

4. Opportunities for fantasy and talk should be particularly plentiful during the elementary years.

5. Physical activity continues to be a strong need throughout all the years of elementary school, but is particularly important during the primary grades.

6. Emphasis on activities that require fine muscular coordination, such as writing, should be minimal during the early elementary years.

7. All youngsters benefit from supportive environments that fulfill physiological, safety, love, and esteem needs. Lack of interest in learning is frequently the consequence of deficiencies in these areas.

8. Expressions of hostility toward adults and each other grow increasingly stronger as youngsters mature, but the need for adult support remains equally strong.

Junior High: 12–15 Years

Most girls have completed their growth spurt by the beginning of this age. Boys, however, may not complete it until later, and sometimes in highly irregular patterns. Since puberty is reached by practically all, concern with physical and psychological changes is intense. This is the period of adolescent awkwardness, self-consciousness, emphasis on appearance. Eating and sleeping habits tend to be poor, although health is usually good. Physical and mental endurance is limited.

The peer group dominates as the source of behavior standards and approval. Students feel a great need to conform to group standards in order to be part of the group. There is great concern over what friends think, and the importance of adults diminishes. Conflict between the generations is common and students begin to confide in friends instead of adults. Socially, girls are more mature than boys, and immature boys tend to cover up feelings of social inadequacy with overly critical attitudes toward girls.

Much moodiness and unpredictability in behavior are evident. This may be due to role confusion as well as inadequate health habits, biological changes, and the like. Boisterous behavior and outbursts of anger are common, many induced by feelings of inadequacy as well as by chemical factors. This age group tends toward intolerance of others and highly opinionated statements— particularly toward parents and teachers whose previous role of supremacy is resented.

At this stage, students are capable of formal operational thought. Abstractions, symbolic modes of presenting materials, generalizing, and theorizing are within their capacities. Nonetheless, a tendency to daydream and fantasize may interfere with maximum cognitive growth.

How Children Differ

The *rate* and *form* of development differ considerably among children. Cultural and social-class environments, as well as sex, account for some of these differences. It should be clearly understood at the outset that differences within a single group are far greater than average differences between them. Probably any identifiable characteristic is present in all variations within a given social grouping. Lower-class child-rearing patterns, for example, range from extreme authoritarianism to extreme permissiveness, just as middle-class child-rearing patterns do. There are boys who are exceedingly aggressive and others who are very passive, and the same is true of girls. Characterizations of differences among groups are based on averages—hence the range of differences among individual group members of the same social group is much larger than the average differences among groups. What this implies is simply that no accurate prediction of an individual's behavior can be made on the basis of his or her cultural, social, or sex group. Each individual is a unique combination of characteristics and traits.

What purpose then does characterization of groups have? It can serve to sensitize teachers. Certain types of advantages and disadvantages are more characteristic of particular groups, and alert teachers can take these into account in planning instruction.

Cultural Differences

Child-rearing patterns differ among cultural groups. Immigrant groups—subcultural groups that have either not been allowed or have not chosen to become assimilated into American mainstream culture—frequently do not have typical American expectations for their children. Many such parents tend to be more authoritarian and to deplore the permissiveness they feel characterizes American child-rearing patterns. The free behavior of American women is offensive to many from Latin American and European cultures. Strict religious sects impose behavior patterns on their youngsters that set them apart from their schoolmates. Children in authoritarian households are less likely to expect acceptance and understanding from adults, and may not be able to relate to their teachers in ways expected of them. The desire for achievement, which is strongly cultivated in middle-class American culture, is frequently at odds with the immigrant groups' stress on family dependence and unity rather than success. This may create problems for their children, who may find themselves torn between the desires of their families and the expectations of the school. Those minority cultures that are asserting a new pride in their distinctiveness are tending more and more to reject the dominant culture. Minority children in the school systems frequently distrust teachers and schoolmates of the dominant cultural group.

Social-Class Differences

Equally important are social-class differences. The middle class, comprised primarily of professionals and white-collar workers, is the dominant social class, and its values are generally accepted as norms. The values of this class

Suggestions for Teaching the Educationally Disadvantaged

Among the many teaching suggestions offered for working with the educationally disadvantaged, which would probably be effective with all children, are:

1. Continual diagnosis to uncover learning gaps and needs
2. Individualized instruction
3. Multiple objectives to include knowledge, skills, values, and attitudes
4. Small units of instruction, arranged in a hierarchy of skills from more simple to more complex
5. Emphasis on concrete, tangible, and overt activity
6. Extensive opportunities for experiences
7. Varied instructional techniques, including games, dramatizations, role-playing, and programmed instructional materials
8. Capitalization on student interests and student-created materials
9. Manageable tasks that can ensure success
10. Positive reinforcement techniques such as praise, progress charts, and even money
11. Maintenance of stable rules and firm control in a positive way in order to establish feelings of physical and emotional safety
12. Show of interest in students' lives—what they do, what they have eaten, how they feel
13. Deemphasis on competition—keeping performance in front of peers to a minimum unless student volunteers
14. Extensive and frequent verbalization by teacher with students

are generally considered to include hard work, responsibility, self-reliance, success, competition, resolution of conflict through nonviolence, and self-improvement through education. Lower-class values—the values of the working and nonworking poor—are different in some important ways. There is greater emphasis on, and indeed approval of, physical aggression—physical competence may be very important for survival. There tends to be less respect for property; sexual activity begins earlier; and generally there is less control over impulses that middle-class children are taught to suppress. Education may pose conflicts for the lower-class child since success may mean leaving friends and family behind. Linguistic patterns differ; lower-class children tend to have smaller vocabularies and less complex verbal patterns and tend to rely on group understanding of common meanings rather than articulated phrases to communicate. Since they are best understood by their own group, they have great fear and anxiety in encountering new situations and people. Coupled with all of this is a narrow set of experiences—lack of reading materials, little or no travel, and no friends outside the immediate group. All of this tends to retard cognitive as well as social development.

Lower-class students do have some advantages over their middle-class counterparts. Practical survival skills acquired under financial and physical hardships, including responsibilities in the care of the house and younger children, induce earlier awareness of adult roles and maturity. Cooperation, lessened competition among siblings, and greater enjoyment of each other, as well as mutual aid that transcends the nuclear family are also more commonly found among lower-class youngsters. And cognitive styles tend to be slow and careful as opposed to facile and clever. Unfortunately, these skills are not rewarded in schools.[5]

Disadvantaged Groups

The term "educationally disadvantaged" has been generally adopted to describe those youngsters who reach school with a lower-than-average number of those skills that are rewarded in school. Among the characteristics usually attributed to them are the following:

1. A slower rate of learning
2. Perceptual, language, and reading deficits
3. Low achievement in school
4. Greater antagonism toward school and teachers
5. Preference for physical rather than verbal experience
6. Greater interest in the practical
7. Less inhibition of aggressive impulses
8. Poor self-image
9. Poor health habits, crowded home conditions, frequent moves
10. Many fatherless homes
11. More emotional problems
12. More frequent victimization by prejudice and discrimination

Although the majority of disadvantaged people in the United States is white, the number of blacks and some other racial groups is disproportionately large. For that reason, some people tend to regard the characteristics listed above as peculiar to minorities. The actual numerical distribution of disadvantaged groups, as identified in a 1967 study, from largest to smallest is: urban whites, urban blacks, rural blacks, rural whites, rural Spanish-Americans, urban Puerto Ricans, American Indians.[6]

What needs to be understood above all is that "educationally disadvantaged" children are not necessarily less capable. Their poorly developed skills are largely the result of lack of instruction and opportunity. They may be slower in progressing through the developmental stages, but they can achieve required school skills given sufficient time.

[5]Further information on this subject may be found in the following sources: Bernstein, B., "Social Structure of Language and Learning," *Educational Research* 3 (1961), pp. 163–70; Corwin, Ronald G., *A Sociology of Education: Emerging Patterns of Class, Status, and Power in the Public Schools* (New York: Appleton-Century-Crofts, 1967), pp. 158–62; Fantini, Mario, and Gerald Weinstein, *The Disadvantaged* (New York: Harper & Row, 1968; Klausmeier, Herbert J., and Richard E. Ripple, *Learning and Human Abilities; Educational Psychology,* 3rd ed. (New York: Harper & Row, 1971), pp. 218–21; Lindgren, Henry Clay, *Educational Psychology in the Classroom,* 4th ed. (New York: Wiley, 1972), ch. 4; Riessman, Frank, *The Culturally Deprived Child* (New York: Harper & Row, 1962; Tenenbaum, Samuel, "The Teacher, the Middle Class, the Lower Class," *Phi Delta Kappan* 45 (1963), pp. 82–86.

[6]R. J. Havighurst and T. E. Moorefield, "The Disadvantaged in Industrial Cities," in P. A. Witty, ed., *The Educationally Retarded and Disadvantaged,* 66th Yearbook, Part I, National Society for the Study of Education (Chicago: University of Chicago Press, 1967), pp. 8–20.

Teaching Suggestions Based on Studies of Sex Differences

1. All youngsters should be encouraged to engage in high-level cognitive tasks and rewarded strongly for them. Less time should be spent in low-level tasks.

2. Environments that reward conformity and docility are good neither for boys nor girls. Boys do poorly in such environments, academically and socially, while girls, who succeed in them more frequently, are encouraged to persist in patterns that are ultimately self-defeating.

3. Both boys and girls should be encouraged to become more autonomous decision-makers, but in early childhood particularly, girls need attention along these lines.

4. While all children need to develop verbal abilities, boys need special encouragement.

5. While all children need to develop visual-spatial and mathematical abilities, girls need special encouragement. In social studies this means more opportunities to work with maps, graphs, tables.

6. Neither excessive aggression nor excessive passivity is desirable for maximum intellectual development. In general, boys are more likely to benefit from some inhibition of their aggressive tendencies, while girls are more likely to profit from the encouragement of aggressiveness.

Sex Differences

The issue of personality and cognitive differences between the sexes has a long history. Characteristically, women have been identified as more emotional, passive, and dependent, while men are purportedly more rational, active, and independent. Physiological and hormonal differences between the sexes are impressive and suggest that they are accompanied by personality and cognitive differences. But many traditional beliefs about the types and degree of differences are simply wrong or inconclusive.

After a three-year study of over two thousand books and articles on sex differences, two leading psychologists concluded that many so-called differences are no more than myths, while others are fairly well substantiated. They believe that the following are *not* supported by the evidence:[7]

1. Girls are more social than boys.
2. Girls are more suggestible than boys.
3. Girls have lower self-esteem than boys.
4. Girls lack motivation to achieve.
5. Girls are better at rote learning and simple repetitive tasks.
6. Boys are more "analytic" than girls.
7. Girls are more affected by heredity, boys by environment.
8. Girls are "auditory," boys "visual."

[7]Eleanor Emmons Maccoby and Carol Nagy Jacklin, "What We Know and Don't Know About Sex Differences," *Psychology Today* (December 1974), pp. 109–112.

These, however, are fairly well established sex differences:

1. Males are more aggressive than females.
2. Girls have greater verbal ability than boys.
3. Boys excel in visual-spatial ability.
4. Boys excel in mathematical ability.
5. During childhood, girls appear to be more obedient to adults.
6. Dominance appears to be more of an issue in boys' groups than in girls' groups.

Individualizing Instruction

In order to meet the differences that exist among students, efforts are being made to individualize instruction. This implies choosing educational objectives and instructional means that can best satisfy the needs of each individual learner.

Maximum individualization of learning occurs when students choose both the learning objectives and learning means. But the concept of individualization includes a range of alternatives, even some situations in which the teacher prescribes both objectives and means. The element that identifies an individualized program is that it is tailored to meet individual needs. Programs differ, however, in relation to whether the teacher or the student makes the choice of objectives and means. Four types of individualized programs are generally distinguished. They are summarized in Chart 3–1 and elaborated below.[8]

Chart 3–1

Four Types of Individualized Programs

	Teacher chooses means	Student chooses means
Teacher chooses objectives	Individually diagnosed learning	Self-directed learning
Student chooses objectives	Personalized learning	Independent study

Individually Diagnosed Learning

In this program the teacher diagnoses student needs, determines objectives for each individual, and prescribes means for attaining them. Suppose, for example, after administering a battery of diagnostic tests, the teacher determines that map skills vary greatly among students. John does not understand latitude and longitude, Mary does not recognize the distortions in the Mercator map, and Jim cannot interpret map symbols. The teacher would then determine for each a dif-

[8]The terms used to describe each type of individualized program are taken with some minor modifications from Jack V. Edling's model as described in Ronald E. Hull, "Selecting an Approach to Individualized Education," *Phi Delta Kappan* 55:3 (November 1973), pp. 169–73.

ferent educational objective and provide means for reaching them.

This type of individualized program is probably the easiest to implement. Its basic requisite is careful diagnosis and the accumulation of self-directed learning activities that can be distributed appropriately. Although these activities may require considerable time to collect and prepare initially, they can be used time and again and supplemented when needed.

Student autonomy, however, is clearly minimal in this situation, since it is the teacher who does all the choosing. Nonetheless, it represents an advance over the standardized program where students are given similar if not identical assignments, regardless of abilities and needs.

Self-directed Learning

In this program the teacher chooses the objective but the students choose the means. This may involve the students' choosing from among a group of alternatives presented by the teacher, the students generating their own means, or some combination of the two. The following is a representative sample of means choices that might be offered to students learning about the concept of "interdependence."

Collect magazine pictures of items that grow and items that have to be manufactured. Arrange a bulletin board with pictures. Give your bulletin board a title.

Tape an interview with (1) your mother, (2) a local businessman, (3) a policeman. Ask questions to find out what they need to do their job, where the things come from, and how they get them.

List as many things as you can observe in the classroom. Next to each, write the place it comes from, who makes it, who pays for it, and where the money comes from.

Find out all the steps it takes to bring a loaf of bread to your table. Write a story about it called "A Loaf of Bread."

Arrange to take a trip with someone to the business section of your town. Stand at a street corner for about an hour and observe all the trucks that go by. Record (1) the product the truck is carrying and (2) the state the truck comes from.

Arrange a field trip to a local pier. Find out the names of the countries from which ships come and the products they bring. With the help of your teacher or another adult, write the information down.

Write an imaginary story describing all the things you would have to do for yourself if you were the only person in the world.

Look at the Yellow Pages of your telephone directory. List all the types of services and stores you think you could do without.

Plan and prepare a mural with a group in which you show how people need each other.

Think of three things you might do to help learn about the ways people need each other. Discuss them with your teacher.

Offering students choices means more work for the teacher since each objective needs to be accompanied by several alternatives. On the other hand, it has the advantage of allowing for divergent student learning styles. Care needs to be exercised, however, to ensure that the means offered do indeed lead to the objective. Thus, for example, in the sample given above, the teacher would have to provide some synthesizing classroom activities, such as periodic class discussions or a class "book," to pull newly learned material together in order to

ensure satisfactory mastery of the concept. Moreover, one must try to overcome the tendency for children to try means with which they have already been successful rather than experiment with new techniques. Thus, some combination of requirements and alternatives may be best in most situations.

Personalized Learning

In personalized learning, the students select the objectives but the teacher selects the means. The selection of objectives may emerge from a range of alternatives suggested by the teacher, suggestions proffered by the student, or some combination of the two.

Suppose, for example, the subject of study is community groups. The teacher may then present the following for student choice:

Ethnic groups	Recreational groups	Women
Business groups	Social groups	The aged
Professional groups	Political groups	Labor groups

Or, if students are learning about Mexico, they might select a topic such as: products, people, trade, history, government, relations with the United States, geography, music, or painting.

In either case, the teacher would have prepared a number of books, maps, films, and other means through which students would be required to learn about the subject area of their choice.

It is generally assumed that when students select their own objectives, learning motivation will be high because they will choose things that interest them.

But this type of program is not without its difficulties. It requires abundant sources and resources so that adequate and varying means can be suggested by teachers to realistically implement objectives. Most individual classrooms cannot hope to do this except in a limited way, and it is questionable whether even most school libraries and resource centers could manage it. Hence this type of program is best realized when all of a school's resources are committed to it, as in the "open school." Another basic problem is that students' choices of objectives may tend to reinforce their immediate interests rather than expand horizons and develop needed skills. The proper balance between student choice and adult imposition on the basis of diagnosed needs must be considered.

Independent Study

In this program the students choose both the objectives and the means, using all available resources—including teachers—to help them develop both. This type of individualization requires the most basic reorganization of classrooms and schools. It involves multiple resources both in and out of the classroom—freely available to students—and a minimum of constraints. Richly endowed book and media libraries, an abundance of manipulative materials, a variety of resource people, adequate and varied types of work spaces, and free student mobility among them are essential. As a total program this succeeds best in open schools. Yet all social studies classrooms can provide opportunities for students to engage in independent study for some of the time. Students' unique interests need to have the opportunity to develop and should be encouraged.

Some Recommendations

Each of the above programs has advantages and disadvantages. Probably no one of them alone can satisfy all needs, and each requires at least some structural changes. Rather than advocate one as the only way to provide maximal benefits—a claim that cannot be substantiated at present in any case—it is more realistic to suggest incorporation of all in some limited ways within any classroom. For some activities, most teachers can manage to do some individual diagnosis and prescription and personalized learning. For some part of the time, students can engage in self-directed exploration or independent study. In short, each of the approaches identified above has enough to offer to make it desirable to incorporate all of them with adaptations in some way within any school program.

Means, Materials, and Techniques

Any individualized program must be accompanied by appropriate means, materials, and techniques. Means includes types of activities in which students should engage; materials refers primarily to learning resources, and techniques to short-term instructional strategies.

Means   Using Bruner's modes of instruction, the means through which students learn can be classified as follows:

1. Enactive means
   A. *Making things* such as candles, puppets, maps, toys, models, furniture, musical instruments, equipment, scenery, jewelry, foods, clothing, dioramas, artifacts
   B. *Physical activities* such as jumping, running, climbing, skipping, kneeling, wrestling
   C. *Creative activities* such as dramatizing, dancing, singing, painting, drawing, sketching, presenting puppet shows
   D. *Simulated activities* such as playing games, role-playing
2. Iconic means
   A. *Observing and interpreting* such things as pictures, films, photographs, film strips, diagrams, maps, graphs, cartoons, exhibitions, artifacts, as well as taking field trips
3. Symbolic means
   A. *Reading* historical books, literature, short stories, essays, case studies, poetry, anthropological books
   B. *Writing* essays, book reports, research papers, compositions, answers to questions, questions
   C. *Listening* to friends, teachers, resource people, speakers, interviewees, dramatic readings
   D. *Talking* to friends, teachers, small groups, large groups

At primary grade levels, the enactive mode should predominate. But care should be exercised to ensure that all three modes are used throughout all of the elementary grades. Hence any program of individualization must include activities that permit learning through enactive, iconic, and symbolic representation. Learning will not only be enhanced for all in this way, but will be particularly useful for students who may be developing more slowly.

Materials   An individualized program requires a rich environment with many materials. Considerable time should be spent teaching students how to use and care for them. The following is a list of basic materials to begin with:

1. Assorted reading materials: textbooks, at least one each of several kinds appropriate for different reading levels and topics; assorted library and trade books; magazines and periodicals; newspapers, booklets, and folders; programmed materials; study prints
2. Assorted maps, map puzzles, and globes
3. Varied art and music materials
4. Records and tapes of stories, songs, historical events, and so forth
5. Original tapes made by students and teacher
6. Commercial games, at least one each
7. Multimedia kits

8. Assorted film strips, slides, and movies
9. Assorted hardware including slide viewers, an overhead projector, an opaque projector, a 16-millimeter sound projector, a small television set for small group viewing, a small radio set with headphones, a Polaroid or other type of camera
10. Blank tapes, slides

Techniques

Above all, individualized instruction depends on independent learning. Students need to be able to pursue their activities without requiring too much help from the teacher, who will be occupied doing other things. Hence any task assigned for individual learning should be characterized by the following:

1. *A set of directions.* These should be clear, succinct, and simple. They should specify such things as where the student is to work, what he or she will need, and standards of work and behavior. Students should be taught beforehand how to operate all special equipment (opaque projectors, tape recorders). It is worth taking as much class time as necessary to perfect these skills.
2. *A statement of objectives.* This should let the student know what he or she is expected to learn and how to demonstrate that it has been accomplished.
3. *A list of content materials.* The teacher should either provide the content materials, or direct the student where to find them. Content materials may include reading, visual, oral, or tactile materials.
4. *Suggestions for further activities.* These should include suggestions to help students reinforce or extend their learning. This might mean doing worksheets, constructing something, interviewing someone, preparing a research report, drawing a map, or some other appropriate activity.
5. *Procedures for self-evaluation.* Since individualized instruction should be completely self-directed, procedures for self-evaluation should also be included. For example, the student might be instructed to compare his or her work with answers written on an answer sheet or recorded on a tape.

The following techniques are being increasingly used to help individualize instruction: (1) task cards, (2) learning packets, (3) programmed materials, (4) learning centers, and (5) learning contracts.

Task Cards

A task card is what its name implies: a card with *one* assigned task written on it. Tasks may cover the gamut of educational objectives. They may be very brief or fairly complex. One set of task cards may be prepared to teach particular social studies concepts; another to help develop skills such as mapping, graphing, and summarizing; still another to develop attitudes and values. Puzzles, riddles, or pictures may be included, as well as directions for sources of additional needed content. In short, the task card is an extremely flexible tool, as diverse as the range of possible means to implement particular learning objectives.

Index cards of varying sizes and colors can be used. They should be clearly

You are an anthropologist
living in the 22nd century.
You find this photo in a time
tube. Answer these questions
in one or more sentences.

1. Describe the object.
2. What is it probably made of ?
3. Where did the material probably come from ?
4. What do you think this object was used for ?
5. What makes you think so ?
6. What kind of people might have used it ?
7. What makes you think so ?

written, preferably typed. Double or even triple spacing is desirable. For students with limited reading skills, pictures and drawings can help supplement verbal symbols.

One advantage of task cards is their easy storage. Teachers can prepare sets of diverse objectives, file them appropriately in neat containers, and have them readily available as needs manifest themselves. Confident that they have on hand at least a set of initiating activities to meet diverse objectives, they need not panic at the thought of individualizing.

The following are examples of task cards:

1. Write a biography of your favorite sports hero.
2. Select a newspaper article from among our class newspapers. Write a summary in outline form. If you need help in making an outline, check with the folder marked "Writing an Outline," which is in the class "Skills" file.
3. Using the Yellow Pages, find out how many doctors and dentists there are in our community. How many are specialists?
4. Using class puppets, prepare a play about frontier life.
5. Prepare a bulletin board summarizing the important news of the week.
6. Choose a game you know well from our "Game Shelf." Try to teach someone else how to play the game. If you are a boy, play it with a girl; if you are a girl, play it with a boy.
7. Who am I? I spent seventeen years in China as an advisor to the Kubla Khan. Although I became very rich, I wanted to return to my home in Venice. I wrote the first European book about China.
8. Find out where these cities are located: Amsterdam, Antwerp, Rotterdam.
9. Find a Mexican recipe and prepare some food for the class.

Learning Packets   Learning packets are essentially extensions of task cards. Like them, they are designed for the acquisition of specific learnings. But they usually include several tasks, as well as materials, cumulatively arranged so as to ensure mastery.

The following are examples of titles for learning packets useful for the elementary social studies program:

Writing a Research Report	Many Kinds of Maps	Time Words
Writing a Book Review	Planning an Interview	Learning to See
Interpreting Graphs	Using the Library	Reading Pictures
Interpreting Maps	Writing an Outline	Using a Newspaper

Discarded workbooks and texts, supplemented by a lively imagination and skill, can help teachers develop packets for a variety of learning situations. Like task cards, once prepared, they can be used over and over.

Learning Centers   A learning center is a designated classroom space in which varied reading, visual, auditory, and tactile materials are gathered with the goal of facilitating an individualized approach to the development of a major learning objective. It is not the same as an interest center, which may simply be a place for students to browse once they have finished their work. The learning center is an integral part of the program of study.

A central concern in the design of learning centers is the identification of the major focus, idea, unifying theme, concept, or generalization. The major theme needs to be general enough to include multiple subthemes and to sustain student interest over time. Each center is usually comprised of several learning stations, and each station is arranged to further a particular part of the whole.

Criteria for Designing Learning Centers

1. They should be designed to attain objectives in all the domains of learning.
2. They should include multiple activities in the enactive, iconic, and symbolic modes so as to appeal to varying student abilities.
3. They should permit self-direction. Instructions should be clear and all necessary materials should be provided. Students should not need help from the teacher.
4. They should be attractive. Maximum space should be provided for displays. Humor, color, and varying formats for different stations will add to attractiveness.
5. They should be self-correcting to the greatest extent possible, but both teachers and students can be involved in the evaluation process as needed. Answer keys should be provided whenever possible.
6. They should allow all participants to be successful.
7. Some stations should be optional. Not all children should be required to do the same activities.
8. Students should be involved in preparing some stations. Two or three teacher-initiated stations are usually sufficient to start—these can serve as springboards for the designing of others as learning proceeds.

Virtually anything can be a suitable theme for a learning center. A few examples of successful themes might include: Your Community, Pollution, Looking at Television, Families, Adapting to Where You Live, Poverty, Africa, Who Are You? Breaking the theme down into individual parts may require a fair amount of thought. For example, the learning center "My Community" might consist of the following stations: People in My Community, People in My Community Help Each Other, People in Other Communities Help Mine, Some Good Things about My Community, Some Things That Could Be Better, Things I Can Do to Help.

Designing a learning center involves steps identical to those used in planning a teaching unit. Begin by identifying three or four generalizations and concepts. Plan for about six learning stations, each one designed to teach a particular generalization, concept, attitude, or skill. Find as many appropriate and varied materials as you can in the three modes suggested by Bruner, and create your own materials as needed. Organize materials and questions along the lines discussed in Chapter 1 and in the evaluation exercises treated in Chapter 9. Chart 3–2 is an example of a learning center concerned with the concept of poverty.

Chart 3–2
Learning Center: Poverty

Major Understandings *(Generalizations)*

1. Poverty is a daily reality for significant numbers of the world population.
2. The causes of poverty are complex, including population growth, inequitable distribution of resources, limited technology, limited land, limited energy, and limited fertilizer.
3. Rich nations consume a disproportionate percentage of the earth's resources. A change in the life style of their citizens could make more resources available to others.
4. Because of the growing interdependence of the earth's population, the problem of poverty is a world concern.

Station 1: The Idea of Poverty

Five or six photographs, each labeled with a letter, are posted depicting relative degrees of poverty and affluence around the world. These may be obtained from newspapers and periodicals. (The issue of *Social Education* published in November–December, 1974, includes some good photographs, as does the *Margin of Life: Population and Poverty in the Americas* by J. Mayone Sycos, Grossman Publishers, 1973.) Children are asked to examine photographs and then answer the following questions: (1) What do you see? (2) Have you ever seen any of the conditions shown in these photographs yourself? Where?

(3) Arrange the photographs on a scale from poorest to richest by writing down photograph letters on this scale:

Poorest (1) _____ (2) _____ (3) _____ (4) _____ (5) _____ Richest

(4) Discuss your answers with other members at your station.

Station 2: Understanding Poverty

Several case studies are presented, either on tape or in writing. They should reflect cases of poverty in different regions of the world with varying economies. The sources cited above are equally useful here. Representative examples might include the following:

Case Study: Rogersville, Tennessee, U.S.A.

Ann Opan Trent is forty-five years old, but according to her doctor she has the body of a sixty-eight-year-old woman. She has cirrhosis of the liver and can barely walk. She lives in a trailer and sometimes needs to slide around to move about in it. Because she was married only thirteen years before her husband died, she does not qualify for Social Security benefits. Her total income is forty-five dollars a month, which she gets in food stamps. She has no money for heat, light, clothes, or any other necessities. Her neighbors sometimes help her out. (Adapted from Tom Tiede, "Public Welfare, Private Pain," *Times Standard,* January 7, 1975, p. 4.)

Case Study: Bali, Indonesia

Gusti Ngurah Ketut Muglong is forty years old and a very respected member of his community. He is a farmer. He owns one-half acre of "wet-rice land" and rents another field about the same size. Although he could produce three rice crops a year, he has enough water for only two. He also raises sweet potatoes. Because the cost of fertilizer is going up, he may be forced to reduce the size of his crop still further.

Muglong has five children ranging in age from one through seven. His wife is expecting their sixth child soon. For breakfast, the family usually has bread and coffee; for lunch and dinner, rice and sweet potatoes. Occasionally they are able to get frogs and fish caught in the canals. Sometimes there are spiced pickles, vegetables, coconut, and fruit.

Muglong and his family eat almost all the food they grow and have little left over to sell. There is no money for clothing, medicine, school, land rent, taxes, fertilizer costs, and other things they need. Muglong has borrowed money to pay for these things and each year he gets more into debt. Sometimes he is able to get some outside work and earn as much as thirty cents a day. (Adapted from James M. Oswald, "Bali: A Case Study," *Social Education* 38:7, Nov.–Dec. 1974, pp. 658–59.)

Case Study, The Sahara Desert

Ibrahim Omar is a Tuareg herder. He has a wife and three living children. In the past six years, the Sahel, or Sahara Desert, has been the scene of a severe drought—no rains have come. Once Ibrahim had one hundred cattle, twenty camels, and forty goats. He was able to exchange his animals for things he needed and for food. When the drought came, all his animals died except the camels. He sold his camels for a very low price to some traders from Dahomey because he was afraid they would die too. Now Ibrahim has nothing.

Ibrahim and his family now live in a distant town where thousands of other families have moved to find work. Conditions are very crowded and hunger is severe. Sometimes Ibrahim finds work and sometimes he begs. This is very humiliating for him. As a Tuareg, he is very proud—he has been taught never to ask for food. (Adapted from Susan J. Hall, "The Sahel: The Shore of Disaster," *Social Education* 38:7, Nov.-Dec. 1974, pp. 659–60.)

Questions that follow readings can include: (1) Locate these places on a map. (2) What problems do all these people have in common? (3) How are their problems different? (4) What kind of help does each one need?

Station 3: Poor Countries: Rich Countries

Pictures and artifacts of measures of economic well-being are arranged conveying the idea of medical services, educational facilities, recreational facilities, food, gadgetry, and so on. Also included is a chart listing the per capita income for several nations of the world, including some of the richest and poorest. Ask the children to list the things they have that are included in the photographs plus any others they can think of. They might prepare a booklet about themselves called "I Never Realized I Had So Much" or something similar. The children can then read a short description of what per capita income is and by examining the chart, pick out the richest and poorest nations. Then ask them to infer what things richer nations have that poorer ones do not.

Station 4: Population Growth

A collection of pertinent graphs, charts, reading materials, and art materials is assembled here. Children are asked to note the title of this station and assume responsibility for arranging and adding to it themselves. They may produce a fact sheet, write poems, design graphs, color maps by population density, and so forth.

Station 5: Grain: A Vital Food Source

Simple graphs and charts illustrate the amount of grain it takes to produce one pound of hamburger, one egg, and one glass of milk; the amount of grain consumed per capita in the United States as compared with average consumption in the world. The children interpret data by answering questions such as: How much grain does it take to produce a pound of hamburger? Why? What other way is there to eat grain? How can Americans change their habits to consume less grain but still get adequate nutrition? Would this solve the world's food problem? Why or why not?

Station 6: Fertilizers

This station includes pertinent research materials on the topic of fertilizers. The children write reports describing how fertilizers affect food production, how energy resources affect the production of fertilizer, and the current distribution of fertilizer throughout the world. Students can be asked to conclude their report with suggestions about what to do (e.g., decrease fuel and energy use, use less fertilizer on lawns, educate others).

Station 7: Food: A World Concern

Tapes, film strips, and printed matter from such sources as the World Food Conference held in Rome in November, 1974, and the United Nations Food and Agricultural Organization, along with copies of press and magazine reports of the conference from November and December, 1974, are the central focus of this station. (See *Social Education* 38:7, November–December, 1974, pp. 683–88, for an excellent annotated list of additional sources plus addresses and costs.) A teacher-made tape can introduce the conference and explain its historic significance.

Station 8: An Idea Box

This station is stocked with blank index cards. Students should be encouraged to write down ideas for solving the problem or general questions about it. These will be the focus of a class discussion at the conclusion of the unit. In addition to encouraging thought about the subject, the idea box gives the teacher some feedback about questions and problems. Students should be free to use this station at any time during the unit study.

Resources for Use at Learning Stations: Poverty

Asimov, Isaac, *Earth: Our Crowded Spaceship* (New York: Doubleday, 1974). A science fiction account that teaches about interdependence through topics such as technological development, hunger, and energy. Grades 5 and above.

Holt Databank System, *Inquiring About Cultures: Studies in Anthropology* (New York: Holt, Rinehart and Winston, 1972). Fourth-grade level text.

Holt Databank System, *Inquiring About Cultures: Studies in Anthropology* (New York: Holt, Rinehart and Winston, 1972). Sixth-grade level text.

The Mini Page. A nationally syndicated four-page newspaper for young readers. It includes numerous issues devoted to the teaching of global interdependence. Available from The Mini Page Publishing Company, Inc., P.O. Box 191, Raleigh, N.C. 27602. Grades K–6.

Powderhorn. Simile II, P.O. Box 1023, La Jolla, Calif. 92073. A game about the unequal distribution of wealth and power in the world. Grades 4–6.

Senesh, Lawrence, *Our Working World: Regions of the World* (Chicago: Science Research Associates, 1973), pp. 381–405. A social studies textbook in which a chapter called "Spaceship Earth: Our Only Home" discusses major problems of the Earth and the need for international cooperation. Grade 4.

Teaching About Spaceship Earth (Intercom No. 71). Center for War/Peace Studies, 218 East 19th St., New York, N.Y. 10033. A role-playing situation in which students pretend they are passengers on a huge spaceship hurtling through space at the speed of 66,000 m.p.h. They run into major problems including inadequate oxygen, polluted water, sickness, mutinies, and unstable technicians. Students have to make decisions about what to do. The analogy between the spaceship and Earth is elicited in debriefing sessions. Grades 3–5.

Wilcoxson, Georgeann, *Balidecer.* John Knox Press, Box 1176, Richmond, Va. 23209. A simulation in which students have to negotiate and trade in order to sustain the population of an imaginary country. Grades 6–12.

Teacher Resources

For the most helpful resource directly applicable for teaching see *Social Education* 38:7 (November–December, 1974).

Programmed Materials

Programmed materials are distinguished by the following characteristics: (1) the material is divided into small sequential steps called frames, (2) each frame requires overt responses from the learner, (3) the student can progress at his or her own pace, (4) there is immediate feedback regarding the accuracy of the response, (5) continuous reinforcement occurs through awareness of progress, and (6) evaluation is based on a written record of performance.[9]

There are two major kinds of programming techniques: linear and branching. In linear models, all students proceed through the same sequence. In branching models, students are directed toward appropriate activities based on the accuracy of their responses. Thus learners who fail to respond correctly to one kind of activity are directed toward those that will reteach it in a somewhat different manner.

Programmed instruction has been used most frequently in the teaching of geography. The following is taken from a linear program in geography:[10]

1. A model is a small copy of some object. A round model of the earth is a globe. A globe is a small copy of the _____.   **earth**

2. A map is a drawing of the earth or part of the earth on paper. If we draw the earth or part of the earth on paper, we are drawing a _____.   **map**

3. Look at the map in Figure 1 [globe, showing Western Hemisphere, with Equator indicated] on page 1 of your map booklet. This is a special kind of map because it shows the earth round, like the globe. We must remember that this is still a map because it _____ drawn on paper.   **is**
   is/is not

4. A sphere is a round, ball-like object. Because the earth is a nearly round, ball-like object we often call the earth a _____.   **sphere**

5. When "hemi" is used before a word, it means "one-half." One-half of a sphere would be called a _____ sphere.   **hemisphere**

6. Since the model of the earth is a sphere, when we divide it in half, we have two hemi_____.   **hemispheres**

Learning Contracts

Individualization is premised on students undertaking much of the responsibility for their own learning. Legitimate concern exists, however, regarding their ability to fulfill this responsibility. The learning contract is one way of dealing with this problem.

The learning contract is a written agreement entered into by the teacher and the student regarding work to be completed. It customarily includes the type of work the student will do and the date by which he will complete it. Students may

[9]William Clark Trow, *Teacher and Technology: New Designs for Learning* (New York: Appleton-Century-Crofts, 1963), pp. 93–96.
[10]Frank MacGraw and Joseph E. William, *Geography of the United States* (Palo Alto, Calif.: Behavioral Research Laboratories, 1964), p. 1. Reprinted by permission of the publisher.

apportion their time as they see fit. Some may wish to alternate periods of browsing and chatter with intense work sessions, while others may prefer regular "work hours." Since they assume responsibility for fulfilling the contract, they must learn to distribute their time appropriately. And the teacher, firm in the conviction that each student will complete his or her task, can then benevolently overlook activities normally constrained in the conventional classroom.

A variation of the learning contract is the student daily lesson plan. Like the learning contract, the student daily lesson plan necessitates agreement between the teacher and the student. Like the teacher daily lesson plan, it breaks down hours and work activities. It is more structured than the contract and is particularly useful in helping children accustom themselves to distributing their time purposefully.

Contracts should be arranged for short periods in the beginning; from two days to a week is long enough to start with. Length of time should vary with the maturity level of the students. Initial tasks should be easy so that the students develop the habit of finishing their work and being pleased with the results. Much preparation is needed to help students assume the responsibility of aportioning their time, but once they have learned how, they can be very successful. Do not expect good results for at least a few weeks.

Work Contract

Student Name: Alan Grey
Teacher: Mary Moore
For period beginning: October 15

Grade: 4
Date: October 10, 1975
And Ending: October 19

Tasks to be completed:

Locate the Tropic of Cancer and the Antarctic Circle on the map grid.

Make a chart showing the number of students in my class living one block, two blocks, three blocks, four blocks, and five or more blocks from school (based on my survey of students in the class).

Read at least 50 pages of my library book *Coming of the Mormons* by Jim A. Kjelgaard.

Learn to spell: Mormons, frontier, transportation, Sioux Indians, the "Hopi Way."

Read the chapter on the American frontier in the text and answer the questions at end of the chapter. Write one question of my own.

Participate in a group discussion with the teacher comparing how the pioneers and the Indians felt about land ownership.

Help prepare the display cabinet.

Modifying Interaction Patterns

The traditional school structure is basically authoritarian. School personnel at all levels are accustomed to "take orders" from those above and "give orders" to those below. Part of the effort in individualizing is directed toward breaking this pattern. Rather than have children receive learning orders from teachers, it is hoped that they will initiate much of the learning themselves. One way to encourage this is to modify conventional classroom interaction patterns so as to establish a supportive classroom climate.

The term *interaction* refers to the verbal and nonverbal communication patterns people use. A supportive classroom climate is characterized by a good deal of student talk—both as response to the teacher or other students and initiated by students. It is also characterized by teacher talk that is primarily responsive—that is, teacher talk that acknowledges and supports student talk. Research evidence strongly supports the conclusion that the pattern that dominates most classrooms is just the opposite. Teacher-initiated talk and very little student talk are the prevailing modes.

Flanders' Interaction Analysis Code

In order to develop supportive interaction patterns, one must become sensitized to one's own verbal patterns. One of the most useful instruments teachers can employ to accomplish this is the Flanders' Interaction Analysis Categories code, shown in Chart 3–3, which functions as an objective measure for the assessment of classroom interaction. Teachers can use it by taping their classes and then analyzing their own role.

Supportive teacher response patterns are included in categories 1 through 3. To "respond," according to Flanders, means "to take action after an initiation, to counter, to amplify or react to ideas which have already been expressed, to conform or even to comply to the will expressed by others."[11] In short, to respond is essentially to support another's talk. To initiate talk, on the other hand, means "to make the first move, to lead, to begin, to introduce an idea or concept for the first time, to express one's own will." This pattern, exemplified in categories 4 through 7, asserts the centrality of the "self."

Flanders found that students working with teachers who used more supportive patterns benefited academically as well as in general attitudes toward school.

The difference between a social studies episode dominated by teacher-initiated talk as opposed to teacher-response talk is illustrated in Chart 3–4. The numbers above the sentences indicate behaviors classified according to Flanders' code.

Note that in the first version the teacher asks for student responses but fails to acknowledge them. In the second version, the teacher acknowledges the first student's definition in a supportive way while simultaneously asking for an expansion of the student's idea. The other responses are treated in the same way. This technique opens up the concept "united"; the first technique closes it.

[11] Ned A. Flanders, *Analyzing Teaching Behaviors* (Reading, Mass.: Addison-Wesley, 1970), p. 35.

Chart 3–3
Flanders' Interaction Analysis Categories* (FIAC)

Teacher Talk	Response	1. *Accepts feeling.* Accepts and clarifies an attitude or the feeling tone of a pupil in a nonthreatening manner. Feelings may be positive or negative. Predicting and recalling feelings are included.
		2. *Praises or encourages.* Praises or encourages pupil action or behavior. Jokes that release tension, but not at the expense of another individual; nodding head, or saying "Um hm?" or "go on" are included.
		3. *Accepts or uses ideas of pupils.* Clarifying, building, or developing ideas suggested by a pupil. Teacher extensions of pupil ideas are included but as the teacher brings more of his own ideas into play, shift to category five.
		4. *Asks questions.* Asking a question about content or procedure, based on teacher ideas, with the intent that a pupil will answer.
	Initiation	5. *Lecturing.* Giving facts or opinions about content or procedures; expressing *his own* ideas, giving *his own* explanation, or citing an authority other than a pupil.
		6. *Giving directions.* Directions, commands, or orders to which a pupil is expected to comply.
		7. *Criticizing or justifying authority.* Statements intended to change pupil behavior from nonacceptable to acceptable pattern; bawling someone out; stating why the teacher is doing what he is doing; extreme self-reference.
Pupil Talk	Response	8. *Pupil-talk—response.* Talk by pupils in response to teacher. Teacher initiates the contact or solicits pupil statement or structures the situation. Freedom to express own ideas is limited.
	Initiation	9. *Pupil-talk—initiation.* Talk by pupils which they initiate. Expressing own ideas; initiating a new topic; freedom to develop opinions and a line of thought, like asking thoughtful questions; going beyond the existing structure.
Silence		10. *Silence or confusion.* Pauses, short periods of silence and periods of confusion in which communication cannot be understood by the observer.

*There is *no* scale implied by these numbers. Each number is classificatory; it designates a particular kind of communication event. To write these numbers down during observation is to enumerate, not to judge a position on a scale.

Source: Ned A. Flanders, *Analyzing Teaching Behavior* (Reading, Mass.: Addison-Wesley, 1970), p. 34. Reprinted by permission.

Chart 3–4
Interaction Episode

Primarily Teacher Initiation Talk

Teacher:

Remember that we talked	5*
yesterday about the fact	5
that the thirteen colonies	5
became the first thirteen	
states. Remember too that we	5
said that they were not really	
united. Jim, can you tell us	4
what "united" means?	

Jim:

"United" means "together."	8

Teacher:

Anyone else?	4

Helen:

"United" means "agreeing."	8

Teacher:

The dictionary defined	5
"united" as "joined	5
together, combined, made	
one." Well, the first	5
thirteen states were more	
joined together in name	5
than in reality. For	
although they now all belonged	5
to a new country called the	
United States of America, they	5
didn't act that way.	

Primarily Teacher Response Talk

Teacher:

Remember that we talked	5
yesterday about the fact	5
that the thirteen colonies	5
became the first thirteen	
states. Remember too that we	5
said that they were not really	
united. Jim, can you tell us	4
what "united" means?	

Jim:

"United" means "together."	8

Teacher:

Yes, "united" does imply	2
"together." Would anyone	3
like to add to that?	

Helen

Yes, but it doesn't mean	
together in all things.	8

Teacher:

Right. Can you explain that	2
a bit?	3

Helen:

Well, a family could be	8
united in most ways but	
still not agree on everything.	8

Mary:

I agree. We're one country	9
but different people have	
different ideas.	

Teacher:

You've raised some interesting	3
points. And also an	3
interesting question. If	3
"united" does not mean	
"together in all things,"	
just what does it mean?	3

*The numbers are recorded at three-second intervals.

Of course, communication among people goes beyond words alone—it includes an enormous number of nonverbal gestures as well. Since the early 1950s a great deal of research has been done in the area popularly known as "body language." It is now fairly common knowledge that we are constantly—and for the most part unconsciously—transmitting signals about our feelings and reactions. The way one sits or stands or moves one's eyes, even minute changes in skin texture, are part of the process of communicating with other people.

Sometimes nonverbal gestures can speak louder than words. They may give messages that contradict what is said. For example, a teacher may say to a student "that's very interesting," while fiddling with a pencil or looking out the window. Students will properly understand this as disinterest despite the teacher's statement to the contrary.

On the other hand, there is ample evidence that the meanings of body movements and gestures are, like spoken languages and dialects, not universal. Arabs and Italians, for example, stand much closer to the persons they are addressing than the British or Germans do. Such differences in body language lead to many misunderstandings between people of different ethnic or racial backgrounds—a white, middle-class teacher may completely misinterpret a statement by a black or chicano student if the body language that accompanies it seems to indicate another intention.

Individual and Small-Group Work

Even where a skillful teacher can elicit student response, the communication flow in a large classroom tends to be like that in Figure 3–3. This arrangement, which characterizes most classrooms, is based on the assumption that the teacher has the most important contribution to make in student learning. Without underestimating the crucial role played by teachers, it is necessary to acknowledge that a large number of students "turn off and drop out" under such a system.

Part of the effort in individualization is aimed at altering this communication flow and increasing student involvement. Small groups, either with or without an adult, are encouraged to exchange learnings with each other. Individual activity allows for concentrated involvement. The large group centered on one person is reserved primarily for those activities that are spectator-like. In short, the individualized classroom is characterized by functional groupings—groupings that appear best to serve the learning objective.

Modifying Organizational Patterns

The conventional elementary classroom is a self-contained unit in which one teacher is assigned thirty or forty students. Each teacher is charged with the responsibility of being equally competent in all the assorted skills required for

Figure 3–2
Communication Flow in Most Classrooms

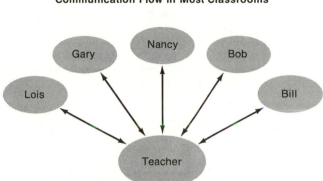

managing a classroom. The range and extent of such skills is suggested in Chart 3–5. The expectation that teachers should be equally skilled in all of them is absurd. Like students, teachers are not standardized products with similar interests and abilities—they, too, are individuals. Rather than continue what appears to be a futile effort to make them all alike, it seems far more reasonable to capitalize on existing strengths by permitting teachers to function in the roles they find most satisfying.

Differentiated Staffing and Team Teaching

The concept of allocating diverse roles for teachers is called differentiated staffing. The most popular form of differentiated staffing is team teaching. Team teaching may take a variety of patterns, but its basic prerequisite is the presence of at least two adults who, together, are responsible for a group of students. One type of team may consist of two teachers, each with equal levels of responsibilities, who combine their classrooms and allocate differentiated tasks. Using a list such as that suggested in Chart 3–5, each teacher would assess his or her own strengths and divide the responsibilities accordingly.

Another type of team might consist of several adults, each with different levels of responsibilities, such as that suggested by Duane Manning.[12] It would include: a *team leader,* who is responsible for introducing new concepts and ideas and is skilled in interpersonal relations as well as curriculum and research; a *senior teacher,* who is responsible for applying innovations in the classroom and for selecting and evaluating teachers in the program, and who is skilled in the arts of teaching and diagnosing learning processes; a *regular teacher,* responsible for the usual functions teachers perform, but relieved of responsibilities for nonteaching tasks; an *intern,* responsible for some limited teaching, grading papers, and supervising activities and study centers; a *teacher aide,* responsible for keeping records, operating audio-visual equipment, doing clerical work, and performing other nonteaching tasks.

[12] Duane Manning, *Toward a Humanistic Curriculum* (New York: Harper & Row, 1971), pp. 72–74.

Chart 3–5
Some Teacher Skills Needed in the Social Studies Classroom

Knowledge

Cognitive and affective developmental patterns of children; instructional strategies in the cognitive and affective domains; methods and content of the social science disciplines; social issues; ways of humanizing structure and content; available physical and human resources; ways of getting additional resources; student and community needs; school and state requirements.

Curriculum Development Skills

Diagnostic Skills

Diagnosing cognitive and affective needs of the student.

Selecting Content

Selecting appropriate concepts, generalizations, values, skills, scenes, and learning objectives on the basis of criteria of relevance, significance, student needs and interests, scholarliness, balance, school requirements, and availablity of resources.

Developing Learning Program

Analyzing necessary prior learnings, identifying required and optional learning experiences, identifying priorities, arranging sequence.

Selecting and developing appropriate learning strategies: expository and inquiry.

Selecting learning materials: books, games, films, realia, skill lessons, furnishings, art equipment, resource people, trips, and expeditions.

Arranging learning environment, including use of teacher and community resources and time.

Providing for individual and group experiences.

Instructional Skills

Working with large groups, small groups, and individuals.

Implementing strategies: expository and inquiry.

Techniques: research, role-playing, simulation games, storytelling, leading discussions, dramatizing, art, using visual media effectively, exploring values.

Interpersonal Skills

Being able to relate to students, staff, other school members, parents, and community.

Public Relations Skills

Being able to communicate with parents, school personnel, and community for purposes of information, support, and acquisition of additional resources.

Technical Skills

Keeping records of individual student progress; assembling catalogs of available materials on the market and in the school district; operating audio-visual equipment; preparing attractive displays.

Evaluation Skills

Measuring student cognitive and affective learning; evaluating the effectiveness of instructional strategies; evaluating learning resources and materials; evaluating the strength of the humanistic component.

Whatever the form a team-teaching arrangement takes, its success depends on one essential premise: the team members must be willing participants. Hence teams should be comprised of volunteers. The self-contained classroom will continue to appeal to some teachers and that choice should be available to them. Experimentation along team patterns can be encouraged with the assurance that teachers may leave after a reasonable time should they find it unsuitable. Caution should be exercised, however, to ensure that it is given a fair chance, for the greater part of the difficulties are encountered in the beginning. With sufficient time, most can be overcome.

The Nongraded School

Placement in grades on the basis of age levels is an administrative convenience, not necessarily an educational requirement. Despite the fact that cognitive, affective, and physical growth is largely a developmental process, the age at which a particular development occurs differs among individual children. A wide range of mental ages already characterizes kindergartners, and differences both in achievement and mental age continue to widen with each successive grade. It is not uncommon to find as much as a six-year difference between the highest and lowest achievers by the time children reach the sixth grade. The nongraded school eliminates grouping children on the basis of age and substitutes grouping on the basis of needs.

Nongraded schools vary in type and form. One type may involve a division of the entire school into two groups, a primary and an intermediate division. All students would enter the primary division at age six, but the termination point, generally considered normal at the end of three years, might be extended. The normal termination point for the intermediate division would be approximately at age twelve, but this too might be extended. Sometimes a nongraded program will apply only to the primary grades. Also possible, although infrequent, is the deliberate inclusion of multi-age groups within a single classroom. One third of the class might be nine-year-olds, one third ten-year-olds, and still another third eleven-year-olds.

Although advocates of the nongraded school emphasize the need for using multiple criteria for determining groupings, the one most commonly used is the reading level. The following is a description of how social studies are taught in one nongraded school where fifteen reading levels are identified to determine groupings:

The program for these levels is built on five central themes. They are: (1) Man and His Natural and Cultural Environment; (2) Responsible Citizenship and Governmental Development; (3) Recognizing and Understanding World Interdependency; (4) Economic Living; and (5) Conflict and Change. Concepts, generalizations, and facts from each of the social sciences are included in each of these. In many instances, concepts will be experienced by children on one level one year, and in the next year, on another level with a different theme.

Each level has a unit title based on the central theme. For instance, the central theme "Man and His Natural and Cultural Environment" has the following units:

Kindergarten	"Living Where We Are"
Nongraded Levels I–IV	"Meeting People from Other Lands"
Nongraded Levels V–VI	"The Concept of Culture"
Nongraded Levels VII–VIII	"Venture Around the World"
Nongraded Levels IX–X	"New Horizons for Desert Land"
Nongraded Levels XI, XII, XIII	"Basic Geographic Skills and Understandings"
	"The U.S., the U.S.S.R., and Canada—A Study in Contrast with a Look Toward the Future"
	"A Geographic Survey of the U.S.—A Regional Approach"
Nongraded Levels XIV–XV	"Basic Geographic Skills and Understandings"
	"Man the Transformer of the Universe"

Each unit has a short introduction which is an overview of the general goals for that unit. The content is previewed and methods are suggested for its teaching; a master list is presented containing the concepts for each social science discipline involved in that theme, along with suggestions concerning which concept is pertinent to which level. An outline of content is developed which may assist the child in understanding the concept. The amount of content to be considered will be necessarily adjusted by the teacher according to the individual abilities of the students.

Ideally, each level should have a unit plan similar to that which customarily has been organized for the entire grade. Such a systematic design, however, does not imply that each level's activities will be prescribed in detail. Quite the contrary, alternatives will be spelled out from among which children will be able to choose.[13]

[13] John D. McAulay, "Social Studies for the Nongraded School," *Social Education* (April 1972), pp. 454–55.

Like many other social studies programs, the one described above is based on unifying themes, concepts, and generalizations. The basic advantage it offers is to ensure that reading materials provided for each level will be appropriate. However, this advantage is more than offset by some serious disadvantages. Thinking levels are not necessarily congruent with reading levels. A youngster reading at Level II may have a Level X conceptual ability. Confinement to Level II group activities may actually retard the child conceptually. Moreover, if the child is older than most of the other children in the group, the feeling of failure may heighten and the general resistance to learning increase. It would appear that the disadvantages of substituting reading levels for age as bases for social studies groupings are greater than any advantages. The conventional age-graded classroom directed by a skilled teacher has potentially more to offer than a nongraded classroom that uses reading levels as the basic criterion for work levels.

Open Education   Open education—also known as the British infant school, the integrated day school, and the open-corridor program—is the model that is most conducive to personalized learning and independent study. Although practiced only infrequently, the principles of open education are not new to American education. Essentially outlined by John Dewey and the Progressivists, they include individualized instruction, supportive interaction patterns, differentiated staffing, and nongrading. However, open education includes more than just these, and at least four other characteristics are worth describing in some detail.

The first—and perhaps most important—of these characteristics has to do with the physical arrangement of the open classroom. It is a *decentralized room with flexible areas,* breaking with the spatial pattern in which the teacher is at the center of activities and establishing a new pattern with several dispersed learning centers (see Figure 3–3).

Making work areas adaptable to different uses is just as important as decentralizing the classroom. Multipurpose furniture, room dividers, tables of varied sizes and shapes, sofas, armchairs, rugs, and benches are only some of the variety of nontraditional trappings. These can be bought, made from boxes and crates, or solicited from community members. Utility, comfort, and adaptability are more important than aesthetics; hence a well-worn table or a room divider made of old sheets is to be preferred over new, breakable "don't touch me" furniture.

The second major characteristic of open education is that there is *considerable student freedom.* Children are free to explore learning centers and move about freely—in their own room, in corridors, in other rooms, and outdoors. But constraints, although kept to a minimum, do exist.

For one thing, the classroom environment itself acts as a constraint. It governs what shall be explored. If cultural interdependence, for example, is the concept chosen for social studies, the classroom environment will include a variety of materials for developing it. However, a fair amount of opportunity is given for individual choice among those environmental offerings.

Figure 3–3
An Open Classroom

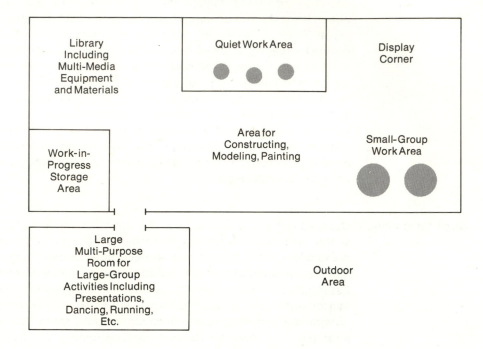

For another, the teacher does not abdicate the role of guide. Through careful diagnosis and evaluation, the teacher assumes responsibility for guiding students into appropriate activities. This may be done informally by observing, commenting, and encouraging students through individual interaction as the teacher moves about the classroom, or through more formal means such as a work contract or student daily lesson plan.

Finally, children are constrained by good sense, consideration of others, and operating rules. Openness does not mean anarchy—undue interference with others and illegal activities are nonpermissable.

A *rich environment* is the third characteristic—but this does not necessarily mean a costly one. It is equally important that the materials be available to the students at all times, that they be renewed and changed, and that they respond to diffuse interests and needs. Requirements of an open classroom are listed in Chart 3–6.

The fourth characteristic is that *individual and small-group work predominate.* Most of the time the teacher circulates among the children, responding to individuals and groups as needed. Only occasionally do they come together in large groups.

When instruction is tailored to meet individual needs, there is less need for large groups to listen to a single adult clarifying something that does not involve most of the students. However, when some students do share a particular learning need—such as writing outlines or working with grids—it may be more effective to have them come together as a small group with the teacher. Small groups are also useful for discussions, sharing ideas, and practicing oral skills. Large groups may also be helpful at times. For example, it is likely that a puppet show or dramatic presentation can be enjoyed by all. Or that the sharing of some student effort—such as an exhibit, drama, or community project—may be appropriate for the entire group. Rules and classroom procedures that affect all students should of course be discussed by all.

In short, learning groups are functionally related to the learning of tasks. If the task is best learned by individual effort, the student should work alone. If it is best achieved through a small group effort, that mode should be used. The criterion for grouping is thus based on student needs and not on presumed teacher or administrative convenience.

Chart 3–6
Some Needs of an Open Social Studies Classroom

Space

Space for large-group activities, for small-group activities, and for individual, quiet activities; unfurnished space for multiple uses; space for storage; outdoor space.

Furnishings

Moveable tables with formica tops, table tops that can be put up or down and are attached to wall, display tables, occasional work tables, comfortable easy chairs, wooden chairs, wooden benches, cushions, rugs, carpets, screens to block off work areas.

Inexpensive materials

String, water, clay, pebbles, sand, crayons, tiles, dowels, pipe cleaners, pencils, pens, felt pens, chalk, paper of all kinds, scissors, erasers, paste, rulers, portable blackboard, paper cutters, spirit masters, paint, easels, knitting needles, yarn, thread.

More expensive equipment

Slide projector, tape recorder, slides and tapes, record player and records, teaching machines, television, duplicating machine, opaque projector, film projector.

Printed materials

Reference books, atlases, fiction and nonfiction books, textbooks, newspapers (many kinds), magazines, pamphlets, mail-order catalogs, book catalogs, graphs, charts, photographs, old newspapers, stamps, posters, artifacts.

Loose worksheets and commercially prepared worksheets (filed according to subject and/or skill levels), labeled photographs, pictures, student work; file boxes with short questions for individual research, skill exercises (arranged according to subject and levels of difficulty), programmed instructional materials; wherever possible answers for self-evaluation should be provided.

Games, maps, globes, charts.

The Processes of Individualizing

Individualizing instruction requires abandoning many traditional school practices in favor of more functional ones. The following is a summary of the specific processes required in making the transition.

1. Abandoning absolute curricular requirements that must be followed by all. Instead, objectives and means should be related to individual needs.
2. Abandoning hit-or-miss methods of instruction that are not suited for all children. Instead, teachers should carefully diagnose student abilities and keep progress reports on each child's development, accomplishments, and activities.
3. Abandoning the position that textbooks must be the dominant instructional tool. Instead, a variety of instructional resources should be employed.
4. Abandoning materials to which students are allowed only limited access. Instead, use many materials and make them freely available.
5. Abandoning the system of dividing the day into periods in which specific subjects are to be studied. Instead, students should organize much of their own time.
6. Abandoning the quiet, single-purpose lesson in favor of a variety of ongoing activities.
7. Abandoning the conventional physical layout with students' chairs neatly arranged to face the teacher. Multipurpose furniture and flexible learning centers replace it.
8. Abandoning conventional interaction techniques. Instead, teachers should respond to student communications in supportive ways that encourage greater student participation.
9. Abandoning the conventional learning pattern of one teacher and thirty-five students. Instead, grouping should be functionally related to the instructional tasks performed, and individual and small-group activities should predominate.
10. Abandoning the concept of the immobile teacher at the focal point of the room. Instead, teachers should move about, helping and observing.

Summary

By the middle of the twentieth century, the American system of education had achieved a degree of organization that must have made it the envy of General Motors and the Pentagon. As many as thirty or forty students were arranged in neat rank and file facing a single teacher who would expound at length on a variety of subjects. A system of time periods, learning levels, assessment, and certification had been evolved that none could fault—except, of course, the students, whose needs were frequently ignored in the process.

In recent years, a number of alternatives have been explored with the intention of shaking up this rigid system and utilizing the natural energy and curiosity of children. It has become clear that all of the components of the present system can be changed for the better and that this can be accomplished in a number of ways. The physical layout of the classroom can be altered, breaking up the rows and creating a number of focal points for individual study. The way the teacher teaches can be altered, shifting from a lecturing, expository approach to a question-and-answer, inquiry-oriented approach. Teachers can be moved around and classes combined, so that each one can do what he or she does best. The hours can be made to correspond to the natural rhythms of the class, movement from one grade level to the next loosened up so that each student can proceed at the most natural pace. In a word, the system of learning can be individualized.

The essential elements of any program of education are (1) what is to be learned and (2) how it is to be learned; the type of program to be followed depends on whether the student or the teacher makes these decisions. Some believe the ideal would be for the student to be responsible for both decisions, but that is rarely practical and not always desirable. When students select what will be learned, the assumption is that motivation is higher because they are doing what they wish to do. Sometimes students select only the means, and frequently the teacher makes all the choices. There are cases in which all of these programs can be useful.

Values

A value . . . is anything—idea, belief, practice, thing—that is important to people for any reason.[1]

Persons have experiences; they grow and learn. Out of experiences may come certain general guides to behavior. These guides tend to give direction to life and may be called values.[2]

Values are at once personal preferences or attitudes and cultural norms or imperatives. As personal preferences or attitudes they are deeply rooted in the needs of the individual, in whatever he considers important and holds dear, in what later becomes his style of life. As cultural imperatives they refer to the pressures and norms which, if properly assimilated and internalized, make man's daily life both efficient and satisfying. . . .[3]

These three statements represent some of the different definitions of "values," a subject that has been the focus of interest of an increasing number of social scientists from all disciplines.[4] Yet despite their divergent approaches, there is little disagreement among scholars that (1) values are central motivators of behavior and (2) values are learned. Moreover, there is general agreement that while values may be classified as belonging to the affective domain—that of attitudes, feelings, and emotions—they exert a powerful influence on the cognitive domain. Precisely what this influence is and how it works is not entirely clear. But there seems to be little doubt that values not only influence what we learn, but how and if we learn. However, those concerned with the place of values in education have not agreed on the very basic issue of whether or not schools have a responsibility for cultivating any values at all.

Values and Education

The relationship between values, learning, and personality has been investigated by many psychologists. Some have concluded that what people remember—as well as their critical abilities in general—is strongly influenced by their values. For example, both Milton Rokeach and Clarence Kemp found that people with "dogmatic" and "rigid" mentalities tend to be weak in analytic thinking and generally less able to memorize data unrelated to their own systems of thought.[5] And a growing number of investigators have come to believe that value education in the classroom can result in more positive personality development as well as contribute to learning. They maintain that it can lead to im-

[1]Corrine Brown, *Understanding Other Cultures* (Englewood Cliffs, N.J.: Prentice-Hall, 1963), p. 95.
[2]Louis E. Raths, Merrill Harmin, and Sidney B. Simon, *Values and Teaching: Working with Values in the Classroom* (Columbus, Ohio: Merrill, 1966), p. 27.
[3]Hubert Bonner, "Scientific Assumptions and Human Values," in Jeremiah W. Canning, ed., *Values in an Age of Confrontation* (Columbus, Ohio: Merrill, 1970), p. 51.
[4]For more information about articles and books that deal with values, see E. M. Albert and C. Kluckhohn, *A Selected Bibliography of Values, Ethics and Esthetics* (New York: Free Press, 1959) and Walter L. Thomas, *A Comprehensive Bibliography of the Value Concept* (Grand Rapids, Mich.: Northview Public Schools, 1967).
[5]Clarence Gratton Kemp, "Effect of Dogmatism on Critical Thinking," *School Science and Mathematics* 60 (1960), pp. 314–19 and Milton Rokeach, *The Open and Closed Mind* (New York: Basic Books, 1960).

proved self-concept,[6] increased "openness" to new ideas,[7] increased acceptance of other nationalities[8] and minority groups,[9] and increased learning.[10] While evidence supporting these particular conclusions is far from definitive, there appears to be little doubt that the affective domain has a strong influence on both personality and learning.

Teaching Values in the Classroom: Some Issues

The crucial importance of values has confronted educators with two major questions: (1) Should values be taught in schools? (2) What specific values should children be helped to learn? Neither question has been conclusively resolved.

Historically, schools have maintained two contradictory positions in answering these questions. Some educators assert that schools should be value-free, or neutral, thus leaving the primary shaping of values to other societal institutions, including the family and the church. Others maintain that the teaching of certain core American values is a legitimate goal of public education.

The Case for Neutrality

Underlying the position that schools should be neutral is the assumption that knowledge itself is neutral. After all, it is reasoned, facts are facts regardless of who states them. And since schools are merely vehicles for the dissemination of knowledge, they can maintain a neutral position. However, as some scholars have pointed out, knowledge is *not* neutral. What is studied, how such studies are interpreted, and how this knowledge is disseminated in the classroom are all value-laden processes.

The fact that social scientists cannot divorce themselves from value postures has been acknowledged by many social scientists, particularly those concerned with the sociology of knowledge. A minor incident that occurred some years ago illustrates one quite obvious type of value imposition. In 1931, a major conference was held by the American Historical Association at which conferees were invited to recommend further areas of research. Among the many topics suggested, only one was concerned with ethnic minorities, "The Civilizing of the American Indian."[11] Not only does this fact reflect a lack of interest in minority people—itself a value—but the language in which the title was phrased implies a

[6]Fannie R. Shaftel and George Shaftel, *Role Playing for Social Values: Decision Making in the Social Studies* (Englewood Cliffs, N.J.: Prentice-Hall, 1967), pp. 33–36.

[7]Hilda Taba, "Education for Independent Valuing," in Alexander Frazier, ed., *New Insights and the Curriculum,* Yearbook (Washington, D.C.: Association for Supervision and Curriculum Development, 1963), pp. 221–40.

[8]Wallace E. Lambert and Otto Klineberg, *Children's Views of Foreign Peoples* (New York: Appleton-Century-Crofts, 1967).

[9]Frank L. Fisher, "Influences of Reading and Discussion on the Attitudes of Fifth Graders Toward American Indians," *The Journal of Educational Research* 62 (November 1968), pp. 130–34.

[10]James Raths, "Underachievement and a Search for Values," *Sociology of Education* 34 (May 1961), pp. 422–24.

[11]David S. Landes and Charles Tilly, eds., *History as Social Science* (Englewood Cliffs, N.J.: Prentice-Hall, 1971), p. 39.

more insidious value. "Civilizing" another person implies the imposition of a superior culture upon a barbaric one. Historians today are neither as oblivious nor as elitist in their treatment of minority cultures. But one can only speculate what judgments will be made forty years from now regarding current values.

That the dissemination process is also value-laden is suggested by these acute observations made by Louis J. Raths and his associates:

> In school and out, he [the student] is told that to cooperate is not only excellent but is practically a necessity in our world. At the same time, he is told that everybody should look out for himself, that if you don't look out for yourself nobody else will. . . . He is told that women are the equal of men, and as he grows up he sees that in many situations they are not. In school he learns a romanticized version of the vigilantes in California history. He comes to believe that they were fine people. And at the same time he is supposed to pledge loyalty to a society that is ruled by law. He learns about some of the great patriots who initiated our revolution, people who stood up and spoke their minds; and while he is learning these things, people close to him advise him to be careful of what he says, not get into any trouble, go along with the authorities, and make the best of whatever the situation is.[12]

It is the recognition that values pushed out the front door inevitably sneak in the back door that has prompted some educators to reexamine the value-neutral position.

The Case for Teaching Communal Values

If values cannot be kept out of the school, the problem then remains of *what* values to teach. The traditional position maintains that Americans share certain basic values. These tend to be identified with such attributes as obedience, responsibility, kindness, cleanliness, honesty, loyalty, self-discipline, self-reliance, and achievement.[13] Since these attributes are equated with "good citizenship," the social studies are frequently charged with the responsibility for their cultivation. But some of these values have become the target of strong criticism.

There is considerable doubt that these values necessarily reflect "good citizenship." Neither Thomas Paine nor Martin Luther King, for example, were noted for their "obedience," but many people would agree that they were exemplary citizens. Moreover, many of these attributes appear eminently suitable for a bureacratic mentality equipped to serve organizations rather than individuals or humanity. Loyalty, achievement, and obedience, for example, have not only generally characterized members of the school system, General Motors, and the Democratic and Republican parties, but also the Nazi party and the Communist party. An identifiable core of American values must assuredly be more than this. A third point to be considered is that Americans are becoming increasingly

[12]Raths, Harmin, and Simon, *Values and Teaching,* p. 21.

[13]The Boy Scouts of America, which claims a membership of more than fifty million "Scouts and former Scouts," describes the attributes of a Scout as follows: "trustworthy, loyal, helpful, friendly, courteous, kind, obedient, cheerful, thrifty, brave, clean, reverent." Boy Scouts of America, *Scout Handbook,* 8th ed. (North Brunswick, N.J.: Boy Scouts of America, 1973), p. 32. For more complete discussions of traditional American values see George D. Spindler, "Education in a Transforming American Culture," in George D. Spindler, ed., *Education and Culture* (New York: Holt, Rinehart and Winston, 1963), pp. 132–47; Michael McGiffert, ed., *The Character of Americans* (Homewood, Ill.: Dorsey Press, 1970); Jules Henry, *Culture Against Man* (New York: Random House, 1963); Robin M. Williams, Jr., "Individual and Group Values," *American Academy of Political and Social Science. Annals* 371 (May 1967), pp. 20–37.

aware of the pluralistic values that exist in their society. The rich and poor, the red, brown, black, yellow, and white, the young and old differ in many of their basic attitudes. While shared values no doubt also exist among these groups, they are not necessarily included in the above list. Finally, the ambiguity of these virtues poses problems. For example, exactly to whom is responsibility and loyalty due? To oneself? To the local community? To the nation? To the world? And exactly what is meant by ''achievement''? Is it financial success? An enduring marriage? Many friends? The advancement of one type of interest frequently depends on a cost to another. In short, many so-called communal values appear neither adequate nor precise enough to meet the needs of our curricula.

Current Responses   Social studies educators respond to these issues in varied ways. First, there are those who continue to believe that values should be kept out of the schools, that value education is an infringement of the civil rights of students and parents.

Second, there are those who believe that value education is indeed essential, but who would carefully refrain from the teaching of specific values. They are ''neutralists'' with a new twist. Their emphasis is on the processes of valuing, or *value clarification.* The strategies they advocate are expressly designed to eliminate the teaching of specific values. This orientation, exemplified by Louis Raths, Sidney Simon, Leland Howe, and Howard Kirschenbaum, is probably the dominant position today.

A variant of the contemporary neutralist position is the orientation concerned with *improving value judgments.* Like those who support value clarification, advocates of this position are concerned that no specific values be taught. Unlike value clarification, however, emphasis is given to developing the abilities that can help people make more rational value judgments. Lawrence E. Metcalf, Jerrold R. Coombs, and Milton Meux are among the exponents of this approach.

Finally, there are the educators who are specifically concerned with *moral education*. This group is admittedly not neutral and advocates the teaching of specific values deemed moral. However, the values they specify bear little resemblance to the list of traditional ones that was given earlier. They recommend that children develop their abilities to make moral judgments based on concern for others and for justice, and the strategies they propose are designed to help students develop these capacities. The prominent exponent of this orientation is Lawrence Kohlberg.

Each of these schools of thought has a contribution to make, and it seems reasonable to assume that teachers need to develop competency in all of them. In the following, these orientations are described in greater detail and illustrative strategies are presented.

Value Clarification

Value clarification is concerned primarily with leading students to an understanding of their own values through self-exploration of their beliefs, attitudes, feelings, and interests. The teacher's role in this orientation is to pose facilitating questions that will help students become aware of their own values and to accept the students' responses without censure or disapproval.

The late Louis Raths was a pioneer in developing this approach. He believed that much asocial behavior and many discipline problems of students are the result of unclear values. His research led him to the conclusion that when students are given the opportunity to engage in value clarification, many of these problems disappear.

Traditional methods of teaching values—such as setting an example, persuading, directing, or even inspiring—fail largely because they are imposed externally rather than demanding that students engage in the process themselves. The value clarification process, Raths said, should help students develop values "that represent the free and thoughtful choice of intelligent humans interacting with complex and changing environments."[14] The process should involve students in the following:

CHOOSING: 1 freely
                 2 from alternatives
                 3 after thoughtful consideration of the consequences of each alternative
PRIZING: 4 cherishing, being happy with the choice
                 5 willing to affirm the choice publicly
ACTING: 6 doing something with the choice
                 7 repeatedly, in some pattern of life.[15]

[14] Raths, Harmin, and Simon, *Values and Teaching*, p. 40.
[15] *Ibid.*, p. 30.

Engagement in the process is not automatic, however, and students need to be encouraged to participate in it. Teachers can help by (1) *responding* to particular student comments and/or (2) *initiating* the process themselves.

Responding to the Expression of Values

Suppose that one of the boys in a class says "I hate my brother." This statement—however strong—is probably not a real value statement; that is, it is probably not a persistent guide to his behavior. The teacher may respond in a number of ways. Perhaps the most typical is to choose to ignore it, presuming that the student will eventually mature and reconsider his feelings. Or the teacher may decide to deliver a short lecture on the virtues of strong family ties. The teacher may even tell the student of similar personal feelings that have since been outgrown. None of these responses, however, will help students clarify values.

Suppose, instead, the teacher responded with a series of questions, something like these: How long have you felt this way? Do you feel this way all the time? Are there any reasons why you feel this way? Does this feeling give you any pleasure? What are you prepared to do about this feeling? What are you doing already? Does it cause you any trouble? Are you ready to continue doing it? In this case, the teacher is asking the student to clarify his feelings, and the student may well come to the recognition that his expressed feelings of the moment do or do not represent a true value.

Several types of student statements lend themselves to this type of interaction. Raths calls them "value indicators"—expressions that suggest something about values but are not yet fully developed. They include:

1. Statements of *goals* or *purposes* (e.g., I'm going to camp this summer, I'm going to run for student president).
2. Statements of *aspiration* (e.g., I'd like to be a soldier when I grow up, I'd like to have a million dollars).
3. Statements of *attitudes* (e.g., Teachers shouldn't give homework, lazy people should be forced to work).
4. Statements of *interests* (e.g., I'm not interested in learning about boats, social studies bores me).
5. Statements of *feelings* (e.g., I'd like to beat that guy up, that's really ugly).
6. Statements of *beliefs* (e.g., I believe trees should not be cut down, anyone who doesn't believe in God is wrong).
7. *Activities* (e.g., John excludes Walter from playing baseball, Mary avoids playing with blocks).
8. Statements that suggest *worries* or *problems* (e.g., I can't do this, I don't want to fight in a war).

Teachers can follow up value indicators with a series of questions, such as those in Chart 4–1, suggested by Raths and his associates:

Chart 4−1
Clarifying Responses Suggested by the Seven Valuing Processes

1. Choosing freely
   a. Where do you suppose you first got that idea?
   b. How long have you felt that way?
   c. What would people say if you weren't to do what you say you must do?
   d. Are you getting help from anyone? Do you need more help? Can I help?
   e. Are you the only one in your crowd who feels this way?
   f. What do your parents want you to be?
   g. Is there any rebellion in your choice?
   h. How many years will you give to it? What will you do if you're not good enough?
   i. Do you think the idea of having thousands of people cheering when you come out on the field has anything to do with your choice?

2. Choosing from alternatives
   a. What else did you consider before you picked this?
   b. How long did you look around before you decided?
   c. Was it a hard decision? What went into the final decision? Who helped? Do you need any further help?
   d. Did you consider another possible alternative?
   e. Are there some reasons behind your choice?
   f. What choices did you reject before you settled on your present idea or action?
   g. What's really good about this choice which makes it stand out from the other possibilities?

3. Choosing thoughtfully and reflectively
   a. What would be the consequences of each alternative available?
   b. Have you thought about this very much? How did your thinking go?
   c. Is this what I understand you to say . . . [interpret his statement]?
   d. Are you implying that . . . [distort his statement to see if he is clear enough to correct the distortion]?
   e. What assumptions are involved in your choice? Let's examine them.
   f. Define the terms you use. Give me an example of the kind of job you can get without a high-school diploma.
   g. Now if you do this, what will happen to that . . . ?
   h. Is what you say consistent with what you said earlier?
   i. Just what is good about this choice?
   j. Where will it lead?
   k. For whom are you doing this?
   l. With these other choices, rank them in order of significance.
   m. What will you have to do? What are your first steps? Second steps?
   n. Whom else did you talk to?
   o. Have you really weighed it fully?

4. Prizing and cherishing
   a. Are you glad you feel that way?
   b. How long have you wanted it?
   c. What good is it? What purpose does it serve? Why is it important to you?
   d. Should everyone do it your way?
   e. Is it something you really prize?
   f. In what way would life be different without it?

5. Affirming
   a. Would you tell the class the way you feel sometime?
   b. Would you be willing to sign a petition supporting that idea?
   c. Are you saying that you believe . . . [repeat the idea]?
   d. You don't mean to say that you believe . . . [repeat the idea]?
   e. Should a person who believes the way you do speak out?
   f. Do people know that you believe that way or that you do that thing?
   g. Are you willing to stand up and be counted for that?

6. Acting upon choices
   a. I hear what you are for; now, is there anything you can do about it? Can I help?
   b. What are your first steps, second steps, etc.?
   c. Are you willing to put some of your money behind this idea?
   d. Have you examined the consequences of your act?
   e. Are there any organizations set up for the same purposes? Will you join?
   f. Have you done much reading on the topic? Who has influenced you?
   g. Have you made any plans to do more than you already have done?
   h. Would you want other people to know you feel this way? What if they disagree with you?
   i. Where will this lead you? How far are you willing to go?
   j. How has it already affected your life? How will it affect it in the future?

7. Repeating
   a. Have you felt this way for some time?
   b. Have you done anything already? Do you do this often?
   c. What are your plans for doing more of it?
   d. Should you get other people interested and involved?
   e. Has it been worth the time and money?
   f. Are there some other things you can do which are like it?
   g. How long do you think you will continue?
   h. What did you *not* do when you went to do that? Was that o.k.?
   i. How did you decide which had priority?
   j. Did you run into any difficulty?
   k. Will you do it again?

Source: Louis E. Raths, Merrill Harmin, and Sidney B. Simon, *Values and Teaching: Working with Values in the Classroom,* pp. 63–65. Copyright © 1966 by Charles E. Merrill Publishing Company. Reprinted by permission.

Initiating the Process

Teachers need not always wait for students to articulate value indicators. They can often initiate the process themselves by asking questions about personal values, such as: Will you smoke when you grow up? What makes you angry? Would you lie to protect a friend?

Or they can ask questions about social concerns, such as: What do you do to help old people? What are you willing to give up in order to save energy? Do you believe girls should play ball with boys? What is the thing you would most like to change in the world if you could?

Or they can ask questions about historical events, such as: Do you believe the U.S. government did the right thing in spending so much money for space exploration? If you had been President Lincoln, would you have declared war in order to save the Union? Whom do you admire more, Booker T. Washington or W. E. B. DuBois?

Indeed, there are few things students study in the social studies that could not be subjected to value clarification.

Techniques for Stimulating Class Participation

Simon, Howe, and Kirschenbaum have described seventy-nine varied techniques to get class involvement in value clarification.[16] The examples in Chart 4–2 are adapted largely from this source.

Some Important "Don'ts"

Value-clarification processes must be conducted in an appropriately supportive atmosphere. Hence, the following "don'ts" should be regarded as imperatives:

1. Don't moralize, criticize, give your own values, or evaluate student values.
2. Don't pressure students into answering. Permit them to not answer.
3. Don't make it an extended discussion. It is not an interview.
4. Don't ask an individual questions that may be more appropriate for a group.
5. Don't make *all* student value indicators (i.e., student goals, aspirations, attitudes, interests, feelings, beliefs, convictions, and activities) an opportunity for value clarification.[17]

Role-Playing

Role-playing can be used as a variant of the value-clarification process. It requires students to spontaneously *act out* value-laden social situations without benefit of script by projecting themselves into the roles and situations. It allows students to see a problem from different points of view by actually "experiencing" it in a dramatic situation. It also confronts participants with the necessity of predicting consequences of behavior, since role-players must make responses to each other as the play unfolds. It can be used as a vehicle for getting students to understand a variety of situations, from historical conflicts to problems that arise in the home and classroom. The primary purpose of role-playing in value clarification, however, is to have students explore their own feelings and attitudes—either through their interpretation of respective roles or in the discussions that follow enactments.

A very fine summary of the rationale and processes of role-playing is given by Fannie R. Shaftel and George Shaftel.[18] They include approximately fifty problem stories that the teacher can use to launch role-playing. These stories revolve around the themes of individual integrity, group responsibility, self-acceptance, and the management of one's feelings.

[16]Sidney B. Simon, Leland W. Howe, and Howard Kirschenbaum, *Values Clarification: A Handbook of Practical Strategies for Teachers and Students* (New York: Hart Publishing, 1972).
[17]Adapted from Raths, Harmin, and Simon, *Values and Teaching*, pp. 51–55.
[18]Fannie R. Shaftel and George Shaftel, *Role Playing for Social Values: Decision Making in the Social Studies* (Englewood Cliffs, N.J.: Prentice-Hall, 1967).

Chart 4−2
Techniques for Stimulating Class Participation

1. Prepare a list of twenty activities in which students normally engage. Circulate the list among all students and have them place a (1) next to the things they like to do, a (2) next to the things they like to do a little, and a (3) next to the things they don't like to do. Ask for volunteers to give their answers and launch your discussion. (A variation of this is to have students number activities consecutively in the order of their preference. Or have students simply mark each with a ''yes'' or ''no.'')

   Example:

   What do you like to do?

   > take walks
   > go to the movies
   > play with a friend
   > watch television
   > read

2. Ask students to make a choice from several alternatives, such as:

   a. If you saw your best friend throw a gum wrapper on the street, what would you do? (1) say nothing, (2) tell your friend not to litter, (3) pick up the wrapper yourself.

   b. Which would you be willing to give up in order to save energy? (1) ten hours of television per week, (2) a vacation trip to Canada, (3) a warm bedroom.

3. Ask students to rank choices according to level of preferences, as in the following:

   Which would you rather be? Mark your first choice with a (1), the next with a (2), and so on.

   > a soldier in the Confederate army
   > an escaped slave
   > a Catholic in a Puritan colony
   > a prisoner of war
   > a seventy-year-old person

4. Take an issue that has been discussed in class and write it on the blackboard. Draw a long line under it. Working with the students, identify two polar positions on the issue, such as always-never, completely agree – completely disagree, or right-wrong, and write them in at each end of the line. Then ask the students to write their names along the line at the point that best reflects their own position.

   People should fight for what they believe in.

   never _____ *always*

5. Have students fill in blanks to complete some provocative statements, such as:
   a. The thing I like most about myself is _____.
   b. The thing I hate most is _____.
   c. One thing I'd be ready to die for is _____.
   d. By the time I'm twenty, I'd like to be _____.
   e. I feel proudest when _____.

Role-playing by sixth-grade students: a husband comes home to find that his wife does not have dinner ready because she had too many things to do.

According to the Shaftels, role-playing consists of essentially the following steps:

1. *"Warm-up."* The teacher introduces the problem and presents the problem story.
2. *Selecting role-players.* Students discuss the characters, and the teacher selects participants on the basis of whether they have strong feelings about the characters or identify with the role.
3. *Preparing the audience to observe.* Nonparticipant observers are directed regarding appropriate listening behaviors that include considering alternatives to behaviors enacted by role-players, which they will have an opportunity to enact later.
4. *Setting the stage.* Participants are reminded of their roles.
5. *Enactment.* The play is performed.
6. *Discussion and evaluation.* Students discuss the play and evaluate role-players' behaviors.
7. *Further enactments.* Same students or others replay the scene considering alternative modes of behavior.
8. *Further discussion.* The new enactments are discussed.
9. *Generalizing.* In some cases, students can be led to make generalizations about behavior.

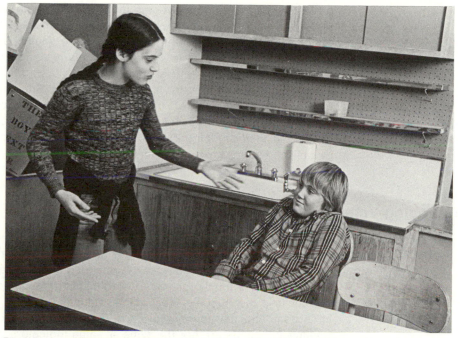

The roles reversed: a working wife returns home to find that her husband does not have dinner ready because he had too many things to do.

Evaluation   The value-clarification approach may indeed make it possible for students to accept and reevaluate themselves in a nonthreatening manner. It may even lead to a reduction in behavior problems as Raths, Harmin, and Simon believe. But there are some disadvantages to this approach, particularly when it is used as the only strategy in value education.

The primary point of analysis and reference is the individual student's own value indicators. The emphasis is on self-exploration. There is no place for the presentation of external influences or evidence that might suggest the inadequacy of the student's values. If a student says "throwing rocks is OK," or "people who were against the war in Vietnam were cowards," the teacher's role is merely to ask some additional questions designed to test these convictions.

This posture has several difficulties. First, it is not at all certain that the teacher's refusal to make a verbal judgment of the student implies the absence of such a judgment. The simple fact of not commenting may be interpreted as acceptance of the student's values. Hence a student may be convinced that the teacher not only accepts him or her as a person, but is also in agreement with the feelings he or she has expressed. And further self-exploration might only convince the student of the soundness of those feelings.

Second, there are some feelings and beliefs that are directly attributable to lack of knowledge. Where this is the case, there appears to be little value in plowing one's ignorance. Thus, for example, students who believe that all war protestors are cowards might gain more from learning something about war protestors than from merely reexamining their feelings. However, as the teacher's role in value clarification is not designed to encompass external information of this sort, the students will have no additional knowledge that might help them to reconsider their beliefs.

This is not to deny that this approach has merit. Students need to feel comfortable in discussing and evaluating their values, and an accepting adult makes this possible. At the same time, it provides teachers with a way to learn a great deal about their students. But to confine all value education to this one approach is to impose excessive limitations.

Improving Value Judgments

In the value-judgment approach, the central point of inquiry is not the students' value indicators, but their value judgments. As in value clarification, there is no attempt made to specify the types of value judgments to be made. But here the emphasis is on rational processes, including the gathering of external evidence, that can help the students improve their value judgments. The teacher's role is to help students develop more rational procedures in such judgments.

Value judgments are not the same as value indicators. Value indicators are expressed goals, aspirations, attitudes, interests, feelings, beliefs, activities, and worries. The subject of a value-indicator statement is "I," as in:

I hate cars.
I disapprove of the President's behavior.
I believe war is wrong in all circumstances.
I approve of stealing at certain times.

A value judgment, on the other hand, is an evaluation of something in which values play an implicit or explicit part. The subject of a value-judgment statement is the thing that is being evaluated, as in:

Cars are bad.
The President behaved badly.
War is wrong in all circumstances.
Stealing is sometimes justified.

A value-clarification strategy focuses on the value indicators of the "I"; a value-judgment strategy focuses on what is being evaluated and on the values that underlie it. If a student says "I hate cars," for example, the teacher can facilitate a value-clarification process by asking questions such as those listed in the left-hand column of Chart 4–3. A value-judgment process can be stimulated by asking questions such as those listed in the right-hand column.

Making Rational Value Judgments

Making rational value judgments involves the following steps:

1. *Identify and clarify the value issue.* Suppose a student says, "War is bad unless you have no other way to get what you deserve." This statement is com-

---

Chart 4–3
A Comparison of Value Clarification and
Value Judgment Questions

Value Clarification	Value Judgment
Statement: I hate cars.	Statement: Cars are bad.
Do you really feel this way?	You believe cars are bad? Why are cars bad?
What do you suppose has caused you to feel this way?	Would you want to see all cars disappear? Why?
Have you considered your feelings carefully?	What do you suppose might be the consequence of this?
Are you prepared to act on your feelings?	Are there any ways cars are good? How?
Have you considered what you might do?	What could be done to take advantage of the good things and eliminate the bad?
	In view of these considerations, do you still feel cars are bad?

---

posed of two value judgments: (a) Wars are bad because of some implied moral value. (b) Wars can be effective in getting what you deserve. Each statement implies a different set of criteria by which it could be evaluated. Moreover, the term "war" itself needs to be clarified. (Does it include "cold" as well as "hot" wars? Guerrilla warfare? Civil disobedience? Or even a "war of words"?) Before any rational value judgment can be made, the issue has to be clarified and the terms explained.

2. *Gather evidence.* Students and teachers should collect as much evidence as they can that might have bearing on the value issue. For the statement "war is bad," for example, facts and generalizations such as the following might be collected:

Over forty million people died as a result of World War I.
Women were given the vote in several countries as a result of changes brought about by World War I.
Over sixty million people died as a result of World War II.
Unemployment decreases during wartime.
Modern wars cost more than wars fought in previous centuries.
America gained its independence by fighting a war.

3. *Evaluate the accuracy of the evidence.* Evidence must be evaluated. Students must learn to ask: Is the statement true? Who says it is? Why should we believe that person? Do other people agree?

4. *Identify the criteria that make the evidence relevant to the value issue.* The ways in which evidence is relevant to the issue need to be made clear. This involves the identification of some value criterion for establishing relevance.

For example, how is the fact that sixty million people died as a result of World War II relevant to the issue of whether "war is bad"? Students might respond that "things that kill people are bad." This then becomes one value criterion for judging the "badness" of wars. The teacher might also ask: "How is the fact that modern wars cost more than wars fought in previous centuries relevant?" To which the students might respond: "Things that cost too much money have got to be bad."

5. *Test the value criterion.* At this point the articulated value criterion must be tested to assess whether it is indeed an all-encompassing value principle. The teacher can stimulate discussion by introducing another type of case in which the value criterion might apply.

You have said that "things that kill people are bad." Suppose you and your family were being attacked by some people with knives and guns. Would you kill them if you had the chance?

You have said that "things that cost too much money are bad." The government spends billions of dollars to help the poor and the sick. Do you think this is bad?

6. *Make a value judgment.* Students can now be asked to make their value judgments. If, for example, the issue under discussion is "Is war always bad?" and war has been defined as "organization for the purpose of fighting where participants are willing to kill or die," one student might conclude that wars are indeed always bad because the taking of a human life is always bad, even when it involves self-defense or the defense of family. Another student might conclude, however, that war is acceptable when human freedom is threatened because the value of freedom is greater than the value of life. The teacher may simply accept these judgments or use them as the bases for launching the process anew. To examine the first student's conclusion, the teacher might encourage the study of a single popular war—such as World War II—and the possible effects if the United States had chosen not to fight. To examine the second student's conclusion, the class might undertake an investigation of nonviolent ways of winning wars, such as those suggested by Gene Sharp in his remarkable book *Exploring Nonviolent Alternatives.*[19] At some point, of course, the teacher must terminate the class discussion and accept student conclusions. At the very least, student judgments at this point should be more rationally based. At the very most, they may lead to further value questions that the participants will continue to explore throughout their lives.

Using a Controversial Value Statement

Teachers can initiate the process of making value judgments by simply introducing controversial value statements in the classroom—the more controversial the better. Such statements should be short, supported on the surface at least by relevant facts, and pertinent to student interests. They can be fictionalized statements, created by the teacher or someone else, actual statements made by famous or not-so-famous people of the past or present, or adapted editorials

[19]Gene Sharp, *Exploring Nonviolent Alternatives* (Boston: Porter Sargent Publisher, 1971).

from newspapers or periodicals. In short, there are many sources from which controversial value statements can be elicited.

The following example is based on a fictionalized statement that is nonetheless reflective of a sentiment held by many people. It concerns the issue of welfare.

Students read.

"People who do not work should not get any money. Many people in this country do not work. Many of them are strong and able, but they would rather take money from the government and do nothing. There was a story I read recently about a young man of twenty-five who just liked to go to the horse races all the time. Yet every month this young man received $150 from the government. Working people pay taxes to the government, which then gives the money to people like this young man. This means that working people are paying lazy people to do nothing."

Teacher: What does this writer believe? What is this writer's *main* belief?

Students identify the issue.

Teacher: What facts does the writer give to support this belief?

Students identify the evidence given by the writer.

Teacher: Is it true that many people do not work? How do you know? Is it true that many of them are strong and able? Is it true that many of them are lazy? How do you know? What facts has the writer left out? Do some people not work for other reasons? What reasons?

Students evaluate facts.

Teacher: Do you think the writer feels that lazy people do not deserve any money at all? Do you think he feels that lazy people should starve? Do you think he feels that all people who do not work should starve? Why do you suppose the writer left out the things you just mentioned?

Students identify value criteria of writer.

Teacher: Do you think lazy people should get money? Why or why not? Do you think people who do not work because they are not able to should get any money? Who do you think should give them money? Why? Do you think lazy people should be forced to work? How?

Students identify own value criteria.

Teacher: You have said that lazy people should not get any money. Suppose your father was a lazy person. Would you agree that he should not get any money?

You have said that people who are sick and cannot work should get money. Suppose a person was not sick in the body, but sick in the mind. Should a drug addict, for example, get any money?

Students test the value criteria.

Teacher: Do you think people who do not work should not get any money? Would you change the statement in any way? How?

Students make value judgments.

Using Conflicting Value Statements   Instead of using just one value statement, the teacher can introduce two opposing statements on the same issue. This immediately sets the stage for verbal conflict — hence a more involving process. The following example concerns the issue of slavery.

Students read.

Today it seems strange that slavery could ever have existed in the United States. Yet even a hundred years after our constitution was written, many people still supported slavery. Many of those who did felt that there were benefits for the slaves as well as for the masters. A white southerner had this to say shortly before the Civil War:

"The chief and by far most important question is, how does slavery affect the condition of the slave? We provide for each slave, in old age and in infancy, in sickness and in health, not according to his labor, but according to his wants. The slave consumes more of the ordinary products than the master and is far happier because even if the business fails he is always sure of support. He is simply sold to another master and participates in the profits of another business. The slave marries when he pleases because he knows he will not have to work any harder if he has a family than he does without a family, and if he dies the family will be taken care of. He is as happy as any human being can be. And why not? He enjoys as much of the benefits of the farm or business as he can. Great wealth brings many additional cares and few additional enjoyments. One can only eat so much. One only needs a certain amount of clothing to keep warm.

"Slaves do not have to compete for employment, as free men do. It is not to the master's advantage to reduce the slave's allowance or wages if he is ill because the slave might die if this happens. The master's feelings for his slave do not allow him to save money when the slave is old. The slaves are all well fed, well dressed, have plenty of fuel, and are happy. They are not afraid of the future and never have to worry about not having enough of anything."[20]

Many other people felt that freedom was more important than any of the benefits that might exist for the slave. Indeed, they strongly doubted that any advantages really existed, and many stories of cruelty and bad treatment were told about slavery. A former slave described her childhood this way:

"I's hear tell of them good slave days, but I ain't never seen no good times then. . . . My mother, she was cook, and I don't recollect nothing 'bout my father. If I had any brothers and sisters I didn't know it. We had old ragged huts made out of poles and some of the cracks chinked up with mud and moss and some of them wasn't. We didn't have no good beds, just scaffolds nailed up to the wall out of poles and the old ragged bedding throwed on them. That sure was hard sleeping, but even that feel good to our weary bones after them long hard days' work in the field. . . . We never seen no money. Guess we'd-a bought something to eat with it if we ever seen any. Fact is, we wouldn't-a knowed hardly how to bought anything, 'cause we didn't know nothing 'bout going to town. . . . On Sunday they made all the children change, and what we wears till we gits our clothes washed was gunny sacks with holes cut for our head and arms. We didn't have no shoes 'cepting some homemade moccasins, and we didn't have them till we was big children. The little children they goes naked till they was big enough to work. . . . Sometimes a slave would run away and just live wild in the woods, but most times they catch 'em and beats 'em, then chains 'em down in the sun till they nearly die. . . . We didn't have much looking after when we git sick. We had to take the worst stuff in the world for medicine, just so it was cheap."[21]

Teacher: What is the issue?

Students identify the issue.

Teacher: What evidence is given to support each stand?

Students identify evidence.

[20]Adapted from George Fitzhugh, *Slavery Justified, by a Southerner* (Fredericksburg: Recorder Printing Office, 1850).
[21]"Jenny Proctor's Story," from *Lay My Burden Down,* edited by B. A. Botkin, copyright © 1945 by the University of Chicago, all rights reserved.

Teacher: Is the evidence accurate? How do we know? How do the statements in each account compare with each other? Which account do you think is more accurate? What makes you think so? Is enough evidence given? What other evidence might be useful?

Students evaluate evidence.

Teacher: If slaves had enough to eat and wear, would slavery then be bad? If slaves were not punished cruelly, would slavery then be bad? Are there any reasons slavery might be good?

Students identify value criteria.

Teacher: You said that when people are beaten, something is bad. Suppose you were trying to get some secrets from an enemy in order to protect your country. Would beating him be a good thing if that were the only way you could get the information? Why or why not?

You said that as long as people have enough to eat and wear, something is good. If someone came along and promised to take care of you for the rest of your life as long as you did everything he wanted, would you be willing to do it? Why or why not?

Students test value criteria.

Teacher: Which statement is closer to your own beliefs? Would you change it in any way?

Students make value judgments.

Evaluation   By focusing on value judgments, students may be led to improve the rational processes with which they make those judgments. They may learn to relate specific decisions to broader value principles and become more aware of their own values as well as those of others.

The emphasis on rationality, however, may hinder or prevent the types of exchanges that can occur in the value clarification approach. Clarification techniques encourage freer and more spontaneous reactions, and can probably cover a wider range of value-laden subjects because of the shorter interaction time. Hence, both approaches are useful.

What neither approach is explicitly concerned with, however, is the development of moral values. Neither approach defines the specific values aimed for, although both imply that some type of moral development is hoped for. The question remains, then, whether it is sufficient to depend on these rather indirect approaches or preferable to complement them with a strategy that is directly concerned with moral development.

Moral Education

Advocates of moral education believe that the value-neutral classroom is impossible. They hold that teachers convey values all the time — even when merely engaged in value-clarification processes or helping students make rational value judgments. At the very least, the teachers are conveying the value that these processes are beneficial.

Nor do the advocates of moral education believe that values are "relative." That is, they do not believe that one set of values is just as good as another.

Some are decidedly superior. Superior values are characterized by a high level of moral reasoning, and ultimately committed to the principles of empathy and justice. The function of moral education should be to develop moral reasoning.

Convention tends to judge morality on the basis of particular behaviors—not on the reasons that accompany them. Conventional morality, for example, will applaud the driver who obeys traffic signals, regardless of whether it is done out of fear of an observant policeman or out of a sense of commitment to the preservation of human life. Conversely, conventional morality will condemn the man who leaves the country to avoid military service, regardless of whether he does it because of fear or for reasons of conscience. These reasons should, however, be taken into account. Moral education, according to this school of thought, should be concerned with helping individuals develop their moral reasoning— not with providing prohibitions and prescriptions for "right" behavior.

Lawrence Kohlberg, the foremost architect of this approach, believes that moral reasoning, like cognitive growth, is a developmental process.[22] He bases this belief on his study of young people from countries around the world, including Great Britain, Canada, Taiwan, Mexico, Turkey, and the United States. He found that regardless of specific differences in culture, similar stages of moral reasoning were discernible in all.

The Stages of Moral Reasoning

Kohlberg identified three major categories of moral reasoning, each of which is age-related. The first category, *preconventional morality,* is characteristic of children between the ages of four and ten. Children of this age can engage in very cruel behavior when no fear of punishment is present, because they have not yet developed a sense of morality. The second category, *conventional morality,* characteristically develops from approximately age ten until age eighteen. It is essentially a conformist orientation. Those in this category are concerned with conforming to and maintaining the social order. Only a small group of adults reach the level of the third category, *postconventional morality.* Its basic orientation is a set of major ethical principles that are not the result of deference to authorities or self-interest. They include the principles of justice and the reciprocity and equality of human rights.

Each of these three categories includes two subcategories, making a sum total of six identifiable stages, as follows:

1. The *preconventional* level (approximate ages: 4–10)

Stage 1: Orientation toward punishment and unquestioning deference to superior power. The physical consequences of action regardless of their human meaning or value determine its goodness or badness.

Stage 2: Right action consists of that which instrumentally satisfies one's own needs and occasionally the needs of others. Human relations are viewed in terms like those of the marketplace. Elements of fairness, of reciprocity and equal sharing are present, but they are always interpreted in a physical, pragmatic way. Reciprocity is a matter of "you scratch my back and I'll scratch yours" not of loyalty, gratitude or justice.

[22]Lawrence Kohlberg, "The Child as a Moral Philosopher," *Psychology Today* 2:4 (September 1968), pp. 25–30. Copyright © 1968 Ziff-Davis Publishing Company. Reprinted by permission of *Psychology Today* magazine.

2. The *conventional* level (approximate ages: 10–18)

Stage 3: Good-boy–good-girl orientation. Good behavior is that which pleases or helps others and is approved by them. There is much conformity to stereotypical images of what is majority or "natural" behavior. Behavior is often judged by intention—"he means well" becomes important for the first time, and is overused, as by Charlie Brown in *Peanuts.* One seeks approval by being "nice."

Stage 4: Orientation toward authority, fixed rules and the maintenance of the social order. Right behavior consists of doing one's duty, showing respect for authority and maintaining the given social order for its own sake. One earns respect by performing dutifully.

3. The *postconventional* level (approximate ages: 18 onwards)

Stage 5: A social-contract orientation, generally with legalistic and utilitarian overtones. Right action tends to be defined in terms of general rights and in terms of standards which have been critically examined and agreed upon by the whole society. There is a clear awareness of the relativism of personal values and opinions and a corresponding emphasis upon procedural rules for reaching consensus. Aside from what is constitutionally and democratically agreed upon, right or wrong is a matter of personal "values" and "opinion." The result is an emphasis upon the "legal point of view," but with an emphasis upon the possibility of *changing* law in terms of rational considerations of social utility, rather than freezing it in the terms of Stage 4 "law and order." Outside the legal realm, free agreement and contract are the binding elements of obligation. This is the "official" morality of American government, and finds its ground in the thought of the writers of the Constitution.

Stage 6: Orientation toward the decisions of conscience and toward self-chosen *ethical principles* appealing to logical comprehensiveness, universality and consistency. These principles are abstract and ethical (the Golden Rule, the categorical imperative); they are not concrete moral rules like the Ten Commandments. Instead, they are universal principles of *justice,* of the *reciprocity* and *equality* of human rights, and of respect for the dignity of human beings as *individual persons.*[23]

In illustrating these developmental stages, Kohlberg uses the following example in relation to the question of human life:

Stage 1: The value of a human life is confused with the value of physical objects and is based on the social status or physical attributes of its possessor. Tommy, age ten: (Why should the druggist give the drug to the dying woman when her husband couldn't pay for it?) "If someone important is in a plane and is allergic to heights and the stewardess won't give him medicine because she's only got enough for one and she's got a sick one, a friend, in back, they'd probably put the stewardess in a lady's jail because she didn't help the important one."
(Is it better to save the life of one important person or a lot of unimportant people?) "All the people that aren't important because one man just has one house, maybe a lot of furniture, but a whole bunch of people have an awful lot of furniture and some of these poor people might have a lot of money and it doesn't look it."

Stage 2: The value of a human life is seen as instrumental to the satisfaction of the needs of its possessor or of other persons. Tommy, age thirteen: (Should the doctor "mercy kill" a fatally ill woman requesting death because of her pain?) "Maybe it would be good to put her out of her pain, she'd be better off that way. But the husband wouldn't want it, it's not like an animal. If a pet dies you can get along without it—it isn't something you really need. Well, you can get a new wife, but it's not really the same."

Stage 3: The value of a human life is based on the empathy and affection of family members and others toward its possessor. Andy, age sixteen: (Should the doctor "mercy kill" a fatally ill woman requesting death because of her pain?) "No, he shouldn't. The husband loves her and wants to see her. He wouldn't want her to die sooner, he loves her too much."

Stage 4: Life is conceived as sacred in terms of its place in a categorical moral or religious order of rights and duties. John, age sixteen: (Should the doctor "mercy kill" the woman?) "The doctor wouldn't have the right to take a life, no human has the right. He can't create life, he shouldn't destroy it."

Stage 5: Life is valued both in terms of its relation to community welfare and in terms of life being a universal human right.

Stage 6: Belief in the sacredness of human life as representing a universal human value of respect for the individual. Steve, age sixteen: (Should the husband steal the expensive drug to save his wife?) "By the law of society he was wrong but by the law of nature or of God the druggist was wrong and the husband was justified. Human life is above financial gain. Regardless of who was dying, if it was a total stranger, man has a duty to save him from dying."[24]

Moral reasoning is a developmental process, but this does not mean that all people inevitably progress to the final stage. People may stop developing at any

[23]*Ibid.,* p. 26.
[24]Lawrence Kohlberg, "Moral Education in the Schools: A Developmental View," *The School Review* 74:1 (Spring 1966), pp. 8–9. © 1966 by The University of Chicago.

one of these stages. Criminal adults, for example, frequently fail to progress past the preconventional level. And many adults—perhaps the majority—probably progress no further than Stage 4, the "law and order" level.

It is possible, however, to help individuals progress from one stage to another. This can occur when they are engaged in frequent discussion about moral issues with others whose moral reasoning is at least one stage above their own. An individual at Stage 3 can respond positively to a Stage 4 argument. The process, however, is not reversible. An individual who has arrived at a particular level does not regress.

Moral Dilemmas

The teacher can help children develop their moral reasoning by introducing discussions concerning moral issues in the classroom. The primary vehicle for doing this is the moral dilemma.

A moral dilemma is a life-like problem in which two value principles are in conflict. The students are asked to choose between one behavior or another and give reasons for it.

A good moral dilemma should include the following elements:

1. It should build on other work in the classroom. This means it should be integrated into the social studies program, not treated as a separate subject.
2. It should be as simple as possible.
3. It should be open-ended, with no obvious or single answer. The objective is to produce cognitive conflict, argument, and disagreement among class members.
4. It should help students focus on the reasoning of the conflict, not the facts.
5. It should be appropriate for the age level of the students.[25]

Generating Dilemmas

Dilemmas can be generated from actual classroom situations, out-of-class issues, or content areas of study—fictionalized or real. The following are some representative examples:

Dilemmas that arise out of classroom experiences of children:

Tommy needs a book to do his homework. His teacher has told him she would send for his mother if he did not finish his work. Tommy's mother works and will be very angry with him if she has to come to school and lose a day's pay. Tommy has lost his book but is afraid to tell anyone because this is the third book he's lost. There are lots of extra books in the room but the teacher has told the children not to touch them. Should Tommy take the book home to finish his homework?

Mary sees her friend John hitting Peter, a young and frail child. She feels sorry for Peter and would like to tell John to quit. But she is new to the school and has few friends. John is one of them and she is afraid of losing his friendship. Should she tell John she disapproves of his conduct or ignore it?

[25]Adapted from Edwin Fenton, Ann Colby, and Betsy Speicher-Dubin, "Developing Moral Dilemmas for Social Studies Classes," unpublished draft (Cambridge, Mass.: Moral Education Research Foundation, October 29, 1974).

Miss Smith has had some money stolen from her purse. She is very upset. She suspects that a student in the class has taken it. She tells the class that if the money is returned by the end of the day, she will ask no questions and forget the whole incident. But if it isn't, she will cancel the class picnic scheduled for the next week. Tim saw Linda take the money. At the end of the day, Miss Smith announces she has not yet received her money. She asks if any of the students know anything about it. Should Tim tell her what he knows?

Fictional dilemmas that arise out of social studies:

Roger lives with his family in the South before the Civil War. His family owns a big plantation that has many slaves. Roger's favorite slave is Joseph, a young man who tells him many stories. One night Roger overhears Joseph telling another slave that he plans to run away to the North where he can be free. Roger knows that his father would lose a lot of money if this were to happen. Should he tell his father what he knows?

William Saws lives with his family in early colonial Boston. He knows that many of his friends and neighbors are very unhappy with British rule and that trouble is brewing. His parents, however, are loyal to the king and feel that the trouble is being caused by a small group who are trying to influence everyone else. One day, Jane, a friend, tells him that a secret meeting is being planned for that evening. His parents were not invited because they are suspected of being untrustworthy and might tell the authorities. Jane tells him not to tell his parents but invites him to come if he can. Should Roger tell his parents about the meeting?

Real historical dilemmas:[26]

The small northern town in California in the 1880s was seething with excitement. Yesterday evening rival Chinese gangs had shot at each other on the streets. A stray bullet accidentally struck and killed a prominent businessman. The angry white citizens threatened to lynch all the Chinese in town. Fortunately, cooler heads prevailed, and all the Chinese were placed aboard a ship for San Francisco. There was one remaining Chinaman in the area; he was Ah Low, who worked for the rancher Tom. Tom's wife had died leaving two small children to raise. Ah Low had become the children's friend and substitute mother. The children loved Ah Low and he had proved to be a faithful friend and servant to Tom. A vigilante committee rode out to Tom's ranch demanding that Tom turn Ah Low over to them. Tom refused and ran the men off the ranch at gunpoint. The men promised they would return for Ah Low and kill Tom if he resisted. Tom must make a decision concerning Ah Low. What should Tom do?[27]

A young Cherokee Indian named Elias had been sent north to a missionary school in Connecticut in the 1820s. It was important to the Cherokee nation to train and educate their young men in the ways of the white man's civilization. The Cherokees had decided to learn the skills of the whites and become farmers, artisans, merchants, and teachers in order to keep their remaining lands. Many whites were angry at the school and its board members because some Indian students had married white girls of the village. They believed that the two races should not intermarry. Elias and Harriet, a white girl of the village, fell in love and announced their engagement. Harriet wanted to become a missionary and help Elias's people. The citizens of the village became very angry and demanded that the school be closed. Harriet's friends and relatives tried to persuade her to cancel the engagement. Strangers wrote angry letters to Harriet and the school board members. The village was gripped with fear and hate, and a mob burned a figure of Harriet in the village square. Her own brother was a member of that mob. Harriet loved Elias,

[26]These historical case studies were adapted by Jane Walstrom, a student in the Department of Education at Humboldt State University, Arcata, California.
[27]Adapted from Lynwood Carranco, "Chinese Expulsion from Humboldt County," *Pacific Historical Review* (November 1961), pp. 329–40.

but she also loved her family and home. Should she marry Elias?[28]

Jim was a young inexperienced hunter on a fur-trapping expedition in the Missouri River wilderness area of 1823. He knew that the trip would be dangerous, but he couldn't turn down the chance for adventure and good pay. That morning Jim and his friend Hugh were hunting for venison to feed the hungry men. Suddenly, Jim heard Hugh screaming in pain and fear! Jim rushed to his friend's aid and saw a grizzly bear mauling Hugh. Jim and the others killed the bear, but not before it had ripped Hugh's body with its sharp claws. Hugh was still alive, but no one believed that he would live. The party could not stop to take care of Hugh, their fort was 500 miles away and winter was closing in. Jim and another man named John volunteered to stay with Hugh until he died, and bury him. Days passed. It began to snow and twice hostile Indian raiding parties almost discovered them. John and Jim were afraid; each day that they stayed became more dangerous, but miraculously, Hugh weakly clung to life. Should John and Jim stay or leave?[29]

A Strategy for Developing Moral Reasoning

Once the teacher has the moral dilemma prepared, there are several steps students should engage in. Basically they are the following:

1. Students read the moral dilemma.
2. Students clarify terminology.
3. Students identify the moral conflict.
4. Students make a tentative decision.
5. Students state reasons for their decision.
6. Students evaluate reasons.
7. Students reaffirm their decision or make a new one.

The largest amounts of time should be spent on steps 4 through 6.

In order to maximize student involvement, the following procedure can be used once step 4 is reached. State the possible courses of action and ask the class members to indicate their initial preferences by raising hands. Put all those in favor of one course of action in one group, all those in favor of the other course of action in another group, and "undecideds" in a third group. Then instruct each group to discuss the reasons for the decision (or indecision) and decide which three reasons are the most important. Have each group appoint one member to write down the reasons and report them to the entire class. Give them a specific time limit for their discussion. At the end of the designated time, regroup the entire class and launch a general discussion based on the conclusions reached by each group.

The Teacher's Role

After presenting the dilemma, making sure the points are clearly understood, and dividing the groups, the teacher's role is minimal. The most important contribution the teacher can make at this time is to help the students keep focused on reasons—not the facts, validity, or actuality of the case. Above all, at no point

[28]Adapted from Dale Van Every, *Disinherited: The Lost Birthright of the American Indian* (New York: Morrow, 1966), pp. 40–53.
[29]Adapted from Don Berry, *A Majority of Scoundrels* (New York: Harper & Row, 1961), pp. 49–69.

should the teacher convey a critical judgment either by word or deed, regardless of his or her own feelings of dismay or even shock at the level of moral reasoning evidenced. If Kohlberg is right, the teacher may rest content in the knowledge that students will develop their moral reasoning abilities quite adequately without assistance. Indeed, should a teacher venture to express his or her own feelings, the attempt is likely to either inhibit further discussion or simply reflect reasoning that is beyond the students' comprehension.

Evaluation   There is, of course, no certainty that the stages identified by Kohlberg actually do reflect a developmental process in moral reasoning. More research is needed to confirm them. However, if we accept the premise that cognitive growth is a developmental process, it appears equally probable that moral reasoning is similarly developmental.

If we accept this premise, certain major implications follow. For one thing, it allows us to depart from the labeling process with which teachers and indeed many adults tend to identify youngsters. Thus, rather than calling a six-year-old "honest" or "dishonest," "bad" or "good" — and thereby suggesting that his or her character has somehow already been shaped — we can interpret the behavior as one point in normal developmental growth. This avoids the peril of reacting in such a way as to reinforce negative behavior. For example, if we define a six-year-old as a "liar" (rather than recognize the child's intense fear of punishment), we may begin to behave in ways that lead the child to assume that the label and behavior are appropriate.

Second, by utilizing Kohlberg's premise we can identify some norms or expected standards for moral reasoning for each age group. Thus, we need not react with dismay if a ten-year-old says "I would lie to a policeman if my best friend stole something," because it is a typical Stage 2 level of moral reasoning. But it may be a legitimate cause for concern if an eighteen-year-old says the same thing.

Three, the premise offers the hope that moral level can be improved by some rather simple processes. No society can sustain itself without at least a conventional morality (Stages 3 and 4). The growing crime rate and generally antisocial behaviors that characterize our times suggest that increasing numbers of people do not even reach this level. If Kohlberg is correct, then the schools may help change the situation by the simple process of discussing moral dilemmas in the classroom.

However, we cannot accept the premise uncritically. More evidence is certainly needed to support not only the analysis of the components of the stages themselves, but also the contentions that moral reasoning can be developed through moral discussions and that the nature of the process is progressive and irreversible. Moreover, there is no evidence at the moment to support the underlying premise that higher levels of moral reasoning will result in more moral *behavior.* And finally, one invidious implication must be noted in Kohlberg's thesis. Kohlberg sees a correlation between cognitive development and moral reasoning — that is, individuals who are more developed cognitively are likely to be more developed in their moral reasoning. This suggests that intellectual capacity and morality are linked; not only that smarter people are capable of higher morality, but that people who are not so smart *cannot* achieve a high level of morality. Taken in conjunction with current efforts that presume to find high cognitive abilities among particular population groups, this has ominous overtones.

Theoretical implications aside, however, the instructional strategy itself appears only beneficial. The discussion of moral issues can certainly do no harm, and just possibly may do a great deal of good as children listen to each other articulate moral standards. Of course, it means introducing yet another component in an already overcrowded curriculum. Here, priorities must dictate policy. Teachers who believe that their major role is the dissemination of facts will be reluctant to take the time to explore values. But those who agree with the idea that the social studies curriculum must have multiple objectives—including value objectives—will find the time for it.

Summary

The development of values is as important as the development of the intellect, and many studies exist that demonstrate a definite relationship between the two. Values affect both the personality and the learning ability of the individual.

Some educators continue to insist that knowledge is neutral and therefore value education should not take place in the classroom. However, it is a simple matter to demonstrate that the many choices that must be made in teaching are all subject to influence by the values of the teacher and the society in which the teacher lives. The question is not whether values should be taught but *how* they should be taught.

Three basic opinions exist presently, and all have something worthwhile to offer. The first, value clarification, holds—perhaps too cautiously—that it is only the techniques of valuing and not the values themselves that should be taught. Thus the teacher should question value judgments made by the students without attempting to suggest specific alternatives, in order to suggest that more consideration be given to those values they claim to hold. The second school of thought also holds that specific values should not be taught but believes that more should be done to develop the skills necessary to make rational value judgments. This school wishes to encourage students to learn to gather and evaluate evidence, to identify the relevant criteria, and to put these to a test before reaching value judgments. The third school of thought takes the most extreme position, holding that a more specific moral education is called for. While the followers of this school also do not wish to advocate values in the traditional sense (such vague and easily distorted attributes as "loyalty"), they do propose that students need to develop basic ethical principles such as empathy and justice.

Any program of moral education must take into account evidence that moral reasoning is a developmental process that goes through a series of stages. These range from a low level of preconventional reasoning, in which values are essentially determined by deference to superior power (such as the parent or teacher holds), to the highest post-conventional level, in which values are determined by decisions of conscience and universal ethical principles. These stages are age-related, but progress from one to the next is not automatic. Development can stop at any stage if the person is not exposed to—or capable of understanding—moral reasoning of the next stage. Schools can be very important in helping people develop moral reasoning by allowing many opportunities for students to engage in discussions of moral dilemmas.

While there is no conclusive evidence to support the superiority of any of the major schools of thought, Kohlberg and his associates have accumulated a good deal of research to support the third opinion, that of a specific moral education. Nevertheless, each of the opinions — and their accompanying strategies — has its virtues, and teachers should attempt to develop skills in all of them.

Social Issues

There are three basic ways of organizing social studies curricula: (1) using the structure of the social science disciplines: their concepts, generalizations, and methods, (2) using the interests and needs of individual students as springboards for inquiry, and (3) using broad social issues. The first is the most pervasive format, incorporated in the majority of social studies programs. The second represents an aspiration heralded by the new "humanists" and reflected in part in the propulsion toward individualization and the "open classroom." The third remains virtually unrepresented in elementary social studies curricula either as fact or aspiration. Nonetheless, it is the approach most congruent with a humanistic curriculum.

While definitions of humanism vary, the issue of a meaningful life is a central concern of humanists today.[1] Paths to a meaningful life are made more available when cognitive and affective learnings are used to illuminate central social concerns.[2] Such learnings need to occur within humanistic structures; that is, in environments that are responsive to individual needs.

Social Science Disciplines as Framework

A curriculum organized around the structure of the social science disciplines emphasizes rational knowledge of the world based on scientific models. Such knowledge is essential for any disciplined inquiry into what is and what can be. But the social science disciplines are primarily concerned with *describing* the world, rather than *prescribing* what ought to be. And while humanists welcome the former, they are more concerned with the latter. Cognitively centered curricula tend to make humanistic concerns peripheral. As Figure 5–1 suggests, they tend to begin and end with cognitive concerns, even if taught in humanistic environments. Using them one can, for example, describe the concept of power without considering whether the use of power can always be justified, how much power an individual should have, or whether power is at all necessary for the public good. A discipline-centered curriculum has much to offer a humanistic curriculum in the way of knowledge—but it is not sufficient unto itself.

Individual Interests as Framework

A curriculum based on individual interests and needs has the advantage of allowing for the development of student autonomy and responsibility. But, as suggested in Figure 5–2, there is no assurance that this form of organization will lead either to mastery of the content of the disciplines or to concern with values and attitudes. A student who chooses to study airplanes, for example, might learn all their types and features and never consider their impact on the quality of life or on the nature of warfare and international relations. That this indeed does occur is attested to by Jonathan Kozol, who had the following to

[1]Eric Weil, *Daedalus* 99:2 (Spring 1970), pp. 237–55.
[2]See George Isaac Brown, *Human Teaching for Human Learning: An Introduction to Confluent Education* (New York: Viking Press, 1971), p. 3.

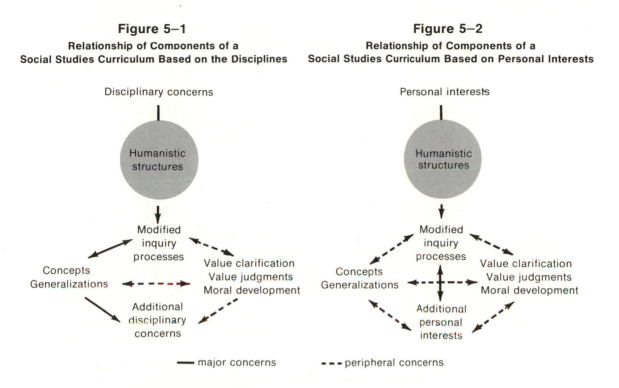

Figure 5–1

**Relationship of Components of a
Social Studies Curriculum Based on the Disciplines**

Figure 5–2

**Relationship of Components of a
Social Studies Curriculum Based on Personal Interests**

say after his extensive observations of free schools where students are given maximum choice:

> In visiting many of the rural Free Schools in the course of these two years, my wife and I repeatedly ask ourselves this question: Why is it, in so many of these self-conscious, open and ecstatic Free Schools for rich children, everyone boasts that he is doing "his own thing" but everyone in each of these schools, from coast to coast, is doing the same *kind* of thing? Why is it, we ask, that "free choice" so often proves to mean the weaver's loom, tie-dye and macrame, that "organic growth" turns out in every case to mean the potter's kiln?[3]

Children do not spontaneously awake one morning and ask to learn of things of which they've never heard, observes Kozol further.[4] Hence, while some student choice and curriculum flexibility are desirable, undue emphasis may lead to intellectual sterility, as well as the inability to recognize or cope with social concerns.

**Social Issues
as Framework**

Implicitly or explicitly, both types of organizational patterns described above make certain assumptions about what constitutes a meaningful or a purposeful

[3]Jonathan Kozol, "Politics, Rage and Motivation in the Free Schools," *Harvard Educational Review* 42: 3 (August 1972), p. 415.
[4]Ibid., p. 419.

Figure 5–3
Relationship of Components of a
Social Studies Curriculum Based on Social Issues

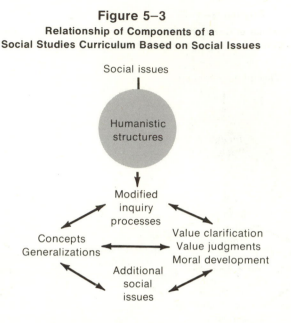

curriculum. The discipline-centered curriculum assumes that the pursuit of rational scientific truth is a purposeful educational experience. The organizational pattern based on individual interests assumes that self-actualization—the realization of one's potential and interests—constitutes the heart of a purposeful education. A curriculum organized around social issues makes still other assumptions about what is purposeful.

A social issues curriculum assumes that meaning is best found through the commitment of one's cognitive and affective energies to significant world concerns. The commitment of social scientists is to scientific truth regardless of its human significance. The social scientist who chooses to study the communication patterns of the Trobrianders may indeed have something ultimately to contribute to solving the problem of war—but the choice of study area will not be based on that concern. The commitment of self-actualizers is to themselves. The skilled flower arranger who is delighted with his work may indeed make life more pleasurable for others, but his commitment stems not from the service he performs but from his own desires.

Of the three types of organization patterns, the one based on social issues is most congruent with a humanistic orientation. A study of social issues must inevitably incorporate both relevant social science knowledge and values, attitudes, and feelings (Figure 5–3). One cannot, for example, study the uses and abuses of technology, or the issue of war and peace, without calling upon the concepts and data of political scientists, historians, sociologists, and other social scientists. Nor can one seek to resolve these issues without first examining one's own basic values. A study of social issues, then, integrates both cognitive and affective elements as it seeks to sensitize students to significant human concerns.

The Need for All Three Frameworks

While the examination of social issues needs to be included in the elementary social studies, it should not be the only organizational pattern used. There is a great deal of value in exploring the disciplines or "doing one's own thing" even when relevance and meaning are not immediately apparent. For one thing, it may simply be interesting. For example, the study of the origin of life, the comparison of human and nonhuman groups, or even historical trivia may have little perceptible importance for contemporary events, but they may simply satisfy the desire for knowledge. For another, what may appear to be irrelevant at the moment may have significance at a later time. It is also important that young people have the freedom to explore what interests them—even when adults doubt its value. Weaving, tie-dying, and macrame are legitimate experiences for children—as is the interest some youngsters have in identifying the names and speed of all types of aircraft. To suggest that all learning in the social studies be directed by one philosophical orientation implies a rigidity that may stifle learning even as it proposes to liberate it. Nonetheless, particular attention needs to be given to the study of social issues because it has been so neglected in the past.

Social Issues in the Elementary Curriculum

By and large, the study of social issues has been confined to higher levels of education. To some degree, it has been incorporated in the more innovative secondary curricula. With the notable exception of the Holt Databank Series, however, attention at the elementary level has been minimal.

Reasons for this scant attention are grounded in disputable claims. It is generally believed, for example, that children are not equipped cognitively to handle the complexity of such issues. Current research, however, suggests that we may be seriously underestimating children's cognitive capacities.[5] Moreover,

---

[5]Edward William Beaubier, "Capacity of Sixth Grade Children to Understand Social Science Generalizations," doctoral dissertation, University of California, 1962, *Dissertation Abstracts* 23:2439–2940 (January 1963); Theodore Kaltsounis, "A Study Concerning Third Graders' Knowledge of Social Studies Content Prior to Instruction," doctoral dissertation, University of Illinois, 1961, *Dissertation Abstracts* 22:1528–1529 (November 1961); Betty Lucille Lowry, "A Survey of the Knowledge of Social Studies Concepts Possessed by Second Grade Children Previous to the Time These Concepts Are Taught in the Social Studies Lessons," doctoral dissertation, State University of Iowa, 1963, *Dissertation Abstracts* 24:2324–2325 (December 1963); Kenneth Orville Penner, "A Study of Fourth Grade Children's Knowledge of Selected Social Studies Concepts Prior to Instruction," doctoral dissertation, Colorado State College, 1967, *Dissertation Abstracts* 28:403A (August 1967).

as Jerome Bruner noted some time ago: ". . . any subject can be taught effectively in some intellectually honest form to any child at any stage of development. . . . No evidence exists to contradict it; considerable evidence is being amassed that supports it."[6] It is also generally assumed that it is in the child's interest to be spared the harsh realities of the real world for as long as possible. To suppose, however, that children are unacquainted with violence, conflict, poverty, and war, for example, is to seriously misunderstood the nature of the child's world. Indeed, there may be reason to believe that realistic encounters with these conditions may help remove shadowy anxieties and fears. Finally, schools in general, and elementary schools in particular, have sought to avoid controversy—an integral part of the study of social issues. Intimidated by assumed and magnified threats, the teaching profession, particularly at the elementary level, voluntarily chooses the safe over the significant.

Perhaps the most compelling reason for the early introduction of social issues is their inevitable influence on basic social attitudes. Evidence suggests that children develop attitudinal postures quite early in life. While many factors influence these postures, cognition plays an important part. In depriving children of knowledge of social issues, we do not fail to contribute to the formulation of values regarding these issues. Instead, we help produce an *inadequate* formulation based on insufficient information.

A peaceful future community requires the solution of the broad social problems that threaten human life. High-level cognitive skills and appropriate attitudes are essential. The elementary school has an important contribution to make toward their development.

Social Issues as Controversy

In a study of the practices and attitudes of American teachers, Harmon Zeigler concluded that the classroom is the very last place controversial issues are discussed.[7] Most American teachers tend toward conformity in their practices. Contrary to popular opinion, however, Zeigler found that it was *not* the community at large that served as the basic inhibiting force. Rather, a strategy of accommodation to *anticipated* trouble kept school functionaries notably silent. In other words, it is frequently the fear of consequences rather than realistic pressures that may keep controversy out of the schools.

This is not to deny that attacks from the public are sometimes real and threatening enough. As social studies texts and strategies continue to promote genuine inquiry, we can expect public reaction to become increasingly suspicious, if not angry. However, certain factors augur well for beleaguered teachers.

Official educational organizations strongly support the notion of academic freedom on all levels of the educational structure. The Board of Directors of the National Council for the Social Studies, for example, adopted a "Position Statement" in 1974 that reads (in part) as follows:

[6]Jerome Bruner, *The Process of Education* (Cambridge, Mass.: Harvard University Press, 1960), p. 30.
[7]Harmon Zeigler, *The Political Life of American Teachers* (Englewood Cliffs, N.J.: Prentice-Hall, 1967).

Basic to a democratic society are the freedoms of teachers to teach and of students to learn. . . .

A teacher's freedom to teach involves both the right *and* the responsibility to use the highest intellectual standards in studying, investigating, presenting, interpreting, and discussing facts and ideas relevant to his or her field of professional competence. As professionals, teachers must be free to examine controversial issues openly in the classroom. The right to do so is based on the democratic commitment to open inquiry and on the importance to decision-making of the expression of opposing informed views and the free examination of ideas. The teacher is professionally obligated to maintain a spirit of free inquiry, open-mindedness, and impartiality in the classroom.[8]

The courts have supported both teacher and student rights fairly consistently in recent years.[9] The National Council for the Social Studies, the American Civil Liberties Union, and other professional groups will frequently provide funds when teachers are caught in litigation. The Meiklejohn Civil Liberties Institute at Berkeley can help with research facilities and practical advice when teachers, administrators, or students are threatened by attacks on their civil liberties.

---

[8]"National Council for the Social Studies Position Statement on the Freedom to Teach and the Freedom to Learn." Approved by the NCSS Board of Directors in 1974. *Social Education* 339:1 (April 1975) p. 240.

[9]See David Rubin, *The Rights of Teachers: An American Civil Liberties Union Handbook* (New York: Richard W. Baron, 1973) for a layman's summary of recent court decisions and *Social Education* 39:4 (April 1975) for a good overview of the entire subject.

Teachers should be aware of these sources of help so that if a forceful stand is necessary, they will feel neither isolated nor helpless. Fortunately, most issues presented in a genuine inquiry manner can be discussed in the classroom without repercussions. The strategy in Chart 5–1 is suggested for teachers who discuss controversial issues in the classroom:

Objectives of the Study of Social Issues

The broad objectives of the study of social issues should include at least:

1. *Recognition of their global impact.* Students need to become aware of the interdependence of all societies in the solution of universal human problems.
2. *Developing cognitive and affective competencies required for their resolution.* Mere "good will" will not suffice. Rational skills based on knowledge tempered by humane considerations are essential.
3. *Increasing sensitivity to their accompanying conditions via moral development.* Students need to become aware of questions of justice and equity.
4. *Developing the desire to solve them.* Students should be moved to want solutions to these problems.
5. *Increasing feelings of potency regarding our abilities to solve them.* All studies of social issues should deal with realistic programs for improvement based on past and present successes, as well as the anticipation of future achievements. Students should come to view themselves as potent agents of change.

The last point, in particular, needs emphasis. Disillusioned and weary adults frequently impose on youth a sense of despair and futility. "Shock" literature, designed to awaken a slumbering population, stresses "gloom and doom" data. Successes receive little, if any, attention. This approach tends to lead to the self-fulfilling prophecy—the consistent prediction of dire consequences leads individuals to behave in ways that ensure them. Achievements must be included in any program based on social issues. Feelings of faith regarding our abilities to solve problems need to be encouraged, and students should be invited to explore and implement changes of their own through actual participation in their communities.

The Nature of Social Issues

What, then, is a social issue? The criteria would seem to include the following:

1. *A social issue affects large portions of the population.* Human problems are considered social issues only when they involve great numbers of people. A personal concern, however, may be a microscopic reflection of a broader problem. Whether or not a family should move to a large city so that the breadwinner may get a higher-paying job appears at first blush a personal concern. Since it is related to the general problems of urbanization, it has social significance.
2. *A social issue is an unresolved and controversial problem.* A social issue is controversial because it is based on divergent knowledge and value claims. For example, the cultivation of group identity may be regarded as beneficial

---

Chart 5–1
A Strategy for Teaching Controversial Issues

---

1. Identify the issue.
2. Identify the many points of view.
   A. What are the factual claims of each side?

   What facts are included? Omitted? How accurate are they? How do they compare with each other? Is the source for the fact identified? Is the source reliable? Can the facts be checked?

   B. What are the value claims of each side?

   How are they similar? How are they different? How do they compare with students' points of view?

3. Check the arguments for their logic.
   A. Do they include any of the following?
      1. Unwarranted generalizations
      2. Unwarranted assumptions
      3. Use of emotional words or name-calling
      4. Exaggerations
      5. Stereotyping
      6. Quotes out of context
      7. Attacks on personalities and motives
      8. Inconsistencies
      9. Unwarranted conclusions
      10. Predictions projected as facts
4. Encourage value clarification.
5. Encourage the formulation of tentative conclusions until more information is in.

---

for purposes of personal well-being and political power. Conversely, it can be accompanied by ethnocentrism and a failure to acknowledge generalized human problems. For some, the value of the former outweighs the latter, while for others it is the reverse.

3. *A social issue is characterized by behaviors and conditions that are judged morally wrong by considerable numbers of the population.* Poverty, pollution, and crime are considered immoral conditions—they offend basic values. The definition of what is "immoral" changes with time, however. War, for example, is becoming increasingly identified as an immoral condition by a large percentage of the population, whereas in the past it was frequently regarded as not only necessary but even useful in building national character.

4. *A social issue is characterized by the belief that the accompanying immoral conditions can be changed.* It is generally believed, for example, that human existence does not require poverty, pollution, or crime. Such conditions are considered amenable to change. On the other hand, death at a ripe old age is not a social issue for it is believed to be inherent in the nature of things.

Social issues cover an extremely wide range of subjects—and they are not necessarily always the ones that are written about in the daily newspapers. Examples of broad social issues that meet the above criteria include: the unequal distribution of resources; the development and control of technology; the balancing of individual, group, national, and international needs; the provision of channels for constructive conflict and the avoidance of war; the reconciling of rationalism with humanism.

Teaching Social Issues

The five examples of social issues given above range from the relatively well recognized to the relatively obscure. For example, world famine and minority concerns have received considerable press attention, highlighting the unequal distribution of resources. Pollution and the depletion of oil reserves—two consequences of technological development—have also received considerable public attention. Not quite so obvious, but no less critical, are the problems that accompany rationally organized societies in which big and centralized structures emphasize efficiency at the expense of individual emotional needs. While an increasing number of people are articulating the need for individual and group identity, relatively few are emphasizing the equally urgent need for global identification if we are to survive on this planet. Finally, the need to eliminate war in a nuclear age is recognized by many, but knowledge of alternative ways of coping with conflict is not widespread.

Despite their complexity, these issues can be effectively taught in the elementary classroom. The following pages elaborate somewhat on each of these topics, suggesting major concepts that can serve as the organizing bases for teaching each, and giving illustrative classroom activities that can help develop them in primary as well as upper elementary grades. Each section concludes with a short list of recommended readings for further teacher information.

One: The Unequal Distribution of Resources

The unequal distribution of the world's resources is a major contemporary problem. Disparities between the "haves" and "have nots" have probably existed since the dawn of human society. What distinguishes the condition today is the growing sentiment that it is basically an immoral condition. It is becoming increasingly unpopular to maintain that the poor deserve to be poor.

The most obvious disparities are based on differences of color, ethnic background, religion, and sex. Groups singled out because of such differences have a disproportionately smaller access to economic resources, education, political power, and leisure. Less obvious are the inequalities suffered by the mentally ill, migrant workers, marginal employees harnessed to dull and routine jobs, abused children, and the aged. Native and black Americans, Puerto Ricans, Chicanos, and 18 million poor whites are among those who suffer particularly in this country. A broader view of the problem reveals that disadvantaged groups

---

Organizing Concepts

The following concepts can be used to organize units of study concerned with the issue of the unequal distribution of resources.

Anthropology
  culture
  socialization
  family
  culture contact

Economics
  scarcity
  poverty
  technology
  goods and services
  labor
  exchange

Geography
  strategic resources
  settlement patterns
  spatial interaction
  population
    characteristics

History
  specific events in time
  change over time
  multiple causation

Political Science
  power
  authority
  law
  rights
  change strategies

Psychology
  needs
  values
  wants
  relative deprivation

Sociology
  social groups
  social relationships
  stratification
  racism
  sexism

---

include the majority of the world's population.

The unequal distribution of resources is not merely a matter of groups, however. Nations also show sharp disparities. North America is the richest region of the world, with a gross national product per capita in 1970 of $4,760. Averages for Latin America, the Near and Far East, Africa, and South Asia for that same year ranged from a mere $510 to an unbelievably low $103.[10] The rich nations of the world consume a grossly disproportionate percentage of the world's energy resources and food, and the gap between poor and rich continues to widen.

Whatever the causes—and explanations vary—these disparities encourage a worldwide ferment from which no nation can escape. Domestic and international violence continues to grow, and the rising expectations of the poor are generally acknowledged as a contributing factor. Genuine reforms of a global nature are clearly called for, and efforts of enlightened national leaders need to be encouraged by a knowledgeable and cooperative citizenry. In addition, individuals have a genuinely important role to play in their own communities and social groups.

[10]Jacqueline R. Kasun, "United States Poverty in World Perspective," *Current History* 64:382 (June 1973), pp. 248–49.

Classroom
Activities

The following activities are representative of only some of the learning experiences that can help develop the concept of inequality.

Primary Grades

Children may be helped to learn the significance of unequal distribution of resources through an experiment in their own classroom. After leading a discussion about the learning resources available to all children in your classroom, you might pose the question, "What would happen if half of the class had books, paper, and pencils, and the other half did not?" Help the children develop hypotheses about what might happen. Then have them set up an experiment to test their hypotheses. Perhaps you could actually have half the class attempt to work without the proper materials. In a culminating discussion, children should be encouraged to generalize their understandings from this experience to other examples of unequal distribution of resources. You might build a file of pictures to help them visualize instances of this phenomenon. Such a file might include a classroom in an underdeveloped nation, an inner-city school, an affluent suburban school, children who must work in the family garden rather than go to school, and a child with a private tutor.

There are many opportunities for children to experience and examine examples of unequal distribution of resources in family life. In a class discussion, raise the following question: "Does everyone in your family eat the same amount of food or have the same amount of money to spend?" In attempting to answer this question, they will need to collect, organize, and analyze pertinent data. Questions of value are bound to arise as children ask whether everyone in the family actually needs the same amount of food or should spend the same amount of money. Perhaps they could then begin distinguishing between those resources that should be equally available to all and those that should be available on the basis of need. Their inquiry into this question probably would lead them into comparisons between families with different standards of living and different life-styles. They should also be encouraged to examine resources and conditions that are nonmaterial, such as health care, love, travel opportunities, and a variety of culturally enriching experiences.

Through the use of pictures, films, stories, or news items, help the children become aware of the unequal distribution of food and clothing among various culture groups in the world. They might be asked to compare what they eat in one day to what a child in a rural, impoverished village of Southeast Asia eats. Have them make charts or graphs to record and interpret their information. If some of the foods typically eaten by impoverished children are available, perhaps the students could try living for a day or two on the amount consumed by those children to gain some firsthand knowledge of this type of inequity. After this experience, the children might develop enough empathy to do something about some of the starving children of the world. They could, for example, contribute money from their allowances to CARE or to one of the organizations that distributes food to hungry people in this country or overseas.

Upper Elementary Grades

Children sometimes fantasize about what they would do if they had a million dollars. They often find it difficult to list all the things they would buy, because the things they really need and want don't cost very much. But there are many people in this country and many more in most other countries who do not have enough money for the things they really need. Have the students make a list of the necessities their family buys each year and the approximate cost. Then compare the average income of families in this country with those in a number of other countries. Further discussion could center around what kind of life the students would have if their family income was drastically reduced, and what could or should be done about such enormous inequities in standards of living.

As you study the history and geography of the United States, differences in the distribution of various resources among the states become apparent. Students can be led into an investigation of these differences and their effects on the ability of states to provide comparable services to their citizens. Make charts and graphs to depict this information. Have students discuss what might be done to equalize these differences if they think they are unfair.

There are large discrepancies among nations in regard to the natural and human resources available to them. Have the students compare three or four nations in this respect and have them hypothesize what would happen if one of the more wealthy nations lost a major natural resource and what would happen if one of the poorer nations gained a major new resource (oil, for example). Have students search for actual examples of these kinds of changes in history. Encourage students to carry on discussions or a mock U.N. debate concerning the unequal distribution of resources among nations. Historically, what methods have nations used to try to correct these inequities? What tactics are some of the national, racial, ethnic, and other minority groups adopting today to improve their access to available resources?

Reading Resources for Teachers

Acuña, Rodolfo. *Occupied America: The Chicano's Struggle Toward Liberation.* San Francisco: Canfield Press, 1972.

Amundsen, Kirsten. *The Silenced Majority: Women and American Democracy.* Englewood Cliffs, N.J.: Prentice-Hall, 1971.

Banks, James, ed. *Teaching Ethnic Studies: Concepts and Strategies.* Forty-third Yearbook, National Council for the Social Studies, 1973.

Burma, John H., ed. *Mexican-Americans in the United States: A Reader.* San Francisco: Canfield Press, 1970.

Cavanah, Frances. *Our Country's Freedom.* Skokie, Ill.: Rand McNally, 1966.

Daniels, Roger, and Harry H. L. Kitano. *American Racism: Exploration of the Nature of Prejudice.* Englewood Cliffs, N.J.: Prentice-Hall, 1970.

Fanon, Frantz. *The Wretched of the Earth.* New York: Grove Press, 1963.

Fellows, Donald Keith. *A Mosaic of America's Ethnic Minorities.* New York: John Wiley & Sons, 1972.

Hamilton, David Boyce. *A Primer on the Economics of Poverty.* New York: Random House, 1968.

Lewis, Oscar. *A Death in the Sanchez Family*. New York: Random House, 1969.

Manhood, Wayne. "The Plight of the Migrant." *Social Education* 37:8 (December 1973) pp. 738–50.

May, Edgar. *The Wasted Americans: Cost of Our Welfare Dilemma*. New York: Harper & Row, 1964.

Myrdal, Gunnar. *The Challenge of World Poverty*. New York: Pantheon, 1970.

Pincus, John A., ed. *Reshaping the World Economy: Rich Countries and Poor*. Englewood Cliffs, N.J.: Prentice-Hall, 1968.

Ross, Arthur M., and Herbert Hill, eds. *Employment, Race and Poverty*. New York: Harcourt Brace Jovanovich, 1967.

Sagarin, Edward, ed. *The Other Minorities*. Waltham, Mass.: Ginn and Co., 1971.

Schusky, Ernest. *The Right to Be Indians*. San Francisco: The Indian Historian Press, 1970.

Sullerot, Evelyne. *Woman, Society and Change*. New York: McGraw-Hill, 1973.

Wax, Murray. *Indian Americans: Unity and Diversity*. Englewood Cliffs, N.J.: Prentice-Hall, 1971.

Will, Robert E., and Harold G. Vatter, eds. *Poverty in Affluence*. 2nd ed. New York: Harcourt Brace Jovanovich, 1970.

Two: Developing and Controlling Technology

Accelerated technological advances have resulted in, among other things, extensive population upheavals, vast pollution, the creation of weapons of holocaustal dimensions, and the emergence of "mass man." On the other hand, technology has made a higher standard of living possible for millions, including broadened educational, aesthetic, and recreational opportunities. How to encourage more of the latter and less of the former is a central issue of our times.

Deforestation; water, air, and food contamination; urban sprawl and rural neglect are problems throughout the world. Unwilling to accommodate to the realities of finite resources, societies have allowed and even encouraged their profligate extraction and use. The energy crisis is but its current manifestation. Unrestrained and exploding population growth promises still greater abuse of the already overtaxed environment. Recently, however, some societies have begun to take the issue of environmental abuse seriously. Sea life again flourishes in the once "dead" Thames, and air pollution in Pittsburgh has declined. Other success stories attest to our ability to solve the problems if we so desire.

Equally important are the effects of technology on the quality of human relationships. Unprepared cultural groups and nations, plunged into modernity, find their traditions threatened and their ecological niches destroyed. These groups are also often the most resistant to international efforts to solve the mutual problems wrought by technological advances. Mere rhetoric on the part of the more modern nations will not be sufficient to convince them that their best interests are involved. Rational, cooperative planning on national and international levels must replace antiquated habits of rivalry and competition if we are to keep from destroying ourselves.

Classroom Activities

The following are representative activities that can be encouraged in the classroom to illustrate the importance of technology in our lives and the problems it may produce.

Organizing Concepts

The following concepts can be used to organize units of study concerned with the issue of technology.

Anthropology
  culture
  culture contact
  cultural similarities
  cultural differences
  ecological niche

Economics
  capitalism
  communism
  socialism
  division of labor
  growth and develop-
    ment
  human resources:
    labor, skills, and
    knowledge

Geography
  resource contami-
    nation
  nonrenewable
    resources
  critical resources
  interdependence
  the earth as an
    ecosystem

History
  specific historical
    events
    (e.g., contact be-
    tween North Ameri-
    can Indians and Eu-
    ropeans, immigrant
    groups, blacks)
  change over time

Political Science
  power
  nationalism
  internationalism
  transnationalism
  negotiation
  laws

Psychology
  attitudes and values
  drives
  needs
  norms
  wants
  conflict
  cooperation

Sociology
  social systems
  educational insti-
    tutions
  religious institutions
  economic institutions
  stability
  change

Primary Grades

In order to help students develop an understanding of the significance of electricity in their lives, have them collect from newspapers, magazines, and advertising materials pictures of all the kinds of electrical appliances and uses they are familiar with. They might organize their pictures in a variety of ways: paste them on a floor plan of a house or school or on charts that show which are used most or least, how much each costs to buy, how much electricity each uses, or their dates of invention. The various sources of electricity and ways of transmitting it may also be explored. Have the students rank several of the more common electrical devices on a scale from most important or useful to least

important or useful. Have them discuss how life would be better or worse (or different) if we did not have certain electrical devices.

The influence of the gasoline engine in our lives would be another investigation that could help young children develop an understanding of technology and its potential benefits and detriments to human life.

A study of modern food technology and the food industry might be initiated by having the students bring in all sorts of food containers, packages, and labels. As they begin reading the labels they will encounter much information, some of it puzzling or incomprehensible, about nutritional values, additives, and preservatives. Through reading about life in the past or talking to senior citizens, they can compare the foods available to us today with those available twenty-five, fifty, or a hundred years ago. Many questions can be raised and discussed concerning the wholesomeness of highly refined and processed foods compared with so-called natural or organic foods.

Upper Elementary Grades

The consumption of energy in this country has risen enormously over the past thirty years. The parents of most children today can probably recall how much lower energy use was when they themselves were children.

1. Have the students list all energy-consuming devices used by their families. Have them ask their parents to help them make a similar list for a family of twenty-five to forty years ago.
2. As a class project, make a chart that shows the energy input for each energy-consuming device.
3. Make graphs to compare energy use today with energy use in the past by typical families.
4. Compare the population in our country today with the population twenty-five to forty years ago. Develop a graph or chart that shows an approximate increase in energy consumption by families over the past twenty-five to forty years.
5. Raise these questions: Where is all this energy coming from? How much more can our energy consumption increase? Is there any limit to the supply of energy? What effect does this enormous increase of energy consumption have on our way of life? On our environment? On the other nations and peoples of the world? What are some ways we can get more energy without damaging the environment? How can we drastically reduce our consumption of energy?

The age of computers is upon us, and all of us are affected in many ways—some obvious, others very subtle. Modern computers can do mathematical calculations in a few seconds that would take humans years to complete. Our phenomenal space-exploration program would not have been possible without the use of computers to design, test, launch, and control rockets and satellites and to interpret data transmitted back to earth from space. Help the students become aware of the benefits and potential dangers of computers by doing some of the following activities.

1. Secure a pocket-sized electronic calculator and teach a few students how to use it. Select a group of able math students and have them race one of the skilled electronic "computer" users in the completion of several difficult math problems. Compare speed, efficiency, and mental burden.
2. List as many ways as the class can think of that computers directly affect our lives.
3. Raise such questions as: Do computers put people out of work? Do computers think for themselves? Who controls computers? Do computers control us? What might our government do to insure that computers work for the benefit of all people? What might we as individuals do to prevent computers from having too much influence or control over our lives?
4. Ask students to write imaginary stories about the uses of computers in the year 2000.

Reading Resources for Teachers

Aids to Environmental Education. Environmental Education, Office of Education, Washington, D.C.

Callahan, Daniel. *Ethics and Population Limitation.* New York: The Population Council, 1971.

Castel, Hélène. *World Development: An Introductory Reader.* New York: Macmillan, 1971.

Chase, Stuart. *The Most Probable World.* New York: Harper & Row, 1968.

Dasmann, Raymond F. *Environmental Conservation.* 3d ed. New York: John Wiley & Sons, 1972.

Ehrlich, Paul R. *The Population Bomb.* New York: Ballantine, 1968.

Ehrlich, Paul R., and Anne H. Ehrlich. *Population, Resources, Environment: Issues in Human Ecology.* 2nd ed. San Francisco: W. H. Freeman and Co., 1972.

Ferkiss, Victor. *Technological Man: The Myth and the Reality.* New York: Braziller, 1969.

Friedland, William, and Dorothy Nelkin. *Migrant Agricultural Workers in America's Northeast.* New York: Holt, Rinehart and Winston, 1971.

Graham, Frank, Jr. *Since Silent Spring.* Boston: Houghton Mifflin, 1970.

Hays, Samuel P. *The Response to Industrialism.* Chicago: University of Chicago Press, 1957.

Idyll, Clarence P. *The Sea Against Hunger.* New York: Thomas Y. Crowell Co., 1970.

Marine, Gene. *America the Raped: The Engineering Mentality and the Devastation of a Continent.* New York: Simon & Schuster, 1969.

Petersen, William. *Population.* New York: Macmillan, 1969.

Rushdoony, Haig A. "Population Growth and the Six-Year-Old." *Journal of Geography,* Vol. 66–67 (September 1968), pp. 367–73.

Servan-Schreiber, Jean-Jacques. *The American Challenge.* New York: Atheneum, 1968.

Terry, Mark. *Teaching for Survival: A Handbook for Environmental Education.* New York: Friends of the Earth/Ballantine Books, 1971.

Vernon, Raymond. *Sovereignty at Bay: The Multinational Spread of U.S. Enterprises.* New York: Basic Books, 1971.

Three: Balancing Everyone's Needs

Both democratic and communistic ideologists supposed that the group distinctions that divide human beings would eventually disappear. Reality, however, has sabotaged this belief. Ethnic, religious, national, and a host of other groupings continue to be the rule all over the world.

Group ties can provide a sense of pride and self-esteem that is essential to human beings—especially so to those groups that have been systematically robbed of these attributes. But they can also be parochial, ethnocentric, and oppressive. Being "white" is clearly not always the equivalent of being right, any more than being "black," "red," or "yellow" is. Where emphasis on group differences dominates and exclusive loyalties are demanded, human communalities dim. A central issue of our time is how to reconcile the need for group ties with the need for global cooperation.

Contrary to popular belief, the assumption of a global identity does not require the abdication of group ties. It does, however, require the assumption of *multiple identities.*

Any human being is simultaneously an individual and a member of many social groups—which may include, among others, a family, a church, an occupational group, an ethnic or regional group, and a country. Multiple group memberships frequently result in conflicting loyalties: a commitment to one's occupation may require spending less time with one's family, a black woman may find herself torn between loyalties to both her race and her sex. Out of such competing loyalties individuals can come to understand others' needs, and exclusivity becomes increasingly difficult to demand. The assumption of multiple identities needs to be encouraged through study and through contact with members of many different groups.

The assumption of multiple identities needs also to be encouraged on the level of the nation-state, if for no other reasons than pragmatic concerns. Generally accepted as the ultimate legal and moral sovereign group, rightfully entitled to ultimate loyalties, the nation-state is nevertheless affected by global realities. Environmental pollution recognizes no borders as it spreads unimpeded from the shores of one nation to another. A small group of oil monopolists in the Middle East can bankrupt all of Europe and Japan. A miscalculation on the part of some small and weak far-off nation may involve us all in a nuclear holocaust. Anyone who is a citizen of a nation-state is, willingly or not, simultaneously a member of the world—and it is this recognition that may yet save us all.

Organizing Concepts

The following concepts can be used to organize units of study concerned with the issue of balancing needs.

Anthropology
  kinship
  group identity
  multiple identities
  cultural similarities
  cultural differences
  national culture
  global culture
  ethnic groups
Economics
  scarcity
  supply and demand
  opportunity cost
  trade
  monopolies
  multinational corporations
  labor
  producer

Geography
  resources
  spatial interaction
  regions
  rural areas
  suburbs
  central cities
History
  specific events in time
  change over time
Political Science
  power
  authority
  representation
  welfare
  rights
  patriotism
  the nation-state
  international relations
  public opinion

Psychology
  aggression
  personal identity
  love
  needs
Sociology
  amalgamation
  the "melting pot"
  assimilation
  integration
  pluralism
  colonization
  ethnocentrism

Classroom
Activities

The following are representative activities that can be encouraged in the classroom to make students more aware of the many, often complex, relationships they have with others.

Primary Grades

Within each classroom there exist many groups of children, in which memberships often overlap. Each child is a member of several groups. In some instances, belonging to a particular group enhances one's individuality; in others, it may actually make one much less of an individual. The students can explore some of these concepts and their implications through a variety of activities.

1. Have the students form groups based on such things as sex, age, or height. Have them discuss how they know which of these groups they belong in and whether these divisions are important or not.
2. Designate more ambiguous types of groups such as good students and less able students, fast runners and slow runners, rich students and poor students. Have the students discuss how they know which group they belong to and whether these divisions are important or not. Also, what problems did they have trying to decide which group to join?
3. Have the students choose between groups that have overlapping memberships. For example, have each child join one of the following groups: boys, girls, good readers, good runners, and those who like school. Ask them to discuss how and why they made their choice.
4. Have the students suggest as many groupings as they can think of that their class can be divided into. Make diagrams to show how a person can belong to more than one group at a time.
5. After the students have participated in some of these activities, have them discuss why people choose to belong to certain groups, clubs, or organizations, what they gain and/or give up by becoming members, and how conflicts arise between such groups.

Members of a family can simultaneously belong to several groups. Help your students explore this phenomenon by doing some of the following activities.

1. Have each student make a chart for his or her family showing the members of the family and groups each belongs to (Boy Scouts, church choir, bowling team, etc.) Discuss reasons for joining these groups. Does belonging to each group help one be a better person? Does one's membership in each group help other people?
2. Have each child make a list of the more abstract kinds of groups his or her family is a member of—racial, ethnic, religious, occupational, educational, and so forth. Discuss how belonging to any of these groups affects their lives, and how other people behave toward them because of their group ties.
3. Collect pictures of all kinds of people and make charts or collages to show these people in a variety of groupings. Have the students discuss how they decided which group to put each picture in.

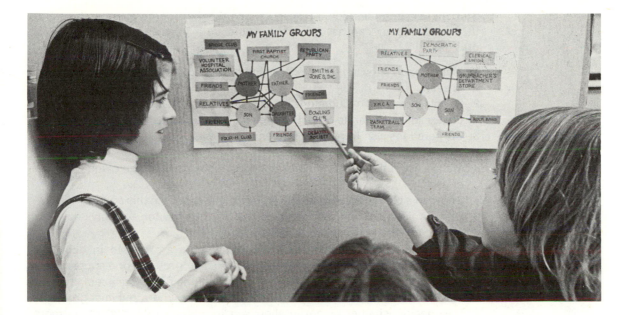

Upper Elementary Grades

Each community has several groups, organizations, clubs, political factions, and so on, that form an important part of that community's social, political, and economic structure. Much of this structure can be recognized through careful reading of the local newspaper. Bring in several issues of the paper and have students do some of the following activities.

1. Cut out all articles, announcements, and advertisements that refer to one or more community groups or organizations. Develop a system for organizing or categorizing these items.
2. Make a list of the names of people who appear in the paper in connection with a particular group, activity, or problem.
3. Find articles that describe problems or issues between two or more local groups and categorize them as political, social, economic, and so on. Develop role-playing or simulation activities that will involve the students in the decision-making process.
4. Discuss the conflicts individuals in a community face when groups they belong to have opposing values or advocate courses of action with which those individuals disagree.
5. Find and discuss examples of conflict that were resolved by peaceful, legal, or other reasonable means.

Many of the laws of our nation are the result of the influence of individuals and groups on members of Congress and the Administration. Almanacs are a convenient source of information about the names and sizes of these groups.

Student research can identify those groups that have large memberships and that consequently can have a strong influence if they are organized for that purpose.

1. Make a chart showing the major occupational groups and numbers of people in each.
2. People in various occupations usually belong to unions, associations, or societies. Make a chart to show the largest of these groups.
3. Corporations also have great influence in our country. List some of them by size of sales or capital investment.
4. Make a list of the major religious denominations and the size of membership of each.
5. Show on a chart the major ethnic and/or racial groups in this country.
6. Discuss potential and real conflicts that might arise for an individual who belongs to more than one of these groups.
7. Develop simulation activities in which students are placed in decision-making positions and must represent a particular group. (For example, have students assume the roles of representatives of the basketball team, the student body, the teachers' association, the parents, and a feminist group, as they decide whether or not to allow weaker players to participate in more games.)

Reading Resources for Teachers

Banks, James A., and Jean D. Grambs. *Black Self-Concept: Implications for Education and Social Science.* New York: McGraw-Hill, 1972.

Carmichael, Stokely, and Charles Hamilton. *Black Power: The Politics of Liberation in America.* New York: Random House, 1967.

Duran, Livie Isauro, and H. Russell Bernard, eds. *Introduction to Chicano Studies.* New York: Macmillan, 1973.

Greenstein, Fred I. *Children and Politics.* New Haven, Conn.: Yale University Press, 1965.

Hines, Paul D., and Leslie Wood. *A Guide to Human Rights Education.* Washington, D.C.: National Council for the Social Studies, 1969.

Latané, Bibb, and John M. Darley. *The Unresponsive Bystander: Why Doesn't He Help?* New York: Appleton-Century-Crofts, 1970.

Ludwig, Edward G. "The Perils of Group Identity," *The Crisis,* Vol. 78 (March 1971), pp. 53–56.

Manning, Charles. *The Nature of International Society.* New York: John Wiley & Sons, 1962.

McNickle, D'Arcy. *Native American Tribalism: Indian Survivals and Renewals.* New York: Oxford University Press, 1973.

Young, Whitney M., Jr. *Beyond Racism: Building an Open Society.* New York: McGraw-Hill, 1969.

**Four:
Conflict and War**

Rather than being undesirable, social conflict may actually be beneficial. As Georg Simmel pointed out more than fifty years ago, conflict is a way of rebel-

---

[11]Georg Simmel, *Conflict,* trans. by Kurt H. Wolff (Glencoe, Ill.: The Free Press, 1955) pp. 17–18.

ling against "tyranny, arbitrariness, moodiness and tactlessness."[11] Lewis Coser says it actually helps groups maintain relationships by "clearing the air."[12] It is not only useful as a means for expressing unpopular and dissenting views and keeping groups together, but perhaps most importantly, it serves to promote needed changes. A world without conflict might simply perpetuate the status quo.

The ultimate methods for resolving conflicts are violence and war. Short of these methods, however, there are many other ways of resolving conflict. Accommodation, negotiation, and bargaining are well-known strategies for the resolution of conflict situations without violence. Even when people, institutions, or nations strive openly to achieve the same goal and resist pressures to accommodate—as they do in a competitive situation—violence can be avoided. Eugene Sharp has identified 197 techniques whereby even acute conflict with overwhelmingly powerful forces may be resolved short of violence.[13] These alternatives must be given fuller consideration in view of the current potential for destruction.

In part at least, alternatives to war are not considered because people tend to regard it as inevitable. This attitude is apparently learned at a very early age. One study reports that out of a sample of third- and fourth-grade American children, only seven percent believed there would be no war when they grew up.[14] Adults tend to believe that "wars have always existed and always will exist." They attribute the cause to some basic flaw in human nature.

How realistic is this assessment? While it is difficult to deny the existence of human aggression, most anthropologists and psychologists do not believe that it must ultimately result in violence. Even Konrad Lorenz, who believes that man finds violence pleasurable, believes that feelings can be channeled into peaceful behaviors.[15] Some people believe that social structures that promote inequities will have to be radically altered before wars cease. But few social scientists accept the view that wars are inevitable. While they may advance different explanations and solutions, most agree that wars can be avoided.

What can schools contribute toward this end? They can help young people examine basic attitudes about conflict and war and expose them to the knowledge of war that social scientists have. They can make students aware of the many ways of resolving conflict short of violence. Perhaps most importantly, they can help young people come to believe in the possibility of a world without war and provide some realistic appraisal of how this might occur.

Classroom Activities   The following are representative activities that can be encouraged in the classroom to illustrate the nature of conflict and ways to resolve it.

[12]Lewis A. Coser, *The Functions of Social Conflict* (Glencoe, Ill.: The Free Press, 1956), p. 47.
[13]Eugene Sharp, *The Politics of Nonviolent Action* (Philadelphia: Pilgrim Press, 1971).
[14]Howard Tolley Jr., *Children and War* (New York: Teachers College Press, 1973), p. 39.
[15]Konrad Lorenz, *On Aggression* (New York: Harcourt Brace Jovanovich, 1966), chapter 14.

Organizing Concepts

The following concepts can be used to organize units of study concerned with the issue of conflict and war.

Anthropology
  evolution
  cultural similarities
  cultural differences
  culture contact

Economics
  competition
  equitability
  trade
  negotiation
  global economic
    concerns

Geography
  resources
  interdependence
  interaction
  settlement patterns
  site and place

History
  specific events in time
  changes over time

Political Science
  power
  authority
  leadership
  citizenship
  national and inter-
    national political
    institutions
  sovereignty
  law
  justice
  political attitudes

Psychology
  aggression
  sublimation
  dehumanization
  scapegoating
  alienation
  perception
  projection
  conflict

Sociology
  conflict resolution
    strategies
  dissent
  passive resistance
  war
  cooperation

Primary Grades

Children in their homes, neighborhoods, and schools typically face conflicts with other persons many times every day. Cooperation is also one of their regular experiences, yet much more attention is given to the conflict situations, especially in the newspapers and on television. Any examination of the conflicts people face might well be complemented, then, by an equally thorough look at how people cooperate to make a better life for everyone.

1. Make a bulletin board display or collage to illustrate examples of conflict and cooperation.
2. Make a picture display with captions to illustrate why people get into conflicts with one another.
3. Make a picture display with captions to illustrate why people work cooperatively to accomplish common goals.
4. Develop several role-playing episodes in which children act out possible resolutions to a conflict situation; for example, a situation in which John and

Jim, two brothers, want to watch different television programs at the same time when only one set is available, or a situation in which twenty sets of crayons must be distributed among thirty students.

5. Role-play episodes in which potential conflicts can be avoided through co-operative efforts.
6. Utilize pictures and discussion to help the students learn such concepts as competition, interdependence, interaction, negotiation, power, leadership, scapegoating, and cultural differences.

Conflict among children in the classroom and on the playground is a common occurrence in the typical elementary school. The classroom, therefore, can become a social science laboratory for the study of conflict and its resolution. Rather than approach this as a special topic to be investigated for a limited time, the study of conflict in the classroom might become a continuous process throughout the school year. Initiate the study on some occasion when a conflict arises that involves a large portion of the class, as when a group of students complains about "unfair" use of the playground equipment by other classes or about specific school rules. Suggest that this problem be studied as social scientists might approach it, by developing a problem-solving model and applying it. Such a model might include these five questions: (1) What is the problem that

caused conflict and what are all the facts related to it? (2) What are some possible ways of solving the problem or of preventing it from occurring again? (3) How shall we decide which possible solution to try first? (4) How and when should we try out one of the possible solutions? (5) How will we know if a solution has worked or should be abandoned in favor of another solution? Some of the following activities can be carried on independently of any particular attempts to resolve a conflict.

1. Make a list of all the conflict situations that have arisen recently and add any new ones that arise. Any time the same conflict occurs again, make a tally mark after it.
2. Select the five most common or frequent conflicts from the above list after one month of tallying. Make a chart which shows how frequently each occurs, how many children are involved, how it was resolved, and whether its resolution was satisfying or acceptable to all involved.
3. Select one of the five most common or frequent conflicts and apply the problem-solving model to it. Develop at least three solution strategies. Do a series of experiments to test each solution strategy. Record the results on a chart.
4. Whenever the opportunity presents itself to have a class discussion about conflicts, raise value clarification questions so that children not only apply a scientific approach to conflict resolution, they also gain an understanding of the value differences which underlie most interpersonal and intergroup conflicts. (How do you feel about this? When did you begin to feel this way? Would you like to see the problem solved? What would you be willing to give up?)

Upper Elementary Grades

Simulation games offer excellent opportunities for exploring the problems of conflict and war. Although many games are available from commercial firms, many teachers and their classes design their own with very satisfactory results. A simulation game deals with a real-life problem in a hypothetical way. A group of decision-makers try to achieve a specific objective within a known structure of roles and rules. Given below are a few situations with potential for conflict which might be developed into simulations.

1. There is a vacant lot in the neighborhood. The owner does not care how it is used and offers to let the children decide. There are three established groups of children in the neighborhood who want to take over the development of this lot.
2. The town of Fairview is a bottleneck on a major highway. The Department of Highways has decided to eliminate the problem by building a freeway through or around the town. Groups of businessmen, civic leaders, homeowners, taxpayers, conservationsts, and others form to try to influence where the new freeway will be built.

3. The small country of Geodelphia is preparing to celebrate its hundredth anniversary of independence from a major European nation. The population of Geodelphia is 30 percent aboriginal stock, 25 percent descendants of the European mother country, and the remainder are a variety of other racial and ethnic groups. The 25 percent from the mother country dominate the country in terms of power, money, and political and social leadership. The other groups have recently been agitating for more equal participation in the affairs and benefits of their country and want this extended to the planning of the centennial celebration.

4. The nations of the world are divided into three factions: the capitalist nations, the communist bloc, and the third world—those nations that are relatively undeveloped and not aligned with either of the other blocs. A new nonpolluting energy process has been invented but can only be developed in the highly technological countries of the capitalist and communist blocs. The most essential mineral ingredient of the process, however, exists only in a few of the third-world countries, who are reluctant to part with it simply because they are suspicious of the wealthier nations. Without this mineral, the industrial-agricultural basis of the developed nations of the world will soon collapse.

Different cultures have different orientations toward conflicts, violence, cooperation, interdependence, and war. What is the modern American cultural orientation? Involve your students in a variety of activities to try to answer this question.

1. Have teams of students observe the playground and record instances of conflict and cooperation. Have them analyze and interpret their data in terms of (a) what conditions led to each instance of conflict or cooperation, (b) what values predisposed the participants to behave either aggressively or cooperatively, and (c) whether one can predict what kinds of situations will lead to violence and what kinds will result in cooperation?
2. Have teams of students interview students, teachers, parents, and others about their views on conflict and cooperation in our culture.
3. Analyze children's television shows for instances of conflict resolution. Determine a ratio between violent and peaceful means of resolving conflict. Infer what effect this might have on children who spend many hours watching these shows.
4. Make a list of the heroes of our country. Determine why they are considered heroes. Is it because they have resolved problems by peaceful, rational means, or by more aggressive or violent methods?
5. Make a chart that shows all the wars the United States has been involved in, the historical causes, and the results of each. Have the students discuss what alternatives to war existed in each case and why our country chose the alternative it did.

Reading Resources for Teachers

Barnet, Richard J. *The Economy of Death*. New York: Atheneum, 1969.

Clark, Grenville, and Louis Sohn. *World Peace Through World Law: Two Alternative Plans.* 3d ed. Cambridge, Mass.: Harvard University Press, 1966.

Coser, Lewis. *The Functions of Social Conflict*. Glencoe, Ill.: The Free Press, 1956.

Fisher, Roger. *International Conflict for Beginners.* New York: Harper & Row, 1969.

Fried, Morton; Marvin Harris; and Robert Murphy, eds. *War: The Anthropology of Armed Conflict and Aggression.* Garden City, N. Y.: The Natural History Press, 1968.

Freeman, Howard. *America's Troubles: A Casebook on Social Conflict.* 2nd ed. Englewood Cliffs, N. J.: Prentice-Hall, 1973.

Larson, Arthur, ed. *A Warless World.* New York: McGraw-Hill, 1963.

Lorenz, Konrad. *On Aggression.* New York: Harcourt Brace Jovanovich, 1966.

Nesbitt, William A. *Teaching About War and War Prevention.* New York: Foreign Policy Association, 1971.

Plano, Jack C., and Robert E. Riggs. *Forging World Order: The Politics of International Organization.* New York: Macmillan, 1967.

Sharp, Gene. *Exploring Nonviolent Alternatives.* Boston: Porter Sargent Publisher, 1970.

Five: Reconciling Rationality with Humanism

The growth of bureaucracies all over the world has been a rational response to social necessities. Large governments, school systems, social service agencies, and businesses can offer a centralized planning and administrative apparatus, capable of servicing mass populations in a highly efficient and impartial manner. But the bureaucratic structure also imposes anonymity and impersonality, with no attention to individual needs that deviate from the norm. Apathy, alienation, irresponsibility, and a general sense of impotence frequently characterize both employees and clients.

However well intentioned, rationally planned change can cause severe hardships. Ecological niches may be destroyed, life-styles disrupted, and social relationships permanently damaged, resulting in increased physical and mental disease. Its effects may be seen in the rural families who become urban slum dwellers throughout the world, displaced by the mechanization of agriculture. Without such changes, however, inequities may remain unchallenged and new problems arise. But the question of whether to change or not to change is a pointless one—change is inevitable. The problem is to direct it in ways that will serve rational and humane ends.

Adequate planning for change needs to include attention to all its multiple effects. Economic considerations are not sufficient. However much a slum-clearing project, for example, may promise liveable housing, it may well be viewed by its intended occupants as threatening to lifelong traditions and friendships. However much more efficient and impartial big government may be, local populations may prefer to pay the higher costs rather than abdicate personal relationships with decentralized political groups. Learning to direct and control change so that we may provide for a qualitatively better human environment is an imperative of our times.

Organizing Concepts

The following concepts can be used to organize units of study concerned with the issue of rationality and humanism.

Anthropology
cultural identity
cultural diversity
modernization
culture change
ecological niches

Economics
division of labor
profit and loss
economic concentration
markets
means of production
automation

Geography
environmental changes
ghettos
rural areas
city areas

History
specific changes over time
specific events in time

Political Science
government
representation
centralization and de-centralization
welfare
citizenship
rights
democracy
communism
socialism

Psychology
alienation
impotence
self-concept
emotional needs
habits
security
values
attitudes

Sociology
bureaucracy
centralization
specialization
standardization
a hierarchy of offices

Classroom Activities   The following activities represent ways that students can be helped to recognize that the resolution of social problems requires both rational and humanistic considerations.

Primary Grades

Helping young children understand the value conflicts that arise from the interplay of rational and humanistic approaches to resolving problems and satisfying basic human needs may be a very difficult task. Since our culture is futuristic and technologically oriented, we are continually exposed to glamorous scientific-technological solutions to human problems. It is not until people become more experienced and mature that they begin realizing that some human problems and needs cannot be met effectively by those means. The activities listed here may, however, help children achieve a more balanced viewpoint.

1. If your school has a cafeteria that most children utilize, discuss some of these questions: Do you enjoy eating in the cafeteria? Why or why not? How does

the food compare to what you eat at home? If you were grown up would you rather cook your own meals or eat in a cafeteria? Is eating in a cafeteria better for some people than eating at home? Why?

2. Take a study trip to a supermarket and then to a small, family owned and operated grocery store. Have the children compare prices on a few essential items. If possible, in each store have them talk to the manager or owner about the store and its customers. Have the children look for differences in the way customers act in each store. When you return to school have a discussion about the differences between the two stores. Try to get children to identify the values each kind of store offers the owners, the customers, and the neighborhood.

3. If you teach in a school that has at least one classroom for each grade level, ask teachers at other grade levels to take part in an experiment with your class. For a day, or perhaps even a week, change each classroom into a one-room school by having children from kindergarten or first grade through the sixth grade in each room. After reading about one-room schools, have the children organize themselves to simulate a country school. When the experience is completed, conduct a discussion about the benefits and drawbacks of each approach to education.

4. Using carefully selected pictures reflecting the following situations, discuss the ways in which people have their needs met and achieve a satisfying life: (a) working in a large factory on an assembly line versus being a craftsman in a small shop, (b) living in a small rural community versus in a large city, and (c) traveling on foot or by bicycle versus traveling in an airplane.

Upper Elementary Grades

As children in the upper elementary grades approach adolescence, they need to prepare themselves for the dramatic, often disturbing changes they will soon encounter in themselves and in their surroundings and routines. They will, more than ever before, experience forces that create conflicts between their sense of individuality and their need for group identity and conformity. One way to help them is to give them opportunities to explore their own needs and desires in relation to the physical and social settings they are in now and will be encountering in the future.

1. They will soon be entering junior or senior high school, which probably will place them in a much larger and less personal school environment. If possible, have them visit the junior or senior high school that they will attend, or have students from those schools visit their class. Have them discuss their concerns and expectations for the new experiences, and ways they can adjust without giving up their own individuality.

2. Have them design a new school and its program so that they have the best of what technology and education have to offer, while at the same time allowing for individual freedom, expression, and satisfaction.

3. Have the children design a new neighborhood or community to replace the one they presently live in. Make lists, first, of the things they need in a community, the things they like to do (individually and in groups), and the modern technological features they would like to incorporate. Have them assess their present community relative to these lists, then design a new one. Be sure to also have them consider the relationship of community design to such social problems as crime, traffic congestion, pollution, drug and alcohol abuse, and lack of neighborliness or community spirit. Their designs and ideas may be executed in pictorial form or in models, or simply presented in discussion. The emphasis, however, should be on making decisions that reconcile rationality with humanism.

Some Resources for Teachers

Alinsky, Saul D. *Rules for Radicals: A Practical Primer for Realistic Radicals.* New York: Random House, 1971.

Dahl, Robert A. *Who Governs?* New Haven, Conn.: Yale University Press, 1961.

Gilboy, Elizabeth. *A Primer on the Economics of Consumption.* New York: Random House, 1968.

Gordon, Kermit, ed. *Agenda for the Nation: Papers on Domestic and Foreign Policy Issues.* Washington, D. C.: Brookings Institution, 1968.

Holtzman, Abraham. *Interest Groups and Lobbying.* New York: Macmillan, 1966.

Huxtable, Ada Louise. *Will They Ever Finish Bruckner Boulevard?* New York: Macmillan, 1970.

Illich, Ivan D. *Deschooling Society.* New York: Harper & Row, 1971.

Katz, Carol. *The Law and the Low Income Consumer.* New York: New York University School of Law, 1968.

Mack, Raymond. *Transforming America: Patterns of Social Change.* New York: Random House, 1967.

Parker, Donald; Robert M. O'Neil; and Nicholas Econopouly. *Civil Liberties: Case Studies and the Law.* Boston: Houghton Mifflin, 1965.

Rolfe, Sidney E. *The Multinational Corporation in the World Economy.* New York: Praeger, 1970.

Rose, Arnold M. *The Power Structure: Political Process in American Society.* New York: Oxford University Press, 1967.

Slote, Alfred. *Termination: The Closing at Baker Plant.* Indianapolis, Ind.: Bobbs-Merrill, 1969.

Trebing, Harry, ed. *The Corporation in the American Economy.* New York: Quadrangle, 1970.

Summary

The use of broad social issues as an organizing framework for the social studies program is probably most consonant with a humanistic orientation. While programs based on the structure of the social sciences emphasize cognition, and programs based on individual interests may have little control over cognitive or affective learning, a social issues organizational pattern integrates both cognitive and affective development. Moreover, inasmuch as it addresses issues that are of vital concern to large numbers of human beings, it permits students to transcend personal concerns. While all three types of programs should be used, particular emphasis needs to be given to the social issues approach because it remains virtually unrepresented in the elementary school.

Five broad objectives should characterize the study of social issues. Students should: (1) recognize the global impact of these issues, (2) develop rational and affective skills necessary for their solution, (3) become more sensitive to the moral questions they pose, (4) develop the desire to solve them, and (5) increase their own feelings of potency regarding both their own and others' ability to solve them. The last point in particular needs to be emphasized. Social issues affect our everyday lives, and they involve behavior that it is generally deemed possible to change. Many issues, however, seem so overwhelming that students (and teachers) can easily become convinced that nothing can be done. If this occurs, nothing will—so be sure to include experiences that demonstrate where somebody's efforts did make a difference.

Because these issues are controversial, social studies teachers need to develop appropriate teaching strategies that are consistent with genuine inquiry and incorporate more than one point of view. The teaching profession needs to insist on a climate of free inquiry even at the elementary level.

When preparing units on specific social issues, one should begin by identifying which concepts from each of the social studies disciplines might be included under the heading. In setting up lesson plans, try approaching the subject in as many ways as possible, stressing active participation by the students.

Additional References for Teachers

The following is a partial list of additional references for teachers. Although all may be useful for the study of social issues, most are also valuable for developing varied types of social studies programs.

General Introductions to Broad Issues

Becker, Howard, ed. *Social Problems: A Modern Approach.* New York: John Wiley & Sons, 1967.

Eisenstadt, S. N., ed. *Comparative Social Problems.* New York: The Free Press, 1964.

Kavolis, Vytautas, ed. *Comparative Perspectives on Social Problems.* Boston: Little, Brown, 1971.

McDonagh, Edward, and Jon Simpson, eds. *Social Problems: Persistent Challenges.* New York: Holt, Rinehart and Winston, 1965.

McLendon, Jonathan C., ed. *Guide to Reading for Social Studies Teachers.* NCSS Bulletin 46, 1973.

Perrucci, Robert, and Marc Pilisuk, eds. *The Triple Revolution Emerging: Social Problems in Depth.* Boston: Little, Brown, 1971.

Wertheimer, Michael, ed. *Confrontation: Psychology and the Problems of Today.* Glenview, Ill.: Scott, Foresman, 1970.

Dictionaries

Ellkot, Florence, and Michael Summerskill. *A Dictionary of Politics*. Rev. ed. Baltimore: Penguin, 1957.

English, Horace B., and Ava C. English. *A Comprehensive Dictionary of Psychological and Psychoanalytical Terms: A Guide to Usage.* New York: David McKay, 1958.

Gould, Julius, and William L. Kolb, eds. *A Dictionary of the Social Sciences*. New York: The Free Press, 1964.

Horton, Burne J., and others. *Dictionary of Modern Economics*. Washington, D. C.: Public Affairs Press, 1948.

Murray, Sir James A. H., and others, eds. *A New English Dictionary of Historical Principles*. 13 vols. Oxford: Oxford University Press, 1888–1933.

Putnam, George P., comp. *Dictionary of Events*. New York: Grosset & Dunlap, 1936.

Stamp, Dudley L., ed. *A Glossary of Geographical Terms*. New York: John Wiley & Sons, 1961.

Webster's New International Dictionary of the English Language. 3rd ed. Springfield, Mass.: G. and C. Merriam, 1961.

Winick, Charles. *Dictionary of Anthropology*. New York: Philosophical Library, 1956.

Zadrozny, John T. *Dictionary of Social Science*. Washington, D. C.: Public Affairs Press, 1959.

Statistical Data Sources

Andriet, John L. *Guide to U.S. Government Statistics*. 3rd ed., rev. and enlarged. Arlington, Va.: Documents Index, 1961.

Schmeckebier, Laurence F., and Roy B. Eastin. *Government Publications and Their Use.* Rev. ed. Washington, D.C.: Brookings Institution, 1961.

United Nations Statistical Office. *Statistical Yearbook,* 1972.

United States Bureau of the Census. *County and City Data Book.* Washington, D.C.: U.S. Government Printing Office, 1966.

———. *Eighteenth Decennial Census of the United States, Census of Population.* Washington D.C.: U.S. Government Printing Office, 1960.

———. *Historical Statistics of the United States.* Washington, D.C.: U.S. Government Printing Office, 1965.

———. *Statistical Abstract.* Washington, D.C.: U.S. Government Printing Office. Published annually.

———. *United States Census of Housing.* Washington, D.C.: U.S. Government Printing Office, 1960.

United States National Office of Vital Statistics. *Vital Statistics of the United States.* Washington, D.C.: U.S. Government Printing Office. Published annually.

Biographical Reference Books

American Men of Science. Tempe, Ariz.: J. Cattell Press.

Current Biography. New York: H. W. Wilson Co.

The Directory of American Scholars. New York: R. R. Bowker.

Who's Who in America. Chicago, Ill.: Marquis Biennial.

Who's Who of American Women. Chicago, Ill.: Marquis Biennial.

Indexes

Biography Index: A Cumulative Index to Biographical Materials in Books and Magazines. New York: H. W. Wilson Co. Cumulated annually.

Dissertation Abstracts: A Guide to Dissertations and Monographs Available on Microfilm. Ann Arbor, Mich.: University Microfilms. Bimonthly.

Education Index: A Cumulative Subject Index to a Selected List of Educational Periodicals. New York: H. W. Wilson Co. Issued annually since 1932.

Index of Economic Articles. American Economic Association. 7 vols. Homewood, Ill.: Irwin, 1961–66.

Index to Legal Periodicals. New York: H. W. Wilson Co.

International Bibliography of Socio-Cultural Anthropology. Chicago: Aldine. Issued annually since 1955.

New York Times Index. New York: New York Times. Published semi-monthly and annually.

Population Index. Princeton, N. J.: Office of Population Research, Princeton University, and the Population Association of America. Issued quarterly since 1935.

Psychological Abstracts. Washington, D.C.: American Psychological Association. Published annually.

Reader's Guide to Periodical Literature. New York: H. W. Wilson Co. Cumulated annually.

Sociological Abstracts. Brooklyn, N.Y.: Leo P. Chall. Published 7 times a year.

Social Science and Humanities Index. New York: H. W. Wilson Co. Cumulated annually.

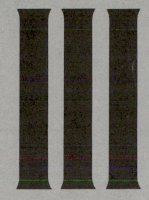

Skills
and Tools

Skills

Skills are the fundamental tools of learning. They are the means whereby independent, autonomous learning becomes possible. Without them, the learner remains helpless, dependent on available authorities to provide the "right" answers.

Social studies skills require complex cognitive processes. They are neither automatic nor mechanical, such as those required in driving a car or typing, for example. They cannot be left to chance. A developmental sequence of instruction explicitly directed toward their acquisition is the best means to ensure successful learning.

Two major categories characterize social studies skills. The first, *basic research skills,* involves the location, interpretation, and organization of data. Such data are primarily found by observing, listening, and reading. The second category, *critical thinking skills,* basically includes the analyzing, synthesizing, and evaluating of data. Together, these skills make inquiry possible.

Fortunately, much effort has been devoted to identifying the subskills of these two categories. However, these identifications are largely based on logical analysis, classroom experience, and subjective judgments, and it is not uncommon to find some divergent listings. A breakdown of the subskills is given in the following pages. While these are gleaned from many sources, including the author's own subjective judgments, one source was particularly helpful. The thirty-third Yearbook of the National Council for the Social Studies, published in 1963, probably remains one of the most comprehensive attempts to identify the skills of the social studies.[1] The information it contains was very useful in compiling the lists of skills at the end of each section of this chapter.

If these skills are to be developed sequentially, it will also be necessary to identify the appropriate grade levels for their introduction. Again, classroom experience and subjective judgments are the primary source for making these decisions. Hence, grade placements in the following pages should be regarded as suggestions only. No teacher can assume that a particular skill has been mastered at a previous grade level. Each teacher must diagnose his or her students to determine their needs. In any case, each of the skills requires continuous development throughout the years of schooling. It is therefore important that social studies teachers, regardless of class assignment, be familiar with the entire sequence of skills.

This chapter is divided into four sections. Each deals with basic research and critical thinking skills as they apply to: observing and listening; reading; map and globe skills; and time and chronology. Each section begins with some preliminary comments and suggested classroom activities. Each section concludes with a detailed listing of specific skills and their suggested point of introduction. As a general rule, higher-level thinking skills are emphasized in the middle and upper elementary grades. However, some attention needs to be given to them as early as kindergarten.

[1]Eunice John and Dorothy McClure Fraser, "Social Studies Skills: A Guide to Analysis and Grade Placement" in *Skill Development in Social Studies* (33rd Yearbook), Helen McCracken Carpenter, ed. (Washington, D.C.: National Council for the Social Studies, 1963).

Guidelines for the Teaching of Social Studies Skills

1. The skill should be taught functionally, in the context of a topic of study, rather than as a separate exercise.
2. The learner must understand the meaning and purpose of the skills and have motivation for developing them.
3. The learner should be carefully supervised in his first attempts to apply the skill, so that he will form correct habits from the beginning.
4. The learner needs repeated opportunities to practice the skill, with immediate evaluation so that he knows where he has succeeded or failed in his performance.
5. The learner needs individual help through diagnostic measures and follow-up exercises, since not all members of any group learn at exactly the same rate or retain equal amounts of what they have learned.
6. Skill instruction should be presented at increasing levels of difficulty, moving from simple to the more complex; the resulting growth in skills should be cumulative as the learner moves through school, with each level of instruction building on and reinforcing what has been taught previously.
7. Students should be helped at each stage, to generalize the skills, by applying them in many and varied situations; in this way, maximum transfer of learning can be achieved.
8. The program of instruction should be sufficiently flexible to allow skills to be taught as they are needed by the learner; many skills should be developed concurrently.

From "Social Studies Skills: A Guide to Analysis and Grade Placement" by Eunice John and Dorothy McClure Fraser, in *Skill Development in Social Studies* (33rd Yearbook of the National Council for the Social Studies, 1963), Helen McCracken Carpenter, ed., pp. 311–12. Reprinted with permission of the National Council for the Social Studies and the authors.

Observing and Listening

While the gifts of sight and hearing are bestowed on most people, observing and listening are skills that need to be developed. The ability to see does not ensure accurate observation any more than hearing guarantees listening.

Students spend most of their school time listening and looking. Teacher talk dominates the school increasingly as students move up the grade ladder. Yet little effort is made to teach observation and listening skills in the same systematic manner that is generally applied to reading skills.

Observation and listening skills center primarily on sensory experiences—on first-hand sensory perceptions mediated through sight, sound, touch, smell, and taste. A fairly detailed listing of observing and listening skills, as well as their suggested point of entry into the curriculum, is given at the end of this section. Many others will occur to sensitive teachers as they work in the classroom. Older students probably need more experiences with this type of skill than younger ones do since these skills frequently weaken as students learn to depend more on written verbal materials.

**Activities
to Develop
Observation Skills**

To introduce students to the importance of observation, arrange an incident. Stage an argument or a magic trick or something of the sort and have it take place without warning. Keep the incident simple and short—no more than several minutes—and use people who are known around the school. Have the "actors" leave at the conclusion of the event, and then raise the following questions: Who was involved? What occurred? Who said what? What was the final result?

Responses to such actions inevitably vary. Stage similar activities, but this time warn the students that an incident will take place that day and give them directions such as: "Observe carefully to see who is involved, what they do, and what the conclusion is." Ask the students for their observations. Were they more accurate this time? Was there greater consensus regarding events? If differences are noted, ask the students to account for them.

The object of the above exercise is twofold: (1) to illustrate in as dramatic a fashion as possible the difficulty of making accurate observations and (2) to get across the point that observing with a purpose in mind makes it easier to be accurate.

Either suggest or ask that the students propose a set of questions to guide their observations. These might include the following: What are the main ideas? What is the sequence of ideas? What supporting evidence or details are given for main ideas? Then provide a series of observation experiences that conclude with the above questions. Such experiences might include showing a series of thematically connected pictures or a filmstrip without commentary, projecting a movie without sound, or taking students for short excursions in the neighborhood.

While observation helps us gather accurate information, what we perceive is frequently guided by our own assumptions and biases. To help students become aware of their own biases, you might show them photographs of scenes that portray different countries in nonconventional ways—for example, a poor farm in the United States, a sophisticated technological plant in Nigeria, an unveiled woman chemist in Egypt, a modern museum in Mexico. Ask the students to choose from a list of names the countries they think each photograph represents; then discuss with them their reasons for their choices. Or you might bring in a set of photographs of individuals whose identity is known to you but not to the students. Have the students speculate on the personality of each person. Or ask some leading questions, such as: Which one is most likely to be a bank president? A teacher? A criminal? Have the students explore the reasons for their choices. Give the correct information at the end of the exercise. This exercise can help students realize how their biases influence their perceptions.

While it is important for students to become aware of their own biases, it is equally important for them to learn to recognize the biases and assumptions of people who prepare visual materials—in textbooks, films, magazines, newspapers, and so on. Have students carefully examine specific types of visual materials. To help them become aware of biases concerning sex roles, for example, ask them to list the types of activities boys, men, girls, and women are shown

doing in textbooks. Ask them if photographs and pictures give a distorted view of the ways people live and act. Have students hypothesize regarding the effects of these illustrations on people's attitudes. Videotape a typical television commercial of the sort directed at children. Show it without sound. Have the students analyze the visual techniques used to sell products. Do the same with advertisements aimed at other groups.

Careful attention to detail can help develop more accurate observation skills. Expose the students to varied visual experiences and ask appropriate questions. For example, you might bring in a set of uncaptioned newspaper photographs and ask them to match the captions to the appropriate photographs. Have them explain the bases for their choices. Or you might project a still picture so that all the students can see it clearly at the same time. Ask students to note as many facts as they can and make inferences about relationships of people in the picture, occupations, climatic conditions, time, and so forth.

Sensitize students to body language. Strike a few poses yourself and ask students to interpret your feelings by the way you sit, stand, move your eyes, position your arms, fingers, legs.[2] Show some movies without sound and have students analyze them along the same lines.

Activities to Develop Listening Skills

Although listening to words is generally emphasized in school, social science data include sounds of all kinds. To help sensitize students to their sound environment, try some of the following.

[2]For a general introduction to the subject see Julius Fast, *Body Language* (New York: Simon & Schuster, Pocket Books, 1971).

Tape a variety of common household sounds: vacuum cleaner, clothes dryer, washing machine, typewriter, and so on. Ask students to identify the objects making the sounds. Ask them to tape other sounds.

Ask the students to close their eyes and identify as many sounds as they hear.

Take the students on a walk, and when back in the classroom, ask them to recall as many sounds as they can.

Provide many opportunities to help students develop their listening skills with words. Radio broadcasts, tapes, oral readings by teacher and students, as well as short teacher lectures, all encourage listening. Guide these experiences by providing such directions as: Listen for main ideas, supporting evidence, and conclusions. Be ready to discuss the feelings and biases of the speaker. List two new things you learned. Be ready to discuss these things with the class.

Accustom students to listen critically and carefully. Help them sort out relevant and irrelevant details. You might do this by reading aloud an interesting article that you have modified by adding some irrelevant points and asking the students to identify these points. Or you might ask students to evaluate each other as they give short speeches, directions, or simple demonstrations. Be sure this does not become a carping exercise. Make the students aware of supportive interaction techniques and encourage them to use phrases and modes of behavior that make people feel good about themselves. Ask the students to evaluate your own way of communicating with them.

Attending to words alone, however, is not sufficient for the interpretation of the spoken language. Inflection, pitch, speed, and tone provide important clues to meaning. Experiences like the following can help sensitize students to these factors.

Bring a tape in a foreign language to class. Pick a speaker who expresses a range of emotions, and ask the students to infer the feelings of the speaker. Then translate the message and examine how it relates to inferences made by students. Another useful exercise is to ask the students to read a simple sentence in English, such as "I want to take a walk," in as many ways as they can to express such emotional states as anger, sadness, and eagerness.

Many assumptions about people are made on the basis of voice alone, particularly when they are not simultaneously seen. Some of these are unwarranted. One way to help students become aware of these assumptions is to bring in tapes of many different kinds of voices: children, adults, various dialects, high- and low-pitched. Ask the students to identify the sex, ethnic origin, age, height, weight, and occupation of the speaker. Compare their responses with the facts and, if possible, with photographs of the speakers. You may succeed in exposing several stereotypes.

Lie detectors operate on the principle that while people can fool us with their words, their bodily reactions will betray them. Explain to your class how a lie detector works, and see if you can get someone to give a demonstration. Inexpensive amateur models based on skin resistance are available. Ask students how reliable they think a lie detector is, and explain how and where it is used.

In short, approach observing and listening skills with the same care as you would all other aspects of the social studies curriculum. Use them as opportunities for gleaning information as well as engaging in higher levels of inquiry.

The suggestions for exercises that were given above have all been experimented with in classrooms, and some have proved highly successful in getting certain ideas across. A word of warning is in order, however. These descriptions were necessarily short and incomplete, and you may not be able to achieve the expected results with all of the exercises the first time you try them. Selecting a film for silent projection, for example, requires a fair amount of care and may be impossible to do well if the school's film library is limited, while the success of tape recording exercises depends in large part on the quality of the equipment used. Do not be discouraged, then, if your first efforts should fail.

Chart 6–1 is a partial list of basic research and critical thinking skills as they apply to observing and listening. Each skill consists of many subskills or parts—not all of which can be learned during the school year. The column on the left identifies some skills and subskills, the column on the right suggests the approximate grade levels at which the skill should be introduced. At each successive grade level, old skills should be reviewed and reinforced.

Chart 6–1
A List of Observing and Listening Skills

Basic Research Skills	**Grades**
Locating Information	
Observes and listens with a purpose	K–1
Identifies main ideas	K–1
Follows directions	K–1
Describes things observed and heard	K–1
Identifies sequence of ideas	K–1
Notes supporting details and evidence	4–5
Takes notes while continuing to observe and listen	7–8
Interpreting Information	
Understands meaning as a whole	K–1
Avoids projecting own ideas	K–1
Distinguishes between important and unimportant details	2–3
Compares information with other sources	2–3
Distinguishes among types of observations and heard sources	4–5
Recognizes advantages and disadvantages of each type of source	4–5
Organizing Information	
Composes titles for things observed and heard	K–1
Selects answers to questions	K–1
Arranges events, facts, ideas in sequence	K–1
Classifies information under main headings	2–3
Uses more than one source to find information	2–3
Selects main ideas and supporting facts	4–5
Writes a summary of main points	4–5
Notes reference source	4–5

Critical Thinking Skills

Analyzing

Sees relationships among ideas and events	K–1
Identifies point of view	K–1
Infers motives, feelings, values, attitudes	K–1
Identifies supporting evidence for a conclusion	2–3
Distinguishes between relevant and irrelevant details	2–3
Identifies bias	4–5
Distinguishes facts from value statements	4–5
Identifies techniques used to persuade or convince	4–5
Identifies assumptions	6

Synthesizing

*Plans a field trip, interview,
visit from a resource person:*

Identifies purpose	K–1
Identifies questions	K–1
Plans procedures	K–1
Expresses appreciation appropriately	K–1
Finds acceptable ways to open and close interviews	4–5

Evaluating

*Evaluates on the basis of the
following criteria:*

Clarity	K–1
Accuracy	K–1
Presentation of different points of view	K–1
Warranted conclusions on basis of given evidence	K–1
Warranted conclusions by comparison with other sources	K–1
Value implications	K–1
Social implications	K–1
Appropriate use of language	4–5
Appeals to emotion	4–5
Consistency	4–5
Logic	7–8
Care in citing documentation, references	7–8

Reading

One out of four students in the United States has significant reading problems. In large city school systems, up to half the students read below their grade-level expectations.[3] Nonetheless, most social studies texts continue to demand high-level reading abilities. If students fail to become interested in them, it is no doubt largely due to the frustration they must feel in attempting to understand words and phrases that are above their level of comprehension.

[3]James E. Allen, "An Address to the National Association of State Boards of Education, Los Angeles, September 23, 1969," in June R. Chapin and Richard E. Gross, eds., *Teaching Social Studies Skills* (Boston: Little, Brown, 1973).

One way to cope with the problem is to rely heavily on other media. But this is a way of evading the issue rather than overcoming it. Using audio-visual aids will not help students read better. Moreover, despite the proliferation of multi-media resources, the necessity for coping with the written word has by no means been reduced. Reading is still the essential component of all social studies programs, and student success in these programs continues to be strongly correlated with reading proficiency.

Reading is a highly complex process. Even at its simplest, it involves complex neurological processes. At its most complex, it includes high-level thinking. To read implies more than the simple translation of letters into sounds—it means active cognitive and affective interaction with symbols. Suggested reading skills in the social studies and the points at which they may be introduced into the curriculum are given in Chart 6–2, beginning on page 193.

Directing a Reading Lesson

Merely directing students to read is insufficient. The assignment of any reading lesson should be preceded by activities that prepare the students for the reading and followed up by activities that reinforce and extend learnings.

The preparation stage is the most important. If this is done well, the other steps will proceed fairly efficiently and easily. First read the assignment carefully yourself and select the most important cognitive and affective learnings as well as skills which you hope will result from the assignment. Introduce the class to new concepts and generalizations and spend as much time as necessary in developing them adequately. Write any difficult words on the blackboard and make sure the students can read and understand them. Concentrate on the particular skills—such as the interpretation of pictures, graphs, and time lines—that are necessary to understand the assignment. When you are reasonably confident the students have mastered the vocabulary and special skills, introduce the reading assignment. Describe its contents briefly and clarify the purpose of the assignment. For example, what points should they look for and why? What questions will they be expected to answer? Will they be expected to write out the answers or simply be prepared to discuss them? Will they be expected to write summaries or outlines? In short, make the purpose of the assignment as specific as possible.

The reading itself can be done independently and silently. But follow it up with activities that will reinforce learnings. Discussions, other readings on the same issue, reading aloud of particular passages, preparation of original projects related to the reading, worksheets, and written tests are examples of follow-up activities. Provide independent help as needed.

Research Skills

Helping students become independent researchers is an important goal in the social studies. Locating, interpreting, and organizing information, as well as analyzing, synthesizing and evaluating it, are essential research skills.

Locating Information Dictionaries are among the most basic social studies reference materials. Keep several different ones in the classroom, including picture dictionaries, special social science dictionaries, and old dictionaries, as well as the usual classroom variety. They are not only valuable for traditional uses—such as spelling, syllabification, pronunciation, and meaning—but also for developing concepts. Compare meanings in several dictionaries and note changes in meanings over time. (An interesting investigation for students would be to find out how dictionary compilers arrive at definitions.)

Identifying appropriate reference sources is a valuable skill. A "reference debate" such as the following is a good way to start.

Allow approximately three sessions on consecutive days for the activity. On the first, divide the class into small groups of three or four students each. Assign each group a different reference source—Group A: dictionaries; Group B: newspapers; Group C: pictorial materials; Group D: almanacs. Tell each group that they will be asked to "sell" their product on the third day. To be successful, they will need to study their product carefully and be able to answer the following questions: How is my product useful in doing social studies research? What makes it better than or different from any other product? Allow groups approximately two work periods, and help each to complete its task. (This process should consume part of the first work period and all of the second.) On the third day, assemble the desks of respective groups in clusters and label each one appropriately. Launch the session by asking each group in turn to describe its product and answer questions.

The newspaper group may point out the up-to-date information newspapers provide about world events, local happenings, and sports. The encyclopedia group might say that encyclopedias are more accurate than newspapers and have much more information about the past. The dictionary group might claim that dictionaries are useful in all kinds of research, because everybody has to be able to spell and know the meanings of words. Opportunities for counter-arguments should be given and the information could be summarized in chart form at the conclusion.

Reference skills should be reinforced with a variety of exercises. To improve the students' ability to identify sources, for example, the teacher might prepare a list of questions and ask the students to determine where the most helpful information could be found. What, for instance, is the best source for finding the names of your state senators? The elevation of Mt. Rainier? George Washington Carver's date of birth? In order to explore a particular reference source in depth, compose a series of questions relating exclusively to it. The World Almanac, for example, contains a vast amount of information. Circulate a worksheet with about twenty questions such as these: How many people living in the United States in 1970 were born in foreign countries? Which is the fastest scheduled train in the United States? Who was the President of Czechoslovakia in 1973? See how many the students can answer in a week.

The quickest and most efficient way to use any reference source is to find out how it is organized. The careful examination of titles is one of the quickest, if not

always the surest, ways to assess content. Try reading a few titles to the class and ask them to infer what the content is. Tables of contents are additional valuable clues. You might circulate just the title and table of contents of several references and ask students to compose a paragraph or two telling what they are about. Students should become accustomed to noting the author and date of publication. The class should discuss how these factors might affect point of view. Students should also become familiar with the function and/or structure of other components including glossaries, indexes, footnotes, illustration lists, italics, and appendixes. Ask the students to compare how these are organized in different sources. They might compare the varied ways footnotes are entered and decide which way is simplest or clearest. A particularly good exercise would be to check some of the footnotes against their sources for accuracy and relevance.

Begin to introduce students to varied reference sources in the early primary grades. Arrange periodic visits to the library so that students become completely familiar with its resources and how to find what they need. Devote several hours each year to the skill of simply locating materials in the library. Assign tasks such as locating specific books, using the *Readers' Guide to Periodical Literature* to find the titles of five current articles on a particular topic, finding three books on a given subject, or combinations of any of these.

To introduce young students to author, subject, and title cards, prepare copies of these on large tagboard. Discuss them in class to make sure students understand their format and function. Give students the opportunity to actually use the library's card catalogue. You might send small groups to the library to locate specific subject matter, asking the librarian, a teacher's aide, or an older student to help them. Distribute three index cards and a book to each student and ask each one to prepare an author, title, and subject card for the book. Encourage students to help each other in the task.

Interpreting and
Organizing
Information

Merely locating information is not sufficient, however. Students need a lot of practice interpreting and organizing information. They must learn to identify the central ideas, to avoid projecting their own ideas on the printed page, and to compare information from one source with another. Does the author really say that? Where did you see it? Are you quoting out of context? Is this your idea or the author's? Questions of this sort help students develop appropriate interpretation skills.

In the early grades, children can simply list two or three main ideas from their reading. As they mature, they can progress from simple sentences to simple paragraphs, each one focusing on a single idea. Written reports might be divided into separate sections with subtitles that clearly delineate the ideas. Thus, in writing about a particular country, for example, subtitles might be used to distinguish information on geography, history, and industry. They should also learn to write outlines and to incorporate quotes, footnotes, and bibliographies in their reports.

Students can learn to assemble research materials so as to have them available when needed. Each student might be provided with a research kit—a shoe box with ruled index cards. Students can use these cards to write down any information they learn from a reference. The first entry should always include the author, title, publisher, and publishing data. The rest of the card would include main ideas, appropriate quotes and page numbers, plus some evaluative notes. Learning how to file information for easy retrieval is essential. A subject-area filing system is best for most purposes. When students have collected approximately ten cards, help them decide on the subject categories and file the cards accordingly. When they are ready to write a report, they need merely retrieve the appropriate cards.

Synthesizing
Reading Activities

Written activities, such as reports, plays, and poems, and oral activities such as discussions, panels, debates, and reports, are good synthesizing activities. Provide many opportunities for students to engage in them.

In preparing written reports, stress the importance of not copying from references, except for purposes of quoting. Teach the students how to give credit for quoted materials. Encourage them to proofread their own materials. Provide immediate feedback to the students by writing comments on their papers to

Chart 6–2
A List of Reading Skills

Basic Research Skills	Grades
Locating Information	
Dictionaries:	
Alphabetizes to third letter	2–3
Uses guide words	4–5
Uses pronunciation keys	4–5
Syllabicates correctly	4–5
Selects appropriate meaning	4–5
Books and other verbal reference materials:	
Uses title as guide	K–1
Uses table of contents	K–1
Reads to find answers to questions	K–1
Selects statements pertinent to topic	K–1
Uses title page	2–3
Distinguishes between storybooks and factual books	2–3
Chooses appropriate books for purpose	2–3
Makes use of headings, topic sentences, summary sentences to select main ideas	4–5
Uses index, copyright date, glossary, appendixes, map lists, illustration lists	4–5
Skims as necessary	4–5
Uses italics, marginal notes, footnotes	6
Newspapers, magazines, pamphlets:	
Recognizes as sources of information	2–3
Selects appropriate materials	4–5
Learns organization	6
Recognizes purposes and coverage of different publications	6
Recognizes and uses many reference materials, including:	
Maps and globes	K–1
Encyclopedias	2–3
Biographies and autobiographies	2–3
Diaries	4–5
Travel accounts	4–5
Letters	4–5
Records of inquests and committee meetings	4–5
Written interviews and polls	4–5
Case studies	4–5
Folk stories and myths	4–5
Songs and ballads	4–5
Academic accounts from various social science disciplines at appropriate levels	4–5
Almanacs	4–5
Atlases	6
Pictorial materials:	
Recognizes as sources of information	K–1

Describes content	K–1
Uses as one source of information	K–1
Graphs and tables:	
Understands significance of title	4–5
Identifies basis on which constructed and units of measure	4–5
Constructs simple graphs and tables	4–5
Charts:	
Understands steps in development	6
Traces steps	6
Compares size and quantity	6
Constructs simple charts	6
Cartoons:	
Recognizes as expressing different points of view	6
Notes symbols used	6
Makes simple cartoons	6
Library skills:	
Uses card catalogue	
Finds materials by subject, author, title	2–3
Notes publication date and publisher	4–5
Recognizes Dewey Decimal System as key to finding book	6
Uses *Readers' Guide to Periodical Literature* and other indexes	7–8

Interpreting Information

Grasps meaning as a whole	K–1
Avoids projecting own ideas	K–1
Distinguishes between important and unimportant details	2–3
Compares information with other sources	2–3
Distinguishes among types of materials	4–5
Recognizes advantages and disadvantages of each	4–5

Organizing Information

Composes a title for story, picture, table, chart, or cartoon	K–1
Selects answers to questions	K–1
Arranges events, facts, ideas in sequence	K–1
Classifies facts, events, ideas under main headings	2–3
Makes a simple table of contents	2–3
Makes an outline of topics to investigate	4–5
Takes notes	4–5
Uses more than one source to find information	4–5
Selects main idea and supporting facts	4–5
Writes a summary of main points	4–5
Uses correct outline form	6
Makes a bibliography	6

Critical Thinking Skills

Analyzing

Sees relationships among ideas and events	K–1
Identifies point of view	K–1
Infers motives, feelings, values, attitudes	K–1
Identifies supporting evidence for a conclusion	2–3
Distinguishes between relevant and irrelevant details	2–3
Identifies bias	4–5
Distinguishes facts from value statements	4–5

Identifies techniques used to persuade or convince	4 – 5
Identifies assumptions	6

Synthesizing

Communicates orally:

Develops an adequate vocabulary	K – 1
Chooses appropriate word	K – 1
Pronounces correctly	K – 1
Keeps to the point	K – 1
Exchanges ideas in a discussion	K – 1
Gives an organized oral report	2 – 3
Uses notes in making oral report	6
Gives credit for quoted materials	6

Communicates in writing:

Applies writing, spelling, punctuation, capitalization skills	2 – 3
Avoids copying from references	4 – 5
Includes bibliography	4 – 5
Gives credit for quoted materials	6
Uses standard English	6
Proofreads and revises	6
Organizes information and ideas clearly	6
Includes footnotes	7 – 8

Problem-solving and decision-making:

Recognizes a problem, an issue, a controversy	K – 1
Suggests a tentative conclusion, solution, hypothesis, prediction, decision, generalization	K – 1
Proposes ways to test the conclusion, solution, hypothesis, prediction, decision, generalization	K – 1
Locates and gathers relevant information	K – 1
Draws tentative conclusions that may support or modify original conclusion	K – 1
Recognizes areas for further study	K – 1

Conceptualizing and generalizing:

Gets the subconcepts and facts	K – 1
Interprets subconcepts and facts	K – 1
Identifies common elements and relationships	K – 1
Induces a tentative concept and generalization	K – 1
Tests concept and generalization against other data	K – 1

Evaluating

Evaluates on the basis of the following criteria:

Clarity	K – 1
Accuracy	K – 1
Presentation of different points of view	K – 1
Warranted conclusions on basis of given evidence	K – 1
Warranted conclusions by comparison with other sources	K – 1
Value implications	K – 1
Social implications	K – 1
Appropriate use of language	4 – 5
Appeals to emotion	4 – 5
Consistency	4 – 5
Logic	7 – 8
Care in citing references and documentation	7 – 8

help reinforce learning. Work returned the next day is much more useful than that returned a week or a month later. Keep copies of written work so that the students can assess their own progress over time.

Provide frequent opportunities for the students to speak in class. The familiar "share and tell" is useful as long as it is not abused or routinized. Encourage the students to talk about their experiences, books they have read, newspaper articles, travel, and so forth. Young children in particular enjoy conducting mock telephone inquiries and exchanges.

Allow many opportunities for oral reports, but be sure to teach the pupils how to be a good audience. Establishing a supportive room climate is very important for helping pupils feel secure in any form of oral communication. It is best to have group oral reports before having individual ones. Be aware of students with speech problems or those who are shy and anxious. They will need your special consideration and guidance.

Help students evaluate their own and others' oral reports. Construct a checklist with students that might include the following questions: Did the introduction arouse interest? Did the speaker make the purpose clear? Was the subject matter interesting? Were the facts accurate? Did the speaker cite references? Was the content well organized? Was the speaker's manner friendly? Could the speaker's voice be heard? Were visual materials clear and appropriate? Was there a summary? Was the speaker able to answer questions adequately? Tape record reports from time to time to help students evaluate themselves.

Maps and Globes

Skills relating to place and space are inherent in the study of maps and globes. The social studies bears a major responsibility for their development.

Elementary social studies have suffered from two major weaknesses in teaching map and globe skills. First, they all too frequently reflect a "spatial provincialism." The United States is treated as the spatial center of the earth and significant concerns are limited to its borders. The new social studies attempts to dispel this erroneous perspective by focusing on the entire globe right from the beginning. When notions of space are limited to local or national borders, distorted views of global issues are inevitable. For example, pollution problems in the United States cannot be solved through American efforts alone. Air and water currents spread pollutants all over the globe. This fundamental spatial recognition has political overtones: the solution of environmental problems depends on planning together with other nations—many of whom distrust each other profoundly. Or if we seriously want to solve the world's food problem, we need to recognize that in part at least it is due to poor transportation systems making food distribution to remote hinterlands difficult and costly. Whether or not the nations of the world can or should address themselves to world transportation problems is again a political issue, but if it is not solved, it is unlikely that the food problem will be solved either.

The other weakness in the traditional approach to these skills is a tendency to emphasize description. Where is it? How big is it? Who lives there? These are examples of essentially descriptive categories. In the new social studies, emphasis is on conceptual skills—on developing major understandings regarding the interrelationships of place, space, and human beings. The new social studies asks questions like: What effects does ghetto living have on its residents? On people living outside the ghetto? How does population density affect personality? How does a country's size affect its political policy? The emphasis is on relationships rather than description.

Maps and globes are the essential tools of the geographer, who uses them to illustrate in highly graphic and efficient ways the complex interrelationships that exist among places, spaces, and human beings. Henry Warman identifies five major geographical concepts that should be used to structure the geography curriculum and can help orient the teaching of map and globe skills:[4]

1. The concept of the life-layer
   This involves the study of the "choice and not-so-choice areas of the earth" where people have settled.
2. Man the ecological dominant
   Man is the chooser of how he uses his particular life-layer. He lives on the surface of the earth, but what is below and above the surface is becoming increasingly important in his decision-making.
3. Culturally defined resources
   The world is objectively real. But how we perceive it and use it is influenced by culture. Economic geography—how people live and how they make their livings—is the focus here.
4. The law of comparative advantage
   A study of the composition and distribution of populations in an area (age, sex, education, ethnicity) affords insight into the types of decisions people make in using their resources.
5. Perpetual transformation
   Both the earth itself and patterns of usage are constantly changing. In reality, there is no one geography but a "geography for every time."

Map and Globe Skills

Skills in the study of maps and globes involve (1) size and shape, (2) orientation and direction, (3) location, (4) scale and distance, and (5) symbols. A detailed listing of some of these and when they may be introduced is given in Chart 6–3 at the end of this section.[5] Classroom activities are suggested below.

Size and Shape

Ask a young child how deep the ocean is, and the answer is likely to be that it is so deep that it cannot be measured. The concept of size puts finite boundaries

[4]Henry Warman, "Geography in the Curriculum," *Education Forum* 31 (January 1967), pp. 167–72.
[5]For a good summary of the research pertaining to children's abilities to read maps, see Haig A. Rushdoony, "A Child's Ability to Read Maps: Summary of the Research," *Journal of Geography* (April 1968) pp. 213–22.

on what is frequently perceived as limitless—a concept of increasing importance in a world that has used its resources as though they were indeed infinite. A concept of geographical size is also essential for understanding historical events and social developments—as well as being able to project realistic alternatives to the problems that result from size. To fully conceptualize size and shape requires many experiences throughout the elementary school years. Size and shape concepts should become a fundamental part of the way in which youngsters orient themselves.

Young children can begin with words that describe the relative size and shape of tables, chairs, and other familiar objects—words such as big, small, deep, narrow, wide, circle, square, and triangle. Familiar objects can be compared. Which piece of chalk is larger? Which book is thicker? Which apple is rounder? A series of objects of graduated size can be presented, and children asked to arrange them from smallest to tallest, from thinnest to thickest. Natural objects outside the room should also be compared—one hill with another, one body of water with another, one tree with another. Comparing unlike objects requires a higher degree of conceptual skill because appropriate measures have to be selected first. How can the size of a body of water be compared with the size of a mountain? Shall we measure depth, height, width, or area? As students mature, more precise measures should replace relative words—with emphasis on metric measures. Students should be urged to "guesstimate" and then compare with actual figures. A pocket claculator can encourage children to manipulate large numbers as they attempt to assess the size of large objects.

Students should be encouraged to hypothesize about the effects of size and shape. For example, how does height among humans affect visual perception or feelings of self-worth? How does the size of a table affect its usage? How does the size of a mountain or the depth of a river influence movements of peoples?

Experiences with the globe should begin in kindergarten and continue throughout all the elementary grades. The globe is the truest way to represent the earth. Relative size and shape are both more accurately portrayed than on any flat map. Students should observe the globe's shape and compare the size and shapes of land masses, bodies of water, continents, and countries. The effects of size on political power and economic resources can be discussed. Does size make a country strong? If not, what does? Does size determine a country's economic wealth? What are the consequences of the fact that the world contains almost twice as much water as land?

In preparation for their work with flat maps, students should be introduced to the concept of size distortions that occur when rounded objects are flattened. Provide them with cut orange peels or something of the sort and ask them to stretch these out on flat paper. Ask them to note what happens. This should help prepare them to understand the limitations of flat maps.

To help students synthesize learnings, have them prepare dioramas, models, or murals in which objects have to be cut or molded according to relative size. Younger children will only be able to roughly approximate proportions, but older students can be expected to be fairly accurate.

Orientation and Direction   Begin orienting students to direction by using relative terms, such as *up, down, above, below, right, left, farther, nearer.* Have children apply these terms by moving objects appropriately according to directions, for example, "put the small block above the large one," "walk two steps to the left," "move the chair further away." Teachers and children might construct an actual maze in which the winner would be the one making the fewest errors while following directions blindfolded.

Cardinal directions (north, south, east, and west) should be introduced in the late primary grades. One way to present the concept is to take children outdoors at noon and have them stand with their backs to the sun. Explain that the direction they are facing is north. Have children then examine the globe and locate the North and South Poles. (Do not use "up" and "down" to explain these terms. "Up" should always be used to mean away from the earth and "down" to mean toward its center.) Explain that the direction "north" is toward the North Pole and that the direction "south" is toward the South Pole. Explain how east, west, and south can be derived if one knows where north is. Show the students a compass and explain how to use it. Have them post signs around the room with the letters N, E, W, S on appropriate walls or make a set of arrows and letters from tape to fix on the floor. Accustom children to explaining where objects are in terms of their true direction. Direct children to place objects in the northern, eastern, western, or southern parts of the room. Explain how the rising and setting sun help in finding true direction.

To reinforce the concept of true direction, take children on a walk in the neighborhood. Both before and after the expedition, point out the direction they will take. Construct a floor map of the walk and orient it correctly.

Ask children to discuss the advantages of knowing true direction. Ask them to follow directions given in two ways—one in relative terms, the other in true directional terms. Which one was more efficient? More accurate? Easier to follow? Would pilots or navigators be able to find their way if they did not know true direction?

Students should develop the habit of describing the location of cities, countries, and continents to each other in terms of true direction. The direction of river flows, winds, air currents, and trade routes should also be identified in this way. Students will thus better understand the courses of pollution flows, migration patterns of animals, and trade routes.

Location Each place on the earth's surface has a relative location as well as latitudinal and longitudinal location. Relative location refers to the position of a place in respect to other places. Latitudinal and longitudinal locations are absolute.

In early primary grades, children should learn to locate familiar objects such as seats in the room or schoolhouse and play areas on a large map drawn by the teacher on the playground or on some other floor surface. Construct many maps with the children of places they know well and have them locate things such as streets near home and school, bridges or tunnels, nearby freeways, and other familiar objects and locales. Students can also locate, on the globe and assorted flat maps, domestic and foreign places they have traveled to or heard of. Posters of foreign places as well as travel brochures can lend meaning and excitement to this activity. The locations of places in the news as well as places specifically associated with studies should be identified in every grade of the elementary school.

The concept of the map grid can be introduced in the intermediate grades. Grids are imaginary reference lines that make accurate map and globe construction possible. One way to introduce students to the concept of the grid is to bring in an unmarked round object, such as a rubber ball, and ask students to transform it into a globe. They can begin by tracing the major continents. Students will quickly note the need for reference points to make this possible.

The effects of location on economic and social relationships should be a primary area of concern. What are the effects of proximity (of people, cities, trade routes, etc.) on social and economic relationships? What factors cause large cities to be located where they are? How has the development of sophisticated media like television and telephones affected relative location? How about sophisticated transportation systems? What is the relationship between the location of particular cities and surface features such as rivers and oceans, mountains, agricultural lands, or mining areas? Students might also compare historical views of location with current ones. Where, for example, did Columbus actually think the New World was? Have them examine very early maps of the Americas. They will thus begin to understand that location is more than a mere descriptive category—that it is in fact of great significance to the course of human development.

Scale and Distance

The concept of scale can be introduced to young children by comparing familiar objects with photographs or with representations drawn on the blackboard. Pupils can construct three-dimensional scenes of familiar places and cut out objects so that they approximate scale size; for example, trees would be larger than people, houses smaller than trees, and so on. To increase sophistication, have them actually draw objects to scale using graph paper. Working in pairs, they can first trace a book on one-inch squared graph paper, then draw the same book on one-quarter inch squared paper after discussing how to do it.

To begin to develop the concept of the relationship between distance and time, have the students count the number of blocks between house and school or other familiar places. Take them on a walk and clock the time it takes to walk one block. Then ask them to estimate how much time it takes to go from one place to another. Or have them pace off a block so each one knows its length in terms of his or her particular stride. Then ask them to find out how many paces it is to the playground from the classroom or other places in the school. Help them figure out how many "blocks" the distance is, and how long it should take to walk it. Ask pupils to estimate how long it would take to get from school to their homes by bus or car. Ask them to use watches to find out actual time, and discuss what accounts for differences. (Buses may take circuitous routes, some streets have stop lights, and so on.) Have children engage in a variety of estimating activities in relation to places. How long should it take to get to the market from school? To the airport?

Maps are drawn in proportion to actual size. The fractional proportion is called the map scale. Three forms of map scales are usually used—fractional, verbal, or graphic. The fractional scale shows the relationship between one unit of measurement and the same unit on the earth's surface. The verbal scale is a statement of the situation as, for example, "one inch equals one mile." The graphic scale is the one most frequently used in elementary school. It is usually shown as a line with divisions that represent units of actual distances on the earth's surface. Students should become familiar with map scales, comparing maps of a particular area drawn to different scales and constructing their own maps of these places on yet another scale.

Students should also become familiar with the scales of globes. A 12-inch globe is constructed on a scale of 660 miles to the inch; a 16-inch globe on a scale of 495 miles to the inch. To find out the scale of a globe, take a measuring tape and stretch it tautly around the globe. This forms a great circle route. The shortest distance between any two points on the globe is along a great circle. Take the length of the tape (the globe's circumference) and divide it into 25,000 (the approximate number of miles around the earth) and you will get the number of miles per inch. Students can then compare air distances via great circle routes with land distances that must take mountains, oceans, and other features into account.

The earth's movements, both rotation around the sun and revolution on its own axis, should be understood. They explain seasons, tides, the changes in the length of days, and aspects of the weather.

Students can begin to understand the concept of time zones by studying them first in the United States. Teachers might divide the classroom into time zones and have students figure out where they would be in the United States. From a study of the time zones in the United States, students might move on to Europe and Asia and then to the world as a whole. They can have fun figuring out what time they would arrive in particular countries if they traveled by air, boat, or train. Travel agencies can supply actual times for comparison.

Symbols   The mapmaker uses a wide variety of symbols to represent things on the earth's surface. Developing skill in using this language of mapping is important.

Young children can begin by making maps of the classroom and neighborhood. They can decide on ways to represent these symbolically on the blackboard, using primarily pictorial and semipictorial symbols. As children mature, more abstract symbols can be introduced.

Compile many different maps in the classroom and have the students carefully examine the symbols used. Have them categorize the symbols in such groups as: symbols that resemble actual things; symbols that represent man-made features such as crops or houses; symbols for elevation, important cities, rivers, population density; and color, contour, and visual relief symbols. Students can prepare a class chart or symbol dictionary in which they note symbols and what they stand for.

A symbol is a conceptual category—hence not only its meaning should be understood but also the grouping it represents. Thus, along with learning the symbol for objects, students should conceptualize them. When the class is studying the symbols for mountains, hills, plains, and valleys, for example, the teacher should bring in photographs and ask the students to identify features they have in common and then group these features. When does a hill become a mountain? How is a valley distinguished from a plain or a river from a railway?

By employing different types of symbols, maps can be used to illustrate much more than just the topography of an area or the relative or absolute positions of objects. There are maps that describe population densities, ethnic breakdown, historical events, the distribution of dialects, climate, soil types, and the per capita consumption of soybeans—among other things. Students should be introduced to this fact by making maps of various types themselves. Virtually any subject dealt with in the social studies lends itself to this kind of assignment.

Students should begin by determining exactly what categories will be most useful in conveying the information they wish to express. Instructed to "make a map that tells something about the people who live on your block," they will have to decide what factors they deem most interesting or important. Should they indicate the number of people in each family, the number of years each family has lived there, the type of house and number of automobiles each has, the profession of each person? If they decide to do the first of these, they might break the information down by age and sex, and devise symbols to indicate these categories. If they are assigned a map on land-usage patterns in their communities, categories might include single-family residences, industrial and manufacturing buildings, streets, vacant lots and other unused land, and public buildings. Or, if they are to demonstrate the distribution of pollutants throughout the United States, categories might include several varieties of air, land, and water pollutants.

Chart 6–3
A List of Map and Globe Skills

Basic Research Skills   **Grades**

Size and Shape

Describes size and shape of globe, room, familiar areas, objects, using relative terms such as large, small, square, round	K–1
Makes a model of a room, house, farm, or other familiar area	K–1
Describes size and shape of mountains, rivers, streams	2–3
Compares size of different states	4–5
Compares size of continents, oceans, land, regions, hemispheres, countries	6

Orientation and Direction

Uses relative terms of location such as up, down, above, below	K–1
Uses cardinal directions on globe, world map, floor map, neighborhood map, classroom map	2–3
Uses compass	2–3
Makes a simple sketch map to show location	2–3
Uses cardinal directions in city and country	4–5
Uses intermediate directions (southeast, southwest, northeast, northwest)	4–5
Compares meridians and parallels on different map projections	4–5
Constructs simple maps, properly oriented	4–5
Describes orientation and direction of river flow, varied routes	6

Location

Locates buildings, school, harbor, park, etc. on street map	K–1
Locates land and water masses on globe	K–1
Locates countries known to students on world map	2–3
Locates land and water masses on a variety of map projections	2–3
Locates hometown, mountains, bridges, streams, oceans, islands on a variety of map projections	2–3
Locates place via longitude and latitude	4–5
Identifies varied climates via latitudinal degrees, coast lines, hemispheres	4–5
Locates equator, tropics, circles, continents, oceans, large islands	4–5
Locates place by number-key system on highway map	4–5
Uses atlas to locate place	4–5
Compares different maps of one place	4–5
Traces routes of travel by different means of transportation	4–5
Describes a trip using direction and location	4–5
Locates several state boundaries, principal rivers, coastal cities, peninsulas, capes, climatic areas, poles, cities, regions, rainfall areas, straits, windbelts	6
Uses map index to locate place	7–8

Scale and Distance

Makes simple scale map of a familiar area; e.g., room, neighborhood, street	K–1
Computes distance in terms of blocks; e.g., from school to home	2–3
Computes distance in terms of time; e.g., from school to home	2–3
Compares actual distances (a block, a mile) with those shown on map	4–5

Determines distances on map by using scale	4–5
Compares scale and distance using different maps of same area	4–5
Compares maps of different areas to note that smaller scale is used to map larger areas	4–5
Compares distance between two points on maps of different scales	4–5
Reads elevation on different maps	4–5
Identifies time zones of U.S. and relates them to longitude	6
Estimates distances using latitude	6
Estimates air distance using tape to measure great circle routes	6
Understands and uses map scale expressed as representative fraction, statement of scale, or bar scale	6

Symbols

Tells which objects are represented in simple map symbols	K–1
Understands color symbols for land and water	K–1
Recognizes symbols on class-made floor plan for table, chairs, street	K–1
Recognizes symbols on picture maps of community, outer space	2–3
Recognizes symbols on globe for oceans, islands, cities	2–3
Uses legends on different kinds of maps	4–5
Identifies symbols used for water features to learn the source, mouth, direction of flow, depths, and ocean currents	4–5
Identifies pictorial symbols such as dots, lines, colors	4–5
Recognizes symbols for mountains, equator, railroads, state boundaries, largest city, capital city, rivers, population, rainfall	4–5
Recognizes symbols for different populations of cities and population density	6
Understands color contour and visual relief maps	6
Uses all parts of a world atlas	7–8

Critical Thinking Skills

Analyzing

Sees relationships suggested by data:

Compares size and shape of familiar objects; e.g., chairs, houses	K–1
Compares distance and time to familiar places; e.g., school, home	K–1
Compares symbols with what they actually represent	K–1
Compares mountains with rivers, travel by ship with plane and other familiar modes of travel	K–1
Compares size and shape of continents, countries, oceans, roads, bridges, mountains	2–3
Compares distances to places studied	2–3
Sees relationships between natural conditions and distance from equator	2–3
Sees relationships between street, towns, cities, countries, continents	2–3
Compares population, rainfall, crops in different places studied	4–5
Sees relationship between physical and political features; e.g., river and state boundary	4–5
Compares size and shape of mountain ranges	6
Sees relationships between any two of the following: surface features, products, climate, precipitation, land features, river systems, land use, political boundaries, regions, agriculture, transportation	6
Compares different shipping routes to Europe or within the United States in different historical times	6

Relates population and economics, population and land features	6
Compares size and location of lands claimed by native American tribes, Spanish, French, English, and Russian in North America	7–8
Sees relationships between climate, soil, vegetation; production and altitudes	7–8
Compares effects of different ocean currents on countries	7–8
Compares metropolitan areas	7–8
Sees relationship between westward routes and natural conditions	7–8

*Identifies distortions in
different map projections:*

Globe	K–1
Mercator	2–3
Polar-centered	4–5
Historical map	4–5
Relief	4–5
Equal area	6
Conic	6
Aerial map	6

Synthesizing

Conceptualizes:

Continent, country, North Pole, South Pole, ocean, sea, globe, road, bridge, hill, mountain, north, south, east, west, up, down, left, right	K–1
City, capital, equator, great circle route, low, middle, high latitudes, hills, plain, valley, northwest, northeast, southwest, southeast, dam, hemisphere, region, delta, oasis	2–3
Province, Tropics of Cancer and Capricorn, Arctic and Antarctic Circles, latitude-longitude, degree, elevation, relief, canyon, plateau coastline, harbor, canal, bay, altitude, revolution	4–5
Peninsula, isthmus, cape, gulf, strait, rapids, swamp, mesa, upland, lowland, reef, watershed, mountain range, precipitation, vegetation	6
Meridian, ecliptic, isobar, continental shelf, solstice, equinox, horizon ring, area	7–8

Generalizes:
Induces or deduces generalizations about
the earth, maps, globes, seasons, climate,
and human activities such as:

Maps are ways of summarizing information	K–1
Objects may be represented by pictures or symbols	K–1
The earth is round	2–3
A large area may be shown on a small map	2–3
There is approximately twice as much water area as land area	2–3
The sun may be used to determine direction	4–5
A wall map does not change true direction	4–5
The earth spins in space	4–5
The earth's rotation causes day and night	4–5
It is hottest near the equator	4–5
Climate becomes colder as we go toward the poles	4–5
Flat maps distort	4–5
A map is really a diagram	4–5

A hemisphere is half of the earth	4 – 5
There are different kinds of maps for special purposes	6
Longitude is related to time	6
Latitude is related to temperature	6
The revolution of the earth causes a change of seasons	6
Oceans influence weather on continents	6
Mountains influence rainfall	6
Our natural environment influences our activities	6
A city must be accessible in order to grow larger	6

Makes maps:

Makes floor maps of objects such as boxes and models or drawn with chalk or crayon or some other substance on floor, some flat material, or earth	K – 1
Draws pictorial maps of local places, ways to get from one place to another, distribution of raw materials, and similar subjects	K – 1
Makes mural maps using paper cut-outs of objects, streets, etc.	K – 1
Outlines wall maps using a projector or a pantograph	K – 1
Puts together jigsaw puzzle maps of states and countries	K – 1
Makes specimen maps using real things such as rocks, dirt, plants	2 – 3
Makes relief maps of plaster, papier-mâché, earth, or other materials	2 – 3
Marks maps and globes with different patterns to show trade routes, boundaries, highways, rivers, and similar features	4 – 5
Makes maps using colors to show physical features, political boundaries, and so forth	4 – 5
Makes maps to show the development of an area or to illustrate a topic such as the westward movement in the United States	4 – 5
Makes maps with symbols to represent telephone lines, television networks, and other systems of communication	4 – 5
Makes maps showing special interests such as cities, parks, rivers	4 – 5
Makes transparent maps to illustrate different subject matter and show relationships when placed over other maps	4 – 5

Evaluating

Evaluates maps on the basis of the following criteria:

Clarity	K – 1
Accuracy	K – 1
Warranted conclusions by comparison with other sources	K – 1
Consistency	K – 1
Care	K – 1
Distortion	K – 1

Time and Chronology

Subjective time is an unreliable measure. Spending an hour in school may seem like a long time to students, while the equivalent hour may seem all too short to a busy mother. Objective time, the application of mathematical and astronomical measures to events, is independent of the personal perception and subjective judgments of the perceiver. The focus on objective time measures has become a necessity in modern societies. It is useful in reconstructing the historical past, enabling us to see how events are related and to hypothesize regarding cause and effect. Probably as important as its roles in organizing the past and present, however, is its function in planning the future.

Time Systems and the Calendar

The earliest experiences with objective time usually occur in the early primary grades when children learn to tell time by the clock. Associating time with a personal activity helps children develop meaningful time concepts, such as: at 9 o'clock we start school, at 12 o'clock we eat lunch, and so on. Chart classroom activities with the students using time measures, and develop plans for the day based on time measures. To begin to understand how other important people in their lives spend their time, ask children to interview their parents to find out what they do at certain hours of the day.

Learning the calendar year and months is also an early primary activity. Keep a large calendar in your classroom. Note holidays, birthdates, and other dates of importance to students. Have them find out how many days or months it is from one important date to another. Add other events to the calendar as the year progresses. Note the relationship of seasons to months.

Relate the passing years to the personal development of students. Ask them to bring in photographs of themselves from other years. Discuss the changes that take place over the years. What things could they do when they were infants? What things can they do today that they could not do when they were three years old?

Keeping a diary is a good way for intermediate students to refine their time skills. Start with short term diaries—of a week or month. Or have students create imaginary diaries out of historical events, such as a week in the life of a child going west on a wagon train. To have students appreciate how significant diaries can become, familiarize them with some famous ones, such as *The Diary of Anne Frank*.

In intermediate grades students begin to focus on dates. They can also begin to understand the basic importance of dates as points of orientation in time, rather than isolated facts. The use of B.C. and A.D. can be introduced in the intermediate years, but it is usually not until the junior high years that students learn to manipulate them adequately.

Events as Chronological Series

In early primary years, pupils should have many opportunities to practice arranging events in sequence. The teacher can present a scrambled group of descriptions, photographs, or pictures of events (such as a simple story or a shopping trip) and ask the students to rearrange them appropriately. Pupils

can be asked to relate stories in sequence: things they did from the time they got up until the morning recess, or other similar activities that depend on sequence. Introduce sequence expressions, such as "first," "second," "third," and use them frequently in class. For example, when lining children up, you might say "Those wearing green socks line up first," or "Joe, you are the first person in line. Please exchange places with the third person." Put the daily schedule on a chart. If variations are made during the day, ask students to identify them.

In early intermediate grades, begin using arithmetical terms to distinguish past from present and future events. Instead of saying "last week" or "sometimes," use precise terms, such as "six days ago" or "ten years from now." Have students compute the length of time between two historical events, for example, the number of years between the American Revolution and the Civil War, or the arrival of the first slave and the Emancipation Proclamation.

To help students understand the sequence of history, try putting a list of famous people or events on the blackboard and ask the students to arrange them according to who lived first or what happened first. Plan a future activity, such as taking a class trip, and ask students to identify what things have to be

Chart 6–4
A List of Time and Chronology Skills

Basic Resource Skills

Time systems and the calendar

Learns to tell time by clock	K–1
Uses names of days of the week in order	K–1
Uses names of months in sequence	K–1
Uses calendar to find dates of special events and to determine length of time between important events	K–1
Associates seasons with particular months in northern and southern hemispheres	4–5
Accumulates some specific date-events as points of orientation in time	4–5
Uses the B.C./A.D. system of chronology	4–5
Translates dates into centuries	4–5

Events as chronological series and differences in duration

Arranges personal experiences in sequence	2–3
Uses expressions of sequence; e.g., first, second, third	2–3
Recognizes sequence and chronology in experiences such as the school day, weekly schedule	4–5
Uses arithmetical terms in distinguishing past from present events; e.g., ten years ago	4–5
Computes length of time between two dates	4–5
Uses a few clusters of date-events to establish time relationships among historic events	4–5
Recognizes sequence and chronology in time lines	4–5
Knows differences in duration of various historical periods	7–8

Critical Thinking Skills

Analyzing

Earth and time relationships:

Sees relationships between rotation of earth and day and night	2–3
Understands time zones as related to rotation of earth	2–3
Understands relationship between earth's revolution around the sun and a calendar year	2–3

Change and continuity in human behavior:

Compares past and present in studying human behavior over time	2–3
Relates new events to known date-events	4–5

Synthesizing

Conceptualizes:

Uses indefinite concepts such as long ago, past, future, before, after, meanwhile	K–1
Uses definite time concepts such as second, minute, yesterday, decade, century	4–5
Understands concept of prehistoric and geological time	7–8

Generalizes:

Generalizes about human behavior through time	4–5

Makes predictions about future based on study of human behavior in past and present	4–5
Communicates orally:	
Relates events in sequence	K–1
Communicates in writing:	
Arranges events in sequence	2–3
Makes a simple time line	4–5
Evaluating	
Evaluates on basis of following criteria:	
Accuracy	4–5
Warranted generalizations regarding human behavior over time	4–5
Warranted predictions	4–5
Precision in use of definite and indefinite time concepts	4–5
Consistency	4–5
Care in citing references and documentation	7–8

done and in what order. Ask them to estimate by what date they think they can have all the work done.

Introduce simple time lines, focusing at first on personal events. Begin by identifying certain key events in students' lives and charting these on a time line. Have them extend this to a family time line dating back to their grandparents. When were their grandparents married? When were their parents born? When were their parents married? Other time lines can emerge directly from their studies.

Selecting key dates as reference points in time is very useful. For example, 1492 (date of Columbus's discovery of the New World), 1789 (George Washington's inauguration as President), 1861 (beginning of the Civil War), 1910 (founding of the NAACP), and 1959 (the first space satellite into orbit) can be very useful in helping focus other events.

Critical Thinking about Time

Students need to use time concepts critically. Once certain basic skills are developed, they can begin to hypothesize regarding the likelihood of events taking place in certain periods and comparing past and present human behavior. Would a good horseman like Paul Revere have a chance to be a hero today? Is it likely that leisure activities were as important in the nineteenth century as they are today? Is it likely that most parents would have been very concerned about their children's education in the eighteenth century? What important changes have taken place in communication? In eating habits? What effects have these had? What changes are likely to take place in the future?

Understanding geological time can lead to fruitful speculations about human evolution. What made human beings human? How do people today differ from people thirty thousand years ago? In what ways are human beings likely to develop further? In what ways do they need to direct their own development so as to avoid problems? Is it possible that life on other planets has evolved in the same way? What importance would this have?

It is relatively easy to explain changes in technology that have occurred over a period of time. But it is far more difficult to get across how ideas have changed. For example, the concept of childhood is relatively new. Where and when did the idea begin? How does it differ now? Or compare the prevailing attitude toward the American Indian today with that of a hundred years ago. Or the situation of women. Students can think of ideas they have that are different from those of their parents and other adults they know. They should try to evaluate these changes. Which are good? Which are not so desirable? And they might consider what additional changes we need in order to live peaceably and in harmony in this world. A critical approach to the time dimension can help youngsters realize that change is inevitable and, to some degree at least, can be shaped by people like themselves as they plan for the future.

Summary

Some of the skills taught in the social studies are essentially the same as those taught in the sciences and the humanities. Observing, listening, and reading, for example, are skills needed in all subjects of the curriculum. However, some skills, such as map reading or understanding the relationships among events in the past, are the particular responsibility of the social studies. Ultimately, all skills involve learning how to obtain and process information.

Students can obtain information in a variety of ways. They may hear it directly from the teacher, read it in a textbook, see it happen, or look for it in one of a great many sources. In obtaining it they must make a series of decisions, some of a more simple nature (such as whether to look in an almanac or a library book) and some of a more complex nature (such as whether or not to believe what they read there). And, finally, they will probably make some use of this information, even if it is only to pass an examination.

Basic research skills in the social studies are concerned primarily with obtaining information, while critical thinking skills involve more internal processing of the information. The basic research skill of locating information, for example, may involve little more than knowing where to find it, while analysis, a critical thinking skill, involves such things as examining the relationships among ideas. Comprehension may be limited to simply identifying the main ideas, while evaluation means making judgments about the merit and validity of those ideas. Organizing information may involve little more than a general classification of the information, while synthesizing requires putting the information together in some unique form such as a written report, a map, or a mural.

Both basic research and critical thinking skills are essential and should be given a great deal of attention throughout the entire course of schooling. Nowhere, however, are they more important than in in the elementary-school years, where they must be introduced at the proper stage, dealt with in sequence, and frequently reviewed. The teacher must never assume that any skill is so simple that it can be easily learned and never forgotten.

Instructional Resources

Instructional resources are the tools of teaching and learning. They provide data that students use in learning. They may require the student to perform concrete physical actions or utilize abstract symbolization skills. Although it is generally acknowledged that children require many concrete sensory experiences, teachers begin to depend on abstractions almost exclusively when their students are still very young. The use of multiple instructional resources can help arrest this unfortunate trend.

Types of Experience

There is probably no instructional resource that falls exclusively into either the concrete or abstract class. But resources can be categorized as *primarily* one or the other. Edgar Dale has constructed a useful model, the Cone of Experience, in which instructional resources are arranged according to degree of concreteness.[1]

As illustrated in Figure 7–1, the base of the Cone, *direct purposeful experiences,* represents those that are primarily concrete, while the apex, *verbal symbols,* represents the most abstract. Dale cautions that increasing levels of abstraction do not necessarily correspond to increasing levels of difficulty. Even though a drawing, for example, is more abstract than a dramatization, it is more difficult to understand *Hamlet* than a picture of a tree. Nonetheless, meaningful symbols depend on concrete sensory experiences and the school must therefore help provide such experiences. And while all students need them, they are particularly important for slower learners and the educationally disadvantaged. A good social studies program will use many of the resources toward the bottom of the Cone, while not neglecting those at the top.

The Cone of Experience served as the organizational structure for this chapter and the following one. Teaching techniques and examples are offered throughout these chapters to illustrate how resources could be used in the classroom.

[1]Edgar Dale, *Audiovisual Methods in Teaching,* 3rd ed. (New York: Holt, Rinehart and Winston, 1969), p. 107.

Guidelines for Using Instructional Resources

1. The resource should be related to an educational objective.
2. It should be appropriate for the maturity level of learners.
3. It should be enjoyable as well as stimulating.
4. It should be adaptable to individual differences.
5. It should provide something that could not be learned as efficiently or meaningfully in another way.
6. Students should be prepared for it with suggestions of what to look for.
7. Teacher and learners should evaluate it together to assess its effectiveness.

Figure 7–1
The Cone of Experience

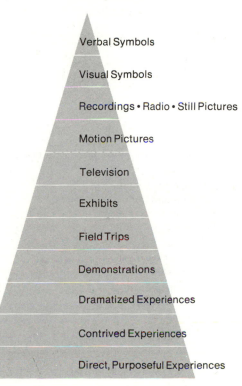

Verbal Symbols

Visual Symbols

Recordings • Radio • Still Pictures

Motion Pictures

Television

Exhibits

Field Trips

Demonstrations

Dramatized Experiences

Contrived Experiences

Direct, Purposeful Experiences

From *Audiovisual Methods in Teaching*, 3rd ed., by Edgar Dale. Copyright © 1969 by Holt, Rinehart and Winston, Publishers. Used by permission.

Direct Experiences

It is generally believed that direct experience is the best way to learn most things. Probably the best way to learn about the political process, for example, is to participate in it, much as the best way to learn about contemporary Mexico is to live there. Obviously not all of the social studies can be learned by direct experiences because of time and space limitations. Students cannot participate directly in the westward movement across the United States any more than they can in Aztec culture. But opportunities for some direct experiences do exist, both within and without the classroom. With a bit of imagination, teachers can expand these opportunities.

Students might actually participate in a political campaign in their community in order to get some understanding of the political process. Or they might design some contemporary Mexican clothing as one way of understanding contemporary Mexican culture. They might construct a model covered wagon that

---

Chart 7–1
Examples of Direct Experiences in the Classroom

Play:
soccer
with toys from other lands
musical instruments

Paint:
a mural of life in an Indian village
a copy of a famous painting
on a piece of stone, like a caveman

Model:
an Aztec sculpture
furniture from a Japanese home
an igloo

Make:
butter
a Chinese meal
a Navaho loom

Participate in:
a school election
an archeological dig
feeding a baby

Sing:
ballads
children's lullabies
folk songs

Dance:
a rain dance
free-form
square dances

Design:
a low-cost apartment
Nigerian clothing
a world flag

Use:
a typewriter
chopsticks
a tape recorder

Weave, sew, or stitich:
a tapestry
a patchwork quilt
a beaded belt

---

could withstand inclement weather and rough routes as well as accommodate a family's needs. They might try modeling in clay an Aztec calendar or an Aztec sculpture. In short, they can sculpt, draw, design, dance, use, and participate in many things through which they can experience some of the content of the social studies more directly. A few examples may be found in Chart 7–1.

Maximizing Direct Experiences
While a direct experience is an invaluable learning tool, it does not of itself necessarily lead to higher thinking and conceptualization. Helping students think about the experience through guided inquiry can give cognitive and affective meaning to sensory exploration. Questions to stimulate inquiry based on direct experiences are given in Chart 7–2. Note that cognitive questions include almost the entire range of educational objectives, while affective questions focus on value clarification.

Contrived Experiences

When direct experiences are not possible, contrived experiences may be offered as a substitute with very useful results. A contrived experience is basically of two types. In one, physical objects such as models, replicas, or specimens are

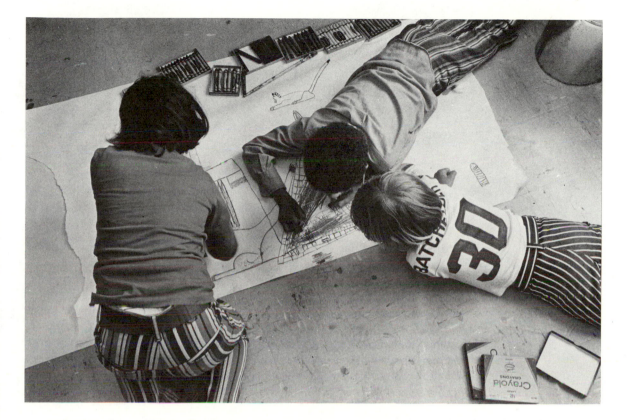

Chart 7—2
Examples of Inquiry Questions Based on Direct Experiences

Cognitive

What does it taste like? Feel like? Smell like? Look like? Sound like?

What are you doing?

What is it for?

How does it compare with ———?

What other things do you need?

Where did you get the idea of doing it this way?

What did you learn by doing it?

Is this the best way of doing it?

What would you suggest to make it better next time?

Affective

How do you feel about this?

Why do you feel this way?

Would you like to do it again?

Would you recommend that others do it?

Is it worth the time and effort?

Is it something everybody should do?

used to suggest another time or place or object. The other basic type of contrived experience is the simulation game, in which some process or event is re-created as an activity. These experiences present, of course, only partial aspects of reality. Models, for example, are either smaller or larger than the real thing and always less complex. Replicas and specimens are always seen outside their environmental context. The reality presented in games is also limited—many of the elements that are characteristic of the real-life situation are omitted. Contrived experiences edit reality to make it easier to understand, but because of this they also present distortions. Hence it is essential to make sure that the students are aware of the limitations of this kind of experience.

Using Objects The limitations of contrived experiences can be turned to an advantage if inquiry strategies are applied when introducing objects to a class. Rather than telling the students what the object is, the teacher can present it as a mystery for them solve in the fashion of Sherlock Holmes. Such unusual objects as an Eskimo snow mask, a Tuareg headdress, or an Australian aborigine's spear-throwing stick provide a basis for reaching a number of useful conclusions about the ways of life of other peoples, the geography of the regions they live in, and their ways of thinking. Decorative objects—or decorations applied to objects that have a specific purpose—can also tell us a great deal about a people. Native crafts, such as the art of making beautiful lamps out of olive oil tins, can offer insights into the economy as well as the ingenuity of the Mexicans or the Spaniards. Objects with a specific purpose, such as postage stamps, can reveal something about the history, beliefs, and achievements of a people—for example, the fact that the government of Ghana would issue a postage stamp to publicize a campaign against malaria is indicative of the goals and priorities of that country. (Stamps can also be used to study what did *not* take place—as, for example, the fact that it was not until 1893 that the United States honored a woman on one of its stamps.)[2]

[2]The woman, however, was neither American nor contemporary, but Queen Isabella of Spain. For an interesting article on this subject, see Richard C. Brown, "Postage Stamps and American Women," *Social Education* 38:1 (January 1974), pp. 20–23.

Chart 7–3
Examples of Inquiry Based on Objects

Cognitive

What is it?

What do you see on it?

What do you suppose it is used for?

Who might have used it? What makes you think so?

Where would these people most likely have lived? What makes you think so?

Can you tell anything about the values of the people who made it?

How does this compare with other objects that serve the same purpose?

What can you say about it in general? Why do you say that?

How do you suppose this compares with the real thing? What else should be included? How can we find out?

Affective

Do you like it? Why or why not?

Do you think the people who made it had a sense of beauty?

Do you think they were intelligent? Why or why not?

Would you like to have it in your home? Why or why not?

Was this a good way of making it? Why or why not?

If you were making something like this, how would you do it?

A Specific Case: Using a Selection of Stamps from Ghana

What years do the stamps cover? How can we find out?

What kinds of themes run through different periods? Why do you suppose these were chosen? Who selects the themes?

How do these themes compare with those of other countries for the same years?

What important events and concerns are not included in this selection? How can we find out if stamps were issued with these themes?

What themes would you expect to find on stamps for this year? Who will volunteer to find out if we are right?

Simulation Games

Technically, simulations and games are two different things. For the purposes of the classroom, however, the terms are sometimes used interchangeably or together. A simulation game may be defined as an environment or situation that imitates or recreates aspects of real life, in which students assume the roles of decision-makers and compete for certain goals.

There are several different ways of classifying games. One typology, identified by Roger Kasperson, classifies them according to the game environment. Games with physical environments, such as baseball or tennis, develop physical skills. Symbolic games deal with symbolic environments, such as numbers and words. Bingo, crossword puzzles, and tic-tac-toe are examples of symbolic games. Social games, which deal with abstract elements of social environ-

> ### Guidelines for Playing Simulation Games
>
> 1. Consider the number of participants, supplies, and physical arrangements before the game begins.
> 2. Brief participants thoroughly as to the nature and goals of the game, as well as the environment in which it is set.
> 3. State the rules clearly.
> 4. Be flexible. Add rules or modify existing ones as you see fit.
> 5. Spend some time in practice sessions.
> 6. Allow adequate time for the game itself.
> 7. Allow students the opportunity to play the game several times.
> 8. Schedule a debriefing session immediately after the last play of the game.

ments, are the content of social studies games. Such abstract elements are generally concepts and generalizations from the social sciences.[3]

Many advantages are attributed to simulation games. Research indicates that they are enjoyed by most children. They can be particularly useful in illuminating difficult concepts regarding the social system or historical events, and valuable skills can be developed through them. Perhaps more important is their capacity for helping participants develop feelings of potency regarding their social environment. The player wins by making a series of social decisions. Since these are similar to decisions required in real-life situations, players can begin to feel that they do have some control over their environment. Actual involvement in decision-making through the legislative process or in resolving social conflicts not only teaches students how certain things are accomplished, it makes them realize that their behavior does make a difference. Equally valuable is the apparent success of simulation games with both fast and slow learners. For the latter, it provides another approach to difficult concepts, reducing dependence on complex reading materials, while the former can play the game at higher levels of sophistication.

The major disadvantage of games is that they present simplified models of reality that may easily lead to distorted views. Games can also have a dehumanizing effect on the learners, since the object is often simply to win, without attention to underlying values and attitudes. However, these disadvantages can be overcome through appropriate debriefing strategies. Many commercially prepared games are accompanied by recommended debriefing strategies. Teachers may supplement these or create their own. An example of a debriefing strategy with both cognitive and affective learnings is given in Chart 7–4.

Evaluating Simulation Games   There are many social studies games currently available but not all will be appropriate to the needs of each class. Nor are they all valid. In some, the major ideas may be inaccurate, while others may purport to teach one thing, but when analyzed, actually teach something else. Rules may be too complicated or the

[3]Roger E. Kasperson, "Games as Educational Media," in William A. Nesbitt, ed., *Simulation Games for the Social Studies Classroom,* 2nd ed. (New York: Thomas Y. Crowell Co., 1971), p. 100.

Chart 7–4
Example of a Debriefing Strategy

Teacher Questions	Student Activities
What goals did each of you have in mind as you made your moves?	Recall goals. Begin to comprehend other players' goals.
Why did you choose that goal?	Clarify values.
Did the moves you made help you realize your goals?	Evaluate consistency of moves with goals.
Did winning mean you had to give up certain things you believe in? If so, which ones?	Clarify values by analyzing "costs" of winning.
Did losing sometimes mean you held on to certain things you believe in? If so, which ones?	Clarify values by analyzing possible benefits of losing.
What facts are included in the game?	Recall facts
Are these accurate? How can we find out?	Evaluate accuracy of facts.
What important ideas does the game involve?	Synthesize concepts, generalizations, main ideas.
How do these ideas compare with what people say in real life?	Evaluate as compared with other authorities.
How do these compare with real life?	Evaluate as compared with real life.
What is missing from the game that would have made it more like real life?	Evaluate by noting omissions.
How might the game be changed?	Propose alternative concepts, generalizations, main ideas.

---

game may take too much time. Teachers need to evaluate games before using them. The following questions can help assess merit.

1. *What are the central concepts, generalizations, ideas?* Are they important for your group? Are they appropriate for your group? Are they amply illustrated? Are they accurately represented? Are the supporting facts accurate?
2. *What choices are available to players?* Are they consistent with the central concepts and generalizations? Do they reflect them accurately? Do they pose real conflicts for the player? Are choices available to many players?
3. *Under what conditions can winning occur?* Is winning the result of consistent decisions made by players? Can players win merely by chance?
4. *What are the rules of the game?* Are they simple enough to be understood? Are they consistent in helping players make sound decisions? Do they allow for distortions? Do they help clarify concepts and generalizations?
5. *How is the game organized?* Is it suitable for large or small groups? Do available space and time blocks accommodate the necessities of the game?

Two Examples Simulation games may be rigorously formalized with specified procedures, such as those described on pages 226–27. Or they may be more open-ended and flexible, as are the *Norules* and *Mini-Society* simulations described below.

Norules

Norules (no rules) is a simple game that was developed to highlight the importance of rules.[4] It is appropriate for all students from the first grade on, but especially for those who have difficulty following or accepting rules. Without any preliminary announcements, the teacher takes a large, blown-up balloon and bats it out to the classroom. Some child will automatically react by hitting it and others will respond similarly. The teacher responds instantly by starting to record names and "points" on the chalkboard. But "points" are to be assigned arbitrarily without any apparent rhyme or reason. Girls might be favored over boys, blondes over brunettes, or blue shirts over other colors. Sometimes points should be given for a specific action, as when the balloon hits the desk; at other times points should be taken off for the very same thing. The befuddled students will try unsuccessfully to figure out what you're up to. After a reasonable amount of time, assemble them for a debriefing session, which might run like this:

Teacher: "What did you think when the game began?"
Pupils: "To hit the balloon." "When you started keeping points, I wanted the girls to win." "I wanted to win!"
Teacher: "How did you feel when you realized that you didn't know what the game was?"
Pupils: "I didn't like it." "I thought it was fun until nothing seemed to make sense."
Teacher: "Was winning the game important?"
Pupils: "Everyone likes to win." "Isn't that what games are for, to win or lose?"
Teacher: "Bill, how did you feel when I never let you score a point?"
Pupil: "I didn't like it at all. I knew I was right, yet you wouldn't let me score."
Teacher: "How did you know you were right?"
Pupil: "Well, I did things that always seemed right before and I've always been good at games, so I should have scored points."
Teacher: "Marcia, why did you quit trying to play?"
Pupil: "No one ever hit it my way."
Teacher: "Who liked the game?"
Pupils: "I didn't!" "I did, because I won."
Teacher: "If we played the game again, do you think you still could win the game?"
Pupils: "I don't know—maybe." "I'm not sure because you kept changing the rules." "I could if you wanted me to."
Teacher: "What were the rules?"
Pupils: "Well, one time you could get points for hitting the balloon." "If it hit the floor you could get points."

[4] *Norules* was developed by George E. Pickett and Jerry K. Larson.

Teacher: "Always?"

Pupils: "No."

Teacher: "How would you suggest the game be changed?"

Pupils: "By making some rules we all liked."

Teacher: "Would making rules solve anything?"

Pupils: "Then we would know how to win."

Teacher: "What purpose can this game serve?"

Pupils: "It can be just for fun." "I didn't think it was any fun!" "Maybe to let us know that rules are necessary?"

Teacher: "How does this compare with real life?"

Pupils: "People like to win." "We have rules so we know how to win." "Sometimes winning is too important—we forget that other things are important too." "Not everyone likes rules." "Not everyone follows the rules."

Teacher: "Does the phrase 'it's not whether you win or lose but how you play the game' seem right to you?"

Pupils: "We've heard that before in sports here at school, but everyone still likes to be a winner." "It sounds right, but I still like to win." "I really don't like poor losers though." "If the game was played fair it's not quite so bad if you lose."

Teacher: "Well, let's make some rules for this game and see if it makes a difference in how you feel about the game."

Mini-Society: An Economic Simulation

Mini-Society, in which the entire class is turned into a simulated economic society that lasts for several weeks or the entire year, goes beyond a conventional game or simulation.[5]

The "society" is launched by the teacher's creation of a "scarcity" situation — of chairs, crayons, or something else usually found in the classroom. A classroom discussion is then held in which students propose means of "allocating" the resource. Eventually, students usually propose "money," and soon the class embarks on a variety of economic projects — printing money, opening businesses and banks, starting a civil service, taxing, possibly even setting up a stock market, and international trading with other classes engaged in the same simulation. Eventually all services in the classroom are put on a pay-as-you-go basis — even the teacher's. All this activity is not in response to a prepared script, but is generated by the students themselves as they simulate the roles of economic producers and consumers.

The program revolves around such economic concepts as scarcity, what to produce, how and for whom to produce it, flow of income, accounting profit and loss, economic profit and loss, factors that determine supply and demand, price ceilings and price floors, competition versus monopoly, money, and inflation. This may sound far beyond the level of the elementary school student, but in fact it is not difficult to understand when a society is constructed from scratch in a classroom.

[5]Marylyn Kourilsky, *Beyond Simulation: The Mini-Society Approach to Instruction in Economics and Other Social Sciences* (Los Angeles: Educational Research Associates, 1974).

The course is intended for fourth through sixth grade, and adaptations have been undertaken to make it suitable at still lower levels. Preliminary assessments are very positive, and it is currently being tried in several school districts throughout California.

A Sampling of Simulation Games

The following is a list of some of the commercially produced simulation games that are available for classroom use. They are arranged by discipline.

Anthropology

Atlantis. Students play the roles of archeologists and discover an ancient civilization (grades 4–8). Portola Institute, 1115 Merrill Street, Menlo Park, Calif. 94025.

Bushman Exploring and Gathering. Adaptation to a difficult environment is illustrated through the gathering and hunting life of the Kalahari Bushmen (grade 5). Education Development Center, 15 Mifflin Place, Cambridge, Mass. 02138.

Githaka. Players attempt to increase the number of cattle in their herds and the amount of pasture space while seeking to improve their social positions. Based on the social system of the Kikuyus of Kenya (grades 4–8). The Learning Center, Social Studies Department, Princeton, N.J. 08540.

Economics

The Columbia River Game. Play is based on an understanding of the economic interests that affect the river—industry, government agencies, and farming—and their interrelationships (grades 4–5). Teaching Research, Oregon State System of Higher Education, Monmouth, Oreg. 97361.

Free Enterprise. Players act as executives in corporations to learn about the free enterprise system (grades 4–9). Instructional Innovations, Redlands, Calif. 92373.

Market. Consumer and seller bargain with each other in a grocery market setting in a game intended to illustrate the way prices are determined in a market economy (grades 6–8). Benefic Press, 10300 W. Roosevelt Road, Westchester, Ill. 60153.

Sociology

Culture Contact. Cultural differences and misunderstandings are studied by role-playing a situation in which modern traders attempt to deal with a preindustrial society (grades 4–8). Games Central, Abt Associates, Inc. 55 Wheeler St., Cambridge, Mass. 02138.

Neighborhood. A game that involves the development of urban areas (grades K–8). Abt Associates, Inc. 55 Wheeler St., Cambridge, Mass. 02138.

Sunshine. Segregation and other urban problems are dealt with in an imaginary city by making the players members of different races (grades 4–8). Interact, P.O. Box 262, Lakeside, Calif. 92040.

Political Science

Election. The typical steps and procedures followed by a candidate for the presidency of the United States are played through by four participants (grades 6–9). Educational Games Co., P.O. Box 363, Peekskill, N.Y., 10566.

The Sumerian Game. One player takes the role of the ruler of a country with an agricultural economy and must make decisions that will improve the situation of the people of the country (grades K–8). Board of Cooperative Educational Services (BOCES), Westchester County, Yorktown Heights, N.Y. 10598.

Pollution. The control of pollution requires that players deal with political, economic, and social aspects of the problem (grades K–8). Abt Associates, Inc., 55 Wheeler St., Cambridge, Mass. 02138.

Dramatized Experiences

Dramatized experiences include a variety of activities. Tableaus, which are essentially picture-like scenes in which the participants are posed against appropriate backgrounds, are the simplest of all; they require a certain amount of research to prepare the scene but no real acting. Pantomimes, involving activities without speech, can become quite complex if the students are good actors. In pantomime one may attempt to communicate things as abstract as feelings—such as love, sorrow, or joy—or one may simply illustrate an activity—such as the preparation of a Hoopa meal or the movements of Bushmen hunting in the desert. Puppetry, using marionettes that slip on the hand or hang from strings, can be employed to recreate folk tales or myths or to perform stories of the students' own invention. Plays, which present human situations or events in condensed form, can be useful when they deal with historic events or such problems as prejudice and discrimination, the search for identity, and the impact of technology on individuals.

Students can create their own dramatized experiences, act out scripts, or observe the performances of others. Each of these activities has its advantages. Creating one's own material may involve both affective learnings and high-level synthesizing activities. Working with carefully chosen scripts can be extremely effective in making certain kinds of points. And simply observing the performances of others can transform spectators into mentally and emotionally active co-participants.

Role-Playing   One of the more recent developments in the area of dramatized experiences is role-playing. In this activity participants are assigned specific characters or

roles to play in specific situations. They create the script themselves while acting out the scene. This technique tends to work best with limited social-conflict
situations such as arguments within a family or the predicament of a black child
torn between friendship for a white child and pressures from adults of both
races that discourage such relationships. (Role-playing as a tool for the development of moral values was discussed in Chapter 4.)

Role-playing can also be put to effective use in other areas of the social
studies as a means of providing a different, more personal insight into historical
or social issues. One might stage, for example, events like that of Chief Joseph
of the Nez Percé Indians discussing with some of the surviving elders whether
or not the tribe should surrender. Or, in the area of government, one might assign students positions on a state budget committee making decisions about
how to allocate funds for highways, education, and care of the aged. A deeper
understanding of the judicial process may be attained through mock courts in
which the students assume the roles of judge, lawyer, plaintiff, and accused.
With a bit of imagination, role-playing can also be used to create historically
impossible situations with provocative results—such as the meeting of a feudal
serf, a slave from an American plantation, and a Calcutta street dweller.

Role playing can be a very effective means for helping students understand
others' points of view. Through assuming the role of another without benefit of

Guidelines for Role-Playing

1. Select a situation that involves many points of view.
2. Be sure students understand the situation.
3. Permit students to pick their own roles. In the beginning choose only volunteers.
4. Remind students of the roles they are to play. The quality of the acting is unimportant—what counts is to truthfully reflect the motives and interests of the character.
5. Play some roles yourself.
6. Discuss appropriate spectator behaviors with the students (e.g., observe carefully, take notes, save your comments for the conclusion).
7. Discuss characterizations at the end of role play with all students. Have the same or other people replay it.
8. See if students can arrive at any generalizations after the performance.

script, students are forced to consider how and why people behave as they do. Such insight can lead to improved communication and more effective strategies for working out problems. Its usefulness has become apparent in many situations, including government, where officials are sometimes charged with playing the roles of international political leaders in gaming situations that attempt to predict reactions to actual and potential events.

Successful role-playing requires very careful planning and class preparation. This is particularly important when first introducing the technique. Unless much attention is given to procedures, students may profit little from the experience.

Demonstrations

A demonstration is an explanation of an idea or skill that incorporates audiovisual materials. The idea may be a concept, a generalization, a process, or even a set of related facts. The audiovisual material may range from chalk drawings on a blackboard to expensive videotape recorders. Demonstration is essentially an expository technique that may culminate in a student activity—as when students apply Japanese brush techniques at the conclusion of a demonstration—or it may be the first step in an inquiry strategy—as when students analyze and evaluate a demonstration of an interviewing technique.

The art of demonstration has been largely ignored in current social studies training programs. But effectively implemented, the demonstration can be a very efficient and enjoyable learning experience. The following examples illustrate the variety of things that might be demonstrated: the effects of the pollution of major water areas on drinking water, illustrated with photographs and charts; the interdependence of farmer and city retailer, with maps to show the transport systems of produce and goods; the impact of the private automobile on the quality of life, which would include such things as photographs of traffic jams and recordings of automobile sounds; how to conduct an interview, which would involve actually holding an interview with someone.

Guidelines for Demonstrations

1. Limit the number of main ideas. Three should be the maximum.
2. Make an outline of the main points and steps.
3. Keep the demonstration itself simple.
4. Be sure equipment is in working order before you begin.
5. Have a rehearsal.
6. Be sure everyone can see and hear.
7. Do not deviate from the main points.
8. Enliven the demonstration with humor, personal anecdotes, and concrete references.
9. Observe the group for signs of confusion and boredom. If these occur, stop and ask the students if you are making yourself clear. Find out what the points of difficulty are and go over them until they are understood.
10. Summarize your main points at the end. A written handout at the conclusion can help reinforce them.
11. Evaluate the demonstration with students through discussion and/or written exercises.

Study Trips

Teaching outside the classroom is becoming widely recognized as an important—if not essential—part of the education process. Although it can be valuable for all students, it is invaluable for those who otherwise rarely venture beyond their homes. A visit to a supermarket or the beach may be a common experience for the average middle-class child, but for some children it may be a unique event. The potential teaching value of the community itself has been largely underutilized. In part this is due to the restrictive policies of many schools, which may involve complicated safety regulations as well as financial questions. But it has also been due in part to the restricted imagination of many teachers. Few are able to see the potential in local visits beyond such conventional trips as to the museum or post office. However, worthwhile study trips may be made to construction sites, churches, other schools, the courthouse, varied residential areas, shopping centers, a factory, a newspaper office, a printing plant, a hospital, a broker's office, a local college, an auto-mechanic shop, a store specializing in the products of a specific country, or just to the next street corner.

An Unusual Study Trip

Most communities offer a variety of interesting possibilities for study trips. Ruth Bassett, an imaginative fourth-grade teacher, was able to "sift" history from a local cemetery with her students.[6] Her example is worth following.

Plan carefully! Visit the cemetery you have chosen for the study trip and familiarize yourself with it. Make notes of the things a child could learn from the

[6]Ruth Bassett, "Reading History from Tombstones," *Instructor* (April 1971), pp. 94–96.

markers. Ask yourself how long a visit will be needed to gain the necessary information. Can you foresee any problems? Are they surmountable?

In the classroom, discuss what information can be found in a cemetery. How would an archeologist explore the area? What shall we look for and what will we need for this exploration? Ask your pupils to talk about do's and don'ts of behavior with their parents. The following day, discuss what their parents had to say. Make a class chart on "graveyard etiquette."

Ruth Bassett had prepared checklists to serve as tally sheets. Each child was to keep age-group tallies of burials: men over sixty, women over fifty, and children under ten. Prior to going they tried to predict what they would find. A tally of the number of soldiers killed in each war was chosen to be a group project, carried out by everyone. To prepare for it, the students did some research on wars and learned about the different war emblems and the official government markers that are placed by the graves of soldiers.

In addition to the tally work, the teacher raised a number of questions about the cemetery itself, pointing out certain epitaphs, the materials from which tombstones were made, and other features. For example, a hitching post led to the question of why people had tied their horses out in the roadway instead of riding them up the hill. The pupils reasoned that if the horses had been taken

Guidelines for Planning a Study Trip

1. Visit the site beforehand to locate specific points of interest.
2. Estimate the time required to get there and back and to explore.
3. Determine whether it is worth the time and effort.
4. Determine whether it will involve any undue strain on anyone. Will it impose on the hosts the need to entertain beyond their means or available time? Is it likely to cause friction between the hosts and the school?
5. Make sure safety needs can be adequately met.
6. Decide whether small groups or the entire class should go.
7. Get consent from appropriate school officials and from parents.
8. Make arrangements with those in charge of the place you will visit.
9. Plan the transportation in detail and arrange to pay for it.
10. Make arrangements for students who cannot go.
11. Get your students interested through discussions, presentations, and so on.
12. Discuss with the students questions that might guide their observations. List and circulate these.
13. Discuss behavioral constraints and consequences of possible violations. Sensitize students to the needs of the people they will be interacting with.
14. Back in the classroom, evaluate the trip with students, consider appropriate gestures of appreciation, and discuss ideas for further learning.

inside the cemetery, they would have eaten the flowers and shrubbery and probably would have knocked over some stones.

The trip was planned for the afternoon. The students took tally sheets, pencils, a few pocket-size magnifying glasses (to be shared), and bags of cookies.

Chart 7–5
Evaluating a Study Trip with Students

Cognitive

What did we learn?

Were we able to answer the questions we had? Which ones?

What things did we not consider in our list of questions?

What things didn't we do that we should have done?

Which other people should we have spoken to? Why?

Did our behavior cause any problems? What?

What other things do we now want to find out about?

Affective

Did you enjoy it?

How did you feel about the people we met?

Would you recommend that others take this trip?

Would you like to do it again?

Would you say it was a good use of our time?

Did you find out some new things about yourself?

Did you discover some new interests? New friends? New likes and dislikes?

Did it change any of your beliefs?

The evaluation was not held until the next day, so that children would first have the chance to talk over this very personal experience with their families.

The evaluation covered many topics. It brought about a discussion of some of the services supplied by today's communities: hospitals, doctors, school nurses, immunization, safe water supplies, and sewage disposal. This was inspired by the tally sheet information, which indicated an early mortality rate for children and young women.

All in all, the children learned something about history, archeology, health, biology, economics, and geology, just from a visit to the cemetery. Ruth Bassett felt that exploring the past in this way gave new dimension to history and its relationship to the students' lives. Similar study trips using the same techniques can be organized to visit such places as an old fortress, an abandoned building, or a modern high-rise apartment house.

Exhibits

Exhibits are materials that have been assembled to communicate a message. They are primarily three-dimensional displays or bulletin board collages, and may include collections of pictures, words, electronic devices, specimens, objects, charts, maps, or any combination of varied materials. The message may be intended for students, parents, or community groups. Its purpose may be cognitive (to give the "facts" or illustrate a concept), affective (to persuade, convince, arouse), or a combination of both.

Good exhibits are self-explanatory and their instructional value does not depend on accompanying explanations. They may be used to initiate inquiry, summarize learnings, illustrate a process, or simply display student skills and talents. An attractive exhibit will command attention without coercion; hence it is an effective means for communicating new ideas. A school that emphasizes frequently changing, skillfully prepared exhibits cannot help but stimulate some independent new interests.

Exhibits may display such things as the concept of culture, facts about Mexican-Americans, the steps in creating a painting, the functions of UNICEF, newspapers from around the world, various occupations, the life of a migrant worker, how to conserve energy, the evolution of technology.

Guidelines for Preparing Exhibits

1. Identify an important central concept, generalization, or main idea.
2. Identify selected subcomponents that reflect the range of the concept, generalization, or main idea.
3. Consider various means of illustrating the subcomponents.
4. Think of a provocative question or statement to attract attention.
5. Keep words to a minimum. The exhibit is primarily a visual device.
6. Place it where it can be easily seen.
7. Use color, textures, push buttons, levers, and so on to add variety and interest.
8. Change exhibits frequently.

**Planning and
Using Exhibits**

Planning an exhibit is essentially a synthesizing activity involving many higher-level thinking skills. Because it depends primarily on visual communication, it is a means for involving students with reading difficulties in higher-level cognitive tasks. Helping children plan a successful exhibit requires some skill. The following questions should be asked to guide them:

1. What is the main idea? Is it important? Why?
2. What should be included? Why are these important?
3. Where can appropriate pictures, objects, specimens be found? Who can help?
4. What title should it have? Is the title clear? Short? Interesting?
5. How can it be made attractive? Is it colorful enough? Is it cluttered? Is it clear? Can people see it easily?
6. Can the words be easily read? Are they spelled correctly?
7. What do other people think about it? How do they think it could be improved?

**Using Exhibits
to Initiate Inquiry**

Asking questions rather than giving answers is a good way to get the students to learn something from an exhibit. For example, the title of an ecology exhibit might be "Is Our Water Safe?" Other provocative questions might include:

What is the source of the water we drink?
How is water analyzed for purity?
Who checks to see if our water is safe?
How often is our water checked?
What can we do to make sure our drinking water is safe?

The exhibit itself might juxtapose magazine photographs of a tall, cool glass of water that looks inviting to drink (though you may have to use a picture from a liquor advertisement to get this effect), a polluted stream, a well, a lake with motorboats on it, a large factory by a river, and a water-purification plant (you may be able to get the last from the public relations department of your local water department). Sources of information useful in answering the questions the exhibit poses could be listed at the bottom of the display: the school nurse, city or county health authorities, health magazines (which should include *Today's Health*), library books, and audiovisual materials.

An exhibit on the resolution of conflicts could begin with the question "You want to fight?" and include the following pictures: a handshake, a courtroom scene, a picket line, a sit-in, a voting booth, a fistfight, a photograph of the most recent war, a picture of two children arguing with each other. The following questions could be posted:

What do all of these scenes have in common? How are they different from each other?
Which ones do you like best? Why?
Which ones happened to you? How did you feel about it?

Do you know anyone who has been in a sit-in? Do you know how they feel about it?

Do you know anyone who has been in a war? Do you know how they feel about it?

Using Exhibits to Summarize

A period of study of the American Indian could culminate with an exhibition of Indian artifacts. This would provide a pleasant and practical change from the books and photographs that comprise the usual extent of such studies and would give the teacher a means of summing up the material that had been covered. (For that matter, it could serve equally well as a way to initiate inquiry.)

Artifacts are obviously easier to encounter in some areas than others, but fellow teachers, members of the community, museums, and local tribes are potential sources that should not be underestimated. Some may even be willing to visit the class and answer questions. Be sure, in any case, to make the display as informative as possible, labeling each item with a description of what it is and what tribe it was made by. Try to find photographs of these and other common objects being used or worn and display them with the artifacts. Don't forget to invite the other classes to view the exhibit.

A study of the conservation of energy could be summarized by an exhibit put together by the students. Several approaches might be taken, of which the simplest would be to have them find pictures to illustrate the title "Ways We Can Conserve Energy." The exhibit could be divided into three sections to cover the school, the home, and the community. Students should be encouraged to try to apply what they have learned by suggesting new ways to conserve energy that were not mentioned in the classes, such as changing business hours or delaying the Christmas shopping season until December.

Using Exhibits to Display Skills

Exhibits can be used to display just about any type of student skill. For example, maps made by students can be displayed along with professionally drafted maps when the class has completed an in-depth study of the various uses and types of maps. A series of questions could be listed that would require using the maps. These might include such things as:

What is the population of New York City?
What is the annual rainfall in Kansas?
What is the climate of Nigeria like?
What countries border on France?
How many things can we tell about Japan from maps 1, 2, and 3?

Using Exhibits to Promote Activities

Attractive exhibits can encourage youngsters to try new things. Reading, for example, is one activity most teachers are eager to promote. Visual displays can make the contents of a book seem more vivid. Photographs and real objects can provide a sense of connection with the real world. For example, a teacher might use photographs of the parents of the students in an exhibit designed to introduce *The Daddy Book* and *All Kinds of Mothers* to a primary grade class.[7]

Place the two books on a stand in front of the exhibit. Stick a large bookmark in each that says READ ME! Questions might be listed on a separate chart: Is a daddy a father? What is your mother's job? What is your daddy's job? Can you find pictures of their jobs in this exhibit? What does your mother look like? Can you draw a picture of her? What does your daddy do for fun? Are all daddies alike? Are all mothers alike? Are they the same all over the world? Why do you think so?

Sources of Exhibits   Commercial firms, museums, civic and educational organizations, and government agencies can be valuable sources for ready-made exhibits. Many local groups and companies may have exhibits on hand or may be willing to prepare them for a school. A number of national sources also exist that offer free or inexpensive materials. References to these sources are often found in the articles and advertising of professional magazines like *Social Education.*

Educational Television

Strictly speaking, educational television refers only to programs that are specifically designed for school use. These are generally accompanied by classroom instructional materials and available only on closed circuits. For practical purposes, however, educational television can be said to include any telecast that educates.

Television programs designed for schools are generally sequenced and accompanied by teacher guides. Like all other instructional tools, some are good and some are bad. Local school offices generally receive lists of available educational television programs. Others can be found in social studies journals like *Social Education.*

Americans All, produced by station KRMA and the Denver Public Schools, is a typical example of an educational television series for elementary and junior-high-school students. It is composed of thirty-one programs designed to enrich knowledge and understanding of the American heritage. *Our Changing Community,* part of the Elementary Social Studies program produced by Valley Instructional Television Association, is directed at the primary grades.[8] It includes twenty-eight lessons aimed at developing basic generalizations about communities and the changes that take place within them. Both programs are accom-

[7]Robert Stewart, *The Daddy Book,* illus. by Don Madden (New York: McGraw-Hill, 1972), and Cecily Brownstone, *All Kinds of Mothers* (New York: David McKay Co., 1969).
[8]*Our Changing Community,* a series of 28 lessons prepared in 1966–67 by the Valley Instructional Television Association, P.O. Box 6, Sacramento, Calif. 95801.

panied by teacher guides suggesting introductory and follow-up activities for students. The Valley Instructional program, however, also includes suggestions for developing student research skills, both through independent study and through class and group projects.

Television programs produced for commercial and public educational networks have not yet begun to be properly exploited as school media. Part of the difficulty is legal—the issue of copyright violations is still being disputed. Another difficulty is that many schools have neither the funds nor the foresight to invest in equipment needed to reproduce telecasts. Actually, the initial expense is not very high, tape is relatively cheap, and anyone can learn the skills to operate the equipment with a minimum of training.

Commercial television is notorious for its shortcomings, but at its best it is superb. Newcasts, special documentaries, dramatizations of biographies and historical events, and even some of the series provide noteworthy social studies material. Thus NBC's "Little House on the Prairie," based on Laura Ingalls Wilder's book, gives valuable insights into such things as education, family life, and health problems of late-nineteenth-century America. "The Waltons," produced by CBS, is a good vehicle for understanding the depression period of the thirties.

Television as an Inquiry Tool

The Delaware Educational Television Network has developed a television series in geography designed to promote inquiry. "If Maps Could Talk" is intended for primary, intermediate, and upper elementary levels. Each unit, approximately fifteen minutes long, is organized around central themes, unifying concepts, and generalizations. The unit begins with a problem that students are invited to explore and solve. Solutions are implicit in the data, which include drawings, scale models, documentary sequences, maps, globes, and related materials. Here, for example, is an outline of "Why Live Here?" the fourth program in the series:

Unifying Concept: Relative Location

Substantive Generalizations
1. Location influences the way we live.
2. Distance is measured in both time and linear units.
3. The significance of a location is dependent upon many factors in addition to linear and time units.
4. Man's decision of where he lives is influenced by social, geographic, economic, political, historic, and psychological factors.
5. Terms used to describe locations (big, far, crowded, etc.) are relative, requiring explanations and comparisons to be meaningfully used.

Methodological Generalization
6. Maps may be used to help clarify, explain, and predict locations.[9]

[9]Richard S. Craddock and Val Arnsdorf, "Geographic Inquiry in the Elementary School via *ETV*," *Journal of Geography* LXX:5 (May 1971), pp. 270–74.

Guidelines for Using Television

1. Scan the weekly program guide to find programs of possible interest.
2. Reserve equipment for use at the appropriate times.
3. Identify the educational objectives the program can be used for.
4. Determine whether the program is suitable for the cognitive and emotional level of students.
5. Decide whether it might be useful for a small group or the entire class.
6. Determine whether the entire program is useful or only parts of it.
7. Arouse student interest with an introductory discussion.
8. Suggest things to look for.
9. Discuss the program afterwards. Be sure to include an evaluation.

The teacher's manual suggests questions to introduce this program:

1. What do you mean by large? small? By old? new? near? far? How do we decide what these words really mean when we use them?
2. In choosing a place to live, what kinds of places would you want to live near, what kinds of places would you *not* want to live near? Why? Can you find a place that is near to or far from all the things you want?[10]

It also provides a number of useful suggestions for bulletin board exhibits, work with maps, study trips, and related activities that can be used to supplement each program.

Motion Pictures

The special virtues of motion pictures and television lie in the ways that they can alter our view of reality. They can transport us instantly from one part of the world to another, even to places that no longer exist. They can recreate the distant past or speculate on the way things will look in the future. They can slow down the movement of the fastest objects and compress events that take months into the space of a few seconds, reduce the earth to the size of a penny and enlarge microscopic details thousands of times. And they can do all these things with an immediacy and sensation of reality that is extremely convincing. A good film or television program is not only an invaluable tool for clarifying complex ideas and abstract concepts, it can also be used to shape attitudes.

Motion pictures have been a basic instructional resource for the past several decades. Whether or not this will change once television and videotape have become established in the classroom is an open question. Because of the size and relative quality of the image, films may still be favored for certain types of materials. The guidelines offered earlier in this chapter for using television apply, for the most part, to the use of motion pictures as well. It is worth adding, however, that because of their relative expense, films should always be previewed when possible.

[10]Ibid., pp. 273–74.

Other Ways of
Using
Motion Pictures

Films need not always be shown in the way the filmmaker intended. Sometimes variations can be quite effective in making certain points or simply in making the students more aware of how this particular medium works. Here are a number of possible alternatives:

1. Show the film without sound. Encourage the students to speculate aloud on what is happening. Then replay the film with sound.
2. Stop the film from time to time and ask the students to hypothesize about what will happen next.
3. Show the film without an introduction and without revealing the title. Afterward, ask the students to suggest fitting titles.
4. Show a film to introduce a unit of study and then show it again at the conclusion of the unit. You will be surprised to discover how much more sensitive the students are the second time around—particularly when the issue is complex and the language somewhat difficult.
5. Invite a local filmmaker in to show and discuss a film.
6. Have the students itemize as much of the factual content of the film as possible. Then have them check it for accuracy against other sources.
7. Stop the film part-way through and ask the students to try to role-play the rest of the story.

Still Pictures

In recent years, still pictures have become increasingly important in the social studies and more emphasis is now being placed on the skills of picture interpretation. In the past, photos tended to be treated as a supplementary source of limited value. Texts were rather sparsely illustrated, and teachers who wished to give their classes a fuller idea of what other times and places were like had to subscribe to magazines like *National Geographic*. Now, however, pictures of good quality are not only commonly incorporated in texts and units, in some cases they constitute a primary source for generating inquiry. For example, the Fideler Company has prepared six *Picture-Bank Resource Centers* that include over 1800 pictures appropriate for the social studies curriculum.[11] A strategy for helping students interpret still pictures is given in Chart 7–6.

Stills are, of course, available from a great many other sources, including the daily papers, different types of magazines, travel agencies, airline companies, government agencies, and the tourist offices of other countries. One must only be careful to select those that are clear enough, large enough, and easily interpreted.

Using Pictures
for Comparisons

Pictures can be excellent vehicles for promoting inquiry through comparisons of objects, events, or people. For example, one can compare photographs of a

---

[11]*Picture-Bank Resource Centers* (Grand Rapids, Mich.: The Fideler Company).

Chart 7–6
Picture Interpretation

Teacher's Questions

Describe the people, the objects, the physical features (land, flora, fauna). What are the people doing? What are the animals doing?

What do you suppose the climate is like? Standard of living? Family life? Population? Technology? Time period?

How might these affect people? Objects? Physical features?

How are people, objects, physical features alike? Different? What is the relationship among them?

What can you say about the picture in general? Where do you suppose it was taken? Who are the people? What are they doing with each other? How can we check to see if this is right?

Do you think this is an adequate representation? Why or why not? Do you think it is accurate? Why or why not? What important things have been omitted? Is it probable that things would have happened in this way?

Student Processes

Students show comprehension by translating into verbal medium.

Students make inferences beyond the data.

Assuming students have studied some of these before, they would be applying old learning to new situations.

Students analyze.

Students synthesize.

Students evaluate adequacy, accuracy, and probability.

A Specific Case: Using a Photo of a Cambodian Village*

Translation: What do you see in this picture?

Interpretation: What do you think the climate is like in Cambodia? What clues in the picture helped you reach your conclusion?

Application: How does climate affect the lives of people in Cambodia?

Analysis: Imagine that you are going to prepare a report about Cambodia. What topics would you include in your report? For which of these topics might you use this picture as an illustration?

Synthesis: Imagine that you live in this Cambodian village. Write a story telling about a typical day in your life.

Evaluation: Imagine that you are selecting pictures to illustrate a report about the changing ways of life in Southeast Asia since World War II. Would you include this picture? Why? Why not?

*SOURCE: *Picture-Bank Resource Centers* (Grand Rapids, Mich.: The Fideler Company).

Cambodian Villagers Many groups of people live in Southeast Asia. These groups differ greatly from each other in language and customs. However, the people are generally similar in physical appearance. ASIA PLATE 39 FIDELER VISUAL TEACHING GRAND RAPIDS, MICHIGAN

person or place that were taken many years apart in order to call attention to the kinds of changes that occurred. A more ambitious project might involve showing two photos or lifelike drawings of the same event or scene with some variations in them and asking the students to compare them. But even the most commonplace subjects can lend themselves to launching a provocative inquiry session. Take, for example, two schoolhouses that are obviously in very different types of communities. If the students are asked a series of questions such as those given below, they can single out the features that provide information about such things as the size of the community, its wealth, and possibly even its values. First ask general questions about one school, then about the other:

What do you see in the picture?
Do you like what you see? Why or why not?
Describe the building. When do you think it was built? What makes you think so?
What do you think it is (was) used for?
How can you tell it is a school?
Do you like this school? Why or why not?
Describe the things you think one might find inside this school.
If you were to go to this school, do you think you would enjoy it?

In what kind of community do you think this school is located? Tell me what you think of it.

Once the students have decided what each of the schools is like, ask questions that will lead to a comparison of the schools:

Which school do you like better? Why?
Which school is in the larger community? Why do you think so?
Which community seems to be more prosperous? How can you tell?
How would you compare your own school to the two schools you have seen in the pictures (size, appearance, community)?

After the question session is over, give the students the facts about each of the schools and compare these with their hypotheses.

Summary

There is an old and oft-quoted saying that goes: experience is the best teacher. Presumably the type of experience referred to is direct experience, the act of doing something—as when someone tries to learn how to ride a bicycle. Unfortunately, there is no saying around to advise us as to what to do in cases in which direct experience is either not available or an impossibility—which, in the social studies, is frequently the case.

A social studies class cannot travel back in history to discover how the Native

Americans lived before the European colonists arrived. They can, however, duplicate some of the conditions and activities of life for some specific tribe—for example, the Narragansett Indians of Rhode Island, whose life and language were documented by Roger Williams in 1643.[12] On the level of direct experience, these activities might include trying to make food and clothing in the same way the tribe did. On the level of contrived experience, the class might examine actual objects preserved from the period or models of buildings based on the descriptions in Williams's book. Other types of experience, such as study trips to museums or the ruins of Native American cities (or to reservations), exhibits put together by the teacher or class, copies of pictures taken by nineteenth-century photographers, and some of the more accurate documentary films about Native American life in the past could supplement this unit of study. Role-playing situations based on the material in Williams's book might be developed to examine the very important differences of belief and way of life that existed between the Narragansetts and the Puritan colonists.

Direct experience may indeed be the best teacher, but it need not be the only one. For the majority of things that need to be learned in the social studies, other resources must be used. This chapter has described types of experiences that come fairly close to the level of direct experience. The following chapter, which concentrates on visual and verbal symbols, is concerned with experiences that are fairly well removed from the concrete level.

---

[12] Roger Williams, *A Key into the Language of America,* reprinted and edited by John H. Teunissen and Evelyn Hinz (Detroit: Wayne State University Press, 1973).

Visual and Verbal Experiences

This chapter, like the preceding one, deals with instructional resources. Visual and verbal symbolic experiences, however, differ from the kinds of experience described in Chapter 7 in that they are more abstract. A visual symbol contains fewer details than, say, a photograph of an object. Verbal symbols rarely contain any clue to their meaning. Most sounds and all collections of letters that are used in speech or writing to symbolize an idea can be understood only by those who are familiar with the conventions of the language being used. It is for this reason that Edgar Dale ranked these two kinds of experience at the very top of his "cone of experience" and why an entire chapter has been set aside here to deal with them.[1]

Visual Symbolic Experiences

Visual symbolic experiences include those visual resources that use symbolic renderings of objects rather than lifelike representations. Photographs, models, movies, and other types of visual resources discussed in the preceding chapter attempt to reproduce the real object in as lifelike a way as possible. Cartoons, charts, and graphs, on the other hand, use picture symbols to represent reality.

Cartoons

Editorial cartoons are among the most effective instructional resources for attracting the attention of students, but they are not always the easiest for children to understand. Cartoons may be very complex in both form and content. They are, by definition, exaggerations of reality, biased to express a particular viewpoint. Worse yet, they frequently resort to stereotypes or unfair misrepresentations of groups or individuals. They are particularly powerful because they combine humor, satire, and ridicule. It is therefore very important to help students develop a critical awareness of these things.

Editorial cartoons are principally of value in teaching current events. They tend to concentrate on the broader, more national issues, and most newspapers print at least one every day. Teachers should make a point of collecting cartoons from several different papers with different political beliefs, so that their students will become more aware of biases and the variety of viewpoints involved in each issue.

Cartoons and Prejudice

Cartoonists have been commenting on controversial issues for a long time. As far back as pre-revolutionary days, American newspapers were making use of satirical drawings to attack individuals and policies, and the commentaries were often rather unfair. In the latter half of the nineteenth century and the early part of the twentieth, with the rise of mass-production printing techniques and a

[1]Dale's Cone of Experience is shown at the beginning of Chapter 7.

The Hartford Times
Ed Valtmann '75

Who is the big fat fellow?
What does "inflation" mean?
What does "recession" mean?
Why is "inflation" pictured as a big fat fellow while
    "recession" is pictured as tall and skinny?
Who is the skinny little man in the middle?
What is the main point the cartoon is making?
Has inflation hurt anyone you know? In what ways?
Has recession hurt anyone you know? In what ways?
Do you think the cartoon is funny? Why or why not?
Do you think the cartoon is giving a true picture of the way
    things are today? Why or why not?
Can anything be done to stop inflation and recession from taking over?
    Can you think of some examples?

broad audience, newspaper and magazine cartoons came to be a powerful weapon. And all too often they were directed at criticizing the new groups of immigrants who reached this country during the period. One after another, the new ethnic, racial, and religious minorities were caricatured in the press and labeled lazy, dumb, conspiratorial, or even homicidal. Chinese, Germans, Italians, Irish, Jews, and Catholics were among the popular victims of the times, and as these groups became assimilated, they tended to join in prejudicial attitudes toward other groups. If direct attacks on minorities have come to be con-

> **Guidelines for Using Cartoons**
>
> 1. Be sure the cartoon is relevant to what is being studied.
> 2. Be sure it is clear and that it is visible to the entire group.
> 3. Ask questions that will test the students' comprehension.
> 4. Analyze the biases and attitudes of the cartoonist with the class.
> 5. Evaluate the cartoon with the students to see if it is more or less in agreement with the available facts.

sidered in poor taste for cartoonists in the latter half of the twentieth century, it does not mean that prejudice itself has disappeared, and teachers must make an effort to make their students aware of the unfairness of popular stereotypes. One very good way to do this is to return to the cartoons of the past. Helping students understand that all groups, including their own, have been the victims of prejudice at one time or another can make them aware that today's victims do not deserve the treatment they receive.

The Anti-Defamation League of B'nai B'rith has collected a series of cartoons from periodicals of the past that illustrate the varieties of prejudice.[2] These have been reproduced as slides and are available from the League's New York office. Teachers could try projecting a few of these for upper-grade students and ask a series of questions with each one. For example:

What minority is being attacked in this cartoon?
What were the historical circumstances that led to this attitude?
Is there a valid basis for this attitude? Is it fair? Why not?
What other minorities were attacked at that time for similar reasons?
Who benefits from such attacks? Who besides the minority suffers?
Does this stereotype still exist today?
Can you give any examples of cartoons or other images that perpetuate this
   stereotype today?

Prejudice is obviously a sensitive topic—many of the students may feel personally attacked because they belong to one of the groups mentioned in the discussion. But prejudicial attitudes develop early, and it is better to tackle them head-on in a classroom atmosphere of rationality and benevolence than to allow them to grow unconfronted on the playground and in the halls.

Charts   A chart is a diagram in which relationships among objects, individuals, events, or processes are represented in a symbolic form. A chart may be as complicated as the flow chart in which the steps between the birth of a bill and its enactment into law are detailed (Figure 8–1). Or it may be as simple as a set of new vocabulary words.

[2]*The Distorted Image: Stereotype and Caricature in American Popular Graphics, 1850–1922* (New York: Anti-Defamation League of B'nai B'rith, 1973).

Figure 8–1

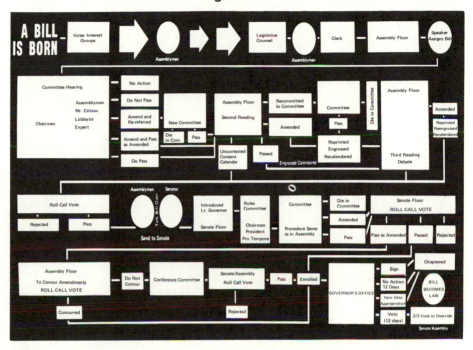

SOURCE: Assemblyman Barry Keene of California. Reprinted by permission.

Charts can be very useful in initiating, developing, or summarizing learnings. They can help summarize information, such as the characteristics of a city or things observed on a field trip. They can demonstrate the relationships among complex concepts, as does the chart of Human Geography (Figure 8–2), in which the interrelationships of people, social values, organizations, work, technology, and environment are diagrammed. Or they can help students make comparisons among such things as different materials needed for different occupations or respective functions of different government agencies. Time charts can help students understand both the sequence of events and time intervals between them. A time chart, for example, might illustrate the sequential relationships of such events as the invention of the cotton gin, the abolition of international slave trade, the Emancipation Proclamation, and the emergence of

Guidelines for Charts

1. Limit them to one central idea.
2. Keep the writing or printing simple and uniform.
3. Make sure the vocabulary is within reading grasp of students.
4. Be sure they are related to ongoing work of students.
5. Change them frequently.

Figure 8–2
Chart Designed to Show Relationships

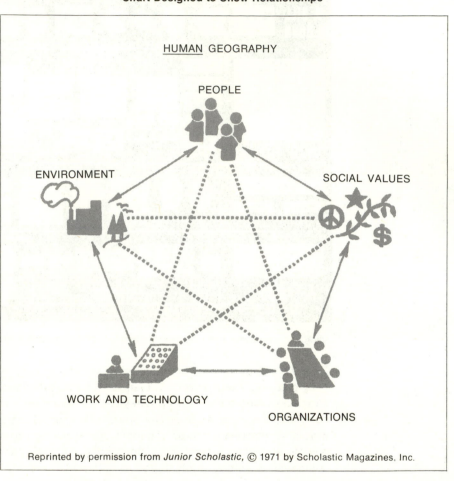

HUMAN GEOGRAPHY

PEOPLE

ENVIRONMENT

SOCIAL VALUES

WORK AND TECHNOLOGY

ORGANIZATIONS

Reprinted by permission from *Junior Scholastic,* © 1971 by Scholastic Magazines, Inc.

the civil rights movement by showing the amount of time between one and another of these events.

Charts are also useful for organizing work in a classroom. They can serve to record the names of committee chairpersons or students assigned to different tasks. They can be used to help clarify directions, such as how to prepare a report or how to greet visitors. In short, they serve many practical classroom uses.

Graphs   Like charts, graphs show relationships among objects in a symbolic form. Graphs, however, are generally confined to showing the quantitative and temporal relationships among objects, and their symbol system is more restricted.

Figure 8–3
Types of Charts

Organizing work

Committee Assignments

Maya: *Melvin, Otto, Shirley, Bonnie,
        Lynette, Keenan, Dwayne.

Inca: *Berney, Brian, Kari, Julie,
        Michele, Ricky, Sherman.

Aztec: *Annette, Ann, Martha, Kim,
        James, Danny, Peter.

Toltec: *Vicki, Helena, Nicole,
        Marina, Robert, Carl, Craig.

*Chairperson

Making comparisons

Farmer	**Fisherman**
Truck-Tractor	Boat
On land	On water
Animals	Fish
Home on farm	Home on boat and on land

Summarizing information

Mexico

Capital: Mexico City
Language: Spanish
Principal seaports: Veracruz, Tampico,
    Acapulco, Mazatlán, Guaymas
Important industries: textiles, food
    processing
Metal exports: lead, copper, silver,
    zinc
Agricultural exports: cotton, coffee,
    cane sugar, wheat, livestock,
    meat, tomatoes, other garden
    products

Reviewing new vocabulary words

Words to Think About

war	crisis
famine	cheat
love	government
hate	power
pollution	liberation
population	energy

The most commonly used symbols in graphs are assorted geometric shapes (e.g., circles, triangles, rectangles), bars, pictorial symbols, pie "slices," lines, and curves.

Although graphs are very efficient ways of organizing quantitative and temporal relationships, and are increasingly used in all of society, they tend to be neglected in the elementary schools. Many reasons contribute to this neglect, including the poor quality of many graphs and their apparent irrelevance to textual material in many cases. Equally important, however, is the fact that interpreting graphs requires the systematic development of cumulative skills—and few teachers apparently think it important enough to devote the time necessary for their students to develop these skills. Students not only need to know the conventions of graph symbols; they should also develop the habit of analyzing and evaluating graphs.

Some types of graphs are easier to understand than others. Simple pictorial and bar graphs are best in the primary grades, with more complex types being introduced in the later grades. By the end of elementary school, students should have experience with all types of graphs. Descriptions of the five types of graphs and examples of ways to use them in the social studies classroom are given below.

Bar Graphs   Young children can be introduced to the idea of graphs through the use of simple quantitative data in their own classrooms. Teachers can make simple bar graphs based on classroom data such as attendance on a given day, the number of spelling and social studies books in the classroom, or the amount of time spent on reading as compared with social studies. When children become sufficiently familiar with simple bar graphs, they can be presented with incomplete graphs, such as that pictured in Figure 8–4, and asked to fill in the missing information. This helps students understand the importance of titles in interpreting graphs. Children can also be invited to make their own graphs with either teacher or students suggesting the data to be graphed. Teachers should avoid using percentages until they feel reasonably sure students have mastered the concept.

Pie Graphs   After bar graphs, pie graphs are the easiest for young children to understand. In this case, the information given has to do with percentages of things, a concept that is fairly clearly expressed by this type of graph. The most effective way of introducing pie graphs is with a real pie, asking the students to determine how

Figure 8–4
A Bar Graph

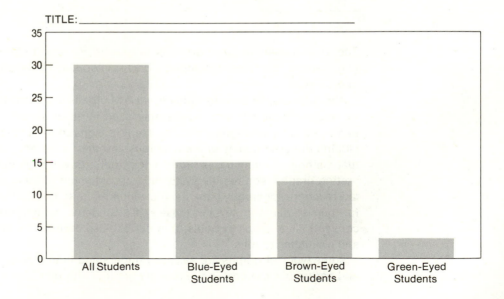

Figure 8–5
Pie Graphs

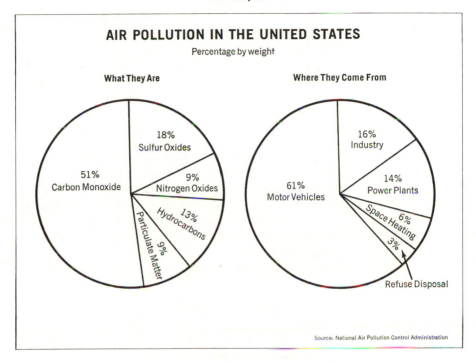

AIR POLLUTION IN THE UNITED STATES
Percentage by weight

What They Are

51%
Carbon Monoxide

18%
Sulfur Oxides

9%
Nitrogen Oxides

13%
Hydrocarbons

9%
Particulate Matter

Where They Come From

61%
Motor Vehicles

16%
Industry

14%
Power Plants

6%
Space Heating

3%
Refuse Disposal

Source: National Air Pollution Control Administration

many pieces should be cut and working out the measurements on the blackboard before the cutting begins. Suitable pie graph subjects include: a state budget, showing what percentages go to education, highways, health, and so on; the exports of a country, illustrating the percentages of manufactured goods, agricultural products, raw materials, and the like; the domestic consumption of energy resources of a given country.

Figure 8–5 uses two pie graphs to show the weight percentages of various air pollutants, as well as the sources from which they come. Graphs like these can serve as powerful data sources to promote inquiry, but before studying the graphs themselves, students must be familiar with the concepts and terms used in them. Then guiding questions like the following can help generate interest:

What is the subject of these graphs?
What substances contribute to air pollution in the United States?
What one substance alone makes up more than half the air pollution in the United States?
What source contributes the most to air pollution? What source contributes the least?
What is likely to happen if more people buy more cars? How could this problem be overcome?

What could industry do to help overcome air pollution? Should government make them do it? Is government trying?

What suggestions would you offer to overcome the problem? What can you do right now? Which suggestions would you give most attention to? Why?

No date is given for these graphs. Is it important to know the date? Why? Do you think the percentages are still the same today? What makes you think so?

Do you think the information on this graph is accurate? Why or why not? How could we check it?

Line Graphs   Line graphs, although the most commonly used type of graph in newspapers and magazines, are somewhat difficult for students to understand, and should only be introduced in the upper elementary grades. Where bar graphs and pie graphs are used to break wholes down into parts, line graphs are used to present the much more complex concept of development over time. They are, in a sense, a series of bar or pie graphs strung together. The line graph in Figure 8–6, which traces a series of price indices over a six-year period, could be used to introduce some complex ideas about inflation with a series of guiding questions like:

What is the title of the graph?

What is a "consumer price index?" Why is it important?

What does the horizontal line stand for? The vertical line?

What years does the graph cover?

What is the lowest consumer price index shown on the graph? When did it occur? Which countries had it then?

What is the highest consumer price index shown on the graph? When did it occur? Which country had it?

Which country had the smallest rise in consumer price index between 1963 and 1969? Which one next? Next?

What can you say in general about the consumer price index in these countries during the years 1963 and 1969? What, do you suppose, caused it?

What do you think happened to the consumer price index in these countries after 1969? How can we find out if this is so?

Do you think a rise in the consumer price index of one country affects the consumer price index of another country? What makes you think so? Why, do you suppose, this happens?

Is this a problem? Who is worrying about this problem? What can be done about it?

Pictorial Graphs   Pictorial graphs are essentially variations of bar graphs. Instead of bars, however, pictorial symbols (sometimes called "isotypes") are used. Their greatest weakness is that they cannot give information as precisely as bar graphs. Note that in the example given in Figure 8–7 the figures of the last farmers in the row

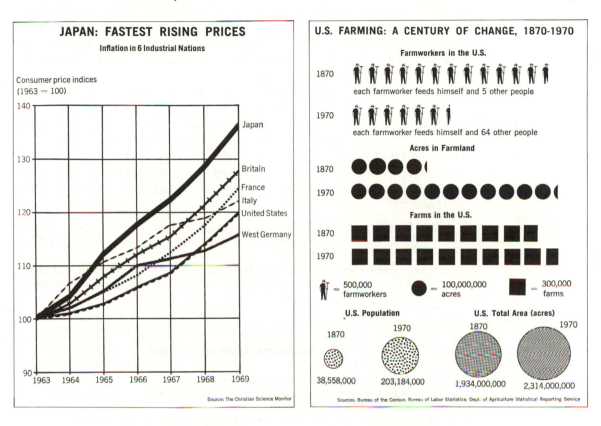

Figure 8–6

A Line Graph

Figure 8–7

A Pictorial Graph

are cut to suggest a fraction, but the exact amount of the fraction is impossible to determine. Nonetheless, pictorial graphs have great visual appeal and can therefore be useful.

Figure 8–7 illustrates how some aspects of farming have changed in the United States during the last hundred years. After questions to determine the basic information given by the graph (e.g., how many farmworkers were there in 1870? In 1970?), questions like the following can lead students to some higher-level thinking:

What can you say about farming in general since 1870?

What do you suppose accounts for the change?

Where did all the displaced farmworkers go? Is this a problem? Why?

Do you think this type of change will continue? What makes you think so?

What are the disadvantages of a change like this? Advantages?

Do you think that farms have gotten larger or smaller since 1870? What makes you think so?

Making Graphs   Students will learn to interpret graphs more easily if they have many opportunities to make them. Try giving them data related to subjects they are studying or, in the lower grades, to things related to their own lives (the month in which each was born, how many brothers and sisters each has, how many and what kinds of pets). Where possible, it is often a good idea to take the data from an existing graph in a book or periodical so that the students will have something with which to compare their finished work.

Usually the most difficult problem the students face is choosing the appropriate graph form. Be sure to give them ample help on this point. The other problems are the same as those cited in the guidelines for making graphs, and a checklist can be prepared to help the students through these phases of the work. While the study of graphs should begin with very simple problems, rather complex ones can eventually be introduced. The following examples require some sophisticated computational skills, but many students can and will rise to the challenge.

In 1900 the world population was approximately one billion. In 1925 it was a little under two billion. By 1950 it had increased to about two and one-half billion, and by 1975 it had reached four billion. How would you graph this?

Out of every dollar spent in 1973 by the federal government, 10 cents went to physical resources, 45 cents to human resources, 32 cents to national defense, 6 cents to interest, and 7 cents to other things. How would you graph this?

Guidelines for Making Graphs

1. Make sure title clearly explains what the graph is about.
2. Be certain that the captions, keys, or scales are clear and do help clarify the elements of the graph.
3. Keep the graph uncluttered and be sure the major relationships stand out.
4. Have scales start at zero so that comparisons and changes are seen in correct perspective.
5. Give the sources and dates of the data.
6. Determine the graph's relevance to instructional materials.

Oral Verbal Experiences

Verbal symbols are more abstract than visual ones, hence their position at the apex of Dale's cone of experience. They can be transmitted in both spoken and written forms, the latter being the most abstract of all since they are really symbols of symbols. That is to say, the written word *chair* is a symbol of the spoken word "chair" — which is itself a symbol of the real object. In this section, we will examine the various kinds of spoken-word experiences that can be used in classroom teaching.

Lectures   The most common form of oral verbal experience in teaching is the lecture. Although this expository means of presenting material has become somewhat discredited in recent years (due mostly to over-use), it can still be an efficient and often quite effective way of presenting information. A few teachers are gifted lecturers who can keep youngsters fascinated, but most need to make a fair amount of effort. The guidelines offered here can be very useful in improving one's lecturing techniques.

Guidelines for Lecturing

1. Keep the presentation short. The attention span of youngsters is limited.
2. Organize material very carefully with clear introduction, development, and conclusion.
3. Give concrete references to illustrate points made.
4. Add interest and relevance by using anecdotes, humor, and examples taken from the lives of children.
5. Incorporate visual materials wherever possible.
6. Reinforce the presentation with some summary activity involving student participation, such as providing a written outline for students to review and opportunities for discussion.
7. Use lectures sparingly.

Resource People   A basic variation on the lecture is to invite someone from outside the school to come in and talk to the class.

While there can sometimes be difficulties about getting resource people during school hours, for the most part individuals or organizations are happy to oblige. In some cases, visitors can be selected by discussing requirements with fellow-teachers and others. As a rule, it is better to decide beforehand which members of the community would be best suited for visits—a letter soliciting names from the parents can result in hurt feelings if offers are not accepted. Among the many kinds of visitors are:

1. Government employees, such as police, social workers, property assessors, postal employees, and county health officials.
2. Government representatives, such as members of the city council, members of the state assembly, senators, and consuls of other countries.
3. Occupational representatives, such as doctors, lawyers, auto mechanics, farmers, cartographers, and factory workers.
4. Ethnic representatives, particularly those who have special knowledge about their heritage.
5. Cultural representatives, such as musicians, composers, poets, painters, photographers, and novelists.
6. Academic representatives, such as political scientists, historians, anthropologists, and economists.

7. Special-interest-group representatives, such as those involved in environmental, political, and economic problems.
8. Family representatives, such as parents (including those who have been divorced or widowed), grandparents, and older brothers and sisters.
9. Community representatives, such as people in the local government, longtime residents, members of planning groups, and museum employees.

Resource people come in many styles. Some come prepared with copious notes and visual materials. Others use a more informal style, depending on student questions to carry them through. Still others have invaluable skills and information but are very reticent. One thing most resource people have in common is the need for help from both teachers and students. To help maximize their effectiveness and make the visit a useful and pleasant experience for all, follow the guidelines given here.

Guidelines for Using Resource People

1. Discuss with the students the desirability of inviting a resource person.
2. Tell the class about the visitor's background and the kinds of questions that can be asked. Have children write these down or prepare a class list.
3. Talk to the visitor beforehand and discuss the group, their interests, and their needs.
4. Prepare the students for the visit by discussing appropriate reception procedures, introductions, note-taking, and so on.
5. Evaluate the experience with the students after the visit. Was it interesting? What have they learned? What else should they explore?
6. Have the class express appreciation for the visit through a class letter, individual letters, tape, or other means.

Interviews   Resource people need not necessarily come to the class. In some cases, representatives of the class can visit the individual and conduct an interview that will later be presented to the other students. Not only does this allow the class to benefit from a greater range of resource people, it also gives them some practical experience in a very useful skill. However, interviews require a fair amount of preparation and a good deal of attention while they are being conducted— otherwise the information will be of little use and is more likely to bore the other students than to interest them. Written interviews are excellent for developing research, organizing, and writing skills, but they should not be attempted before the students have had a lot of practice at conducting spoken interviews. In these days of electronic marvels, the portable cassette tape recorder offers the best means of conducting interviews, for not only does it make it possible for the participants to maintain a conversation at normal speed, it also reproduces the many variations and modulations of speech that convey a great deal of the meaning in conversations.

> ## Guidelines for Interviewing
>
> 1. Decide in advance the specific questions you want to ask. Write them down and discuss them with others.
> 2. Call or write for an appointment. Introduce yourself and give the purpose of your intended visit.
> 3. Listen carefully during the interview. Remember, you are there to hear what the interviewee has to say.
> 4. Take notes during the interview or immediately afterwards.
> 5. Thank the interviewee when you leave.
> 6. Report back to class regarding what you have learned.

The following is an excerpt from a taped interview conducted by a twelve-year-old with a senior citizen in a local rest home. It is a bit of "oral history."

"I was a tally man on the wharf there. I worked for P.L. (Pacific Lumber) forty years. My work started down there, that's where I started—you go down there and there was just boat after boat with the big sails, that's when the sailing boats came in—"

"Go ahead, please."

"Yes, the big sailing boats used to come in when sometimes you'd be sitting on the wharf there. . . ."

"Didn't they used to have a whaling port down in Fields Landing?"

"Oiling?"

"No, whal--ing? Whales, where they bring whales?"

"I'm sorry I can't get that."

"You know, whales, big fish."

"Whales, oh my yes, they used to have a place where they cut 'em up down at Fields Landing. You want a chunk of whale to eat, you'd go over when they was cutting 'em up and rendering the lard out of 'em. They'd give you two or three big slabs of it, it wasn't bad meat. Another thing down there, oh boy, was the clams. All you had to do was go down the bay there, and right now clams. Oh, it was good then! And crabs, we used to work on the boats and go down there, get some crab nets, small ones, put 'em down and tie them to the posts they tied the boats to, run 'em down to the bottom of the bay, bait 'em with most anything, pull 'em up and have our crabs!"[3]

Learning about the industries and times of the community in such an interesting way was a valuable experience for this student and her classmates. The discussion that followed her taped conversation was the beginning of an extended study of the history of the Humboldt Bay area.

Ballads and Songs

Most of the verbal information about the past (or present) that is available to teachers and students is the work of professional writers. Little popular material exists from which we can discover how ordinary people felt about life in a given time or place. One of the few sources is music, the songs and ballads that groups or individuals have composed in their own idioms and preserved from one generation to another in more or less the original form. Popular music from

[3]The interview was taped in 1974 by a student of Barbara Maxon, teacher and vice-principal at South Bay Elementary School, Eureka, California.

Chart 8–1
Using Songs to Teach Social Studies

Good News, Member

Good news, member, good news, member,	1
Don't you mind what Satan say,	2
Good news, member, good news, member,	3
I heard from heaven today.	4
My brudder have a seat and I am glad,	5
My brudder have a seat and I am glad,	6
Good news, member, good news.	7
My Hawley have a home in Paradise,	8
My Hawley have a home in Paradise,	9
Good news, member, good news.	10

After the students have learned the song, ask the following questions:

Line 1: What is good news? What is a member? Can you be a member?

Line 2: What do you think "Don't you mind" means? Why do you think so? Who do you think Satan is? Why?

Line 3: Why do you think this line is repeated?

Line 4: What does "I heard from heaven today" mean to you? What do you suppose it means in the song?

Lines 5 and 6: What is a brudder? What could the seat be? Why do you think so? Would Paradise be something pleasant? Why do you think as you do?

Lines 8 and 9: Who could Hawley be? Is this possibly the name of a pet or person?

Line 10: What would be good news to a slave? How would it feel to lack freedom to do as one chooses? Do you ever feel restricted? If yes, in what ways? Is it by your choice? Can you do anything about it?

Sing the song again. Then follow up with:

Do you think this tempo fits this slave song? Why or why not?

Did you know that slaves used their music to express their feelings and even pass on messages to fellow slaves?

What good news could they pass on to another slave?

What do you think the good news was that is mentioned in this song? Why do you think so?

(Review previously asked questions.) Would you change any of your answers to these questions now? If so, which ones? Why?

Can people be owned today? Why or why not?

In what ways can a person have control over another? Is this good or bad? Explain.

How do you think it felt to be a slave? Explain in detail.

Follow-up activities:

Write your own slave song(s) creating a new way to pass a message.

Do some research and find evidence of other societies that have had some form of slavery. Contrast these to the slavery system in our past history.

other countries can also tell us something about the people of those lands or about human beings in general. Lullabies such as the "Aizu Lullaby" of the Japanese, the Nigerian "Sleep My Baby," and the American "Rock-a-bye Baby" express the tenderness toward children felt in most cultures. And rock music of the sixties, so popular with young people, tells about their generation's attitudes toward love, war, work, and life in general.

. The use of songs and ballads in teaching has the additional advantage of involving the students in an enjoyable activity that transmits something of the feelings of the people who created the song. The example in Chart 8–1 shows how a song created by black slaves in nineteenth-century America can be used to develop the concept of slavery by giving the students some idea of what it was like to be a slave.

The following are useful teacher resources for songs and ballads of historical and social significance:

Ballads of the Revolution. Sung by Wallace House. Folkways Record FH 5801.

Denisoff, R. Serge. *Songs of Protest, War and Peace: A Bibliography and Discography*. Los Angeles: Center for the Study of Armament and Disarmament, California State University, 1973.

Dietz, Betty Warner, and Thomas C. Park, eds. *Folk Songs of China, Japan, Korea.* New York: John Day Co., 1964.

Glass, Paul. *Singing Soldiers: A History of the Civil War in Song.* New York: Grosset and Dunlap, 1969.

Langstaff, John. *Hi! Ho! The Rattlin' Bog: And Other Folk Songs for Group Singing.* New York: Harcourt Brace Jovanovich, 1969.

Leodhas, Sorche Nic. *A Scottish Songbook.* New York: Holt, Rinehart and Winston, 1969.

Lord, Donald C. "The Slave Song as a Historical Source," *Social Education,* November 1971.

Rockwell, Anne. *Savez-Vous Planter les Choux? and Other French Songs.* New York: World Publishing Co., 1969.

Sackett, Samuel John. *Cowboys and the Songs They Sang.* New York: William R. Scott, 1967.

Yurchenco, Henrietta, comp. *A Fiesta of Folk Songs from Spain and Latin America.* New York: G. P. Putnam's Sons, 1967.

Written Verbal Experiences

A wealth of written materials can be used or adapted by teachers who are ready to abandon the textbook as the sole instructional resource. They include:

letters	biographies	case studies
newspapers	autobiographies	written interviews
travel accounts	diaries	polls
journals	plays	data sheets
magazines	myths	calendars
pamphlets	legends	records of inquests
scientific and academic reports	poems novels	and committees

These are the types of materials that social scientists use as data sources in their investigations of our social environment. Nevertheless, they are rarely brought up in textbooks that discuss the results of such investigations (although this is beginning to change). This is a most unfortunate situation, for much of the pleasure of the social sciences lies in discovering these materials and learning from them.

Letters written by famous people like Thomas Jefferson can be exciting because they often reveal something of the motivation behind behaviors and important historic events. But the letters of ordinary people are also often valuable sources, as in the case, for example, of the descriptions and reactions expressed by immigrants to this country in writing to family and friends back home. Fortunately, many such letters have been preserved and are available for study by sociologists, anthropologists, and historians. Many social scientists have also taped interviews with those who cannot write, and have recorded the myths and legends and stories that often reveal the basic attitudes and values of a people—their fears, hopes, and sense of historical identity. Scientific and academic reports of the past and present reflect the changes in the perception of social phenomena over time, affected by the existing views and definitions of

I am Jennifer Moore. I am a girl. I live with my mommy and daddy. My mommy's name is Clarice and my daddy's name is Bill. I am going to be a witch for Hallowe'en. I will scare mommy and daddy. I will go trick or treating. I will be lying on the couch watching T.V.

such things as race, causation, intelligence, and culture. Records of government and other public meetings are usually available for study, as are a surprising number of other sources. Even an ordinary telephone directory can be an exciting source for learning about a particular city.

Tapping these many sources obviously requires that teachers be familiar with them—there is probably no substitute for the well-read and well-informed teacher who is an eager inquirer. However, more and more of these materials are becoming available in textbooks, and teachers might save themselves a lot of time and effort by reviewing the current offerings. Remember that many of these materials may have to be adapted to the reading levels of elementary school students. This is not, however, as difficult a task as it might at first appear to be. Simplifying complex materials becomes relatively easy with just a bit of practice.

Space does not permit a review of all of the resources listed above, but a few are discussed in greater detail in the following pages. They may suggest ways to adapt other types of written resource materials.

Written Interviews   Interviews, polls, and surveys have become very important tools of social scientists. They are particularly favored by political scientists and sociologists, who use them to assess public attitudes toward issues as diverse as the desirable location of a park and the misuse of political power. They are also commonly used by the news media, which query the public on many events of national and local interest. Political parties, advertising agencies, and many other groups rely on these techniques to tell them whether or not a product will sell, a television show is popular, or a political position should be abandoned. Data of this sort can be analyzed with students. Past and present attitudes toward war, for example, can be compared and reasons suggested for the changes. Methods used by the interviewer can be discussed. Was the sample large enough? Did it include all types of people? Were the questions clear?

In order to fully understand this technique, students should have the opportunity to conduct their own surveys. Interviews can be conducted with other class members, students from other classes, friends and relatives outside the school, and even with strangers at shopping areas or other neighborhood centers. They may range from the informal written summary of a session with a single subject (discussed previously) to the formal collection of data from a number of interviewees using a written questionnaire. Written questionnaires are among the best tools for collecting systematic data on a given subject of interest and students should become familiar with this technique.

Although questionnaires frequently look simple once prepared, they are not easy to construct. One of the most difficult parts of the project is to determine exactly what the purpose of the questionnaire is and the type of information needed to fulfill the purpose. Questions have to be carefully selected and precisely written so as to avoid confusion. These essential preliminary steps help students clarify their thinking and usually take considerable time. After writing the questionnaire, students should test it with some friends to determine whether it is indeed clear and understandable. Selecting the sample can also provoke considerable thought. Obviously, not everyone can be interviewed. How many would be enough? Should the sample include different age groups? Which ones? Males as well as females? Different ethnic groups? Collecting the data is fun for most youngsters, but be sure to stress the importance of taking the interview seriously. Teach them how to introduce themselves and give them ample opportunity to practice what they are going to say before actually attempting an interview. When all the data are collected, have the students summarize and analyze them. Were the findings surprising? In what way? Did they run into any problems? What kinds? Would they rewrite some questions if they were to do it again? Why and how?

Interviews of this type can serve very practical purposes. Suppose, for example, a class is charged with proposing some ideas to celebrate "Brotherhood Week." Among the ideas the students suggest is more study of different ethnic groups in the United States. One student thinks it is important to learn more about Chinese Americans. Another says that they are going to do that next year. What emerges from a series of claims and counter-claims is that nobody really knows what ethnic groups are actually studied in the school, so the class decides to conduct a survey to determine this information. They then prepare a questionnaire to structure the survey.

Questionnaire

Interviewer _____ Date _____

Grade level of person interviewed _____

Our class is doing a study to find out which groups in the United States students in this school have studied. We need your help to get this information. Your name will not be used.

	Have studied.	Want to learn more about.
Afro-Americans	_____	_____
Mexican Americans	_____	_____
Native Americans	_____	_____
Puerto Ricans	_____	_____
European Americans	_____	_____
Chinese Americans	_____	_____
Japanese Americans	_____	_____

Instructions:

1. Put a check in column 1 next to each group you have studied something about.
2. Put a check in column 2 next to each group you would like to learn more about.
3. Are there any other groups not listed above that you would like to learn something about?
   List them here: _____

The Case Study   A case study is a detailed presentation of a personal or group experience that includes a value conflict. The purpose of the study is to have students analyze the underlying values and clarify their own values as they make decisions. It is a dramatic way to highlight conflicting interests through the personalization of different points of view. Case studies are sometimes included in social studies textbooks, but teachers should not hesitate to prepare their own. They can use their own knowledge of community events, local and national newspapers, periodicals, fiction and nonfiction sources for ideas.

The case study can be presented in a number of ways. It may simply be typed up and copied and handed out to the students. It may be read aloud. It may even be presented in a fairly spectacular way with slides or photographs and recordings. The most important things to remember about presentation, however, are clarity and brevity — get directly to the point.

The more difficult part of using case studies is the discussion that follows. Students may be all too ready to make quick decisions about the situation presented. So before asking for decisions, have the students do the following:

1. Identify and clarify the problem.
2. Identify the various alternative solutions and their probable benefits and disadvantages.
3. Take a position and defend it.
4. Discuss the positions taken by other students.

If you can, try to establish this procedure as a normal step in dealing with case studies — and other value conflicts that arise in the classroom. This may, with luck, become a habit for the students. And always remember that the students must reach their decisions for themselves. Having others make their decisions for them is something that should *not* become a habit.

An Example of   The easiest way to develop a fictional case study is to begin with fact. Take a
a Case Study   local event or a newspaper story about another city and adapt it. Change names, places, and, at times, the situation itself. A problem involving water pollution might be turned into one about air pollution or even zoning problems. The following is a fictionalized case study based on a real community event in a residential area of a small but growing town.

> Smithsville is a small housing district in the south of Oregon. Ten years ago, the City Council bought ten acres of land in the center of the district for the purpose of developing it into a recreational area at some future date. Meantime, the land was left in its natural state — full of large trees, nature trails, and some wild life. While some people are happy to leave it as it is, others would like to see it developed into a children's park. The City Council has to make a decision within a month.
>
> Mrs. Green, the mother of two children, ages 4 and 6, argued before the City Council at the last meeting: "I need a safe place where my children can play. They need swings and slides and a place to play ball. Right now, there is no place for young children to play, except on the street." (About 25 percent of the families in Smithville have young children.)
>
> Mr. Johnson, a school teacher, has a different point of view. "Smithville used to be a

beautiful place—full of tall trees and greenery. Now it is just full of homes and there is hardly anything green to be seen. We need to protect our environment—and everyone can enjoy the park as it is now."

Mrs. Ray, an elderly widow living on a fixed income, wants to keep the park as it is too: "It would cost thousands of dollars to build a park for young children. This means added taxes which older people, like myself, just can't afford. Let's keep things as they are."

High-school students enjoy the park as it is: "Right now, my friends and I can hang around the park and have a good time. If it becomes a place for little kids, where will kids my age go?"

But people who live next to the park are not entirely happy with the kids who "hang around" the park. Joseph Wright's house is right next to the park and he says: "High-school kids come to the park at night and make a lot of noise. They leave lots of cans and litter—some of it on my front lawn. A park for small children would be better supervised."

If you were a city councilman, how would you vote?

Historical Case Studies

Case studies that draw on actual historical events can be doubly useful, not only allowing the teacher to combine value clarification with the teaching of history but also presenting history in a way that is vivid and memorable. Presenting the students with the facts about an event in the past and asking them to make a decision on that basis is a provocative way of introducing many important issues. The discussion of other positions is expanded to include not only those taken by other members of the class but those taken by the individuals who took part in the event; the identification and evaluation of alternatives becomes a much more crucial issue since it involves real historical choices. However, care must be taken to select issues that are significant and open to more than one alternative. Where possible, it is probably better not to reveal the historical choice until the students have made their own decisions. Like the choice made by a teacher, the choice made by a president of the United States is likely to be accepted as correct whether it was or not.

One good source for historical case studies is the two-volume *Selected Case Studies in American History.*[4] Among the figures featured in the first volume are Davy Crockett, Christopher Columbus, Thomas Jefferson, Queen Isabella, and John Smith. The second volume deals with a variety of issues, including the Sand Creek Massacre of 1864, the Freedom Rides of the 1960s, the case of the Amish and the schools, and the right to keep and bear arms—an issue that was dramatically highlighted by the Kennedy assassination. Although designed for eighth grade, these materials can be adapted for use by younger students by simplifying the language and using only some of the documents.

Each case study in the collection is accompanied by a short introduction, a development of the event, and questions. The case is presented as a problem in which excerpts from historical documents are used to help students make a decision. Thus, for example, in the case called "Who Fired That Shot?" (referring to the first shot fired at Lexington in 1775), both sides of the case are

[4]William E. Gardner, Robert W. Beery, and James R. Olson, *Selected Case Studies in American History* (Boston: Allyn & Bacon, 1969).

> ## Guidelines for Writing Case Studies
>
> 1. Select a study objective.
> 2. Select an appropriate event that illustrates conflicting values.
> 3. Put the event in appropriate language. Use maps, diagrams, photographs, and other media to clarify points where necessary.
> 4. Keep the study short and omit irrelevant details.

presented. Readings from British as well as American sources are offered, including statements by eyewitnesses, newspaper accounts of the time, and even present-day textbooks used in the two countries.

Data Sheets   Data sheets are useful collections of relevant *facts* that can easily be prepared by the teacher for classroom use. They may include statistical data, significant dates and events, descriptive materials, or whatever facts are called for. They should be concise and to the point, and classroom discussions should be held to interpret, analyze, and evaluate the materials. Chart 8–2 gives an example of a typical data chart and the types of questions that might be asked to stimulate a class discussion. It requires fairly sophisticated thinking and is aimed at upper-level elementary grades.

Data sheets can be generated from a great many sources and can reflect a great many things. As long as they present a possibility for comparison, data sheets may deal with all sorts of subjects and materials. For example:

1. Historical events arranged in chronological order.
2. A set of photographs titled and dated to indicate what happened in a certain place at a certain time — as, for example, a building site.
3. A series of quotes by different people with different points of view — or one person whose point of view has changed several times.
4. A series of headlines taken from different newspapers about the same event.

Literary Materials   Literary materials such as novels, plays, poetry, and legends can be used in the social studies to provide experiences with emotional depth and encourage feelings of empathy and knowledge. Good writers are able to add a dimension to the human experience that makes people and concepts meaningful and rich. A library corner in the classroom can make such materials easily accessible. Care should be taken to change materials frequently, and opportunities should be provided for free reading time. Works that pertain to subjects being studied by the class can be assigned to the entire group and then discussed. When books are read by individual students, the teacher should attempt to discuss the book, however briefly, with the student. Questions such as those in Chart 8–3 can be used to guide the discussions. (See Appendix B for a partial list of fiction and nonfiction books suitable for elementary social studies.)

Chart 8–2
Using a Data Sheet to Study World Population

World Population Data Sheet
(Population in Millions)

Region	1971	2000*
World	3,706	6,494
Africa	354	818
Asia	2,104	3,777
North America	229	333
Latin America	291	652
Europe	466	568
U.S.S.R.	245	330
Oceania	20	35

*U.N. estimate.

Source: The Population Reference Bureau, Inc., Revised Edition, August, 1971.

The following questions can help guide subsequent inquiry:
Locate these regions on the map. Read the numbers in the first column. Second column.

What kinds of data are included in the graph? What does "U.N. estimate" mean?

Which region had the largest population in 1971? Which region had the smallest population? Which region is likely to have the largest population in the year 2000? How much larger is this than the next largest one? Why is this number an estimate?

What can you say in general about the rate of population growth in different regions? What kind of effect might this have on food supplies? Energy supplies? Health? Housing? Can we be sure?

Is the growth of populations a problem? Why?

Newspapers   Much rhetoric has been devoted to the need for an informed public in a democracy. Nonetheless, the mass of the American public remains sadly uninformed about national and world affairs. The newspaper is one of the most important sources of current information, and it can prove a very useful tool in the classroom. Intelligently used by an enthusiastic teacher, it can be an exciting instructional experience for students, and may help stimulate valuable lifelong habits.

Newspapers can do the following:

1. develop the concept of interdependence among communities, states, and nations.
2. illuminate worldwide social issues.
3. make students aware of the contributions of various cultures around the world and the conditions under which other human beings live.
4. illuminate the processes of power and decision-making and inform regarding the individuals who make decisions.

Chart 8—3
Questions to Help Students Deal with Literature

Cognitive	*Affective*
What is one new word or fact you learned?	Did you like it?
What does the author mean by the title?	Would you recommend that others read it?
What was the most important problem the character(s) had to face? How did he or she solve it?	How did you feel about the character? Was the character real? What makes you say so?
Can you think of other ways the character could have solved this problem?	Did you feel the character was like you or different from you?
Can you think of an experience you've had in which you've felt the same way as the character?	If you were faced with the same problem, what would you have done?
What lesson do you think the story (book, essay, etc.) teaches?	
Do you believe the story really happened? What makes you think so?	

---

5. inform as to technological developments in science and medicine.
6. keep alive the perception of the relationship of past and present events.
7. make students aware of the functions of a free press in a democratic society.
8. affect basic attitudes and value judgments.

Newspapers, however, will do none of the above unless teachers make conscious efforts to use them with as much care as they would other types of instructional resources. The "let's discuss current events today" approach all too often leads to boredom as students tire of exchanging ignorance. The following suggestions have been experimented with in classrooms and have proved very effective in stimulating interest.

Keep a variety of papers around for browsing. Not just local, but out of state, ethnic group, and foreign papers can be of interest to the students.[5]

Allow time for reading and encourage clipping. Urge students to add to the collection by bringing newspapers from home.

[5]Sources for the most commonly used classroom periodicals are:

Xerox Education Publications, Inc., Education Center, Columbus, Ohio 43216. *My Weekly Reader,* Grades K–6; *Current Events,* Grades 7–9.

Scholastic Magazines, Inc., 902 Sylvan Avenue, Englewood Cliffs, N.J. 07632. *News Pilot,* Grade 1; *News Ranger,* Grade 2; *News Trail,* Grade 3; *News Explorer,* Grade 4; *Young Citizen,* Grade 5; *News-time,* Grades 5 and 6; *Junior Scholastic,* Grades 6, 7, 8.

The Civic Education Service, 1733 K Street, N. W., Washington, D. C. *The Junior Review,* Grades 7 and 8.

The New York Times, 229 West 43rd St., New York, New York 10036. *The School Times* (published twice a month), middle grades.

Help students keep a newsfile. Have them arrange it according to topic. This will help in-depth coverage of significant events as well as provide a ready reference for alternative viewpoints on a given topic over time. Be sure to note date and source on all articles. Don't try to cover more than two or three major topics or the filing will take up too much time.

Have students maintain a news bulletin board. Put it in a prominent place and change it daily. Include headlines, cartoons, maps, photographs, and blown-up articles. Remember that small print discourages readers. Encourage the students to add their own comments, materials, cartoons, and other relevant information. Draw attention to the display frequently.

Provide time for a daily news discussion. Keep the activities varied and try to cover a broad range of subjects.

Hold debates. Should the President veto this bill? Should the new freeway be built? Give the panel of "experts" some time to prepare and allow for general student participation. Be sure to include all points of view.

Simulate television newscasts. This might take the form of a summary report at the end of the week. Provide an imitation microphone and allow the students ample time to prepare. Encourage the use of tapes, photographs, and other media to enliven the presentation.

Interview an "expert." Ask students to select an event or topic and study it carefully. Then arrange for the class to interview the "expert."

Role-play a given event. Set the scene, assign parts, and have the students act out the roles based on what they have read about the individuals in the newspapers or weekly newsmagazines. Conflict between world leaders based on actual or imaginary situations is usually the easiest—and most instructive—type of news role-playing to perform.

Give a report yourself. Don't hesitate to report the news yourself from time to time, especially the larger, more complex events.

Focus on one topic. To avoid random reporting of unrelated topics, let students choose subjects for concentration in advance. Spend the news period on one topic instead of many. Have students report from many points of view.

Prepare a monthly news summary. Synthesize learnings by having the class prepare its own monthly newspaper. Include student cartoons, editorials, advertisements, and so on.

When making oral presentations, students should be encouraged to deliver the news extemporaneously. Discourage reading recitations. A few well-spoken sentences are better experience for the student making the presentation, and they are also more interesting for the rest of the class.

Developing Newspaper Skills

Learning how to read a newspaper intelligently requires several skills. Teachers should ask their students to do the following:

1. *Find out the facts about the newspaper.* Who publishes it? Where does the publisher live? How long has it been in existence? Does it have a point of view? What is its circulation? Who are the editorial staff? What sources does

Guidelines for Preparing News Summaries

Students should include these points:
1. What happened?
2. Who was involved? Give names and occupations or titles where appropriate.
3. Where did it happen? Locate it on a map.
4. When did it happen?
5. Why did it happen?
6. What's important about it?
7. What vocabulary words are needed to explain it?

it depend on for news? Associated Press? United Press International? Local reporters? Syndicated columnists?

2. *Learn the format.* Where are the most important stories located? Where is the editorial page? Sports page? Entertainment? Special columns? Local news? International news?

3. *Evaluate the scope.* What percent of the space is devoted to local news? National news? International news? Does the paper focus heavily on violence? Does it include cultural events? Civic affairs? Education news?

4. *Evaluate the contents.* Are the statements generally accurate? Are sources of information identified? Do headlines describe the account accurately? Are photographs clear and adequately labeled? Are editorials interesting and well written?

5. *Evaluate for bias.* Does the paper distinguish between fact and opinion? Does it present more than one side of the issue? Does it include a section where readers voice their opinions? Do these include opposing points of view? Do articles try to excite or just report the facts?

Textbooks   Even though a great many other resources such as newspapers and case studies have been introduced into the classroom in recent years, textbooks continue to play a major role in social studies instruction. A good textbook can be extremely helpful in presenting material, while even a bad one can function as a basis for study if the proper inquiry modifications are made.

The teacher who is in the position of being able to influence the adoption of new texts can do a great deal to improve the quality of education in his or her school by making a careful study of the available texts. A list of questions to be asked in considering the principal factors is presented in Chart 8–4.

Another Factor: Minorities

In addition to the factors listed in the chart, there is another of at least equal importance. Unfortunately, it has only recently been given any real attention by

publishers, and, for the most part, the improvements have been so limited that this factor is not yet considered crucial enough to be added to the list of major considerations affecting adoptions. It should, however, be borne in mind.

Minorities continue to be inadequately treated in most textbooks. Although black Americans are no longer excluded from texts, and most of the negative stereotypes of the past have finally been eliminated, the changes have rarely resulted in more than a neutralization of racial images. Little or nothing is said of the rich African heritage or the pluralistic communities of American blacks. Worse yet, Native Americans and those of Japanese, Chinese, or Hispanic heritage are still largely ignored. And even when they are presented, the image of them as "outsiders" tends to prevail.

Minority religious groups are also usually ignored or their images distorted. The Jewish faith, for example, is often treated as some kind of prehistoric religious phenomenon. The same may be said of Buddhism and other Eastern religions. The prevalent point of religious reference is Christianity. But even within this framework, only a selected few Christian groups are represented. Little attention if any is ever given to the variety of religious sects that characterize this country.

Chart 8—4
Evaluating Social Studies Textbooks

The cognitive component

Concepts and generalizations

Are these clearly defined and organized? Are they powerful? Do they reflect an interdisciplinary, multidisciplinary, or single-discipline orientation? Does one orientation dominate? Are the concepts closed or open? Is the full range of the concept suggested? Are examples included? Do the examples reflect reality? Are they relevant to student experiences?

Facts

Are they accurate? Do they adequately support concepts, generalizations, main ideas? Are they recent? Are authoritative sources identified?

Social Issues

Are any of the concepts, generalizations, and facts important in understanding major social issues? Have such relationships been made clear? Are alternative points of view included?

Skills

Is adequate attention given to skill development? Are skills introduced sequentially, with sufficient attention to cognitive and affective development? Are inquiry skills fostered? Divergent as well as convergent thinking?

The affective component

Value Clarification

Are the issues presented amenable to value clarification? Is the material presented with enough emotional impact to stimulate value clarification? Is a strategy for value clarification identified? Is it used sufficiently throughout the text?

Value Inquiry

Does the text present issues that are amenable to value inquiry? Does it promote decision-making based on alternative value judgments?

Moral Development

Does the text include materials that help students grapple with moral issues? Are these appropriate for students? Are they significant? Timely? Relevant?

Scope

Do the topics and areas encompass the global community? Do they include varied cultures and sub-cultures? Which ones will need to be supplemented? Does the scope include a range of social issues? Which ones will need to be supplemented?

Sequence

Are concepts and generalizations arranged sequentially on increasingly complex levels? Are major learnings sufficiently reinforced throughout the grades?

Instructional Strategies

Are these identified? Are many strategies used? Are they primarily expository? Varied inquiry strategies?

Instructional Resources

Are these multimedia? Is their cost worth it? Can the text be used independently of them? Does the text include pictures, graphs, charts, tables, cartoons?

Meeting Student Needs

Does the text provide for individual differences? What is the reading level? Is the content presented in an interesting way? If the material is intended for slower readers, is the conceptual level high enough? Is the material relevant to student experiences and background?

Technical Attributes

Is the print clear and legible? Paper too glossy? Photographs attractive? Charts clear and uncluttered? Format consistent? Does it include an adequate table of contents? Index?

Cost and Availability

Is the cost competitive? Is it readily available? Are examination copies available?

There is one other group that deserves special attention in this context, and it is, ironically, composed of a majority of the citizens of this country. Women have been represented in virtually every textbook ever published, but the treatment given them has been extremely biased. Even today, when publishers are very conscious of the problem, textbooks continue to ignore the contributions of women and to perpetuate stereotypical roles. Less readily noticed, but no less pernicious, is the use of masculine singular pronouns to represent both sexes.

There is clearly a need to integrate the experiences of all minorities into the areas of the social studies, just as there is a need to integrate their experiences into our national life. Today's textbooks are a major factor in shaping the attitudes of tomorrow's citizens toward one another, and teachers who are sensitive both to omissions and distortions can play an influential role in changing attitudes by providing a balanced viewpoint and by bringing pressure to bear on those publishers who do not make the effort to improve their texts.

The following guidelines are offered to help evaluate the treatment of minorities in textbooks:

1. Do the verbal and visual contents reflect multi-ethnic groups in the past and present?
2. Do they reflect the role and contribution of various religious groups in the past and present?
3. Do they reflect the role and contribution of women in the past and present?
4. Is the information current and accurate?
5. Is each group presented in such a fashion as to promote a positive self-image?
6. Does the material reinforce ethnocentric views?
7. Does the material reflect the view that problems relating to these groups have all been solved? Are problems presented truthfully annd realistically?
8. Are historical and contemporary figures presented in such a way that both their strengths and weaknesses are made manifest?

Current Textbooks

The following is a partial listing of some current textbooks available in the social studies.[6]

Family of Man. Project Social Studies, University of Minnesota. Edith West, editor. Selective Educational Equipment, Inc. (K–12)

Emphasis is on anthropology, sociology, and geography, although other disciplines are given some attention. The series has a contemporary focus and reflects a culturally pluralistic orientation.

Holt Databank System. William R. Fielder, editor. Holt, Rinehart and Winston, 1972. (K–6)

An interdisciplinary series that most closely approaches an open inductive inquiry approach. It uses multiple media, includes many contemporary social issues not traditionally found in elementary texts, and is generally well and interestingly written.

Man: A Course of Study. Social Studies Curriculum Center, Education Development Center. Peter Dow, editor. Curriculum Development Associates, 1970. (Grades 5 and upwards)

This one year course of study centers around three questions: What is human about human beings? How did they get that way? How can they be made more so? It depends on multiple media, particularly films, and anthropology is its disciplinary focus.

The Social Sciences: Concepts and Values. The Center for the Study of Instruction. Paul F. Brandwein, editor. Harcourt Brace Jovanovich, 1970. (K–8)

This is essentially a multidisciplinary text with emphasis on conceptualizing and generalizing. Not much emphasis on social issues, but culturally diverse groups receive some attention. The text is well organized, and teacher guides include questions to promote higher inquiry. Some value clarification is included.

Taba Program in Social Science. San Francisco State College. Mary C. Durkin and Norman E. Wallen, editors. Addison-Wesley, 1972. (1–8)

This is an interdisciplinary series with some focus on contemporary issues and cultural diversity. Although basic attention is given to concepts and generalizations, affective concerns are included.

World Studies Inquiry Series. Robin J. McKeown, Director. Field Educational Publications, Inc. (7–12)

Although this series is designed for grades 7 and upwards, it is directed at below-level readers. Focus is on contemporary issues, and despite the simple reading level, inquiry questions tap higher-level thinking. There are three paperback books that can be used for a one year source of study or integrated as appropriate for a study of Latin America, Asia, and Africa.

---

[6]For further evaluation of these and other textbooks, see *Social Education* 36:7, November 1972 (whole issue); Irving Morrissett, "Third Report: Ratings of 24 Social Studies Materials," *Social Education* 39:2, February 1975, pp. 96–99; William W. Joyce, "Minorities in Primary-Grade Social Studies Textbooks: A Progress Report," *Social Education* 37:3, March 1973, pp. 218–33.

Evaluation

Evaluation

Evaluation, the process of making judgments about the value or merit of things, is something human beings find impossible to avoid. Living requires decisions and decisions require evaluations. Educational systems are certainly in no position to avoid making evaluations. For one thing, the people who support them have a habit of wanting to feel that they are getting something for their money. Then there is the fact that colleges are selective in their admissions, and grades and test results are among the simplest and most direct bases for making decisions of that sort. Teachers, of course, are required to evaluate students by assigning grades. Even, however, when they choose to present materials in one form or another or emphasize one point over another, they are making judgments regarding the merit of things. And not to be overlooked is the type of evaluation that students consistently engage in—of teachers, programs, and themselves. No doubt there is much that is wrong with the evaluation process in education, but the issue is not to abandon it—a futile effort in any case—but to put it to more appropriate use.

The Functions of Evaluation

To understand evaluation, one must examine not only its techniques but its functions—and educational evaluation has many. Assigning grades, motivating student achievement, diagnosing learning disabilities, and discovering when to modify instructional strategies are among the most commonly cited. But there are other functions that are not as frequently mentioned.

Overt and Covert Functions

What we say we are doing when we attempt to evaluate are the *overt functions*. There are, however, *covert functions* as well—ones that are not publicly stated, that are frequently unrecognized and unintended, and that would probably be largely unacceptable to teachers, parents, and students. For example, an overt function of assigning grades is to help students assess their progress. A covert function, however, is to assign students to occupational roles and social class, for grades are of crucial importance in determining who goes on to vocational or professional studies. And while many people may accept the first function as a legitimate one, they may find the second highly objectionable. Chart 9–1 lists a number of overt and covert functions of educational evaluation. The reader will no doubt be able to add to it.

The overall function of educational evaluation should be to help students learn. But in order to do this, it is essential to be certain that the functions we articulate are the ones we are actually implementing. We must ensure that covert functions are exposed, and, wherever they are detrimental to student learning, discouraged. This requires that teachers cultivate a broad perspective and a willingness to subject both traditional and innovative educational practices to critical scrutiny.

Chart 9–1
The Functions of Educational Evaluation

Overt

To enable pupils and parents to judge performance (grading)

To group students for more efficient learning

To retain or promote students in order to facilitate learning

To motivate achievement

To diagnose learning disabilities

To modify course objectives in accordance with student needs

To modify instructional strategies, techniques, and resources

Covert

To punish and reward
To assign occupational roles and social class

To track students
To facilitate administrative procedures
To ease the burden of preparation for teachers

To punish and reward
To avoid the necessity of individualizing instruction
To maintain standardized means of dealing with individuals

To control student behavior
To ensure conformity

To label students
To legitimate a negative self-image
To justify to others student failures

To placate discontent
To keep standards low and easily attainable

To innovate for innovation's sake
To achieve recognition, special funds, and jobs
To conform to current fads

Diagnostic, Formative, and Summative Functions

Benjamin Bloom and his associates proposed a three-part classification of the functions of educational evaluation, each associated with a different process.[1] The first of these, *diagnostic* evaluation, occurs before instruction begins. It is designed to assess the students' skills, needs, and the like for the purpose of prescribing appropriate learning objectives. *Formative* evaluation occurs during instruction and is intended to identify what the students have not mastered in order to adjust future learning experiences. *Summative* evaluation occurs at the end of instruction. Its purpose is to assign a grade or to assess overall success in meeting learning objectives. Diagnostic and formative evaluation are the most useful for student learning, for at these stages mastery is still possible. Summative evaluation is the least useful because instruction has ceased. Oddly enough, emphasis has usually been placed on summative evaluation, and the other two functions have been given much less attention than they deserve. (Questions to guide evaluation during each of the three stages are identified in Chart 9–2.)

[1]Benjamin Bloom et al., *Handbook on Formative and Summative Evaluation of Student Learning* (New York: McGraw-Hill, 1971).

Chart 9–2
Questions to Guide Diagnostic, Formative, and Summative Evaluation

Diagnostic Evaluation (Pre-Instruction)

Students What are their immediate needs?

What are their interests?

What are their present cognitive, affective, and psychomotor developmental stages?

What strengths do they have that can be capitalized on in the classroom?

What social problems do they need to know about?

What future competencies are they likely to need?

What skills need further development?

What are their learning styles?

Teachers What are their interests and how can these be used in the classroom?

What academic competencies do they have? Which need further development?

What are their teaching styles? Do they need modification?

What instructional strategies are they skilled at? Which need modification?

What interaction skills are they best at? Which require further development?

Schools What legal constraints exist?

What are the informal and formal rules? How do these influence the classroom?

Who are the decision makers? How can they be helpful?

What resources are available and how can they be obtained?

Curricula Are goals significant? Broadly stated? What basic values do they reflect? Do they include cognitive, affective, and psychomotor goals?

Does subject matter reflect what is academically important, globally significant, and of interest to students and the community?

Are objectives consistent with goals? Are they expressed behaviorally?

Are instructional strategies diverse? Are they inquiry oriented?

Are instructional techniques varied?

Do instructional resources tend to be abstract? Do they include many of a more concrete nature?

Are evaluation techniques varied? Are they reliable? Valid? Are opportunities provided for diagnostic, formative, and summative evaluation?

Communities What problems and issues trouble the community?

Who are influential sources in the community? Can they help?

What ethnic groups live in the community?

What life-styles does the community encompass?

What values are reflected in the community?

What are its human and nonhuman resources? How can these be identified? How can they be utilized?

Formative Evaluation (During Instruction)

Students Are students mastering the assigned task?
Which parts of the task are not being mastered?
Can students help explain difficulties?
Can students help choose new tasks?

Teachers What teacher behavior should be modified to help students master assigned tasks?
How are students involved in suggesting teacher behavior modifications? In what other ways could they be?

Schools What additional resources can be provided to help students master tasks?
Where are they available in the school? How can they be obtained?

Curricula Do objectives need modification?
Do instructional strategies need modification?
What other instructional techniques can be used?
Are instructional resources adequate? What additional ones can be used?
Should the present evaluation techniques be modified? Should others be added?

Communities Can they provide additional resources that will help the students master tasks?

Summative Evaluation (Post-Instruction)

Students How well have students achieved cognitive objectives? Affective objectives? Psychomotor objectives?

Teachers Which teacher interests were of most help in achieving the desired results?
Which academic competencies were of most help?
Which teaching styles were most effective?
Which instructional strategies were most effective?
What types of interaction patterns produced the desired results?

Schools How did legal constraints affect results?
How did formal and informal rules affect results?
Which decision-makers were of most help?
Which resources were most effective?

Curricula How have curricular components helped students master objectives?
Which instructional strategies were most effective? Least effective?
Which instructional resources were most helpful? Least helpful?
Were evaluation techniques reliable? Valid? Varied? Who was involved in the evaluation process?

Communities How has the community helped the students master the different objectives?
Which community resources were most helpful? Least helpful? Which ones should be considered next time?
Has instruction helped meet community needs? How?

The Components of Evaluation

There are three essential components of the evaluation process: an object, a measure, and a standard. To evaluate means simply to make a *judgment* based on a measure of an object in relation to some standard.

Objects   As students are the focus of the educational system, it is hardly surprising that they have traditionally been the most common objects of evaluation. But if we conceive the goal of evaluation in schools to be the achievement of the most effective education of students, then it follows that we must also evaluate the other elements of the system that contribute to that end: teachers, schools, communities, and curricula. For example, Mr. Smith, who teaches in a suburb of New York, may have a student who is very much interested in the history of cartography but is a poor reader. There may be no books available in the school with a high enough conceptual level and a low enough reading level, but if Mr. Smith knows the school and the community, he may be able to get the materials he needs. Ms. Jones, a teacher in a rural town, may be asked to develop a social studies curriculum. Her knowledge of the community convinces her that what the students need to develop above all is a sense of being able to accomplish things. Her ability to modify and revise the assigned course will depend at least in part on her knowledge of the formal and informal rules that govern the school. In both cases, student learning abilities are strongly influenced by factors outside the students. And such influences can often make the difference between success and failure.

Measures   Measures are the instruments used to assess objects. In schools, measures consist primarily of written tests, but they may also include classroom work samples, checklists, interviews, and so on. They provide the basis for establishing initial standing, assessing results, estimating the degree of change over a period of time, and discovering any discrepancies between actual and intended results.

It is essential to remember that measures can be faulty and must therefore be frequently evaluated themselves. The two basic criteria for evaluating measures are reliability and validity. Reliability is concerned with the consistency of a measure—that is, would it produce the same result if given under different circumstances and at a different time? Validity is concerned with the degree to which a measure actually measures what it is intended to.

A single measure, such as a written test, rarely satisfies reliability and validity criteria. The student may, for example, be worried or tired at the time of a test, and it is quite possible that the same result would not be produced under different circumstances. Or a measure designed to assess one type of behavior may actually measure another, as in the case of students who fail to perform adequately on comprehension tests because they have reading problems. Because of these considerations, educators are now calling attention to: (1) the need to use *multiple* measures in evaluating a single characteristic, (2) the need for greater skill in constructing *valid* measures, and (3) the need to use a *variety* of measures. The last includes (but is not limited to):

standardized tests	checklists	questionnaires
teacher-made tests	rating lists	anecdotal records
individual and	tapes	work samples
group interviews	panels	discussions
autobiographies	diaries	

Standards

Standards are the criteria against which objects are measured. And in the case of the evaluation of students, this may mean anything from one teacher's idea of what a class should be capable of to the average score of a nationally administered examination. But two kinds of standards are of particular interest to educators at present, each one associated with a different type of evaluation process. One type, called normative evalution, uses norms as standards. The other, called criterion-referenced evaluation, uses specified criteria as standards.

Normative Evaluation

Standards used in normative evaluation are generally numerically derived scores from tests administered to large numbers of students. The standard in this case is the norm, which is usually a numerical average derived from a wide range of scores. The purpose of normative evaluation is to assess the abilities or knowledge of an individual or group in relation to the norm. It is a way of comparing the achievement scores of one student or group of students with others. Most schools use some type of normative evaluation process in assessing student achievement.

Properly used, normative evaluation can be helpful. It can be used by a particular school or teacher to determine appropriate future programs. For example, if students of John Ellen Elementary score below the norm in map reading skills this year, more effort in that area may be prescribed for next year. Or if many schools prove to be greatly disadvantaged in some skill, the state or federal government may be persuaded to allocate monies for special programs.

But normative evaluation has come under sharp criticism in the past few years for some very good reasons. For one thing, it tells us little about what a student actually knows about a subject—only how the student scores in comparison with others on a particular test. For another, the samples from which norms are derived are frequently inadequate. Norms are supposed to reflect average performances of a large population of students—some even presume to reflect the whole nation of students. In order to arrive at norms, however, tests are not given to all students but only to samples who are supposed to reflect the larger group. If the sample is inadequate, then the norms do not really reflect the performance of this larger group.

The most serious criticism, however, concerns the uses to which normative evaluation has been put. Because the very nature of a norm requires that some students will be above it and some below, normative evaluation is often used to make offensive comparisons among students, teachers, and schools. When students score higher than the norm, everyone is clearly pleased. Students feel good about themselves and the teachers and the schools tend to be credited with their success. Conversely, when students score below the norm, they tend to be stigmatized and the teachers and schools are blamed. In some cases, however, schools might actually have contributed to a great deal of student learning, depending on the types of skills students already had.

Criterion-Referenced Evaluation

Criterion-referenced evaluation is a very different type of evaluation process. Standards used in criterion-referenced evaluation are specified criteria that are concretely stated. To illustrate, critical thinking is a frequently invoked standard in evaluating student achievement. But critical thinking is a highly abstract standard — it does not specify exactly what it consists of. On the other hand, a standard like "differentiates between fact and value statements" is quite specific. The purpose of criterion-referenced evaluation is to evaluate student achievement in relation to specified standards — not numerical norms.

There are many advantages to criterion-referenced evaluation. For one thing, it emphasizes learning of a particular subject matter, not comparison of students with one another. For another, it helps eliminate some of the subjectivity that frequently plagues the evaluation process. Both teachers and students can understand a standard that states "differentiates between fact and value statements" while most will not be at all sure what is meant by "critical thinking." Finally, criterion-referenced evaluation lends itself to successful learning experiences for all students. Its basic assumption is that when standards are appropriate and teaching is adequate, all students can achieve success. When students fail, it is because either the standards or the teaching have been inappropriate. Hence, rather than leading to comparisons that are bound to reflect badly on some students, criterion-referenced evaluation emphasizes feelings of adequacy among students.

Behavioral Objectives and Criterion-Referenced Evaluation

An educational objective is a statement of general intent about the results of instruction. There is a direct link between educational objectives and criterion-referenced evaluation. When an educational objective is stated specifically it implies a standard by which learning will be evaluated. When we say, for example, that the objective of a primary unit on communities is "to teach students to understand the ways neighbors help each other," we are implying that we will evaluate the success of our teaching by the way students understand this. The problem, however, is that while this objective is a good deal more specific than simply saying that our objective is "to teach students to understand community interdependence," it is still not specific enough.

For one thing, the subject of the statement is the teacher—it is the teacher who will teach. But our real interest is not to evaluate the teacher, but the learner. And there is not necessarily a connection between what the teacher thinks is being taught and what the student is actually learning. For another, we are not really sure what is meant by the word "understand." How will we know when and if the student "understands." Will it be sufficient if students merely listen while the teacher explains? Will the students have to answer some questions or perhaps prepare a mural? In short, exactly what will the students have to do in order to show that they understand? And how many things will they have to know about neighbors helping each other before we decide they have successfully achieved the objective? Three? Five? Ten? In order to introduce greater specificity in the process of writing educational objectives and to make criterion-referenced evaluation really possible, some educators have advocated the use of behavioral objectives.

Behavioral Objectives   A behavioral objective is a statement of specific intent regarding the results of instruction. At least three criteria are usually required for stating behavioral objectives. Each one should: (1) state what the student will be able to *do* if the objective is mastered, (2) state under what *conditions* the student will be able to do it, (3) identify the *extent* to which the student will be able to do it.

The first criterion emphasizes an observable behavior that can be seen by any objective viewer. Many behaviors are internal and therefore nonobservable. "Thinking," for example, is a nonobservable behavior. "Labeling," on the other hand, is observable. An observable behavior can be evaluated; a nonobservable behavior cannot.

Other examples of nonobservable behaviors are:

know	recognize	gain insight
understand	appreciate	enjoy
become aware	perceive	develop skill

Examples of observable behaviors are:

define	state	choose
list	select	describe
match	identify	arrange
label	translate	summarize

The second criterion, the conditions, are the "givens" under which the student will be asked to perform the behavior. In many cases, the conditions students are given considerably alter the nature of the task. For example, students can be asked to describe the problem of the American colonists before or after hearing a presentation by the teacher, viewing a particular film, or reading the textbook. A statement of conditions adds specificity to the behavior.

The third criterion, the extent, refers to the minimal level of success required in order to consider the task mastered. For example, if the students are given four questions to answer, it may be sufficient that they answer only three correctly. Or the teacher may specify the extent of success for the entire class by requiring that 80 percent of the students shall be able to answer three out of four questions correctly.

These are examples of statements of behavioral objectives that fulfill the three criteria:

> Given the following list, the student will distinguish between the fact and value statements by marking each with an "F" or "V" with 75 percent success:
>> People should learn about their communities.
>> About 75 percent of the population of the United States lives in cities.
>> It would be very good if more people moved to the country.
>> The government should do more to help solve problems in cities.

> When presented with a list of occupations including doctor, farmer, store owner, lawyer, judge, tool maker, baker, the student will differentiate between those who mostly perform an economic service and those who mostly produce an economic product by listing each in appropriate columns, with 100 percent success.

Observable Behaviors in the Cognitive Domain

Behaviors can reflect cognitive or affective processes. Smiling, for example, is a behavior that suggests enjoyment—an affective process. Defining a word, however, is clearly a cognitive process.

Cognitive behaviors can reflect different levels of thinking. For example, recalling the names of the Indian tribes of southwestern California involves memory primarily. But identifying the unwritten assumptions of a given article is obviously a more complex cognitive behavior. If our educational intent is to involve students in all types of thinking processes, our behavioral objectives should reflect this.

To what degree then is it possible to specify behaviors that correspond to different levels of cognition? Stated another way, is it possible to write behavioral objectives that will really reflect higher levels of thinking? Unfortunately, we cannot do so with certainty. But with the help of the Bloom *Taxonomy*, it is possible to generate a list of behaviors that appear to correspond to different levels of cognition. They are given in Chart 9–3. A word of caution: a behavioral objective needs to be read in full to make a proper judgment of the cognitive level. "Classifies," for example, is listed as analysis behavor, which indeed it is under certain circumstances. When students have to pull apart a description of a

---

Chart 9–3

Representative Behaviors in Each of the Categories of the Bloom *Taxonomy:* Cognitive Domain

Knowledge

recite	locate	alphabetize
copy	quote	repeat
define	read	reproduce

Comprehension

act out	interpret	state in own words
substitute	illustrate	determine implications
extrapolate	qualify	summarize
infer	rephrase	translate

Application

apply	generate	manipulate
construct	use	solve
demonstrate	explain	give an example

Analysis

classify	dissect	identify assumptions
deduce	divide	identify causal relationships
differentiate	group	identify elements
discriminate	sequence	identify techniques

Synthesis

combine	plan	hypothesize
compose	devise	conceptualize
propose	design	generalize
formulate	organize	integrate

Evaluation

assess	rank	weigh alternatives
decide	appraise	conclude
judge	resolve	justify

community's resources in order to arrive at some classification system, they are analyzing. But it can also be a comprehension behavior—as when students are first presented with a definition of renewable and nonrenewable resources and then given a list of resources to classify accordingly.

Here is an example of the ways in which observable behaviors might be used to suggest different levels of cognition as applied to the study of social power. The first step, reciting, represents the lowest level of complexity, and each succeeding step represents a higher one.

1. Students *recite from memory* three types of power identified on the previous day (knowledge).
2. Students *give the meanings* of the three types of power *in their own words* (comprehension).
3. Students *give examples* of each type from their own lives (application).
4. Students *identify the main differences* among the three types of power (analysis).
5. Students *propose alternative* types of power (synthesis).
6. Students *appraise the validity* of the types they have learned and their own alternatives (evaluation).

Behavioral Objectives in the Affective Domain

Educational objectives are not limited to the cognitive domain. Most educators try to achieve affective objectives as well. Some teachers, for example, are not content that students simply understand what cooperation and democracy are; they also want them to appreciate these things. Affective terms like "appreciate," "enjoy," "become interested in," "value," "become concerned with" are commonly used in the preparation of educational objectives. But there is obviously great difficulty in evaluating whether students really do "appreciate" or "enjoy" something. The same questions that caused concern about vague cognitive terms have been raised in relation to the affective domain. What exactly do students do? And under what conditions and to what extent do they have to do it before the teacher can claim success? The answers are important if criterion-referenced evaluation is to have any meaning in the affective domain.

Bloom's *Taxonomy* was clearly helpful in suggesting behaviors that appeared to correspond to levels of cognition. What was required was a similar taxonomy in the affective domain, and such a taxonomy did indeed exist. Using the same type of methodological analysis, David Krathwohl's group was able to identify five basic categories of affective objectives.

1.0 Receiving (Attending).
   One is sensitized to the existence of certain phenomena and is willing to attend to them.
   1.1 Awareness.
   1.2 Willingness to receive.
   1.3 Controlled or selected attention.

2.0 Responding.
One is not only willing to attend, but does so actively.
2.1 Acquiescence in responding.
2.2 Willingness to respond.
2.3 Satisfaction in response.

3.0 Valuing.
One accepts a value and commits oneself to it.
3.1 Acceptance of a value.
3.2 Preference for a value.
3.3 Commitment.

4.0 Organization.
One organizes the value into a system by determining how it compares with other values one holds and deciding which are dominant.
4.1 Conceptualization of a value.
4.2 Organization of a value system.

5.0 Characterization by a value or value complex.
One integrates the values into a total world view and behaves consistently with relation to those values.
5.1 Generalized set.
5.2 Characterization.[2]

Unlike cognitive objectives, which are organized in a hierarchy of increasing complexity, the affective categories are organized according to the degree of internalization. That is, each one represents a further stage in the adoption and application of values in one's own life. Thus, those persons who are merely willing to receive a value such as the desirability of a democratic form of government value it considerably less than those persons who have integrated it into their total world view.

But what types of behaviors are manifested at different degrees of internalization? Concretely, what does the person who merely receives a value (such as the desirability of a democratic form of government) *do* in contrast with the person who has become characterized by the value? An individual in the receiving stage may be just willing to listen—while one who is characterized by this value may consistently apply it in relationships with other people. Behaviors that appear to correspond to the varying degrees of internalization identified by Krathwohl and his associates are given in Chart 9–4.

With the above orientation in mind, it is possible to write behavioral objectives in the affective domain. The following are examples:

When given a verbal list of class rules, 80 percent of the students listen attentively.

When presented with the opportunity to choose learning activities, 80 percent of the students choose social studies at least 50 percent of the time.

When asked to state their values, all of the students voluntarily advocate a point of view at least once during the year.

---

[2]Copyright © 1964 by David McKay Co., Inc. From the book *Taxonomy of Educational Objectives: Handbook II—The Affective Domain,* by D. R. Krathwohl, B. S. Bloom, and B. B. Masia, pp. 176–85. Reprinted with permission of David McKay Co., Inc. Lines in italics adapted by the author.

Chart 9–4
Representative Behaviors in Each of the
Categories of the Krathwohl *Taxonomy:* Affective Domain

Attending

show knowledge of something by stating it   listen
submit   view
consider   tolerate
participate   observe

Responding

express pleasure or satisfaction at responding   obey
express enjoyment by doing or verbalizing   cooperate
comply willingly   contribute
acquiesce willingly   volunteer
respond consistently   ask questions

Valuing

communicate the value to others   offer
persist in doing   choose
accept responsibility for doing   support
participate actively   advocate
initiate   promote

Organization of Values

identify the characteristics of a value   relate value to other values
order the priority of the value   distinguish among values
state how things should be   apply value to new situations
weigh alternative behaviors in relation to compare values
     the value

Characterization by a Value or Value Complex

behave consistently in relation to the value
judge phenomena consistently in relation to
     the value

The following is an example of different degrees of internalization as applied to the general objective "students will become concerned about world events:"

1. Students *listen* to teacher discuss news articles of world events in class (attending).
2. Students *ask questions* following discussion (responding).
3. Students *publicly advocate* that everyone should become more familiar with world events (valuing).
4. Students *identify benefits* of knowing about world events and compare these with alternative uses of time (organization of values).
5. Students *consistently participate* in activities that keep them informed about world events (characterization by a value complex).

A Critical Look at Behavioral Objectives

The extensive effort that has emerged in regard to behavioral objectives has fulfilled a real educational need. By adding this degree of specificity, it becomes possible to make realistic use of criterion-referenced evaluation and all its benefits. But like other innovations, the use of behavioral objectives is not without its disadvantages — at least one of them quite serious.

One disadvantage has to do with the amount of time required to write them — time that might be better spent in other work. However, it is primarily at the beginning that efforts are maximum. Once a teacher is skilled in the technique, the writing of behavioral objectives requires little more time than that usually needed to prepare any type of thoughtful objective. Moreover, outside resources that prepare pools of objectives from which teachers can draw are becoming available. For example, the Instructional Objectives Exchange at the University of California in Los Angeles currently offers such items as the following:

Study and Reference Skills (K-12) includes 117 objectives in study skills (following directions, notetaking, summarizing, and organizing) and reference skills (alphabetizing material, using the library, common reference books and mass media sources).

Geography (K-9) includes 97 objectives on major geographical concepts, map and globe skills, geographical features, climate, land change, time zones, communication, weather, earth and sun relationships, and transportation.

Anthropology (4–6) includes 45 objectives in introductory anthropological concepts and such content areas as prehistory, the record of culture, the nature of culture, genetics, evolution, and race.

Related to the issue of time is the question of whether it is indeed necessary to specify objectives in such detail in order to make criterion-referenced evaluation possible. In the strict sense, criterion-referenced evaluation probably requires the fulfillment of all three criteria of behavioral objectives: a behavioral verb, the statement of conditions, and the extent of achievement needed. However, in many cases it is quite possible to dispense with the last two. The extent of achievement needed is frequently a rather arbitrary choice. Why, for example, is 80 percent acceptable and not 60 percent? Or, for that matter, why settle for anything less than 100 percent? Moreover, when preparing a detailed lesson or unit plan, the conditions are specified in the plan itself. Hence, it adds little to specify them in the objectives as well. In short, the classroom teacher can achieve a high enough level of specificity for most classroom purposes by simply stating what the students will do.

Another disadvantage derives from the fact that it is much easier to write behavioral objectives for very low levels of cognition than for higher ones. It is also quite difficult to write them in the affective domain. As a result, teachers have tended to emphasize low-level cognitive skills — in effect trivializing learning. However, using behavioral objectives can actually help eliminate the trivial and the insignificant. Adequately trained teachers who have specified in writing what they expect students to be doing can discover for themselves whether they are emphasizing memory and comprehension at the expense of higher-level cognitive and affective behaviors.

Some critics maintain that behavioral objectives favor closed or convergent learning. But this objection stems from a misunderstanding of their nature, for behavioral objectives can be written so as to reflect either convergent or divergent intentions. The following are examples that reflect divergent intentions:

> Given a set of conflicting accounts of the causes of the Civil War, students will offer their own hypotheses and support them with evidence.
>
> Following a demonstration of the problems of traffic congestion in a downtown area, students will propose plans to solve the problem.
>
> Given the completion of a unit of study about the community, students will choose and implement a means to communicate what they have learned.

Critics also point out that behaviors we can observe are not real indicators of higher-level cognition or values. On the level of psychomotor or low cognitive skills, behavior is a good indicator of achievement. One either knows how to jump or not; one can either recall what Lincoln said in the Gettysburg Address or cannot. In assessing higher cognitive and affective levels, however, we inevitably rely a good deal on inference — that is, we cannot be sure that the behavior really reflects the thought processes we intend. For example, if one asks a student to compare the way of life of the Ashanti with that of modern Americans, one can only infer that the answer is based on analysis. It is also possible, however, that the student is only recalling something heard elsewhere. This is even more obvious in the affective domain. The student who is forcefully advocating the need for economic opportunities for all groups may be doing so not out of a sense of commitment to the value, but to the grade. It is thus quite true that one needs to be very careful in interpreting what behaviors actually mean. But it seems far better to at least attempt some correspondence between behavior and intent than to abandon the effort entirely.

The most serious and justifiable criticism of behavioral objectives is the use that has been made of them by state and federal agencies. Increasing control over education is being assumed by the federal and state governments at a time when the demand for accountability is being heard throughout the nation. People want evidence that schools are really accomplishing what they say they are. Philosophically, this may appear proper. But operationally, this demand may take the form of increased outside control. The state may require schools to produce lists of behavioral objectives before beginning instruction. This takes many hours and obviously cannot be redone frequently. At the end of instruction, schools are required to show evidence of their successful accomplishments. Teachers may find themselves harnessed to objectives they know to be outdated or to objectives formulated before diagnostic evaluation of their current students could occur. The evidence may also be used as reason to dismiss teachers or withdraw funds from "unsuccessful" projects and experiments. All this would only encourage teachers to set low-level objectives and marshal all their instructional efforts toward these minimal achievements. Moreover, there is nothing to prevent state agencies—made up of politicians who may seek or reject professional advice—from selecting objectives that are politically expedient or those consonant with their own values. It is true that this last condition has always existed, but the potential for political control appears infinitely greater when behavioral objectives are to be specified. Teachers must guard carefully against this type of misuse.

Some Recommendations

All things considered, behavioral objectives can be a highly valuable educational tool. They do help clarify what it is we expect of students, and they make it easier to establish priorities. Above all, they allow criterion-referenced evaluation, which is a very important factor in making students feel a sense of accomplishment. However, a few important points must be kept in mind.

First, use behavioral objectives judiciously. They are not the only answer and they should not take up too much of your time. Like all reforms, this one must necessarily be made gradually.

Second, not all lessons have the same requirements. Some benefit from being more specific, some do not require it. Don't feel compelled to apply all three criteria if all that is needed is a bit of clarification.

Third, be on guard against infringement by outside groups, which could turn behavioral objectives into constraints on professional autonomy and make the whole process detrimental to students and overall educational goals.

And finally, bear in mind that there are many problems yet to be worked out. If you begin to feel that the creation of behavioral objectives is a mere verbal game, either change your approach or stop writing them.

The Techniques of Evaluation

It is generally assumed that the appropriate evaluation chain parallels the school's hierarchical chain of command: superintendents evaluate principals, principals evaluate teachers, and teachers evaluate students. But for the past few years educators have been calling attention to the need to complement this process by having each group evaluate the one above it as well.

The purpose of reciprocal evaluation should not be to punish or condemn. Rather, its purpose should be to improve the conditions for learning. As all who are involved in educating learn to use evaluation as an honest attempt to do better, the morale of educators—as well as their quality—is likely to improve.

Above all, recognition needs to be given to the role of the student as evaluator of all the other elements of the educational process. Students, after all, are the most directly affected. Failure to include them in the evaluation process is analagous to a doctor prescribing medication for a patient without asking what the problem is. Unfortunately, this has too often been the case.

Evaluating Students

Since students are the principal concern of schools, it is inevitable that most evaluation will be directed at them. And the main point to be kept in mind is that it is their progress that is to be evaluated, not their flaws. Comparisons, especially those that lead to negative or offensive conclusions, are to be avoided.

The two primary techniques for evaluating students are tests and observation. Each is useful in diagnostic, formative, and summative evaluation.

Standardized Tests

By and large, tests are of two types: standardized and teacher-made. Sometimes, however, students and teachers may combine efforts in constructing a test. According to Lee J. Cronbach, a standardized test is "one in which the procedure, apparatus, and scoring have been fixed so that precisely the same testing procedures can be followed at different times and places."[3] Standardized tests are usually employed for normative evaluation, but they can be useful for diagnostic purposes. When administered at the beginning of the school year and carefully analyzed for student strengths and weaknesses, they can help in determining learning objectives.

The most common types of standardized tests are those that measure cognitive abilities and achievements. The former, however, have been severely criticized during the last few years as not being sufficiently valid or reliable and, more important, because they are often used as grounds for discrimination against the educationally disadvantaged. There is a vast amount of literature on the subject, and every teacher would do well to become acquainted with it. It is unlikely, however, that standardized tests will ever be entirely discredited. They do have their uses and, if proper care is taken in selecting them, there is no reason why schools cannot benefit from them. Chart 9–5 lists some major tests in the social studies. Examples of standardized cognitive tests available in the social studies are given on the following pages.

[3]Lee J. Cronbach, *Essentials of Psychological Testing*, 3rd ed. (New York: Harper & Row, 1970), p. 27.

Chart 9–5
Standardized Cognitive Tests in the Social Studies

Test	Grade Level	Description	Publisher
Ralph C. Preston and Robert V. Duffey, *Primary Social Studies Test*	1–3	Tests social studies understandings in primary levels. Requires no reading or writing on part of children.	Houghton Mifflin Co., 2 Park St., Boston, Mass. 02107
Sequential Tests of Progress, Level 4	4–6	Measures understanding and abilities to read and interpret maps, graphs, the printed word, relationships among facts, concepts, and trends.	Educational Testing Service, Princeton, N.J. 08540
Understanding of Basic Social Concepts from the Iowa Tests of Education Development	3–9	Measures understanding of selected concepts in the social studies.	Science Research Associates, 259 Erie St., Chicago, Ill. 60611
The Progressive Tests in Social and Related Sciences, Parts I and II, Elementary Battery, Form A	4–8	Measures knowledge of American heritage, people of other lands and times, geography, and basic social processes.	Bureau of Educational Research and Service, State University of Iowa, Iowa City, Ia. 52240
Metropolitan Achievement Tests in Social Studies	5–6 7–9	Measures general social studies knowledge and skills. Two levels.	Harcourt Brace Jovanovich, Inc., 757 Third Ave., New York, N.Y., 10017
Nationwide Current Events Examination	4–8	Measures knowledge of current events.	Educational Stimuli, 2012 Hammond Ave., Superior, Wis. 54881
Emporia Geography Test	4–7	Measures knowledge of place locations and other geographical information.	Bureau of Educational Measurements, Kansas State Teachers College, Emporia, Kans. 66801
Modern Geography and Allied Social Studies	6–10	Measures knowledge of vocabulary, economic and human relations, place geography in the United States and the world, and related information.	Same.
History: Every Pupil Scholarship Tests	5–6		Same.
Stanford Achievement Test	4–9	Measures knowledge of facts.	Harcourt Brace Jovanovich, Inc., 757 Third Ave., New York, N.Y., 10017

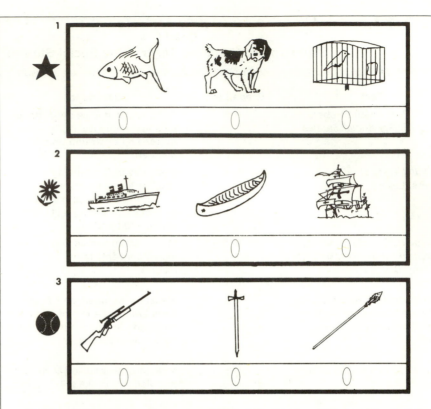

Tell the children to turn the page and look at the first box of three pictures at the top on the left. Be sure they fold the booklets so that only page 2 is visible.

(The boxes of pictures are numbered in the pupils' booklets for your use. Do not read the numbers aloud to the pupils. The symbols which appear in the pupils' booklets and at the beginning of each test question are the pupils' references.)

Page 2

Say:

(1) "Put your finger on the star. Make an X on the picture of a pet for which you need a license."

After a few moments, say again:

"Make an X on the picture of a pet for which you need a license."

Wait until most of the pupils have finished marking their answers and then go on to the next item. Follow this procedure throughout the administration of the test.

(2) "Put your finger on the flower."

"Make an X on the picture of one of Christopher Columbus' ships."

After a few moments, repeat. When most of the children have finished marking their answers, go on to the next item.

(3) "Put your finger on the ball."

"Make an X on the picture of the weapon that men used first."

(Repeat.)

From *Primary Social Studies Test,* Teacher's Manual, by Ralph C. Preston and Robert V. Duffey. Copyright © 1967 by Houghton Mifflin Company. Reprinted by permission of the publisher.

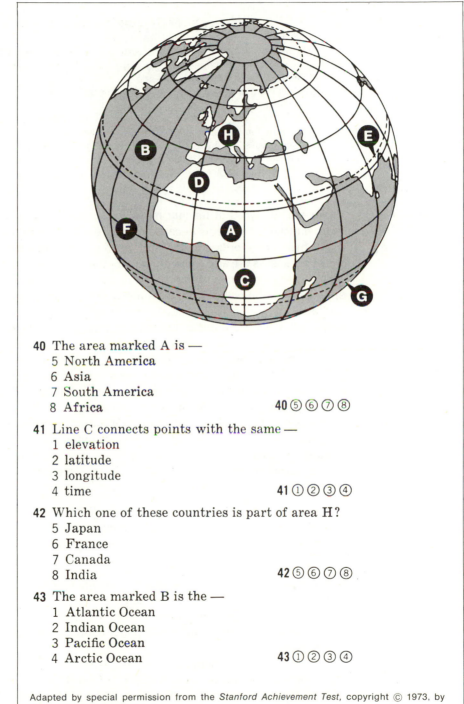

40 The area marked A is —
   5 North America
   6 Asia
   7 South America
   8 Africa   **40** ⑤ ⑥ ⑦ ⑧

41 Line C connects points with the same —
   1 elevation
   2 latitude
   3 longitude
   4 time   **41** ① ② ③ ④

42 Which one of these countries is part of area H?
   5 Japan
   6 France
   7 Canada
   8 India   **42** ⑤ ⑥ ⑦ ⑧

43 The area marked B is the —
   1 Atlantic Ocean
   2 Indian Ocean
   3 Pacific Ocean
   4 Arctic Ocean   **43** ① ② ③ ④

> ### Guidelines for Selecting Standardized Tests
>
> 1. Make sure the test reflects the social studies content of the curriculum.
> 2. Check that the language level is appropriate for the group to be tested.
> 3. Find out if the test is a reputable one.
> 4. Read the teacher's manual carefully to assess the reliability and validity as well as the uses of the test.
> 5. Find out how the test can be used to supplement other measurement techniques.
> 6. Make sure the test will serve a learning purpose.
> 7. Obtain a sample copy for study and take the test yourself. This is the most concrete way to judge what it really does.

Teacher-made Tests

There are two types of teacher-made tests: essay and objective. The essay is more difficult for students because it requires them to organize their responses using their own words and expressions in as complete and accurate a way as they can. Essays are also more difficult for teachers to evaluate unless they have determined in advance precisely the relevant criteria by which to measure responses. Theoretically, essay tests are best for measuring analysis, synthesis, and evaluation objectives. Actually, however, most elementary and junior high school students find it difficult to express themselves adequately in writing and therefore tend to write as little as possible. While students need to be encouraged to develop essay skills, a test is not the ideal time or place to practice.

Objective tests are short-answer tests. They can be used for diagnostic, formative, and summative evaluation purposes. They offer the advantages of providing a quick overview of student accomplishments, requiring little writing on the part of the students, being quickly scored, and being useful for measuring higher as well as lower cognitive levels (although it is admittedly far more difficult to measure the higher levels). There are basically four types of short-answer objective tests: simple recall, alternative response, multiple choice, and matching.

The *simple recall* test is intended to measure the students' ability to remember important names, dates, and other finite information. The test items are usually presented in the form of a question or a sentence with a missing word. Specific guidelines are:

1. The question form is preferable to the statement form.
2. In lower grades, ask for one word only.
3. Avoid using "a" or "an" before a blank.
4. Avoid questions that require only general intelligence to answer, rather than knowledge.
5. Be sure only one response can be the correct one.
6. Put the blank at the end or near the end of the statement.
7. Keep blanks of uniform length so as not to provide clues.
8. Put blanks in straight column at one side for ease of scoring.

In *alternative response* tests the student is asked to choose between two alternatives only one of which is correct. The most common variety is the "true-false" form. Specific guidelines are:

1. The number and order of true and false statements should be random.
2. The truth or falsity of a statement should depend on a single point (e.g., Lincoln was responsible for the Emancipation Proclamation, rather than Lincoln was responsible for the Emancipation Proclamation and the Civil Rights Bill).
3. Avoid negatives, such as *no, never, not.* These confuse students.
4. Avoid clues such as the following words: generally, usually, should, may (these are usually "true"); all, alone, always (these are usually "false").
5. Avoid using the same language as the textbook.
6. Avoid trick questions.

The *multiple choice* test is a slightly more complex version of the alternative response type. It usually consist of a stem and three or more possible choices. The student is asked to select the best one. Specific guidelines are:

1. The stem should be intelligible standing alone.
2. The stem should include a single problem only.
3. The stem should contain all the information necessary for a solution.
4. The stem should include relevant information only.
5. Offer a minimum of three choices.
6. Correct choices should be randomly placed.
7. Put choices in logical order (e.g., from smallest to largest, alphabetically).
8. Keep choices brief.
9. Make all choices plausible.
10. The correct choice should be clearly right.
11. The positive form is preferable. Be sure to underline negatives (e.g., Which is <u>not</u> an example of interdependence?).

The *matching* test consists of a stimulus column and a response column. Students choose the correct answer from the latter in response to a question in the former. Specific guidelines are:

1. Responses should be in logical order (e.g., small to large, numbers arranged sequentially).
2. Each column should have a heading common to all entries in that column (e.g., authors and works, people and achievements).
3. If there is only one answer for each stimulus, include at least three extra responses. However, if an answer can be used more than once, there is no need for this.
4. Use numbers for the stimulus column, capital letters for the response column.
5. Directions should state what relationship exists between columns.
6. The number of items in each column should be no smaller than five and no larger than ten.

Objective Tests and Complex Educational Objectives

It is commonly assumed that objective test items can measure only the lowest levels of cognition—primarily memory. While objective tests have indeed been used mostly for this purpose, it is quite possible to write objective test items that measure higher levels of cognition. Admittedly, this requires some effort and imagination—but given the fact that essays cannot be used extensively in the elementary school, it is a worthwhile skill to develop. Moreover, most students enjoy taking tests that ask them to think, rather than just remember. Examples of objective test items for different grade levels and lower and higher educational objectives are given below.

Knowledge. On this level, the behavior being measured is essentially recall of learnings in a form very similar to the way they were originally encountered. Such learnings might include terminology, facts, rules, trends, generalizations, and so on. The form in which the information was originally presented is important. If students merely heard the information before the test and have not seen it in writing, the written form may pose problems. They may not be able to recognize the words. It is, of course, an assumption governing all tests that students will be able to read them. When in doubt, the teacher should read the questions aloud.

---

1. The column on the left is a list of important black Americans. The column on the right is a list of activities these people are best known for. Match the activity with the right person by filling in the correct number in the space provided. Choose only *one* activity for each person.

People	*Activities*	
1. Martin Luther King, Jr.	A. Abolitionist	_____
2. James Baldwin	B. Author	_____
3. Shirley Chisholm	C. Representative	_____
	D. Scientist	_____
	E. Civil rights leader	_____
	F. Composer	_____

2. Which social scientist is most likely to study what happens to prices when people have less money to spend? Mark the correct letter in the space provided.
   (a) an economist (b) a geographer (c) a political scientist (d) a sociologist _____

3. Each of the following sentences is either true or false. If the sentence is true, circle the T next to the sentence. If the sentence is false, circle the F.

T	F	Before the Europeans came to North America, there were over 1000 Indian languages.
T	F	The Iroquois lived in the northeastern part of what is now the United States.
T	F	All Indian tribes were governed by a chief.
T	F	Europeans brought the horse to North America.
T	F	The Indian population today is about the same as it was before the Europeans came.

Comprehension. Tests on this level may require students to change the phraseology from the form originally encountered, translate from one symbolic medium to another, interpret, or extrapolate. Changing the phraseology generally involves writing something in the students' own words or selecting a phrase from multiple choices that best describes a given communication. Translating from one symbolic medium to another may mean putting a graphic, picture, or map message into words or vice versa. Interpretation involves recognizing the main ideas of a communication. Extrapolation means determining the consequences or implications of a communication. Along with knowledge, comprehension is a common purpose in objective tests.

---

1. Circle those things that *all* persons have.

   eyes   a nose   dresses   beds   a language
   ideas   children   television sets   toys

2. This is a map of Australia. Study it carefully and then fill in the correct answers to the questions below:
   (a) The name of the capital is _____ .
   (b) The largest city in Australia is _____ .
   (c) The city with the greatest population density is _____ .

3. Each of the following terms is an important idea in American history. Define each term in one or two sentences. Use your own words.

   republic

   _____

   _____

   _____

   federation

   _____

   _____

   _____

4. Read the following paragraph carefully. Then read the sentences underneath the paragraph. If the sentence is true, circle the T. If it is false, circle the F.

   Maria spends most of her time helping her mother in their home. Like her friends, she grinds corn, cooks beans, sews clothing, and looks after her younger brothers and sisters. Girls in the village of Pueblo begin to do the work of women at a very early age so that they will know everything they need to know when they are married and become mothers. In Pueblo, married women are very highly respected.

   T   F   In Pueblo, much of a girl's education takes place at school.
   T   F   In Pueblo, girls may choose from many occupations.
   T   F   It is expected that girls in Pueblo will learn how to sew.
   T   F   It is expected that girls in Pueblo will marry.

Application. An application test item requires that students apply an abstraction they have learned to a *new* situation. An abstraction may be a concept, generalization, principle, idea, or so on. Students are given a problem they have not encountered before and in responding to it demonstrate their ability to select and apply an appropriate abstraction. Application questions are very important, for merely having the knowledge or comprehension of something does not necessarily mean having the ability to use it. However, a single item in an objective test would not be sufficient to determine whether a student can actually apply the abstraction.

---

1. If Stings, a local automobile showroom, sold you a car that did not run well, which of the following would you have the right to do? Mark an *X* in front of each correct answer.

   _____ Complain to the store owner.
   _____ Put a sign on your car saying "Stings sells bad cars."
   _____ Complain to the Better Business Bureau.
   _____ Block the entrance to Sting's so people could not get in.
   _____ Break Sting's window.
   _____ Write a letter to the local newspaper.

2. If you were a Puritan child, you probably would not be allowed to use all of these. Mark an *X* in front of the things you would probably <u>not</u> be allowed to use.

   _____ shoes
   _____ a watch
   _____ a television set
   _____ a Bingo set
   _____ a sewing machine

3. Write in the level of government *(local, state,* or *federal)* that is most likely to be in charge of the following:

   (a) providing sewers   _____
   (b) keeping safety standards on trains that travel
       between New York State and New Jersey   _____
   (c) declaring war   _____
   (d) improving highways and freeways   _____
   (e) putting in traffic lights on city streets   _____

4. Jim needs to do a report on the uses of airplanes. He is supposed to get information from three different types of sources. Suggest three specific sources of different types that can help him find out about his topic.

   a. _____

   b. _____

   c. _____

5. The three pictures below all illustrate an idea that can be said in one word. Look them over carefully and then write the word in the space provided under the pictures.

   [Three pictures of different types of conflict—e.g., two boys arguing, a group of picketers in front of a business establishment, a war scene.]

Analysis. Tests of analysis behaviors emphasize the breakdown of material into its parts and the recognition of the relationships among the parts. They may also involve the recognition of the techniques used in the material. The line between comprehension and analysis behaviors is not very sharp. Analysis usually requires a more complex level of comprehension. Sometimes analysis approaches evaluation, as when the student is asked to make a "critical analysis" of something. In test items in which the objective is to assess analysis, students can be presented with familiar or unfamiliar materials (such as a written passage, a graph, a set of data, a photograph) and then asked to distinguish and compare the elements that relate either to the content or the form. The basic assumption is that students have not done this before in relation to that particular material.

---

1. These are all *tools*. Look at them carefully. Then answer the questions I will read aloud to you by writing the correct letter next to the number of the question.

   A. [a picture of a wheelbarrow]   B. [a picture of a crane]
   C. [a picture of a dolly]

   1. Which one can lift the heaviest things?   1. _____
   2. Which one is hardest to make?   2. _____
   3. Which one costs the most?   3. _____
   4. Which one is best for taking dirt away from a backyard.   4. _____
   5. Which one is best for moving a refrigerator into your home?   5. _____

2. Ms. Jones is trying to convince a group of young people that things are getting better for black Americans and will continue to improve. To make this point, she shows them the following graph:

   [A bar graph showing the average earnings of black Americans from the years 1950 to 1970.]

   What *assumption* is she making? Underline the correct answer.

   (a) That earnings in the future will follow the same patterns.
   (b) That the government will do more to help black citizens.
   (c) That whites will help blacks.

3. Mr. Smith is having an argument with a friend about women and jobs. He says:

   "I wouldn't be against a woman earning what a man does if she was worth it, but let's look at the facts. All over the world women earn less than men. Now if this is the case everywhere, there must be a good reason for it. And let's look at what's happening to crime. If women were home taking care of their children, we wouldn't have as many kids wandering around getting into trouble. Would you like your son and daughter to come home to an empty house? What do you suppose would happen to them if there was no one loving to come home to? If you ask me, women who want to work instead of being at home where they belong are just selfish and irresponsible."

   Identify three techniques Mr. Smith is using to convince his friend.

   1. _____

   2. _____

   3. _____

Synthesis. An objective test is not the best instrument for measuring synthesis behaviors. Actually, no test situation is very good for doing this. Synthesizing behaviors involve the production of a unique communication such as that required in writing an essay, producing a plan, or deriving a set of abstract relations. Such activities generally require a high level of creativity and are best accomplished under optimal conditions that are relatively free of restrictions. Test situations impose time constraints and are also usually accompanied by a high level of student anxiety. Nonetheless, some synthesizing behaviors can be measured through objective tests. The assumption governing all types of synthesizing questions is that they are not based on mere recall, but actually require hypothesizing, conceptualizing, generalizing, or any of the other behaviors associated with synthesizing.

---

1. At the front of the room are four pictures of *desert life*. What can you say *in general* about them? Put an *X* in front of the correct answer.
   [Pictures of: an Antarctic setting with people dressed very warmly against the cold; a shopping center in New Mexico—light clothing, sunny and warm, modern transportation system; Bedouins in the Negev in traditional clothing; Mongol nomads of Siberia in front of a yurt.]

   _____ Cities do not develop on deserts.
   _____ People who live in deserts are poorer than people who do not.
   _____ People living in similar environments may use them in different ways.
   _____ The climate in desert areas is very similar.

2. Mr. Smith and Mrs. Jones are trying to decide whether Aleutia is a "free" country. Suggest three standards that could help them decide whether it is really a "free" country.

   1. _____

   2. _____

   3. _____

3. Ellen Mack took many notes in class when the teacher was talking about the Civil War. While reviewing her notes to prepare for a test, she discovers many incomplete phrases. The phrases Ellen found are listed below. Read them carefully. Think of three categories in which you can group them. Write the name of each category next to I, II, and III. Then write the appropriate phrases from Ellen's notes under each category.

   Ellen's Notes

   abolition of slavery
   to get slavery into the territories
   the Battle of Bull Run
   the Emancipation Proclamation
   the right to secede from the Union
   the North won
   the Gettysburg address
   General Grant made commander in chief of all Union armies
   President Lincoln assassinated

   I _____   II _____   II _____

Evaluation. Evaluation behaviors require the making of cognitive judgments based on standards that are either given to students or which they determine themselves. Although evaluation is necessarily connected with affective judgments, the emphasis is on cognition. Cognitive standards may be internal (such as logical accuracy, consistency, proof, adequacy) or external (such as efficiency, utility, or comparison with other work in the field). An evaluation behavior requires that the students use criteria in rendering the judgment. The important thing is the reasons given for the judgment and not the judgment itself. Such reasons need to clearly support the judgment. Although recognition type questions (such as multiple choice or alternative responses) can be posed, they may suggest answers students might not have thought of otherwise.

1. Mr. Tristram Thumbnail, a member of the Health, Education, and Welfare Department, has to make a recommendation regarding how the Department should spend its money next year. The Department has received some additional money to distribute among children and the aged. Mr. Thumbnail is told by a reliable source that the numbers of needy children and aged will increase by about the same amount next year. He receives the following information in an office memo:

COST OF LIVING FOR CHILDREN AND AGED (IN DOLLARS PER YEAR)

	Children		Aged	
	Last Year	This Year	Last Year	This Year
Food	500	600	550	660
Housing	600	660	1500	1650
Medical Care	150	170	600	720
Clothing	500	550	300	330
Other	500	550	500	550
Total	2250	2530	3450	3910

Mr. Thumbnail wants some additional bits of information before he reaches a decision. Below is a list of things he considered. Write "yes" next to each bit of information he probably chose. Give reasons for your choices below.

(a) The name of the source that provided the information.   _____

(b) The feelings of other workers in the Department of Health, Education, and Welfare.   _____

(c) Some figures regarding the cost of living for adults between the ages of 21 and 45.   _____

(d) An estimate of costs for the aged and children for next year.   _____

(e) The definitions of "child" and "aged" used by the source.   _____

2. Here is a painting done by John Trumbull, an American artist who lived at the time of the American Revolution. It is a painting of the Battle of Bunker Hill.

Do you think it is an accurate account of the Battle? Circle one answer.

No   Partly   Yes

Give three reasons for your answer.

> ### Guidelines for Constructing Objective Tests
>
> 1. Test only for important items. Eliminate trivia.
> 2. Write the test items simply, clearly, and specifically.
> 3. Don't try to make the questions tricky.
> 4. Avoid using the same wording as the textbook.
> 5. Focus on only one item in each question.
> 6. State the directions clearly.
> 7. Make sure there is enough space for the answer.
> 8. Group similar question types together (all true-false in one place, all matching in another, etc.).

Observation　A careful observer can learn a great deal about students simply by watching them on the playground, in the hallways, at lunch, and in the classroom. But *casual observation,* the simple noting of student behavior, is subject to error. The fact that Johnny appeared to be busy with his map construction the last time you looked may persuade you erroneously that he really knows what he is doing. The thing you recall best about Karen is that she seemed to know a lot about the Grand Canyon, but you may have overlooked the fact that she never participates in discussions about anything else. *Systematic observation* is more reliable. It involves planning for cumulative observations that are recorded in some form, such as checklists, anecodotal records, rating scales, or interviews.

Checklists

The most common—and simplest—form of systematic observation is the checklist. The various behaviors and activities are itemized on a list and checked off once they have been accomplished or exhibited. Checklists are useful for diagnostic, formative, and summative evaluation in all of the domains of learning.

A typical checklist for recording skills might be compiled from those listed in Chapter 6 and set up as shown in the partial example below:

Time Skills

	Joe	Kathy	Sandy	Ron
Tells the time by the clock	X	X	X	X
Uses names of days in week in order	X		X	
Uses names of months in sequence	X	X		X
Uses calendar to find dates of events		X		X
Uses calendar to find time between events	X	X		

A teacher can focus on a different child during each class discussion and use this as a basis for a follow-up interview with the student. During the interview itself, care needs to be taken to emphasize positive points while areas that need improvement should be considered tactfully.

Contribution to Class Discussion

Name: _Bill Thymes_   Date: 10/23   Yes   No

	Yes	No
Participated in discussion	X	
Answered questions.	X	
Asked questions.		X
Asked for clarification.		X
Challenged factual evidence, accuracy, logic.	X	
Summarized points of view.		X
Accepted criticism.		X
Made the same point many times.	X	
Made an unclear statement.	X	
Made a personal attack.		X
Made irrelevant statements.	X	

Students, however, should be encouraged not to depend exclusively on others for evaluation. A primary requisite for growth is learning how to develop self-evaluation abilities. Teachers can develop checklists that help students evaluate themselves. For example, before beginning a sequential instructional series on library skills, the teacher may circulate a list of specific activities to be performed by each student, who then checks off each item as it is completed. Equally important is having students generate such checklists themselves. By creating checklists that emphasize specific behaviors, students can learn to avoid vague labels such as "bad" or "good," while simultaneously learning to identify specific criteria that make something "bad" or "good."

Guidelines for Making Checklists

1. Decide what general objectives you wish to measure.
2. Identify the specific behaviors or activities for each general objective.
3. List all of the items on a master chart.
4. Photocopy or print as many copies of the chart as you need.

The checklist below was developed jointly by a teacher and students who were concerned that small-group discussions were going nowhere. Approximately ten minutes at the end of each group session was devoted to an evaluation process by the students based on the checklist.

How Good Was Your Small-Group Work?

What was the task?
What was discussed?
What parts of the discussion had nothing to do with the task?
Did everyone have a chance to contribute?
Did anyone make fun of anyone else?
What tasks were completed?
What still needs to be done? Who can help?
How much more time do you need to finish the task?

Rating Scales

A rating scale is a variation on the checklist. It enumerates particular behaviors that the teacher measures by marking the *degree* to which the students exhibit them. The scale can be expressed numerically—for example, by using numbers 1 through 5 to stand for the minimum and maximum exhibitions of the behavior —or in the constant-alternative form in which a word or phrase describes the degree of the desired behavior, as in the following:

Problem-Solving Behaviors

Name: *John Doe*

	Usually	Often	Sometimes	Never
1. Able to recognize and state a problem.	X			
2. Able to state a hypothesis.		X		
3. Can collect appropriate data.	X			
4. Able to interpret and evaluate data.		X		
5. Able to evaluate relevance of data to hypothesis.			X	
6. Able to modify hypothesis on basis of data when called for.			X	

Ratings scales can help teachers observe affective behaviors more carefully, with a view toward intervening when such behaviors are troublesome either to the student or to others. Many judgments about affective behaviors tend to be impressionistic. A child who is noisily quarrelsome, for example, is much more obvious than one who is quietly so. A rating scale can help assess such behaviors more accurately with the purpose of modifying them. If Lynn, for example, complains of feelings of social isolation, data collected by an observant teacher using a checklist such as the one suggested below, can help determine whether or not she is really a social isolate. Such data can serve as a springboard for discussions with Lynn. The checklist might reveal that she is not really the isolate she feels herself to be, in which case the teacher might explore with Lynn the types of expectations she has of others. Or the checklist might show that Lynn does not invite others to participate, which may suggest that she needs to do so more often.

Social Relationship with Peers

Name: *Lynn Johnson*

	Usually	Often	Sometimes	Never
1. Plays alone during recess time.			X	
2. Pairs off with one child only during recess time.		X		
3. Is invited by other students to participate in play activities.			X	
4. Is invited by other students to participate in classroom work activities.			X	
5. Invites others to participate in activities.				X
6. Makes statements or gestures to others indicating displeasure about relationship with other children.		X		

Anecdotal Records

The anecdotal record is a written account of a single significant student behavior observed by the teacher. These can provide continuing in-depth records of children's interests and activities. Because they require considerable work, however, they are probably best used sparingly. Writing something about a different child each day can help focus on individuals without putting too much of a burden on teachers. Maintaining anecdotal records particularly carefully for youngsters with learning problems may reveal patterns that can be modified.

Jim Leonard 2/13

Jim raised the question in class today whether the story of George Washington and the cherry tree was true. This was the first time Jim has spoken up in class voluntarily. When I asked him what he thought, he replied he didn't believe it. I asked him if he'd like to hear what others say about it and he said yes. I told him we'd look in the library tomorrow for some information on the story. I plan to encourage him to report his findings to the class.

Sara Brown

9/30	Showed no apparent interest in studying about Mexico.
10/5	Fingered a Mexican basket John had brought in and asked him some questions.
10/15	Could not find a topic she was interested in working on.
10/17	Asked if she could borrow the book on the Mayas I read in class today.
10/20	Returned the book today saying it was too hard to read. I made an appointment to see her during lunchtime tomorrow.

Interviews

Interviews between teachers and individual students or groups are helpful in diagnosing cognitive abilities and interests as well as measuring progress. They can also be used simply to inform, as when a student needs help in locating sources for a particular project.

Properly used, interviews afford valuable opportunities for closer contact with the students, who will tend to see them as an indication of personal interest on the part of the teacher. Interviews should therefore never be treated as a form of punishment. ("See me about your work after class today—it's not going very well.") They can serve to provide the teacher as well as the students with useful information, but only if the teacher encourages the students to speak—and learns to listen to them.

Self-Reporting Techniques

Self-reporting techniques are tools that students may use to observe and report on their own behaviors. Checklists and rating scales can be used for self-reporting, but autobiographies, diaries, and questionnaires are also useful.

Autobiographies and Diaries

An autobiography is a written or oral account of the student's life as seen by the student. Younger children can be encouraged to tape their autobiographies while older children may be able to write them. However, the information will not be of much use unless it is understood that it will be treated as confidential.

Diaries are cumulative accounts of student activities written by the students themselves. These may be structured (as when the teacher specifies the form or the type of content to be included) or unstructured (as when the student chooses both the form and the type of content). Diaries can help students think about some high point of their day, discover a new interest, or evaluate how well they've used their time in school. The most important thing to remember about diaries is that there should be a good reason for writing them. If you are not planning to use the information for some purpose, the students may soon come to think of them as a waste of time.

Questionnaires

Students can also report about themselves by answering questionnaires prepared by the teacher. These can be used for a variety of purposes. The following questionnaire was designed to identify general interests:

1. I like to spend my spare time _____
2. The thing I do best is _____
3. The thing I enjoy most in school is _____

4. The thing I enjoy least in school is _____

5. What I would really like to study about in school is _____

Questionnaires can also be used to help students make evaluations of other students' attitudes and beliefs. The following example is from a questionnaire that was given to a group of fifth graders. They were not asked to identify themselves. The results were later shared with the class.

Underline the term that best describes how you feel about a person who does the following things:

1. puts gum on the seat of a chair
   hate   don't like   don't care   like
2. talks back to the teacher
   hate   don't like   don't care   like
3. makes fun of old people
   hate   don't like   don't care   like

4. cheats on tests
   hate   don't like   don't care   like
5. doesn't obey the rules in a game
   hate   don't like   don't care   like
6. steals candy from a store
   hate   don't like   don't care   like

Classroom Samples

Students are asked to do a great many exercises in the course of a year. Keep samples of each one's work in order to measure progress and needs. The students should be encouraged to look over them periodically so that they too can evaluate how much they are learning.

Evaluating Teachers

The most important variable affecting student success is the teacher. More than materials, curricula, and expenditures per pupil, the teacher is the significant school determiner of student success.

Many people are convinced that good teachers are "born," not made. This presumption of genetic inadequacy implies that poor teachers are doomed to inflict their weaknesses on hapless students. While good teaching may indeed be more art than science, it is possible to specify some characteristics and behaviors that any professional, given the will, can learn and develop. Most important is that teachers be willing to evaluate themselves—and in an atmosphere that encourages evaluation for growth.

Teacher Characteristics and Student Success

The most commonly used criteria for teacher evaluation are compatibility standards—measures of how well the teacher observes the rules and gets along with others. Is the room neat? Is the teacher liked? Does he or she dress conservatively? Are his or her opinions controversial? However, these characteristics have little to do with student success, and as John Gauss suggested more than a decade ago, Socrates himself would probably have failed.[4] The standards by which teachers should be evaluated are those that can be shown to be correlat-

[4]John Gauss in *Saturday Review*, July 21, 1962, p. 47.

ed with student success. Just what these are remains subject to some dispute, but recent studies have suggested that certain teacher characteristics are far more likely to affect student success than others. (A list of characteristics and their relative importance is given in Chart 9–6.) A few of the results are quite surprising. For example, it appears that there is little relationship between how much a teacher knows about a given subject and how successful that teacher's students will be. This may simply mean that knowledge is not enough, that it must be accompanied by other characteristics if it is to make any difference. This certainly does not mean that ignorance is a virtue—though these findings may eventually lead to a shift in emphasis in the requirements of education departments and schools. For the moment, however, the list must be considered tentative. Further research may very well challenge many of these findings.

Self-Evaluation Perhaps the most effective means of modifying teacher characteristics and behavior is self-evaluation. For one thing, it requires the teacher to be involved at every stage of the evaluation, not merely to read the report of some other per-

---

Chart 9–6
Teacher Characteristics and Student Success

Teacher Characteristic	Relationship to Student Success
Variety of instructional strategies and techniques	Positive
Task-oriented behavior	Positive
Clarity of expression	Positive
Enthusiasm	Positive
Reasonable use of indirect techniques	Positive
Structures information	Positive
Probes student responses	Positive
Mild criticism	None
Simple praise	None
Experience	None
College grades	None
Knowledge of subject matter	None
Student participation	None
Harsh criticism	Negative

SOURCE: Compiled from Lee Ehman, Howard Mehlinger, and John Patrick, *Toward Effective Instruction in Secondary Social Studies* (Boston: Houghton Mifflin, 1974), ch. 11; Barak Rosenshine and Norma Furts, "Research on Teacher Performance Criteria," in *Research in Teacher Education: A Symposium,* ed. B. Othanial Smith (Englewood Cliffs, N.J.: Prentice-Hall, 1971), pp. 37–72; Bruce J. Biddle and William J. Ellena, eds., *Contemporary Research on Teacher Effectiveness* (New York: Holt, Rinehart and Winston, 1974); and Ned A. Flanders, *Analyzing Teaching Behavior* (Reading, Mass.: Addison-Wesley, 1970).

son. Another point, which may well be as important, is that it is essentially not threatening to the person being evaluated.

How does one go about evaluating oneself? Memory alone is clearly insufficient because we are so given to selective recall. Objectivity requires assistance from tape recordings or videotape recordings of lessons played back for study. The latter, of course, are preferable because they make it possible to examine nonverbal forms of interaction, but the former are sufficient for most purposes.

Using recordings may prove difficult at first, but a little practice and a good checklist will make it much easier. Several lists of teacher behavior are available in the multivolume anthology called *Mirrors for Behavior*.[5] The Flanders' Interaction Analysis Categories discussed in Chapter 3 is included in the anthology along with many others. Chart 9–7 offers a checklist of questions based on the teacher characteristics in Chart 9–6.

No matter what the teacher's skills or knowledge, little will be accomplished if the student feels incapable of accomplishing anything. In many cases, student learning disabilities are linked with a negative self-concept.

Three student characteristics have been identified as strongly correlated with success. The first is, of course, a *positive self-concept*. If a person lacks a feeling of his or her own value, it will greatly influence behavior and inevitably lead

[5]Anita Simon and E. Gil Boyer, eds., *Mirrors for Behavior* (Philadelphia: Research for Better Schools, 1967).

Chart 9–7
A Checklist of Teacher Behaviors

Variety of instructional strategies and techniques

Do I use many types of instructional strategies?
   Are some inquiry oriented?
   Do questions I pose elicit high-level cognitive behaviors?
   Do I elicit divergent as well as convergent responses?
   Do I include opportunities for value clarification? Moral development?
Do I use a variety of instructional resources and techniques?
   Do instructional resources include many of a more concrete nature?
   Do I provide opportunities for individualized learning?
Do I use a variety of evaluation techniques?

Task-oriented behavior

Do I keep students oriented to the task at hand?
Do I permit long irrelevant digressions?
Do I introduce irrelevant ideas?
Do I convey the impression that I expect students to be able to master the task?

Clarity of expression

Do students have to ask many questions calling for clarification?
Do I repeat myself often?
Do I ask a question and then offer more information before students can answer?
Are my plans and units well organized? Do the parts fit together?
Do I clarify in my own mind important points and connecting sequences?

Enthusiasm

Am I interested in what I'm doing? Do I convey this interest?
Am I interested in what students are saying? Do I convey this impression?
Am I interested in the subject matter? Do I convey this impression?
Do I think what I'm doing is important? Do I convey this impression?
Do I hold high expectations for learners? Do I convey this?

Indirect techniques

Do I acknowledge student ideas by repeating or rephrasing them slightly?
Do I relate student ideas to other student ideas?
Do I include student ideas in summaries and discussions?
Do I praise and encourage student work and ideas?
Do I accept without hostility student frustration, anger, tension?
Do I recognize student pleasure and approval?

Structures information

Do I review pertinent previous learnings?
Do I introduce new information by connecting it to what has happened before?
Do I summarize learnings at the conclusion of a lesson?
Do I point out important parts?
Do I make transitional statements to indicate the conclusion of one part of a lesson
   and the beginning of another?

Probing student responses

Do I ever ask students to clarify their responses, statements, questions?
Do I ask for elaboration of student statements at times?

to abandoning all efforts to improve. The other two factors, which clearly grow out of the first, are an *openness to new experiences* and a *positive view of the future.*

Parents and environment have the largest effect on children's attitudes toward their own ability to succeed, but teachers can still make a difference. Much of the time, unfortunately, that difference is negative. Hectic schedules, discipline problems, and many other factors prevent the teacher from developing a strong program to encourage a positive student self-image. Teachers need to make every effort to check their own behaviors. Chart 9–8 suggests teacher behaviors that can enhance feelings of worth among students.

Evaluation by Colleagues

At some point teachers may feel the need to supplement self-evaluation techniques with evaluation by outsiders. Most teachers neither benefit from nor enjoy the annual visit in which some summative evaluation of the teacher's effectiveness is undertaken by the principal. Many teachers report that such days tend to be nonrepresentative of actual classroom behaviors since both teachers and students are usually tense and anxious. Yet some type of outside evaluation is usually necessary—preferably by someone knowledgeable. The best and most available candidates for fulfilling this need are probably other teachers.

Much too frequently teachers fear the judgment of their colleagues, who they secretly suspect must be more competent. However, if teaching is conducted in a supportive climate in which evaluation is regarded as a positive technique for helping each other, there can be considerable benefit for all. Teachers should encourage colleagues to visit their classrooms and suggest that such visits be reciprocal. Visiting teachers can avail themselves of casual observational tools

---

Chart 9–8
Checklist of Teacher Behaviors
That Influence Student Affective Characteristics

Do I provide many opportunities for successful achievement?
Do I avoid competitive activities that reflect negatively on the students?
Do I encourage students to make decisions?
Do I include alternatives so that the students can make decisions?
Do I provide opportunities for the students to influence classroom decisions?
Do I spend time helping students develop strategies to influence decision-makers in the school and community?
Do I encourage students to express their feelings?
Do I provide opportunities for expressive behavior through music, dance, and art?
Am I willing to share my feelings with students?
Do I permit students to follow their own interests?
Do I encourage students to try new things? Do I make sure that new experiences will reinforce feelings of worth?
Do I spend time with students discussing the future? Do I put more emphasis on the opportunities for improvement than on the dangers?
Do I emphasize that they have a worthwhile contribution to make?

or the more systematic ones suggested in this chapter. Obviously, the support of principals is required to release the visitors from their other duties during this period. Many will arrange for substitutes if they understand the purpose.

Evaluation by Students

In the last analysis, no one spends as much time evaluating the teacher as the students do—and no single block of opinion may be more important. Teachers can benefit greatly from a better knowledge of students' reactions both to materials and to teacher behavior. And the evaluation process can also be used to encourage positive self-concepts by emphasizing the value of the students' opinions and by making reforms or changes in response to specific suggestions. From time to time students can be invited to hold free-wheeling sessions that evaluate the program of studies just completed and, by extension, the techniques and behavior of the teacher. They can even be trained to observe teacher behavior using a checklist of specific actions and attitudes, a technique that would not only help the teacher's self-evaluation, but give the students practical experience in the systematic and scientific observation of human behavior.

The simplest and most direct way to obtain student evaluations is the questionnaire, which can direct responses into specific areas and limit them to a uniform value scale. Questionnaires can, however, be very misleading. Unless one is careful, it is quite easy to end up limiting the questions in ways that will only elicit the responses one wishes to hear. The following is an example of an objective questionnaire that might be repeated several times. Once the students have become familiar with the questions, their responses at the close of any lesson are likely to concentrate on these points, and this particular questionnaire will become superfluous.

Our discussion today helped me to learn	a little	an average amount	a lot
Students spoke	too little	the right amount	too much
I would like the teacher to talk	less	the same amount	more
The discussion helped me change my feelings	not at all	a little	a lot
I would like to have lessons like this	less	as often as we have been	more

Evaluating Other Elements

To restate a point made near the beginning of this chapter—and it is one well worth emphasizing—students and teachers should not be considered the only elements of the educational system that require evaluation. The schools themselves, the communities served by (and serving) the schools, and curricula are all very much in need of frequent evaluation if the system is to function well. The responsibility for such evaluations is not likely to be assigned to teachers, except perhaps as members of a committee, but it is undoubtedly worth the individual teacher's time to make at least a superficial assessment of the situation. In any case, the most useful guidelines are likely to be those developed by the NCSS Task Force on Curriculum Guidelines, which have been reproduced on the following pages. They are extremely flexible and can be used to evaluate not only district-wide programs but those of a given school or even a classroom.

Evaluation Checklist

The letters following each question indicate the most likely sources for evaluation. *R* includes curriculum reports and plans, position statements, faculty and student handbooks, student newspapers, memos, records or instructional materials available and used, formal evaluation data collected on student competencies; *T* refers to teachers; *S* refers to students; *C* refers to community and parents; *O* refers to classroom and out-of-classroom observations.

RATING			SPECIFIC GUIDELINES
Strongly	*Moderately*	*Hardly At All*	
			1.1 Are students involved in the formulation of goals, the selection of activities, and the assessment of curriculum outcomes? S T
			1.2 Do the school and its teachers make steady effort, through regularized channels and practices, to identify areas of concern to students? S T
			1.3 Do students have choices within programs? S T
			1.4 Do all students have ample oppourtunity for social studies education at all grade levels? R T
			2.1 Does the program focus on the social world as it actually is? R T C
			2.2 Does the program emphasize pervasive and enduring social issues? R T
			2.3 Does the program include analysis and attempts to formulate potential resolutions of present and controversial problems such as racism and war? R T
			2.4 Does the program provide intensive and recurrent study of cultural, racial, religious, and ethnic groups? R T C
			2.5 Does the program offer opportunities to meet and work with members of racial and ethnic groups other than their own? R T C
			2.6 Does the program build upon the realities of the immediate school community? R T C
			2.7 Is participation both in school and out considered a part of the program? R S C
			3.1 Does the program emphasize valid concepts, principles, and theories in the social sciences? R T

RATING			SPECIFIC GUIDELINES
Strongly	*Moderately*	*Hardly At All*	
			3.2 Does the program develop proficiency in methods of inquiry in the social sciences and in techniques for processing social data? R T O
			3.3 Does the program develop students' ability to distinguish among empirical, logical, definitional, and normative propositions and problems? R T O
			3.4 Does the program draw upon all of the social sciences and the history of the United States and the Western and non-Western worlds? R T
			3.5 Does the program draw from what is appropriate in other related fields such as psychology, law, communications, and the humanities? R T
			3.6 Does the program represent some balance between the immediate social environment of students and the larger social world? R T
			3.7 Does the program include the study of man's achivements and those policies contrary to present national goals? R T
			3.8 Does the program include a careful selection of that knowledge of most worth? R T
			4.1 Are objectives carefully selected and formulated? R T
			4.2 Are knowledge, abilities, valuing, and social participation all represented in the objectives of the program? R T
			4.3 Are general statements of goals translated into specific objectives conceived in terms of behavior and content? R T
			4.4 Are classroom instruction and materials based upon clearly stated objectives? R T O
			4.5 Does classroom instruction enable students to see their goals clearly in brief instructional sequences and lengthy units of study? T S
			4.6 Are objectives reconsidered and revised periodically? R T
			5.1 Do students have a wide range of learning activities appropriate to the objectives of their program? R T

RATING			SPECIFIC GUIDELINES
Strongly	Moderately	Hardly At All	
			5.2 Do activities include formulating hypotheses and testing them by gathering and analyzing data? R T O
			5.3 Do activities include the processes of making decisions about socio-civic affairs? R T O
			5.4 Do activities involve students in their communities? S T C
			5.5 Are learning activities sufficiently varied and flexible? T S
			5.6 Do students perceive their teachers as fellow inquirers? S
			5.7 Are activities carried on in a climate which supports students' self-respect and opens opportunities to all? S T O
			6.1 Does the program have a wealth of appropriate instructional resources? R T O
			6.2 Do printed materials accommodate a wide range of reading abilities and interests, learning activities, and sources? R O
			6.3 Is a variety of media available for learning through many senses? R O
			6.4 Do classrooms draw upon the contributions of many kinds of resource persons and organizations representing many points of view? T O C
			6.5 Do activities use the school and community as a learning laboratory? T O C
			6.6 Does the program have available many kinds of work space? R O
			7.1 Does the program help students organize their experiences? R O
			7.2 Are learning experiences organized in such fashion that students learn how to continue to learn? R O
			7.3 Does the program enable students to relate their experiences in social studies to other areas of experience? T S O
			7.4 Does the formal pattern of the program offer choice and flexibility? R S

RATING			SPECIFIC GUIDELINES
Strongly	*Moderately*	*Hardly At All*	
			8.1 Is evaluation based primarily on the school's own statements of objectives? R
			8.2 Does assessment include progress in knowledge, abilities, valuing, and participation? R
			8.3 Does evaluation data come from many sources, inside and outside the classroom? R
			8.4 Are evaluation procedures regular, comprehensive, and continuous? R
			8.5 Are evaluation data used for planning curricular improvement? R T
			8.6 Do evaluation data offer students help in the course of learning? T S
			8.7 Are both students and teachers involved in the process of evaluation? S T
			8.8 Is regular re-examination of basic curricular goals an integral part of the evaluation? R T
			9.1 Does the school provide appropriate materials, time, and facilities for social studies education? R T C
			9.2 Do teachers try out and adapt for their own students promising innovations? R T
			9.3 Are the basic purposes of social studies education as clearly related to the needs of the immediate community as to those of society at large? R C
			9.4 Do teachers participate regularly in active social studies curriculum committees with both decision-making and advisory responsibilities? T
			9.5 Do teachers participate regularly in activities which foster their competence in social studies education? R T
			9.6 Do teachers have social studies consultants available for help? R T
			9.7 Can teachers and schools rely upon a district-wide policy statement on academic freedom and professional responsibility? R T C

SOURCE: National Council for the Social Studies Task Force on Curriculum Guidelines, "Social Studies Curriculum Guidelines," *Social Education*, December 1971, pp. 867–69. Reprinted with permission of the National Council for the Social Studies.

Summary

Evaluation was one of the prime targets of educational reformers of the 1960s, and understandably so. Traditionally it had amounted to little more than the testing and grading of students, a process that—in spirit at least—resembled the factory assembly line. Students were (and still are) sorted out, set on different tracks, and pretty much assigned a rank in society long before they had even graduated. The more radical critics of the system viewed evaluation in much the same way that citizens of a dictatorship view the police, and a number of schools and universities experimented with dropping evaluation in part or in whole.

But evaluation cannot be dispensed with altogether. In the end, the principal objective of education is progress—both on the level of the individual and on the level of the society—and evaluation is the only way we can chart progress. Used intelligently, the tools of evaluation can be very valuable aids to teacher and students alike.

The two most important points to remember about evaluation are: (1) it should always be used to *benefit* the student, and (2) the student is only one of several elements to be evaluated.

Several things can be done to make evaluation beneficial. First, teachers should assess the reasons for evaluation and make sure that they really are what they are intended to be. (If a teacher claims, for example, to be trying to discover what a student's learning disabilities are when in fact the intention is simply to confirm that the student is not worth any further effort, the student will be unnecessarily harmed.) Second, teachers should play down evaluation for the purposes of grading and concentrate instead on using it to diagnose the students' abilities and disabilities and to discover during the course of studies just what is being learned and what is not being learned. Third, teachers should emphasize the evaluation of students in relation to a specific educational objective (criterion-referenced evaluation) rather than in relation to each other. Finally, teachers should bear in mind that knowledge and comprehension are not the only things that must be evaluated. The attitudes and involvement of the students—the affective domain—are also crucial elements of the educational process. A teacher whose students manage to learn a lot is not really successful if those students develop generally negative attitudes toward learning.

As for the other major point, anything that affects what or how the students learn must be subject to evaluation. The teacher, the books, the classrooms, even the community must be frequently assessed in order to discover ways to balance or improve the situation. The students themselves should have an active role in this aspect of evaluation because they are the most directly affected and their point of view is invaluable.

V

The Unit Plan

Unit and Lesson Plans

The two most basic tools for organizing what is to be learned—and the materials to be used in teaching it—are unit plans and lesson plans. The primary function of these plans is to provide a systematic approach to a specific area of study, an approach that will integrate learning experiences in such a way that educational objectives can be achieved. Stated another way, plans are ways of overcoming fragmentation and randomness.

An instructional plan is a proposal, not a recipe. Its objective is not to provide an immutable and rigid set of classroom experiences. Learning opportunities that occur by chance should not be passed over because they fail to fit the plan. Although it may appear to be a paradox, the teacher with a plan is in fact probably in the best position to exploit a serendipitous moment. Rigidity may be far more common among those who have given little thought to planning.

Types of Units

Units are plans for the organization of studies over an extended period of time. They may be as long as the entire school year or as short as a week. Most typically, they are of several weeks' duration. Lesson plans are subdivisions of units and are limited to the activities of a single day.

Resource and Teaching Units

There are basically two different kinds of units—the resource unit and the teaching unit. The *resource unit* is a comprehensive guide in a particular area of study. It suggests many possibilities from which the teacher may choose, and can often be adapted to many different grade levels. Resource units are frequently prepared by teams that may include social studies educators, academicians from the social sciences, and educational psychologists as well as teachers. Sometimes they are prepared by classroom teachers. The *teaching unit* (also called the "experience unit" or "problem unit") is designed for a specific group of students. It may be adapted by a classroom teacher from an available resource unit, or drawn up from scratch.

Resource units are available from many different sources. Social studies textbooks are among the most easily obtained. Several professional textbooks include resource units,[1] as do magazines and journals like *Social Education* and *The Instructor.* Local, county, and state publications and the libraries and curriculum laboratories of local universities can be useful sources of programs and ideas for units. National institutes and organizations such as the Educational Resources Information Center Clearinghouse (ERIC) are also

[1]Of particular interest are: Lavone A. Hanna, Gladys L. Potter, and Neva Negman, *Unit Teaching in the Elementary School: Social Studies and Related Sciences* (New York: Holt, Rinehart and Winston, 1963); Wilhelmina Hill, *Selected Resource Units—Elementary Social Studies: Kindergarten–Grade Six* (Washington, D.C.: National Council for the Social Studies, 1961); and John U. Michaelis, *Teaching Units Based on the Social Sciences* (Chicago: Rand, McNally and Co., 1966).

valuable sources, as are the National Council for the Social Studies (NCSS) and the Association for Supervision and Curriculum Development, both of which often offer units at the conferences they sponsor. (See Appendix A for a more detailed listing of sources.)

Episodic Units

At times it is useful or convenient to prepare shorter units that cover a limited area in just a few days. These episodic units, as they are called, may be self-contained entities that are not related to the rest of the material being studied or, more frequently, they may be designed to fit into an on-going instructional plan. They are flexible and easy to adapt, so that new materials can be included without the need for major program revisions. Some episodic units are available commercially, but they are usually planned by individual teachers to fit specific needs.

The Massialas units on population dynamics are typical of episodic units.[2] The program is concerned with having students explore and make rational decisions about population matters—an issue of utmost concern at present. But rather than develop a self-contained unit on this issue, the designers chose to make it possible to incorporate the unit into any eighth-grade course on American history. Chart 10–1 lists the population topics developed in each episode of the Massialas program and the related history topics with which each can be used.

The Elements of a Unit

The following elements are generally included in all units, although they may be called by different names:

A statement of goals
Identification of content areas
Identification of scenes
Identification of specific objectives
A title
Proposed instructional strategies
Recommended instructional techniques and resources
Proposed evaluation techniques
References and resources for teachers and students

Goals

Goals are the long-range objectives of a program. They are basically statements of intent regarding the overall aims of instruction. Goals may be determined by any of a number of groups and individuals, some of which are more powerful than others in directing school experiences.

[2]*Resource Material Development: Population Dynamics in Eighth-Grade History,* Bryon G. Massialas, Director (Tallahassee, Fla.: Florida State University, 1974).

Chart 10–1
Resource Material Development
Population Dynamics in Eighth Grade American History

History Topics	Population Topics
1. European exploration of the New World	Early stages of the demographic transition; components of population change.
2. European colonization of the New World	Population distribution and settlement patterns; population characteristics of settlers.
3. The Late Colonial Period	Comparisons of factors affecting population size between the English and the colonists; effects of high birth rates on population growth in the colonies.
4. Union under the Constitution	Taking a population census under Article I; comparisons made between the census of 1790 and 1970.
5. Westward movement, Civil War, and Reconstruction	The changing regional balance of the population; black migration from the south; westward migration.
6. The rise of the cities and industrialization	Rural/urban differentials in the population; industrialization and the urbanization of America.
7. America becomes a world power	Immigration as a component of population change.
8. United States and world affairs	The United States in the third stage of the demographic transition; the infusion of technology into developing countries and its effect on population growth.

SOURCE: *Resource Material Development: Population Dynamics in Eighth-Grade History.* Byron G. Massialas, Director. Tallahassee, Florida: Florida State University, 1974.

Legal authority to determine goals and programs rests primarily with state governments. It is usual for each state to issue curricula guidelines every few years for all of the schools within its jurisdiction. In recent years, these guidelines have tended to become more flexible, allowing the school districts more autonomy in determining their educational programs. However, the state reserves the right to intervene.

Although the state is the ultimate legal authority in determining goals, other parties do exert influence. For example, educational projects financed by the federal government are usually accompanied by goal statements and programs of their own. Schools receiving such funds are therefore constrained by the conditions of their contractual arrangements with the federal government. The latter's role has increased considerably over the last few years as federal expenditures on education have increased.

Another powerful influence is the professional teacher organizations. The National Education Association (NEA), comprised of almost one and one-half million members, can bring a great deal of pressure to bear. The National Council for the Social Studies (NCSS), one of the many subgroups of the NEA, is very important in shaping the goals of social studies education. Its influence is felt through its numerous publications and through conferences in which researchers, professors of education, administrative school personnel at state and local levels, and teachers participate. Goals articulated by the NCSS are frequently adopted by individual states as guidelines in preparation of their social studies curricula.

Individual scholars working in universities and colleges also exert influence through the publication of their research and their participation in professional organizations and educational committees. A particularly persuasive or powerful individual may actually shape curricular goals for some time, as John Dewey once did. More often, however, it requires a group of scholars with similar points of view to make a difference.

In spite of all these outside influences and authorities, the classroom teacher is ultimately the most powerful individual involved in the process of planning units. By selectively omitting, emphasizing, or modifying elements of state programs, the teacher determines what is actually implemented. Teachers frequently fail to use this power—sometimes because they fail to consider their *own* goals for social studies instruction.

None of the groups or individuals mentioned above operate in a vacuum. They themselves are influenced by changing social and political pressures and by new educational developments and research. Hence, goals continue to change.

Changing Goals   In the past three decades, surprising changes have taken place in the attitudes of social studies educators. Different ideas and ideals have slowly shifted both the scope and the focus of goals in social studies teaching. This change is suggested by the materials in Chart 10–2, which compares the goals of three influential authorities. The Carr and Wesley list is representative of the 1950s, the Michaelis list—although not published until 1972—is probably the best summary of goals in the decade of the sixties, while the list prepared by the National Council for the Social Studies in 1971 may be setting the standard for the seventies.

All three lists are concerned with knowledge, ability, and value objectives. But *only* the NCSS list is concerned with student involvement in all levels of activities in the community—categorized as *social participation*. The report of the NCSS Task Force on Curriculum Guidelines argues that if students are to become effective and potent agents of change, they need to learn appropriate skills through actual participation in society—and not within "the two covers

Chart 10–2
Goals of Social Studies Instruction

The 1950s (Carr and Wesley)

Knowledge

To become a judicious consumer.

To understand principal economic, social, and political problems.

To learn about vocational activities and opportunities.

To understand the interdependence of peoples and groups.

Values

To respect the rights and opinions of others.

To assume social and civic responsibility.

To act in accord with democratic principles and values.

To become a happy member of a home.

To make intelligent adjustments to change.

To understand and promote social progress.

Abilities

To be skillful in securing, sifting, evaluating, organizing, and presenting information.

To get along with individuals and groups.

To use basic social studies skills.

To exercise critical judgment.

The 1960s (Michaelis)

Conceptual Objectives

To develop understanding of data, concepts, themes, and generalizations.

To develop understanding of democratic beliefs essential to our way of life.

Affective Objectives

To identify, describe, and demonstrate in individual behavior and group activities the attitudes, values, and feelings of individuals who value objectivity, search for creative and divergent views, are sensitive to moral values, value democratic beliefs, respect duly constituted authority and due process of law, are self-respecting and show respect for others, are open-minded, cooperative, and creative.

Inquiry Objectives

To develop competence in using modes, methods, and processes of inquiry.

Skill Objectives

To develop competence in using basic skills in the social studies.

The 1970s (NCSS)

Knowledge

To demonstrate the power of rationally based knowledge in illuminating personal and social needs.

To provide knowledge about the real world.

To help students see patterns and systems in the environment.

To demonstrate the worthiness of personal and social judgments.

Valuing

To provide opportunities for free examination of value dilemmas underlying social issues and student problems.

To provide opportunities for clarifying value conflicts within and between individuals and groups.

To help students realize that different cultures have different values.

To contribute to student's feeling of competence and sense of identity.

Abilities

To emphasize higher level intellectual abilities.

To develop data processing skills.

To develop social competencies.

Social Participation

Involve all students at all levels in community activities.

Adapted from: Edwin R. Carr and Edgar B. Wesley, "Social Studies," in Walter S. Monroe, ed., *Encyclopedia of Educational Research,* rev. ed. (New York: Macmillan Co., 1950), p. 1219; John U. Michaelis, *Social Studies for Children in a Democracy* (Engelwood Cliffs, N.J.: Prentice Hall, 1972), pp. 8–11; and the NCSS Task Force on Curriculum Guidelines, "Social Studies Curriculum Guidelines," *Social Education,* Dec. 1971, pp. 856–60.

of the textbook and the four walls of the classroom."[3]

Major differences may be seen in the objectives identified in each category. Under values, for example, both Wesley-Carr and Michaelis specify the values they believe schools should teach. The NCSS Committee, on the other hand, emphasizes the *processes* of valuing. Whereas educators in the fifties were fairly confident of the values they wanted to impose on students, and those in the sixties only somewhat less so, educators in the seventies are responding to different pressures. Justifiably disturbed by the belated recognition that accepted school values tended to reflect white middle-class culture, today's educators have become sensitized to pluralistic values that characterize the multiple ethnic and socioeconomic groups of America and the world in general. Rather than impose a uniform value system, they advocate encouraging students to engage in value clarification processes as they explore a number of value systems. Simultaneously, however, they would encourage each school to actively practice its own legitimate value system with behavior that emphasizes human dignity, is free of racism and bias, supports self-respect and opportunities for decision making, and encourages general humanistic concerns.

All of the lists are concerned with the development of higher and lower cognitive abilities and skills. Michaelis divides these into inquiry objectives and basic social studies skills objectives. The NCSS Committee simply calls them higher level intellectual abilities and data processing. More interesting are the differences in the social abilities specified in each. Carr and Wesley concentrate on the ability to "get along," a theme that is essentially continued by Michaelis, who wants students to be able to work in groups, carry out plans, adhere to group standards, and so on.[4] The emphasis in the NCSS document, however, is not on "getting along," but on developing "effective interpersonal relations." While the Committee does not specify precisely what this phrase means, they do suggest that it includes effective communication, coping with conflict and authority, sensitivity to the needs of others, and the ability to assume both leader and follower roles. In short, the emphasis appears to be a shift from accommodation to more assertive yet sensitive behaviors.

The knowledge category, considered first in each of the lists, also reflects change. While it may legitimately be argued that all three lists are concerned with social and personal problems, the NCSS document makes these problems the *central* knowledge concern of the social studies. The Committee went so far as to argue that any knowledge included in the social studies should be justified by its claim to contribute to the illumination of social and personal needs. Knowledge that cannot do this should, by inference, be omitted. This stand is in direct opposition to the demands of some educators of the sixties who insisted that the social studies were identical with the study of the social sciences and that what was legitimately included in the latter should be included in the former. In what might be considered a final blow to the social science

[3]The NCSS Task Force on Curriculum Guidelines. "Social Studies Curriculum Guidelines." *Social Education,* December 1971, p. 859.
[4]John U. Michaelis, *Social Studies for Children in a Democracy* (Englewood Cliffs, N.J.: Prentice Hall, 1972), p. 10.

purists, the NCSS Committee argued that any and all rationally based knowledge, from whatever discipline and from that "emergent knowledge" not yet incorporated within any of the disciplines, is appropriate for the social studies. Equally important is the Committee's insistence on dealing with knowledge areas that convey human failure—such as slavery and imperialism—as well as achievement.

If the NCSS document is a barometer of this decade, it seems fair to predict that we will see greater emphasis on process goals in cognitive, affective, and social objectives and increased concern with real social and personal issues— even at the elementary level. This would be entirely in keeping with the needs of an age in which the products of knowledge quickly become obsolete and overwhelming social issues threaten human existence. It is also basically congruent with the orientation of this book.

Content

Whereas "goals" refer to the broad, overall objectives of the social studies unit, content objectives are more specific. Knowledge, skills, attitudes, and values are among the most commonly identified content elements. There is a special need to identify content for the category of social participation, proposed by the NCSS Committee.

Knowledge Content

Knowledge content generally includes the *concepts, generalizations*, and *major understandings* that are to be developed throughout the unit. The criteria for selection of knowledge content vary with desired goals. For example, a unit that is concerned with developing an understanding of geography will identify some of the major generalizations and concepts of that discipline as its knowledge content. Such is the case in these selected generalizations and concepts from the Fifth Grade Course on Regional Studies developed at the University of Minnesota:[5]

Generalizations:

Phenomena are distributed unequally over the earth's surface, resulting in great diversity or variability from one place to another. No two places are exactly alike.

Temperature is affected by such factors as distance from the equator, elevation, distance from warm water bodies, prevailing winds and physical features which block winds from certain directions.

Man uses his physical environment in terms of his cultural values, perceptions, and level of technology.

Population is distributed unevenly over the earth's surface; many of the land areas are thinly populated.

Concepts:

Globalism	Culture	Interrelatedness
Location	Climate	Cultural use of environment
Water	Change	Urbanization

[5]"Teacher's Guide to the Fifth Grade Course on Regional Studies," Project Social Studies Curriculum Center, University of Minnesota, Minneapolis, 1968.

A unit that is concerned with developing an understanding of social issues is more likely to be multidisciplinary or interdisciplinary in nature. The following are representative examples of generalizations or major understandings that could become the knowledge content in such units:

Controlling War and Maintaining Peace

Social conflict has both beneficial and negative effects on the relationships among individuals, groups, and nations.

Social conflicts can be resolved in many ways.

Nation-states offer both benefits and liabilities to individuals and groups.

Individuals, groups, and nations are geographically, politically, economically, and socially interdependent.

Implementing world peace will probably require some political, economic, social, and psychological change on the part of governments and individuals.

Developing and Controlling Technology

Technological development has both negative and positive effects on the quality of life among individuals, groups, and nations.

The accelerated pace of technological development in the last fifty years has left many individuals, groups, and nations unprepared to cope with its many side-effects.

Unchecked technological advances in a competitive environment threaten the life-support systems of our entire planet.

Values influence the development and use of technology.

Skills as Content

The selection of skills for any group of students depends both on the knowledge content and the consideration of the skill developmental sequence of the social studies. For example, where knowledge content focuses on geography it is likely that map skills will be called for. However, the particular map skills that can be developed differ according to grade levels. (See Chapter 6 for a detailed listing of skills.)

Attitudes and Values as Content

The learning of knowledge content cannot occur without reference to values. Students will develop attitudes toward the subjects they study as they learn, whether this is intended or not. Increasingly, efforts are being made to identify desirable attitudes and values and to develop ways to make them a part of the learning of a unit. This type of content may reflect the development of particular attitudes, such as:

an appreciation of diverse cultural styles
a curiosity about social data
a positive self-image
acceptance of the tentativeness of knowledge

Or it may reflect emphasis on valuing processes by providing opportunities for students to do such things as:

identify their own values
identify values that they are prepared to act on
evaluate their own decisions for consistency with the values they express
examine the morality of specific decisions

Social Participation as Content

The restriction of learning to the school environment not only limits the variety of experiences available for meaningful learning, but also tends to encourage civic and personal passivity. The development of potent citizens—those able to effect change in their environments—requires involvement in the civic environment. Little attention has been given this content area, but there is clearly a need for it. Social participation content might include the following opportunities:

to participate in a political campaign of a candidate of the student's own choice

to do volunteer work in a social agency that helps the elderly, young children, the handicapped, or the ill to take part in an educational campaign in the community

to participate in or observe during the planning stages a local community effort directed toward solving some community problem

to observe and record traffic patterns, types of work, sources of pollution problems

to interview and talk to assorted individuals and groups

to plan and implement responsible protests, circulate petitions, make formal requests

Scenes

Scenes are the areas or settings selected for study. Two types of scenes are commonly distinguished in making selections. The first is the *general scene,* which is frequently recommended by state and county curriculum guidelines. It is usually based on the concept of the expanding social environment of the maturing child. The other is the *particular scene,* or specific setting selected for study. For example, the general scene for grade one tends to be the family; the particular scene might be an urban black family in the United States, a rural family in Japan, or a suburban family near Paris. Similarly, the general scene of the community (a second-grade-level scene) might be particularized to include comparisons of rural communities in England and Israel and urban communities in the United States and Southeast Asia.

An interesting variation in the pattern of the selection of general scenes for study was introduced in the California Social Studies Framework of 1974. While the Framework identifies ten areas, or scenes of study, that must be covered in the K – 12 sequence, it goes on to say that they may be used in *any* of the grade level blocks. It is up to the local districts to decide the sequence in which the scenes will be arranged. The ten general scenes identified are:

1. Individual and group development

   Needs and wants
   Issues: maturational, family life, drugs
   Values: attitudes and self-identity
   Individual and group relations

2. Ethnic cultures within and outside the United States
3. Local, state, and national regions
4. American heritage
5. Social and natural environments
6. World cultures and civilizations
7. Political systems of the United States and the world
8. Economic systems of the United States and the world
9. Contemporary issues
10. The roles and contributions of women and ethnic groups[6]

[6]*Social Science Education Framework for California Public Schools,* Report of the Statewide Social Studies Framework Committee (Sacramento, Calif.: California State Board of Education, 1974), pp. 20 – 28.

Whether or not local districts will be able to construct meaningful organizational patterns other than the expanding environment remains to be seen. The Framework, however, should make it easier to adapt those units of study that do not fit into the expanding environment sequence.

Criteria for Scene Selection

Many things must be taken into account when selecting scenes for study, from the present needs of the individual student to the needs of that future world in which the students will one day live. The following criteria should be considered in selecting scenes.

1. *The needs and interests of the students should help determine the selection.* Interests can be identified from student concerns and pleasures. Needs are not as easy to identify; teachers must try to determine which areas of learning may help students in adapting to and dealing with their immediate and future environments. For example, students of varied ethnic backgrounds are often interested in exploring their own cultures. However, students from one ethnic culture need to know about others. Social service agencies, such as welfare agencies, housing authorities, or the Chamber of Commerce may interest only those students who interact with them, but these agencies should be understood by all citizens.

2. *Development must be taken into account.* Younger children, for example, are less able to relate to historical chronology, particularly of the recent past, than are older children. While complex events can probably be taught with some intellectual integrity at any age, it may be wise to postpone them for a later age. Thus, the study of the Vietnam war is probably better suited for older children, but social conflict within a family or community can be studied at younger age levels.

3. *The total curriculum must be considered.* Since state, county, and school curricula are constructed for the entire sequence of study from kindergarten through twelfth grade, the selection of particular scenes should take account of previous and anticipated studies. There is not much point, for example, in focusing on black Americans with a group of fourth graders who studied this group the previous year—though it may be wise to resume this study with greater complexity at the seventh-grade level. If, however, no provision at all has been made for the study of some key group, such as women or the elderly, that group can and should be used as the particular scene at any level and in any situation in which it seems applicable.

4. *Diverse minority groups, both within and without the United States, should be represented.* Within the United States this should include such groups as black Americans, Native Americans, Chicanos, Puerto Ricans, and Asian Americans. These groups, constituting approximately fifteen percent of the American population, have long been neglected or distorted in textbooks and other media. The study of women as a group is also essential. A cross-cultural perspective through the study of minority groups in other lands can

lead to fruitful comparisons and deeper understandings. Although materials for teaching about the experiences of these groups are becoming more available, teachers will often have to search for or construct their own materials.

5. *Study of the non-Western world requires special attention.* Studies reveal that American children are woefully unaware of much of the non-Western world. The greater part of the world population lives in areas other than the West, and their existence affects world affairs with increasing impact. It is imperative that efforts be made to include these areas for study.

6. *The world should be viewed as a community.* The concepts "near" and "far" have changed significantly in the technological age. Youngsters need to become aware of the world community as well as their own local communities. More and more, human beings are becoming part of a global community—in fact, if not yet in spirit. Consciousness of this fact should begin at as early an age as possible.

7. *There should be a balance of past, present, and future.* While it may be argued that the social studies have tended to concentrate too much on the past, undue focus on the present also presents problems. Without a sense of the past, people may develop a sense of rootlessness and noncontinuity—

and even a lack of concern with the future. The present can probably never fully be understood without understanding the past. And youngsters at an early age can be helped to develop a sense of community by studying the relevant past and present, as well as the anticipated future.

Selecting a Unit Title

A unit title will generally reflect the particular scene or some major concept developed in the unit. "Familes Around the World," "Native Americans," "Early America," and "City Problems" are representative titles. Titles should be chosen to succinctly convey an impression of the content to be covered in the unit.

Objectives

Having identified goals, content, and scenes, the unit developer must now translate these into a set of learning objectives. Learning objectives are statements of intent about learner achievement at the end of a given period of time. More and more frequently, learning objectives are being written in terms of student performance or behavior—that is, descriptions of what students will do in order to demonstrate mastery of the intended learning.

Terminal Objectives

A terminal objective is a statement of intent regarding learner achievement at the conclusion of a unit of instruction. Such statements are derived from the content of the unit. Let us suppose, for example, that one content area for a unit on inequality is covered by the generalization "Resources are distributed unevenly among groups," and that the particular scenes are blacks and women in the United States. The terminal objective might then be: "Students will generalize regarding the distribution of resources among blacks and nonblacks, women and men in the United States." Or if one content area for a unit on environmental problems is the generalization "Upsetting the balance of nature can have an adverse effect on human existence," and the selected scenes are plant and animal habitats, then the terminal objective might be: "Students will identify human problems that have resulted from our interaction with plant and animal habitats."

Enabling Objectives

The terminal objectives can only be achieved if a set of smaller tasks are mastered first. This means that the unit developer must attempt to analyze each terminal objective in order to identify the subobjectives that must first be mastered. These subobjectives are generally called *enabling objectives*—they presumably will enable the student to arrive at the terminal objective. They may be stated in rigorous behavioral terms (as described in Chapter 9) or in modified behavioral terms (as in Charts 10–3 and 10–4). For most units, the modified form is acceptable, since the relevant conditions and criteria will generally be specified elsewhere in the unit.

Deciding what the enabling objectives are is not an easy task. A good deal of

considered judgment is required. For example, when using the terminal objective "Students will generalize regarding the distribution of resources among blacks and nonblacks, women and men," the unit developer is faced with a series of fairly difficult questions. What exactly do students need to be able to do in order to accomplish the final task? They obviously have to know what a "resource" is. But resources can be economic, social, geographic, political, or even psychological—does the teacher want the students to deal with all of these? And since the generalization implies that comparisons are to be made among groups, the students will require some kinds of measures. What measures should the unit include? Income? Consumption patterns? Memberships in prestigious organizations? Representation in political office? And shall comparisons include both present and past measures? After all, there are indications of some upward trends and the unit developer does want to be encouraging, even though he or she may simultaneously want the students to understand the realities of the situation. These are just some of the considerations the developer will have to take into account. Moreover, the process must be repeated for each objective in all of the categories—knowledge, skills, values, attitudes, and social participation.

Examples of how a unit developer might finally resolve the questions raised above for units on inequality and environmental problems are given in Charts 10–3 and 10–4.

Chart 10–3
Objectives for a Unit on Inequality

Knowledge
Resources are distributed unequally among individuals and groups in many societies.

Terminal Objective
Students will propose generalizations regarding the distribution of economic resources among whites and nonwhites and women and men in the United States.

    Enabling Objectives
    Students will define the term "resource."
    Students will define "economic resource."
    Students will propose measures by which the distribution of economic resources can be compared, such as income, jobs, consumption patterns.
    Students will compare distribution of economic resources for whites and nonwhites, women and men in the United States.
    Students will propose tentative generalizations regarding the distribution of resources among groups studied.
    Students will evaluate accuracy of generalizations by comparing with other data and information.
    Students will select generalizations that are in their judgment most consistent with the evidence.

Skills

Terminal Objective
Students will further develop line graph skills.

    Enabling Objectives
    Students will identify graph title.
    Students will identify titles of horizontal and vertical axes.

The purpose of the resource unit developer is to provide a broad selection of materials for the classroom teacher. Classroom teachers, however, must take into account the needs of their particular group of students. They must carefully evaluate what must be included or supplemented and what can be omitted.

Selecting Instructional Strategies

A deliberate effort should be made to vary instructional strategies within a unit. However, since inquiry strategies tend to get short-changed generally, particular concern should be given to them. Selection of appropriate strategies depends on a variety of factors including objectives, availability of resources, and psychological considerations. Primary objectives—those of central significance—are probably best served by inquiry strategies. It is here that students need to exercise their highest critical abilities. Since inquiry strategies encourage higher thinking processes more than the other strategies do, they are the most useful in achieving primary objectives.

Students will identify the units of measure.

Students will translate units into words.

Students will identify the main idea of the graph.

Students will compare relationships such as increasing, decreasing, larger, smaller among graph data.

Students will identify trends.

Values and Attitudes

Terminal Objective

Students will clarify their personal values regarding economic inequality.

Enabling Objectives

Students will express their feelings about the distribution of economic resources among selected groups.

Students will listen to the feelings of others.

Students will compare their feelings with those of others.

Students will decide whether their feelings on this subject are consistent with other values they hold.

Students will decide whether they are willing to act on their feelings.

Social Participation

Terminal Objective

Students will freely engage in some community or school activity that they consider useful in order to further explore or implement their values.

Enabling Objectives

Students will propose types of community or school participation activities that might help them further clarify or implement their values.

Students will evaluate the advantages and disadvantages of each activity.

Students will be given the opportunity to choose one activity in which to participate.

With the help of the teacher, students will work toward implementing the activity.

Open Strategies   Open strategies—those that encourage divergence—are appropriate when the content area itself is subject to divergent conclusions—as, for example, when one is dealing with value clarification processes, which are by their very nature divergent. However, open strategies are also applicable to knowledge areas. Many, if not most, knowledge claims are subject to divergent counterclaims, and students should be encouraged to examine them carefully. For example, among the reasons most commonly advanced for the American Revolution is the desire for independence, self-government, and freedom. Some interpretations, however, emphasize economic self-interest and personal advantage.

Closed Strategies   Closed strategies are best suited to convergent objectives. The acquisition of the skills necessary to locate reference books in the library or to interpret map symbols calls for convergence. Knowledge objectives such as ''The United States is comprised of multiple ethnic groups'' or ''Different families have different rules'' also call for convergence.

Chart 10—4
Objectives for a Unit on Environmental Problems

Knowledge

Terminal Objective
Students will identify human problems that have resulted from our interaction with plant and animal habitats and propose solutions.

   Enabling Objectives
   Students will identify examples of how human beings interfere with animal and plant habitats.
   Students will identify ways in which human wastes pollute the environment.
   Students will recognize types of land features that are erosive due to misuse.
   Students will identify natural resources that if completely exhausted can never be produced again.
   Students will name some problems that have resulted from human interaction with the environment.
   Students will propose solutions to problems.
   Students will evaluate solutions.

Skills

Terminal Objective
Students will develop observation skills.

   Enabling Objectives
   Students will identify purposes of observation before making trips to a neighboring forest area and to a garbage dump.
   Students will take notes during study trip describing things observed.
   Students will hypothesize about relationships among things observed and human activities.

Inductive Strategies   Given what we know about young children, inductive strategies are probably most suitable for the elementary school. According to Piaget, youngsters in the primary grades are basically in the preoperational stage, while those in the intermediate grades are in the concrete operational stage. At both these levels, youngsters require concrete experiences in order to deal meaningfully with their environment. Only when they reach the formal operational stage, approximately by age eleven, are children able to deal with abstractions that are not supported by concrete experience. An inductive strategy begins with as concrete an experience as possible. Hence, it is generally more appropriate for the elementary grades.

Deductive Strategies   Deductive strategies can sometimes be very effective, provided they ultimately progress to levels of adequate concreteness. For example, a teacher might well begin a study of rules by explaining: "All people have rules. Some rules are written down but others are not. Sometimes, it is hard for people to realize they are following a rule. Rules are ways of acting that people think are good." The

Students will evaluate the proposition that things observed on the trip can be considered to exist in other places and will suggest reasons why or why not.

Values and Attitudes

Terminal Objective
Students will explore their own attitudes about the importance of the problem and the right of governments to make laws to constrain people's behavior in order to conserve the environment.

Enabling Objectives
Students will express their feelings about the importance of the information they have learned.

Students will voluntarily state their views regarding the rights of people to use the environment as they see fit.

Students will decide whether or not legal authorities should have the right to make laws that constrain people's activities in relation to the environment.

Social Participation

Terminal Objective
Students will freely engage in some community or school activity that they consider useful in order to further explore or implement their values.

Enabling Objectives
Students will identify agencies in the community that are working toward the solution of environmental problems.

Students will communicate in writing with an agency of their choice to find out more about its activities.

With the help of the teacher, students will visit selected agencies of their choice, talk with involved individuals, and decide whether or not they wish to become further involved.

---

teacher might then go on to give examples of written and unwritten rules in the classroom and ask the students to give examples of written and unwritten rules in their families. Finally, the teacher might take the class on a trip through the school for the purpose of being able to identify, through observation, other rules—for example, students are in classrooms, the principal and other administrators are in their offices, exhibits are confined to certain places, supplies are kept in certain places, and so on.

Other Considerations

Even expository strategies have their place. A good presentation or demonstration, enlivened by visual materials, artifacts, or sound, can keep children vitally interested and learning.

Time and materials also influence strategy selection. Open inductive strategies require the most time, hence they are probably best reserved for primary objectives. Inquiry strategies require a great many resources, a factor that will sometimes discourage teachers from using them. Careful planning can ensure that resources are available at appropriate times.

Selecting Instructional Resources

Some of Piaget's ideas about the ways children learn are supported by the findings of Jerome Bruner, a noted experimental psychologist. Bruner has identified three ways that people learn: through *enactive,* or direct, experiences, through *iconic,* or pictorial, experiences, and through *symbolic,* or highly abstract, experiences. Learning experiences that incorporate all three modes are the most effective. Instructional resources should be varied, provide opportunities for all three levels of learning experiences, and include both concrete and abstract experiences.

The question of cost must also be considered in selecting resources. Very expensive materials can frequently be replaced by less expensive ones, and knowledge of the community and other sources can be helpful in finding adequate substitutes. But false economy can lead to unsuccessful learning.

A Proposed Format for Planning a Unit

Unit title

Grade level

Introduction
Rationale, concerns, psychological considerations

Terminal Objectives
  A. Knowledge:
    Major understandings, generalizations, concepts
  B. Skills:
    Basic research, inquiry, social
  C. Values and attitudes:
    Value clarification and inquiry processes, attitudes
  D. Social participation:
    School and community

Daily Lesson Plans
  A. Enabling Objectives
    1. Knowledge
    2. Skills
    3. Values and attitudes
    4. Social participation
  B. Instructional Strategy
    1. Teacher activities
    2. Guiding questions
    3. Student activities
  C. Needed Materials
  D. Formative Evaluation Techniques

Summative Evaluation Techniques

Background Materials and References for Teachers

Additional Materials for Students

Evaluation Techniques   Opportunities for both formative and summative evaluation should be provided for in the unit. Teachers cannot escape their responsibilities for assigning grades if they teach in the public school, but formative evaluation — which offers opportunities for assessing how instruction could be improved — should be built into the program. Evaluation should be an ongoing process, not reserved for the end of the unit with a view toward assigning a grade.

Evaluation techniques should not be limited to paper and pencil tests. Indeed, such tests should be used sparingly. Teacher observation, checklists, small group discussion, anecdotal reports, and other evaluation techniques suggested in Chapter 9 should be incorporated. Multiple evaluation techniques are better than single ones because they are more valid and reliable.

It is important to allow sufficient time when giving tests of any sort. Essay tests are generally difficult for elementary-age students. Techniques for assessing synthesis objectives, such as writing a poem or painting a mural, require considerable thought and effort.

Paper and pencil evaluation techniques, particularly for younger children, should call for minimal writing. The short-answer objective test, when skillfully constructed, can be used to evaluate higher-level as well as basic objectives.

Examples of Units

Excerpts from three different units are given here. The first was designed by a classroom teacher concerned with developing awareness of Native American culture. The school in which this unit was taught is located in a small town in northern California where many Native Americans live. The second unit is from a comprehensive resource unit designed by a group of specialists. It is the result of a well-financed federal project that concentrated on geographic concepts. The third unit, on women, was written by the author of this textbook.

Laytonville Indians

Grade Level: Primary Grades 1–3
Estimated Number of days required: 90
Date: 6-15-72

Indian Life Changes of the Laytonville Indians
Main Idea or Generalization:
  Changes in social group organization occurred over time as a result of interaction with other groups in their homes, clothes, food, work and play.

Concepts:
  Indian life in the community.
  Community needs for work and play.

Values:
  To have children learn to accept and respect alternative ways of life for all kinds of people.

Skills:
Improve Vocabulary   Critical Thinking Skills
Written Comprehension   Oral Communication
Map Making and Reading   Art Work
Oral and Silent Reading   Writing Creative Stories

Behavioral Objectives: Children should be able to:
Identify houses of different uses, clothing and food of yesterday and today, see the change in culture of everyday life in the world. Relate: tell the difference in preparing food from yesterday to today. Identify the change in work and play, home, clothes, and food.

Concept	Guiding Question	Teacher Activities	Solicited Education Objectives
CUSTOMS			
Economic needs	What kind of money was used?	Show pictures of strings of dentalium or other shells used.	Comprehension
	What color were the shells?	Display strings of beads on bulletin board. Describe shells: Yellow, white, gray-natural markings, handmarked, long shells, round shells.	
	What color was most valuable?	Hupa: marked white shells most valuable.	Analysis
	Were the shell beads used in any other way? How?	Show slides of beads. Explain that they had been used originally as ornaments, and became an article of exchange, or money.	Synthesis
	What other articles were used for money?	Show articles that may have been of value to them, such as Turquoise in the case of the Pueblos, blankets by the Navajos. Hupa used woodpecker scalps.	Comprehension
	What kind of money is used in Laytonville today?	Use flannel board prints to identify money: Dollar, Dime, Nickel, Penny.	Knowledge
	How do we use money?	Make store, use play money to buy and sell family needs.	

Concept	Guiding Question	Teacher Activities	Solicited Education Objectives
CUSTOMS			
		Students bring empty cartons to help supply the store.	
	Do we have a bank in Laytonville?	Tell class, Yes, that there is a Laytonville Branch of the bank of Willits.	
	What is the name of the bank?	Make Savings Books and Checks to be used in play store. Show film of *A Bone for Spotty.* Go on a Field Trip through Laytonville, stopping at the store and bank.	Comprehension
Recreational needs	What is going on in the picture?	Show transparencies & pictures of Indian festivals, Indian dances, games of children, Indian women tanning skins, drying meat, gathering berries, wood and making clothing, weaving baskets for cooking and clothing.	Comprehension
	Did the Indians have times for play? Fun? Happiness? Are they smiling? Are they sad?	Ask resource person to talk about Indian life in Laytonville.	Analysis
	What kind of games do we play in Laytonville today that may be like the ones played years ago?	Relate and compare games: stick game, dances, running games. Play other games.	Comprehension
	What game do you like best?	Draw a picture of the game you like to play best.	Analysis
	Do you like to play our Treasure Hunt game?	Play game.	

From *Laytonville Indians,* a unit plan by Reta Terrell, teacher, Laytonville Elementary School, Laytonville, California (Chiles J. Smith, Principal; Richard E. Matlock, Vice-principal), 1972.

The South: Birmingham Case Study and the South As a Region

[Grade 5. The first part of the unit is concerned with illustrating the impact that the discovery and utilization of a natural resource can have on the development of a city. In the latter part of the unit, students examine the region of the South as a whole, and try to identify criteria that distinguish it from other regions of the country. The letters **G** and **S** stand for "generalization" and "skill."]

Objectives

G. Every place has three types of location: a position, a site, and a situation.

G. Location is a position which sets a phenomenon at a specific point on the earth's surface, usually designated by an abstract grid and described in terms of latitude and longitude.

S. *Use atlas index to locate places.*

S. *Applies previously-learned concepts and generalizations to new data.*

G. Site relates a phenomenon to the detailed setting of the area it occupies.

S. *Sets up hypotheses.*

S. *Interprets map symbols.*

S. *Tests hypotheses against data.*

G. Precipitation is affected by factors such as distance from bodies of warm water, wind direction, temperature, ocean currents, and physical features which force winds to rise.

G. Temperature and seasonal differences are affected in part by distance from the equator; temperature ranges are smaller near the equator than further away from it.

G. Places in the interior of continents tend to have greater extremes of temperature than places along the coast.

G. Nature changes the face of the earth through physical and biotic processes.

G. Soil in a particular place is affected by the *type of basic rock in the region, the climate,* vegetation, erosion, *wind, glaciers,* and rivers which move soil, *as well as by how man treats the soil.*

G. Vegetation and what can be grown is affected in part by soil.

Content

1. We examine the areal location of Birmingham.
   A. Birmingham is located in the south-eastern portion of the United States at about the 33rd parallel North, in the interior of the continent.

   B. Birmingham is located in a humid subtropical climatic zone; it is not in the main cotton-growing zone.
      1. It is warm much of the year.
      2. It has 50–60 inches of rainfall annually.
      3. Red-yellow lateritic soils have developed in this region.
      4. Birmingham is outside of the main cotton-growing area.

Teaching Procedures

1. If possible, have your music teacher use some of the songs of Stephen Foster the day before you plan to introduce this unit. As an alternative you might play a record of Stephen Foster's music and have them sing along. After they have been singing about Alabama, Louisiana, and Kentucky, ask your students to point to these states on a large wall map of the United States. Now ask they what part of the United States they are in. Emphasize that Alabama (and Birmingham) are in the southeastern portion of the U.S. When you later call this region "The South" you will need to explain that it was literally the southern part of the U.S. during Colonial days.

2. Have pupils use an atlas index or their student almanac to locate Birmingham's latitude and longitude. Then have pupils locate the city on a physical-political map of the United States.

   Ask: From what you already know about climate and from Birmingham's location, what would you expect to find true about temperatures and rainfall in the Birmingham area? Why? Have pupils check their guesses against temperature and rainfall maps or climatic maps. (Review the use of the legend and symbols used to show temperature and rainfall patterns.)

   Ask: What kinds of vetetation might you expect to find in the region? Why? What kinds of soil would you expect to find? Why? What kinds of crops might you find grown in this region? Why? Have pupils check their guesses against soil, vegetation and agricultural products maps. Ask: Does Birmingham lie within the big cotton producing area? Do pupils think Birmingham would be a typical city of the cotton South, with cotton mills as an important industry?

Materials

Record of Stephen Foster's songs.
Physical-political wall map of the U.S.

Atlas
"Student Almanac"

Temperature map of U.S. or region. Rainfall map of U.S. or region. Or climatic map of U.S. or region. Soils map of U.S. or region. Vegetation map of U.S. or region. Agricultural products maps of U.S. See also maps in Borchert and McGulgan, *Geography of the New World* to examine the many patterns in the South.

SOURCE: Project Social Studies. University of Minnesota, Minneapolis, 1967. Developed under a grant from the U.S. Office of Education; Project HS-045.

Women and Sex Roles

Grade Level: Primary and Intermediate   Time Required: 4 weeks

Rationale

Sexism, discrimination against individuals based on biological gender, is a phenomenon that characterizes many societies. Traditional ideology perceives the proper role of women as home-bound. Yet, more than 70 percent of the women in the United States work during some time in their lives, mostly out of economic need and primarily at low-paying jobs. Educational, political, and economic institutions have consistently discriminated against women. One consequence has been that society at large has failed to avail itself fully of one of its most valuable resources—the talents and abilities of half its population. Another has been the entrapment of both men and women in rigid roles with few opportunities to choose alternative ones.

Opportunities to increase options for both women and men depend on many factors. Knowledge of the facts and processes of sexism needs to increase, as does knowledge of ways to overcome it. This is largely a cognitive matter. Equally important is the development of those types of attitudes that will make change possible. This is largely an affective matter.

Sexist attitudes begin at a very early age. Almost from birth children are socialized to accept appropriate roles based on sex identification. This process shapes youngsters' aspirations and visions of themselves in ways that endure throughout adulthood. Hence, early intervention is needed if current attempts to broaden the roles of both women and men are to succeed.

Terminal Objectives

Major Understandings

1. Both women and men make major contributions to society.
2. The contributions that women make have been less rewarded financially than those made by men.
3. Roles that women and men play are learned through the processes of socialization.
4. Roles assigned on the basis of sex identification have little biological justification.

Skills

1. Students will develop observation skills through observing the activities of men and women.
2. Students will develop reading interpretation skills through the process of analyzing selected reading materials for sexist biases.
3. Students will propose hypotheses to explain why the economic rewards of men and women in our society differ.
4. Students will evaluate traditional role activities on the basis of their biological necessity.

Values and Attitudes

1. Students will clarify their own values regarding desired activities for boys and girls.
2. Students will propose an appropriate response when faced with a moral dilemma in which a boy must choose between hurting the feelings of a girl he likes by not inviting her to participate in an activity or losing his male friends.

Social Participation

1. Students will select a community organization concerned with the problem of sexism that they would like to learn more about.
2. With the help of the teacher, students will visit the organization they have chosen.
3. Students will decide whether they want to do something on their own about the problem.

Major Understanding:	Roles assigned on the basis of sex identification frequently have little biological justification.
Enabling Objectives:	Students will identify activities that girls and boys do.
	Students will distinguish between those activities that are usually done by girls and those usually done by boys.
	Students will evaluate whether or not these distinctions are based on biological differences between the sexes.
	Students will identify what girls and boys can learn how to do.

Teacher Activities	*Guiding Questions*	*Student Activities*
Today we're going to try and find out about girls and boys. Let's begin by having each one of you think carefully about things you do.	What things do you do?	Recall things they do.
(Lists approximately 10 responses on blackboard; e.g. eat, play baseball, sew, watch television.)	Let's look at these words. What things do boys usually do? What things do girls usually do?	Distinguish between activities usually done by boys and those usually done by girls.

Teacher Activities	*Guiding Questions*	*Student Activities*
I'll mark those things that girls usually do with a "G," things that boys usually do with a "B," and things that both usually do with a "GB."	(Pointing to "G" words:) Why do girls usually do this? What does it take to do it? Do boys have it? Can they learn it? (Pointing to "B" words:) Why do boys usually do this? Can girls do it? What does it take to do it? Do girls have it? Can they learn it?	Propose explanations for differences among usual activities. Analyze skills required to do the activity. Evaluate whether skill is associated with biological differences between the sexes.
There are many things you cannot do right now although you can learn how to do them. Some people give up before they even try. I'm going to show you some pictures of things that women and men do. (Shows on opaque projector activities in which women and men are engaged; e.g. taking care of children, typing, driving a truck, playing football.)	(Following each picture:) Is this something only boys can learn how to do? Why or why not? Is this something only girls can learn to do? Why or why not? Are you sure? How can we find out?	Analyze skills required to do the activity. Evaluate whether skills are associated with biological differences between the sexes.
	(At conclusion of picture discussion:) How many things can you think of that both girls and boys can do?	Summarize activities.

Summary

When educators speak of units, they generally mean written plans for organizing learning experiences to achieve specified learning objectives over an extended period of time. They may be referring to resource units, which are broad, comprehensive plans that are intended to apply to a fairly diverse sampling of students. Or they may be referring to teaching units, which are designed for a particular group of students.

Resource and teaching units share certain basic elements. Both contain statements of goals, content, scenes, and specific objectives. Both also recommend instructional strategies, teaching techniques and resources, evaluation techniques, and additional references for both teachers and students.

Social studies goals, the long-range objectives of social studies instruction, are subject to change over time, and unit plans need to reflect these changes. Content objectives (knowledge, skills, attitudes, and social participation) must necessarily be consistent with these goals. Terminal objectives are long-term statements of intent regarding learner achievements at the end of a unit of instruction, based on the content selected for study. Enabling objectives are short-term statements of intent regarding learner achievements. A terminal objective can only be achieved by mastering all of the enabling objectives. Instructional strategies are ways of organizing learning techniques and resources so that students can achieve these objectives. These need to be varied and flexible. Evaluation techniques help identify whether or not objectives are being mastered.

Since the goals of social studies education are not and cannot be fixed, it is important that teachers examine their own goals critically and write or adapt unit plans accordingly. Teachers will need to examine state and county guidelines in order to assess the degree of flexibility allowed. They also need to be aware of the ideas expressed in publications by other influential sources, such as the National Council for the Social Studies, individual scholars, critics, and other teachers. The trend toward greater autonomy for teacher planning is already evident in some states. Informed teachers will be able to take advantage of these opportunities to plan social studies programs that will be exciting and relevant to students and consistent with scholarship, social needs, and humanistic concerns.

Appendix A
Organizational Sources For Social Studies Teachers

General Sources

National Council for the Social Studies: 1201 Sixteenth Street, N.W., Washington, D.C. 20036

This is the principal professional organization of social studies teachers. It publishes *Social Education,* a monthly journal, *The Professional,* a quarterly newsletter, and the *Yearbook.* It also publishes bulletins, pamphlets, and assorted other materials.

Social Science Education Consortium: 855 Broadway, Boulder, Colorado 80302

This is a nonprofit educational organization of social scientists and educators. It provides both services and publications. The *SSEC Newsletter* is available free. The *Data Book* analyzes social studies products in some detail.

The Educational Resources Information Center Clearinghouse for Social Studies/Social Science Education (ERIC/CheSS): 855 Broadway, Boulder, Colorado 80302

This invaluable resource is a clearinghouse for a wide range of educational materials, published and unpublished, including documents, social studies units and guides, project reports, and so forth. Monthly indexes called *Research in Education* and *Current Index to Journals in Education* provide guides to available materials. These can be found at most college and university libraries. Much of the material is on microfiche and some libraries that do not have their own complete collections have entered into lending arrangements with others.

Social studies centers at universities

These centers employ professionals who are primarily engaged in developing and testing new instructional materials in the social studies. For information, write to the director of each center and request that your name be put on the center's mailing list.

   Center for Education in the Social Sciences, University of Colorado, 970 Aurora, Boulder, Colorado 80302

   Lincoln-Filene Center for Citizenship and World Affairs, Tufts University, Medford, Massachusetts 02155

   Social Studies Curriculum Center, Carnegie-Mellon University, Pittsburgh, Pennsylvania 05213

   Social Studies Development Center, Indiana University, 1129 Atwater, Bloomington, Indiana 47401

Embassies and consulates

Each embassy and consulate generally will provide a good deal of information about the nation it represents. *Permanent Missions to the United Nations,* a list of all members of the United Nations missions and the addresses of the missions, can be obtained by writing to the UN Sales Section, Room LX2300, United Nations, New York 10017. A similar directory of embassies in Washington, D.C., *Diplomatic List,* is available from the U.S. Government Printing Office, Washington, D.C. 20402.

Government agencies

The Department of Labor, the U.S. Department of the Interior, the U.S. Department of State, the Internal Revenue Service, the Bureau of Indian Affairs, and many other governmental agencies provide useful social studies materials upon request. A biweekly newsletter entitled *Selected U.S. Government Publications* provides information about publications. The newsletter can be obtained by writing to the Superintendent of Documents, U.S. Government Printing Office, Washington, D.C. 20402.

Publishing companies

Commercial publishers will be happy to provide catalogs, promotional materials, and sometimes free samples. Listings can be obtained from *Social Education* and *Literary Market Place.*

Specialized Sources

Anthropology

American Anthropological Association: 1703 New Hampshire Avenue, N.W., Washington, D.C. 20009

Economics

American Economic Association: 1313 Twenty-First Avenue, South, Nashville, Tennessee 37212

American Federation of Labor and Congress of Industrial Organizations (Pamphlet Division): 815 Sixteenth Street, N.W., Washington, D.C. 20036

Changing Times Education Service: 1729 H Street, N.W., Washington, D.C. 20006

The Joint Council on Economic Education: 1212 Avenue of the Americas, New York, New York 10036

National Consumer Finance Association: Educational Services Division, 1000 Sixteenth Street, N.W., Washington, D.C. 20036

New York Stock Exchange: School and College Relations, 11 Wall Street, New York, New York 10005

The Environment

Environmental Action, Inc.: Room 731, 1346 Connecticut Avenue, Washington, D.C. 20036

National Wildlife Federation: 1412 Sixteenth Street, N.W., Washington, D.C. 20036

The Population Council: 245 Park Avenue, New York, New York 10019

Population Reference Bureau: 1755 Massachusetts Avenue, N.W., Washington, D.C. 20036

Ethnic Studies

Afro-American Studies Resource Center: Circle Associates, 126 Warren Street, Roxbury, Massachusetts 02119

American Jewish Committee: Institute for Human Relations, 165 East 56th Street, New York, New York 10022

Anti-Defamation League of B'nai B'rith: 315 Lexington Avenue, New York, New York 10016

Association on American Indian Affairs: 432 Park Avenue, New York, New York 10016

Foundation for Change, Inc., 1619 Broadway, New York, New York 10019

UW System Ethnic and Minority Studies Center, University of Wisconsin, Stevens Point, Wisconsin 54481

Geography

The Association of American Geographers: 1710 Sixteenth Street, N.W., Washington, D.C. 20009

National Council for Geographic Education: Room 1226, 111 West Washington Street, Chicago, Illinois 60602

History

The American Historical Association: 400 A Street, S.E., Washington, D.C. 20003

The History Teacher, a journal published by the Society for History Education at the Department of History, California State University, 6101 East Seventh Street, Long Beach, California 90840.

Law

Law in a Free Society Project: 606 Wilshire Boulevard, Suite 600, Santa Monica, California 90401

The National Center for Law-focused Education: 33 North La Salle Street, Room 1629, Chicago, Illinois 60602

Special Committee on Youth Education for Citizenship, American Bar Association: 1155 East 60th Street, Chicago, Illinois 60637

Political Science

The American Political Science Association: 1527 New Hampshire Avenue, N.W., Washington, D.C. 20036

Citizenship Education Clearinghouse: 411 North Elizabeth Avenue, St. Louis, Missouri 63135

League of Women Voters: 1730 M Street, N.W., Washington, D.C. 20036

Lincoln-Filene Center for Citizenship and Public Affairs: Tufts University, Medford, Massachusetts 02155

Teaching Political Science, a journal published by SAGE Publications: P.O. Box 776, Beverly Hills, California 90210

Psychology

The American Psychological Association: 1200 Seventeenth Street, N.W., Washington, D.C. 20036

People Watching, a journal published by Behavioral Publications, Inc.: 2852 Broadway-Morningside Heights, New York, New York 10023

Sociology

The American Sociological Association: 1722 "N" Street, N.W., Washington, D.C. 20036

Teaching Sociology, a journal published by SAGE Publications: P.O. Box 776, Beverly Hills, California 90210

World Affairs

African-American Institute, 866 United Nations Plaza, New York, New York 10017

The Asia Society: 122 East 64th Street, New York, New York 10021

The Center for Teaching International Relations: Graduate School of International Studies, University of Denver, Denver, Colorado 80210

Center for War/Peace Studies: 218 East 18th Street, New York, New York 10003

Foreign Policy Association: 345 East 46th Street, New York, New York 10017

The Information Center on Children's Cultures: U.S. Committee for UNICEF, 331 East 38th Street, New York, New York 10016

Institute for World Order: 11 West 42nd Street, New York, New York 10036

Intercultural Social Studies Project: 3 Lebanon Street, Hanover, New Hampshire 03755

Pan American Union, Nineteenth Street and Constitution Avenue, Washington, D.C. 20006

Service Center for Teachers of Asian Studies: Ohio State University, 29 West Woodruf Avenue, Columbus, Ohio 43210

Appendix B

Additional Reading Sources For Students in the Social Studies

Biography

Baumann, Hans. *Alexander's Great March*. Translated by Stella Humphries. New York: Henry Z. Walck, 1968. Grades 6–8.

Bontemps, Arna. *Frederick Douglass: Slave-Fighter-Freeman*. Illustrated by Harper Johnson. New York: Knopf, 1959. Grades 5–7.

D'Aulaire, Ingri and Edgar P. *Abraham Lincoln*. Illustrated by the authors. Garden City, N.Y.: Doubleday, 1939, 1957. Grades 2–5.

Epstein, Sam, and Beryl Epstein. *Harriet Tubman: Guide to Freedom*. N.Y.: Dell, 1975. Grades 3–5.

Fisher, Aileen Lucia, and Olive Rabe. *We Alcotts; the Story of Louisa M. Alcott's Family as Seen through the Eyes of "Marmee," Mother of Little Women*. Decorations by Ellen Raskin. New York: Atheneum, 1968. Grades 5–8.

Kyle, Elisabeth. *Great Ambitions: A Story of the Early Years of Charles Dickens*. New York: Holt, Rinehart and Winston, 1968. Grades 7–9.

Liss, Howard. *The Making of a Rookie*. Glossary of Pro Football Terms. New York: Random House, 1968. Grades 6–9.

Preston, Edward. *Martin Luther King: Fighter for Freedom*. Garden City, N.Y.: Doubleday, 1969. Grades 8 and up.

Stoutenburg, Adrien, and Laura Nelson Baker. *Listen America: A Life of Walt Whitman*. New York: Scribner, 1968. Grades 7 and up.

Sullivan, Wilson, and Frank Freidel. *Franklin Delano Roosevelt*. New York: American Heritage/Harper & Row, 1970. Grades 6 and up.

Williams, Jay, and Bates Lowry. *Leonardo da Vinci*. New York: American Heritage, 1965. Grades 6 and up.

Wyatt, Edgar. *Cochise: Apache Warrior and Statesman*. Illustrated by Allan Houser. New York: McGraw-Hill, 1953. Grades 4–6.

Earth, Sky, and Space

Ames, Gerald, and Rose Wyler. *Planet Earth*. Illustrated by Cornelius DeWitt. Racine, Wis.: Golden Press, 1963. Grades 6–8.

Archer, Sellers G. *Rain, Rivers and Reservoirs: The Challenge of Running Water*. Illustrated with maps and photographs. New York: Coward-McCann, 1963, 1969. Grades 5–7.

Bendick, Jeanne. *Space and Time*. Illustrated by the author. New York: Franklin Watts, 1968. Grades 2–4.

Bergaust, Erik. *The Russians in Space*. Illustrated. New York: Putnam, 1969. Grades 5–9.

Brindze, Ruth. *The Story of Our Calendar*. Illustrated by Helene Carter. New York: Vanguard, 1949. Grades 4–8.

Burt, Olive. *The First Book of Salt*. Illustrated with photographs. New York: Franklin Watts, 1965. Grades 4–6.

Goodheart, Barbara. *A Year on the Desert*. Illustrated by Mel Hunter. Englewood Cliffs, N.J.: Prentice-Hall, 1969. Grades 5 and up.

Jennings, Gary. *The Earth Book*. Philadelphia: Lippincott, 1974. Grades K–3.

Keen, Martin L. *The World Beneath Our Feet: The Story of Soil*. New York: Messner, 1974. Grades 4–6.

Marshall, James. *The Air We Live In; Air Pollution: What We Must Do About It*. Matthew Brennan, consultant. New York: Coward-McCann, 1969. Grades 6–9.

Newell, Homer Edward. *Space Book for Young People.* Illustrated by Anne Marie Jauss. New York: McGraw-Hill, 1968. Grades 7–9.

Schneider, Herman and Nina. *Rocks, Rivers, and the Changing Earth.* Illustrated by Edwin Herron. New York: William R. Scott, 1952. Grades 5–8.

Schneider, Leo. *Space in Your Future.* Illustrated. New York: Harcourt Brace Jovanovich, 1961. Grades 4–6.

Smith, Frances C. *The First Book of Conservation.* Illustrated by Rene Martin. New York: Franklin Watts, 1954. Grades 4–6.

Talley, Naomi. *To Save the Soil.* Illustrated. New York: Dial, 1965. Grades 4–6.

Zim, Herbert S. *What's Inside the Earth?* Illustrated by Raymond Perlman. New York: Morrow, 1953. Grades 4–9.

Folktales, Fairy Tales, and Legends from Around the World

Alger, Leclaire. *Sea-Spell and Moor-Magic: Tales of the Western Isles by Sorche Nic Leodhas.* Illustrated by Vera Bock. New York: Holt, Rinehart and Winston, 1968. Grades 4–7.

Artzybasheff, Boris. *Seven Simeons: A Russian Tale.* Illustrated by the author. New York: Viking, 1961. Grades 4–6.

Belpre, Pura. *Ote, A Puerto Rican Tale.* Pictures by Paul Galdone. New York: Pantheon, 1969. Grades Ps–3.

Carlson, Natalie Savage. *The Talking Cat and Other Stories of French Canada.* Illustrated by Roger Duvoisin. New York: Harper & Row, 1952. Grades 1–6.

Colum, Padraic. *Children of Odin.* New York: Macmillan, 1930; 1962. Grades 4–6.

Courlander, Harold, ed. *The King's Drum and Other African Stories.* Illustrated by Enrico Arno. New York: Harcourt Brace Jovanovich, 1962. Grades 4–6.

Durham, Mae. *Tit for Tat and Other Latvian Folk Tales.* Illustrated by Harriet Pincus. New York: Harcourt Brace Jovanovich, 1967. Grades 4–6.

Green, Roger Lancelyn. *Tales of Ancient Egypt, Selected and Retold.* Illustrated by Elaine Raphael. New York: Henry Z. Walck, 1968. Grades 6–9.

Grimm Brothers. *German Folk Tales.* Translated by Francis P. Magoun, Jr., and Alexander H. Krappe. Southern Illinois University Press, 1969. Grades 3–5.

Harman, Humphrey. *Tales Told Near a Crocodile: Stories from Nyanza.* Illustrated by George Ford. New York: Viking, 1967. Grades 3–6.

Matson, Emerson N. *Longhouse Legends.* Illustrated by Lorence Bjorklund. Camden, N.J.: Thomas Nelson, 1968. Grades 4–6.

Mehdevi, Anne Sinclair. *Persian Folk and Fairy Tales.* Illustrated by Paul E. Kennedy. New York: Knopf, 1965. Grades 4–6.

Nyblom, Helena Augusta (Roed). *The Witch of the Woods: Fairy Tales from Sweden.* Illustrated by Nils Christian Hald. Translated by Holger Lundbergh. New York: Knopf, 1968. Grades 4–6.

O'Sullivan, Sean, ed. *Folk Tales of Ireland.* Translated by the author. Chicago: University of Chicago Press, 1969.

Sechrist, Elizabeth (Hough). *Once in the First Times; Folk Tales from the Phillippines.* Retold. Illustrated by John Sheppard. Philadelphia: Macrae Smith, 1969. Grades 4–6.

Siddiqui, Ashraf, and Marilyn Lerch. *Toontoony Pie and Other Tales from Pakistan.* Illustrated by Jan Fairservis. New York: World, 1961. Grades 4–6.

Singer, Isaac Bashevis. *The Fearsome Inn.* Illustrated by Nonny Hogrogian. New York: Scribner, 1967. Grades 3–6.

Spellman, John W. *The Beautiful Blue Jay and Other Tales of India.* Illustrated by Jerry Pinkney. Boston: Little, Brown, 1967. Grades 4–6.

Stamm, Claus. *Three Strong Women: A Tall Tale from Japan.* Illustrated by Kazue Mizumura. New York: Viking, 1962. Grades 3–5.

Traven, B. *The Creation of the Sun and the Moon.* Illustrated by Alberto Beltran. New York: Hill & Wang, 1968. Grades 4–6.

Food, Shelter, Transportation

Anderson, William R. *First Under the North Pole: The Voyage of the Nautilus.* Illustrated with photographs. New York: World, 1959. Grades 4–6.

Benenson, Lawrence A. *How a House Is Built.* Illustrated by Richard Lewis. New York: Criterion, 1965. Grades 4–6.

Berry, Erick. *Eating and Cooking Around the World: Fingers Before Forks.* Illustrated with photographs. New York: John Day, 1963. Grades 4–7.

Burns, William A. *A World Full of Homes.* Illustrated by Paula Hutchinson. New York: McGraw-Hill, 1953. Grades 4–7.

Coggins, Jack. *Nets Overboard: The Story of the Fishing Fleets.* Illustrated by the author. New York: Dodd, Mead, 1965. Grades 5–7.

Corbett, Scott. *What Makes a Plane Fly?* Illustrated by Len Darwin. Boston: Little, Brown, 1967. Grades 3–6.

Frisch, Rose E. *Plants That Feed the World.* Illustrated by Denny McMains. Princeton, N.J.: Van Nostrand, 1966. Grades 4–6.

Lee, Laurie, and David Lambert. *The Wonderful World of Transportation.* Garden City, N.Y.: Doubleday, 1960. Grades 4 and up.

Lewellen, John. *Helicopters: How They Work.* Illustrated by A. W. Revell. New York: Crowell, 1955. Grades 4–6.

Maps

Epstein, Sam and Beryl. *The First Book of Maps and Globes.* New York: Franklin Watts, 1959. Grades 4 and up.

Hirsch, S. Carl. *The Globe for the Space Age.* Illustrated by Burt Silverman. New York: Viking, 1963. Grades 5–8.

Marsh, Susan. *All About Maps and Map Making.* Illustrated with maps and photographs. New York: Random House, 1963. Grades 5–7.

Rinkoff, Barbara. *A Map Is a Picture.* Illustrated by Robert Galster. New York: Crowell, 1965. Grades K–2.

Tannenbaum, Beulah, and Myra Stillman. *Understanding Maps: Charting the Land, Sea and Sky.* Rev. ed. Illustrated by Adolph E. Brotman and with photographs. New York: McGraw-Hill, 1969. Grades 6–9.

Work

Alterman, Hyman. *Counting People: The Census in History.* Charts and graphs. New York: Harcourt Brace Jovanovich, 1969. Grades 7 and up.

Anderson, Lonzo. *Bag of Smoke: The Story of Man's First Reach for Space.* Illustrated by Adrienne Adams, New York: Knopf, 1968. Grades 4–6.

Asimov, Isaac. *Great Ideas of Science.* Illustrated by Lee Ames. Boston: Houghton Mifflin, 1969. Grades 7 and up.

Bate, Norman. *Who Built the Bridge?* Illustrated. New York: Scribner, 1954. Grades K–3.

Buehr, Water. *Treasure: The Story of Money and Its Safeguarding.* Illustrated by the author. New York: Putnam, 1955. Grades 4–6.

Burt, Olive W. *The Story of American Railroads and How They Helped Build a Nation.* Illustrated. New York: John Day, 1969. Grades 5–9.

Cooke, David C. *How Paper Is Made.* Illustrated with photographs. New York: Dodd, Mead, 1959. Grades 4–6.

Doherty, Charles Hugh. *Tunnels.* Illustrated by Michael Baker. Des Moines: Meredith Corp., 1968. Grades 6–9.

Epstein, Edna. *The First Book of the United Nations.* Rev. ed. New York: Franklin Watts, 1966. Grades 7–10.

Fehrenbach, T. R. *The United Nations in War and Peace.* Illustrated, maps. New York: Random House, 1968. Grades 6–9.

Fisher, Leonard Everett. *The Doctors.* Illustrated by the author. New York: Franklin Watts, 1968. Grades 4–7.

Glassner, Sherwin S., and Edward N. Grossman. *How the American Economic System Functions.* Illustrated by Michael A. Norman. Westchester, Ill.: Benefic Press, 1968. Grades 5–7.

Greene, Carla. *I Want to Be a Dentist.* Chicago: Children's Press, 1960. Grades 1–3.

———. *I Want to Be a Musician.* Chicago: Children's Press. 1962. Grades 1–3.

———. *Soldiers and Sailors: What Do They Do?* Illustrated by Leonard Kessler. New York: Harper & Row, 1963. Grades 1–2.

Ipcar, Dahlov. *Ten Big Farms.* Illustrated by the author. New York: Knopf, 1958. Grades K–4.

Lent, Henry Bolles. *Agriculture U.S.A.: America's Most Basic Industry.* New York: Dutton, 1968. Grades 5–8.

Liebers, Arthur. *You Can Be a Carpenter.* New York: Lothrop, Lee & Shepard, 1973. Grades 4–6.

Mathieu, Joe. *Big Joe's Trailer Truck.* New York: Random House, 1974. Grades K–3.

Ray, E. Roy. *What Does an Airplane Crew Do?* Photographs by Martin Harris. New York: Dodd, Mead, 1968. Grades 4–7.

Schneider, Herman and Nina. *Let's Look Under the City.* Reading, Mass.: Addison-Wesley, 1954. Grades 3–6.

Shay, Arthur. *What Happens at a Television Station.* Photographs. Chicago: Reilly & Lee, n.d. Grades 1–3.

———. *What Happens When You Mail a Letter.* Photographs. Chicago: Reilly & Lee, n.d. Grades 1–3.

———. *What Happens When You Put Money in the Bank.* Photographs. Chicago: Reilly & Lee, 1967. Grades 1–3.

Torbert, Floyd J. *Policemen the World Over.* Illustrated by the author. New York: Hastings House, 1965. Grades 4–6.

Wells, Robert. *What Does a Test Pilot Do?* Photographs and charts. New York: Dodd, Mead, 1969. Grades 3–7.

The United States

Arbital, Samuel L. *Cities and Metropolitan Areas.* Mankato, Minn.: Creative Educational Society, 1967. Grades 5–9.

Cheney, T. A. *Land of the Hibernating Rivers: Life in the Arctic.* New York: Harcourt Brace Jovanovich, 1968. Grades 6–8.

Epstein, Sam and Beryl. *The First Book of Washington, D.C., The Nation's Capital.* New York: Franklin Watts, 1961. Grades 4–6.

Holland, John, ed. *The Way It Is.* Foreword by J. Anthony Lukas. New York: Harcourt Brace Jovanovich, 1969. Grades 5 and up.

Pedersen, Elsa. *Alaska.* Roscoe E. Bell, consultant. New York: Coward-McCann, 1969. Grades 6–9.

Sasek, M. *This Is Washington, D.C.* Illustrated by the author. New York: Macmillan, 1970. Grades 4 and up.

Schwartz, Alvin. *Old Cities and New Towns: The Changing Face of the Nation.* New York: Dutton, 1968. Grades 6–8.

Silverberg, Robert. *Ghost Towns of the American West.* Illustrated by Lorence Bjorklund. New York: Crowell, 1968. Grades 3–6.

United States History

Alderman, Clifford Lindsey. *Witchcraft in America.* New York: Messner, 1974. Grades 4–6.

Carlson, Vade. *John Wesley Powell: Conquest of the Canyon.* Eau Claire, Wis.: Harvey House, 1974. Grades 4 and up.

Cavanah, Frances, and Elizabeth L. Crandall. *Freedom Encyclopedia: American Liberties in the Making.* Illustrated by Lorence F. Bjorklund. Skokie, Ill.: Rand McNally, 1968. Grades 4–7.

Colby, Carroll B. *Historical American Landmarks: From the Old North Church to the Santa Fe Trail.* New York: Coward-McCann, 1968. Grades 4–8.

Cooke, David C. *The Planes the Allies Flew in World War II.* New York: Dodd, Mead, 1969. Grades 5 and up.

Dalgliesch, Alice. *America Begins: The Story of the Finding of the New World.* Illustrated by Lois Maloy. New York: Scribner, 1958. Grades 4–7.

Davis, Burke. *Yorktown, The Winning of American Independence.* Illustrated with photographs and maps. Evanston, Ill.: Harper & Row, 1969. Grades 5 and up.

Dickinson, Alice. *The Boston Massacre, March 5, 1770: A Colonial Street Fight Erupts Into Violence.* New York: Franklin Watts, 1968. Grades 5–9.

Falkner, Leonard. *John Adams: Reluctant Patriot of the Revolution.* Illustrated by Jerry Contreras. Englewood Cliffs, N.J.: Prentice-Hall, 1969. Grades 5 and up.

Foster, Genevieve. *George Washington's World.* Illustrated by the author. New York: Scribner, 1941. Grades 5–7.

Freeman, Mae Blacker. *Stars and Stripes: The Story of the American Flag.* Illustrated by Lorence Bjorklund. New York: Random House, 1964. Grades 2–5.

Fritz, Jean. *And Then What Happened, Paul Revere?* New York: Coward-McCann, 1973. Grades K–6.

Kerman, Gertrude. *Cabeza de Vaca, Defender of the Indians.* Eau Claire, Wis.: Harvey House, 1974. Grades 4–6.

Knight, Ralph. *The Burr-Hamilton Duel, July 11, 1804: A Tragedy That Stunned the American Nation.* New York: Franklin Watts, 1968. Grades 5–8.

McNeer, May. *Profile of American History.* Maplewood, N.J.: Hammond, 1965. Grades 5 and up.

Speare, Elizabeth George. *Life in Colonial America.* Illustrated by Charles Walker. New York: Random House, 1963. Grades 5 – 9.

Tunis, Edwin. *Colonial Craftsmen and the Beginnings of American Industry.* Illustrated by the author. Cleveland: World, 1965. Grades 6 and up.

Native Americans

(For additional listings write to Haskell Institution, Publications Service, Lawrence, Kans. 66044, and Association on American Indian Affairs, A Preliminary Bibliography of Selected Children's Books, 432 Park Avenue South, New York, N.Y. 10016.)

American Heritage, eds. *The American Indian.* New York: Random House, 1963.

Amon, Aline. *Talking Hands: Indian Sign Language.* Garden City, N.Y.: Doubleday, 1968.

Baldwin, Gordon C. *How the Indians Really Lived.* New York: Putnam, 1967.

Bleeker, Sonia. *The Sioux Indians: Hunters and Warriors of the Plains.* New York: Morrow, 1962.

Clark, Ann Nolan. *In My Mother's House.* New York: Viking, 1941.

Felton, Harold W. *Ely S. Parker: Spokesman for the Senecas.* New York: Dodd, Mead, 1973. Grades 4 – 6.

Harrington, I. L. *Nah-Le-Kah-De: The Story of a Navajo Boy.* New York: Dutton, 1937.

Hofsinde, Robert. *The Indian and His Horse.* New York: Morrow, 1960.

————. *Indian Picture Writing.* New York: Morrow, 1959.

Lavine, Sigmund A. *The Games Indians Played.* Dodd, Mead, 1974. Grades 4 – 6.

Lucas, Jannette M. *Indian Harvest: Wild Food Plants of America.* Philadelphia: Lippincott, 1945.

McSpadden, Joseph Walker. *Indian Heroes.* New York: Crowell, 1950.

Marriott, Alice Lee. *Sequoyah: Leader of the Cherokees.* Eau Claire, Wis.: Hale, 1956.

Thompson, Hildegard. *Getting to Know American Indians Today.* New York: Coward-McCann, 1965.

Wheeler, Arville. *White Squaw: The True Story of Jennie Wiley.* Boston: Heath, 1959.

Wyatt, Edgar. *Cochise, Apache Warrior and Statesman.* New York: Whittlesey House, 1953.

Black Americans

Beim, Jerrold. *Swimming Hole.* New York: Morrow, 1951. Grades K – 3.

Chernow, Fred B. and Carol. *Reading Exercises in Negro History.* Elizabethtown, Pa.: Continental Press, 1968. Grades 3 – 6.

Clayton, Ed. *Martin Luther King, Jr.* Englewood Cliffs, N.J.: Prentice-Hall, 1964. Grades 3 – 6.

Derricotte, E. P., and others. *Word Pictures of Great Negroes.* Washington, D.C.: Associated Publishers, 1941. Grades 3 – 6.

Jackson, Florence. *The Black Man in America.* New York: Franklin Watts, 1974. Grades 4 – 6.

Johnston, Johanna. *A Special Bravery.* New York: Dodd, Mead, 1967. Grades 3 – 6.

Meriweather, Louise. *Don't Ride the Bus on Monday: The Rosa Parks Story.* Englewood Cliffs, N.J.: Prentice-Hall, 1973. Grades K – 3.

Stratton, Madeline R. *Negroes Who Helped Build America.* Boston: Ginn, 1965. Grades 3–6.

Wilson, Beth P. *Muhammed Ali.* New York: Putnam, 1974. Grades K–3.

Other Ethnic Groups

Blue, Rose. *We Are Chicano.* New York: Franklin Watts, 1973. Grades 4–6.

Brahs, Stuart. *An Album of Puerto Ricans in the United States.* New York: Franklin Watts, 1973. Grades 4–6.

Raskin, Joseph and Edith. *The Newcomers: Ten Tales of American Immigrants.* New York: Lothrop, Lee & Shepard, 1974. Grades 4–6.

Reit, Seymour. *Rice Cakes and Paper Dragons.* New York: Dodd, Mead, 1973. Grades K–3.

Rivera, Geraldo. *Puerto Rico: Island of Contrasts.* New York: Parents' Institute, 1973. Grades K–3.

Webb, Robert N. *America Is Also Irish.* New York: Putnam, 1973. Grades 4–6.

White, Florence M. *Cesar Chavez: Man of Courage.* Champaign, Ill.: Garrard, 1973. Grades 4–6.

Women

Burt, Olive. *Black Women of Valor.* New York: Messner, 1974. Grades 4–6.

Goldreich, Gloria and Esther. *What Can She Be?: A Lawyer.* New York: Lothrop, Lee & Shepard, 1973. Grades K–6.

————. *What Can She Be?: A Newscaster.* New York: Lothrop, Lee & Shepard, 1973. Grades K–6.

————. *What Can She Be?: An Architect.* New York: Lothrop, Lee & Shepard, 1974. Grades K–6.

Gridley, Marion E. *American Indian Women.* New York: Hawthorn, 1974. Grades 7 and up.

Heyn, Leah. *Challenge to Become a Doctor: The Story of Elizabeth Blackwell.* Old Westbury, N.Y.: The Feminist Press, 1971.

Levenson, Dorothy. *Women of the West.* New York: Franklin Watts, 1973. Grades 7 and up.

Merriam, Eve. *Boys and Girls, Girls and Boys.* New York: Holt, Rinehart and Winston, 1972. Grades K–3.

————. *Mommies at Work.* New York: Knopf, 1961. Paperback: Scholastic Book Services, 1973. Grades K–3.

Other Lands, Other People

Bahija, Lovejoy. *Other Bible Lands.* Nashville: Abingdon Press, 1961. Grades 5–7.

Bleeker, Sonia. *The Tuareg: Nomads and Warriors of the Sahara.* Illustrated by Kisa J. Sasaki. New York: Morrow, 1964. Grades 4–6.

Carew, Dorothy. *Portugal.* New York: Macmillan, 1969. Grades 6–9.

Chubb, Thomas Caldecott. *The Venetians: Merchant Princes.* New York: Viking, 1968. Grades 6–9.

Comay, Joan, and Moshe Pearlman. *Israel.* Illustrated with photographs. New York: Macmillan, 1964. Grades 5–9.

Dunbar, Ernest. *Nigeria.* New York: Franklin Watts, 1974. Grades 4–6.

Erdoes, Richard. *Ireland: Bewitching Wonderland.* Illustrated with photographs by the author and old prints. New York: Dodd, Mead, 1968. Grades 5–8.

Gidal, Sonia and Tim. *My Village in Spain.* New York: Pantheon, 1962. Grades 4–6.

Harrington, Lyn. *Greece and the Greeks.* Photographs by Richard Harrington. Revised edition. Camden, N.J.: Thomas Nelson, 1968. Grades 6–9.

Kaula, Edna Mason. *The Land and People of Kenya.* Philadelphia: Lippincott, 1968. Grades 5–9.

Laure, Jason and Ettagade, *Joi Bangla: The Children of Bangladesh.* Farrar, Straus & Giroux, 1974. Grades 4 and up.

May, Charles Paul. *Chile: Progress on Trial.* Camden, N.J.: Thomas Nelson, 1968. Grades 6–9.

Miller, Richard, and Lynn Katoh. *Japan.* New York: Franklin Watts, 1969. Grades 5–8.

Rau, Margaret. *Our World: The People's Republic of China.* New York: Messner, 1973. Grades 4–6.

Ritchie, Paul. *Australia.* New York: Macmillan, 1968. Grades 6–9.

Schloat, G. Warren, Jr. *Uttam, A Boy of India.* Illustrated with photographs. New York: Knopf, 1963. Grades 4–6.

Singer, Isaac Bashevis. *A Day of Pleasure: Stories of a Boy Growing Up in Warsaw.* New York: Farrar, Straus & Giroux, 1969. Grades 7–10.

Sternberg, Martha. *Japan: A Week in Daisuke's World.* Macmillan, 1973. Grades K–3.

Weiss, Hugh. *A Week in Daniel's World: France.* Photographs by Sabine Weiss. New York: Macmillan, 1969. Grades PreK–3.

Historical Fiction

Alcott, Louisa May. *Little Women.* Illustrated by Barbara Cooney. New York: Crowell Collier & Macmillan, 1955. Grades 5–11.

Bulla, Clyde Robert. *John Billington, Friend of Squanto.* Illustrated by Peter Burchard. New York: Crowell Collier & Macmillan, 1956. Grades 3–6.

Caudill, Rebecca. *Tree of Freedom.* Illustrated by Dorothy Morse. New York: Viking, 1949. Grades 4–7.

Dalgliesh, Alice. *Adam and the Golden Cock.* Illustrated by Leonard Weisgard. New York: Scribner, 1959. Grades 3–6.

DeAngeli, Marguerite. *Thee, Hannah!* Illustrated by the author. Garden City, N.Y.: Doubleday, 1949. Grades 3 and up.

Edmonds, Walter, *The Matchlock Gun.* Illustrated by Paul Lantz. New York: Dodd, Mead, 1941. Grades 5–7.

Gates, Doris. *Blue Willow.* Illustrated by Paul Lantz. New York: Viking, 1940. Grades 5–7.

Wilder, Laura Ingalls. *Little House in the Big Woods.* Illustrated by Garth Williams. New York: Harper & Row, 1932, 1953. Grades 4–7.

Index

Index

A 6
B 7
C 8
D 9
E 0
F 1
G 2
H 3
I 4
J 5